Threading the Bible
Old Testament

Threading the Bible
Old Testament

Requests for information should be addressed to:
Duranno Press, 95 Seobinggo-Dong, Yongsan-Gu, Seoul, 140-240 Korea.

ISBN-10: 89-531-1204-9 03230
ISBN-13: 978-89-531-1204-9 03230

Threading the Bible
Old Testament

B. J. Moon

Duranno

Contents

Forward I

Behind the Scenes of the English version preparation

During my five-year tenure as a Foreign Diplomat in both Washington, D.C. and New York, I had the privilege of being invited as the guest speaker at Revival Gatherings or Bible Seminar events held by Korean churches on approximately over 150 occasions. On these visits I learned about the difficulties confronted by resident pastors in dealing with the English Ministry within the local Korean churches. The common concern among all pastors was that college students as well as youth groups (1.5 generation or 2nd generation of Korean Americans) did not read the Bible. I was even more alarmed by the fact that these young adults had no interest at all in knowing the Bible.

If this situation continues it is probable that in about 10-20 years Korean churches will become like many American churches. Big buildings with only handful elderly people in regular attendance. My heart was compelled to do something about it. With that in mind, I had the vision to translate my book entitled "Threading the Bible" into English so that the 1.5/2nd generations could read the English version of this book and gain an understanding of the Bible. Simultaneously, at the suggestion of numerous pastors who also realized the remarkable recovery of passing on the faith of respective parents to the next generation, the birth of translating the Korean version to English was activated. Through God's grace, Young-Hee Park, who was given a bilingual gift and was also a member of the Leaders Bible Study Group that I was leading at the time, volunteered to take upon the task of translating the book. With her commitment and dedication, the whole process took 8 months and has finally come to reality at this point of publication.

In spite of what occurred behind the scenes, now that the book is published in English it is my desire and hope that Christians throughout the world will benefit in their understanding of the Bible from Genesis to Revelation. This book was written in attempt to assist the reader to capture and follow God's message with interest, enthusiasm and grace. Especially in the 21st century, many people are losing hope in the future because of economic crisis, but I pray that through this book my readers will realize the only hope to overcome hardship and difficult situations in the world is to hold on to God's Promise (the good news) Ultimately, recovering vision for a prosperous future.

My deepest gratitude in Christ to Deacon Young-Hee Park for her diligence in translating this book with the passionate love of Jesus. I would also like to extend my thanks to Dr. Chang-Woo Lee and Deacon Tim Yoon for their assistance in this project and to Dr. Won - Ho Jhe for his help in the reviewing and editing process.

I give all glory to our Lord Jesus!

Elder
B. J. Moon

Forward Ⅱ

Until All Our Churchgoers are Changed with the Word of God

In spite of being a Christian from birth, a big blow of realization hit me at the age of 40 when I was working at the Korean Mission to the United Nations in Geneva, Switzerland. The big blow was my lack of knowledge of the Bible.

Upon my return to Korea, I was determined. Without missing a day, my feet automatically led me to Onnuri Church as soon as I got off from work. Obviously, there were many relatives, friends, and classmates that I wanted to spend time with since I was living abroad for quite a number of years. But I wrestled off all those temptations and instead spent my days attending and even setting up various types of Bible study programs at Onnuri Church. I literally ran after each study groups available at the church. Then one day in the fall of 1994, my eyes caught the wording of an ad on the wall: "Strategy Pursuit of the Bible in 40 Days-Capture the Threading of the Bible!" My heart was totally captivated. I was overwhelmed when I read this ad and exclaimed, "This is it! It's exactly what I need." I couldn't help myself but to think God had prepared this seminar for me. I was desperately yearning for a deep and abiding study. A study that was systematic and organized for easy understanding. The expectation and joy was difficult to hide so I immediately registered for the seminar.

Then later I was diagnosed with stomach cancer. God made me hold on to Him by bringing me near to the valley of death. It was during this time the Holy Spirit was poured onto me, giving me the gift to teach the Word of God. With the encouragement of God's guidance, I started my first Bible seminar of "Threading the Bible" in Beijing, China while going through my cancer treatments. The seminar took place wherever my feet led me. Reflecting back, almost 10 years have flown by but if feels like only yesterday.

My heart stops and my mouth speechless by God's amazing love poured onto me through the Holy Spirit. God has transformed me into a person waking the dawn with shedding tears of prayer each morning. It has become a joyful mission for me to alert the believers in teaching them to begin each day with early morning prayers at church before going out to the world.

In early 2005, with God's grace I was able to hold a 'Threading the Bible' seminar in New York where thousands of people gathered after attending respective Sunday services from various churches. Unfortunately, many other religious institutions strongly opposed it because of my occupation as a government official. The Bible study lasted 5 weeks. At the urging of many people yearning to understand the Bible, this has prompted me to put together a 'reference' handbook that could be used alongside the Bible. Most Christians have been encouraged to study the Word of God, yet many have not been shown how.

I thank God for giving me an opportunity and enabling me to widen the scope to spread the Word of God through this project. The importance of it was proven by a letter received from a man who was serving a one year term in prison in Korea. During this time he had read the Bible 20 times in 8 months and was about to complete his 21st reading in a week. He wrote in his letter that the Bible was difficult to comprehend and confessed that in spite of reading the Bible numerously he felt no significant impact at all. Instead, it made him more frustrated than ever. While going through moments of turmoil, he came across my book *Early Bird Christians* and found out about the Bible study with a twist--a methodical approach for easy understanding. He was asking for help in understanding the Bible so that he could explain to those in prison. A prisoner who did not believe in God approached him being fully aware that he was reading the Bible day and night and threw him a question, "Do you feel at peace when you read the Bible?" His response was, "Quite honestly, I don't know." He felt that he had missed his opportunity in evangelizing this prison mate and felt greatly frustrated. I was convinced that if I wrote a tutorial book on Bible study it would be of great help in assisting those who find themselves in unpredictable situations.

I have been approached by publishers frequently in the past and my excuse was that time was not on my side. But through the works of God, I find myself doing something that was unthinkable. Fortunately, Duranno Press was kind enough to consolidate all the notes taken from my previous studies which I was able to organize it from time to time. Again, I praise God for His grace.

My primary goal is to emphasize each individual's ability to read the entire Bible so that they may experience God's love and grace. Furthermore, for the readers to be able to realize and know what the 'good purpose' (Philippians 2:13) is all about. Needless to say, there are many Bible study materials available. I believe the Holy Spirit will lead and help those who yearn for a deep understanding and abiding relationships with God to live out the truths. God will reveal Himself to them so that they will discover new ability, strength and confidence.

Regardless what level of faith or whatever situation a reader may be in, I pray that through this book, all churchgoers and believers may be able to read the 66 books of the Bible with ease along with the grace and inspiration of God. I earnestly hope that this book will not only ignite the readers' attempt to know God but also allow them to challenge the ongoing questions and puzzling quests raised and interact with the Bible. May each reader experience the existence and grace of the Holy Spirit to guide his journey into the spiritual world.

I want the readers to use this book as a reference guide so that when reading the Bible, each individual may hear the voice of God by applying the truth to our life. In His inspired Word, God has given us everything we need to know about life and godliness. I look forward to the days ahead that from all parts of the world, praise will be given to God for His grace and glory.

I owe my gratitude to Reverend Jin-So Yoo (Presently Senior Pastor at All Nations Church in Los Angeles) for teaching me such an insightful 'formularized' Bible study. My deepest gratitude to Reverend Yong-Jo Ha (Presently Senior Pastor at Onnuri Church in Seoul, Korea) for his continued support in enabling me to deliver the Word at the church and always being there for my spiritual guidance and growth. I thank, in the name of Christ, Reverend Chun-Soo Lee (Presently Senior Pastor at Inchon Sansung Baptish Church) for teaching me the structure of spiritual theology. Without a doubt, it would have been impossible to transfer my lecture notes to a book if it wasn't for these precious people. I also want to convey my love to my wife, Jong-Sook Park, for her dedicated prayers during my lectures and most importantly, for her sharp and impeccable commentary feedbacks never failing to remind me to focus on alignment with God. Additionally, I want to thank the staff members at Duranno Press and Deacon Shin-Hee Han, for her drafting work. Lastly, I would like to thank Elder Byung-Ik Lee of the Ezra Missionary Group who helped me wrap up this project from my official government assignment in New York.

I hope that this book will help future generations of readers to understand the Bible afresh.

I give all glory to our Lord Christ!

Elder
B. J. Moon

UNDERSTANDING THE STRUCTURE: OPENING THE THREAD OF THE BIBLE

First of all, I'd like to introduce how we are going to study the Bible and the reason why we need to study it. You will realize that it is not all about increasing knowledge when studying the Bible.

Knowledge is not Faith Yet

"Is there any way I can grasp the entire scope of the Bible starting from Genesis to Revelations!"

"I'd like to organize my knowledge of the Bible better."

"I want to live the Christian life faithfully but have not experienced the strong impact of the Holy Spirit working within me so I feel frustrated and inadequate. Fear tosses me around whenever conflicting uncertainties arise in front of me and quite instantly, worries and despair takes over my heart. I really want to meet the living God through the Bible so I may have a bedrock faith knowing that God is with me."

Bible is the most widely distributed and read book in the world. Each person's level of faith is different based on each individual's Bible study and experience. Some may have studied selectively choosing a particular book like Genesis from the Old Testament or the book of John from the New Testament, and some choosing a theme or character from the Bible. Others may have different motives but the bottom line is that it does not matter. The most important point is that the purpose of studying the Bible must not remain as mere knowledge. The knowledge of the Bible may be a requirement but clearly it is not faith itself. Problems occur for many people because they are confused in their faith and the knowledge of the Bible.

Many believers know that Jesus had shed blood on the cross for our sins and His resurrection delivered us from judgment and gave us eternal life. This is strictly the knowledge of the Bible, not faith.

"Since I believe in the crucifixion of Jesus, I know that I will end up going to heaven after I die so let me just believe enough for me to reach there."

This is the very confusion that many believers encounter when they limit themselves to the technical knowledge of the Bible. Surely they have attended church strictly according to their academic level of knowledge for many years. One day, a wife was inspired by the Holy Spirit and decides to give tithes, 1/10th of her husband's income to the church. The husband who was attending the church with knowledge got very angry and said, "Do you realize what kind of money that is? It's my hard earned money! We're entitled to go to heaven anyway so why bother? Let's just believe up to that degree. Besides, tithing is done by those 'special' people who have great faith. We don't have to be like them." The wife received more grace as time passed and said to her husband, "Honey, no matter how tired we are, we must pray at early dawn. Without doing it, how can we possibly live in this turbulent world? So, let's pray in the early morning together." The husband blurts out in response, "Are you out of your mind? You know perfectly well how tired and busy we are! We don't even have enough time to sleep and you're telling me to go to church at early dawn? There's so much to be done in the morning. Let the fanatics do that. People like us don't have to do it. Besides it's written in the Bible that we go to heaven anyway."

This is a classic misunderstanding many churchgoers have. It is true that the entire Bible contains the Word of God and the literal writings of it but it is more important to meet God who reveals

Himself through His Word. "~for the letter kills, but the Spirit gives life." (2 Corinthians 3:6) We must be able to interact with God's Word, absorbing its truths and letting God engrave His truth in our heart, mind and life through the Holy Spirit. By the inspirational movement of our heart, we can then give tithes willingly and pray at early dawn. The movement of the Word (=energy-Hebrews 4:12) activates us. Those who have faith will not recklessly waste God's given grace.

I sincerely pray that this book will contribute to equipping each reader in their circumstances of everyday life and that Holy Spirit will guide them into His truth by providing the first step of conviction to God and His Word and to its relevance and power to transform their life. By giving hope to where there's despair and filling that 'gap' in their heart with God's love. Anyone who takes the time can see and understand what God has given us in His Word and how it applies to us today.

This book follows closely with the flow of the Bible and has been put together for easy application, understanding or interpretation of the Bible involving special corners:

1. The book has been structured into 40 Days of Self-Study so that you may grasp the threading of the Bible in 40 days. If you were to digest a day's worth then you will be able to 'Thread' the Bible in 40 days (in case a week = 40 weeks).

2. Thoughts for daily application have been set up in a corner entitled Spiritual Search Specifically, Spiritual Search is also referred as the 'Stream of Grace' where many people have received grace from listening to my seminar. Therefore, I believe this corner will provide great help for those dealing with conflicts both spiritually and secular.

3. Another corner of Knowledge Search has been set up for additional biblical explanation.

4. Important geographical place appears frequently in the Bible can be verified in the Map making it easier and refreshing in understanding the Bible

5. A link between the Old and New Testament has been set up as

the "Threader." Focusing closely on this corner will enable you to 'thread' the link between the Old and the New Testament.

I sincerely hope that this Bible 'Threading' guidebook will allow readers to hear the voice of God. Let the weary spirit be brightly lit, empty spirit be filled but above all, through passionate love and inspiration, my readers to meet God in their hearts through this book. May your reading lead you to understand and become sensitive to His heart. Always remember: It is the indwelling Holy Spirit who guides us into all truth, who takes the things of God and reveals them to us.

Why is the Bible Difficult to Understand?

The typical standard bible study is divided into three categories:

First is studying according to the 'books.' It doesn't matter which book one chooses to study whether it's the book of Genesis or a book from the New Testament. The so-called 'QT' is also one type of a Bible study according to the books.

Second is 'theme' related studies. Choosing a theme such as What is faith? What is salvation? What is resurrection? And so forth.

Third is a selective study of 'biblical character'. Such as: Life of Abraham; Life of David; Moses, Apostle Paul, etc.

Many times we commit ourselves to read the entire Bible and start with great enthusiasm until we reach the mid-portion of the book and find ourselves 'stuck.' For example, it was pretty much a smooth reading from Genesis up to Exodus 24 and then suddenly from chapter 25 you find yourself stuck. Measurements of half cubits long, one and half cubits wide... then suddenly the design of the tabernacle is mentioned and while things become more complicated, the instructions to use certain materials in the construction follow. It doesn't stop there. Out comes the method of offerings and once you reach Leviticus, you're more confused than ever. All those resolutions made in the New Year about reading the entire Bible ends within one or two months which brings you back to square one.

Why is it difficult to continuously read the Bible? Obviously if one is moved by the Holy Spirit, reading the Bible becomes less of a problem, but for the majority of us, the reasons are as follows:

First, the reason why the Bible cannot be read easily is because it is not a story of a continuous history. One story does not connect with the other. But if you look closely, there clearly is a 'thread.' You will realize that there is a flow from Genesis to Revelations. Therefore, we must follow the flow of the history and penetrate into the Bible focusing on 'God's redemptive work.'

Second, we have not seen any of the structures mentioned in the Bible before. This is like a person reading a television manual without ever having seen the television before. Reading the different types of offerings in Leviticus is just like listening to an instructor when none of us have seen a tabernacle before making our heads turn even as we read the Bible. We find ourselves skim reading and turning the pages quickly.

Third, we have no clue in understanding what sort of position or situation each biblical characters were in, let alone understanding the Bible. Such as what made King David pray in such a passionate way and what made Apostle Paul write such determined letters? Our heart will never be moved without knowing the circumstances.

Fourth, we do not know the biblical geography. We are overwhelmed with the names of countries like Syria, Assyria and Aram as we read the Bible. At first glance, Syria and Assyria look like the same country to us making it difficult to understand. All the Bible characters moved according to the Word of God. After Adam's fall, he was thrown out to the eastern part of Eden and at God's calling, Abraham obeyed and left his home country (Haran) for the land of Canaan where God instructed. Quite naturally, we come across various geographical names while reading the Bible. And quite frankly, those names are difficult and foreign to us. It is also surprising that not many people are interested in finding out more about the different Middle Eastern territories while reading the Bible. But amazingly enough, as you open the map and follow through it you will come to realize how closely the loving hands of God and His guidance is upon our lives.

First Build the Backbone According to the Time Period

In order to thread the Bible, we will first follow the 'historical period approach.' The formation of the 'backbone' was the first method I learned from my Bible study. I have applied this method in this book, knowing what wonders it did for me from my own experience. The fact that I could visualize the entire picture of the Bible was just amazing. I felt like a blind man who could see! It was unbelievable.

Second, the focus will be adding 'flesh' to the Word as it unfolds in detail. As time passed, the scope of forming the outline was evidently progressing and helpful in my Bible study but in my heart I felt frustrated. "Wouldn't it be wonderful if someone could add the 'flesh' to the backbone starting from the Creation in Genesis to Revelations? Then surely it would be a great help to those who are unfamiliar with the Bible or to those who have been churchgoers for many years but have trouble organizing it in their head."

My initial thought was that a great minister or a theologian would be ideal to take over this task. But under God's plan, I have taken up this role. This all happened quite naturally when I organized a Bible study group among young adults during my assignment in China. Therefore, my Bible study approach is consisting of the 'bone' of a body that is based on Reverend Jin-So Yoo's book entitled 'Strategy Pursuit of the Bible in 40 days' and the 'flesh' of my own, focusing on how to apply the Word into our daily lives.

Third, we will follow the biblical geography as we go through the 66 books of the Bible. The once complicated biblical map will become easy and simple as we start connecting each place through our own drawing. Simultaneously, we will learn and inspect how each character in the Bible moved according to the Word of God as well as their livelihood.

Drawing the Biblical Map in 30 Seconds

By following their movements in a geographical manner, we can feel the love of God as He interferes and guides through the livelihood of these people. I always draw a map and follow their tracks during my lecture to open the minds of people. That is one of the reasons why a periodic biblical map is essential in this book. Let's try to draw the biblical map in 30 seconds. (I must reveal that this method has been originated by Reverend Jin-So Yoo, author of *Strategy Pursuit of the Bible 40 Days*.)

First, draw a big 'bread' on the left corner and insert a 'fork' from the lower part the bread. Then, draw a chicken leg on the right side-the meat hanging upside down with a foil paper wrapped on the leg itself. Beneath the chicken leg, a pig's foot is drawn in a slanted position. Bear in mind that it must be drawn in a specific way: the left sticking up higher than the right. Pay attention that the right foot of the pig must be parallel with the left. Lastly, on the right corner, draw a picture of a cobra with a wagging tongue sticking out. This completes the drawing of a biblical map in 30 seconds! Once finished, we will follow the tracks of the biblical characters as we go along. Below are main territories:

1. Egypt - Country of Spirit of Sun
2. Babylon (Iraq) - The Middle Eastern territories believe in the moon especially they regard the 'full moon' very important.

There was an incident when I was working in Geneva. In Geneva, the International Committee of the Red Cross is referred to as the

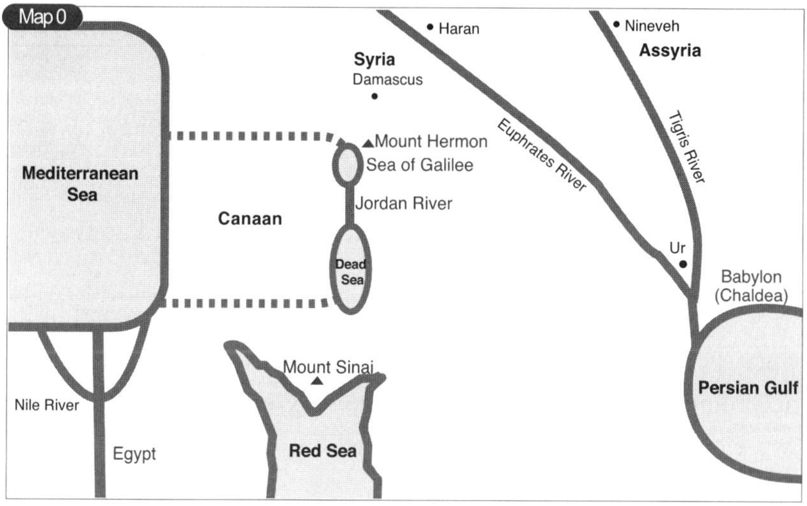

Biblical Map in 30 Seconds These are the names of territories that will appear in our study. Once familiar with it, you will experience the biblical characters coming alive.

Red Cross and the Chinese people without a choice also refer to it as the Red Cross. Red Cross exists in almost all countries. But only in the Middle East they call it the Red Full Moon. All other countries symbolize the Red Cross with a cross except in the Middle East where they symbolize it with a red crescent moon. Why do you think they would draw such a moon? In the Middle East, a 'moon' symbolizes the plains of Mesopotamia. They believe the fertile land is formed by the rivers of Euphrates and Tigris resembles a crescent moon. For this reason why they refer this area as the crescent moon. The northern part of the plains of Mesopotamia where Euphrates and the Tigris River intersect is Assyria, a country of the moon and also referred to as Babylon.

Eventually Assyria destroys the Northern Israel and later Babylon takes over the plains of Mesopotamia after destroying Assyria. The Southern Judah falls in the hands of Babylon--Iraq, today. This is the country that destroyed Israel and took them into exile.

"The sun will not smite you by day, nor the moon by night." (Psalm 121:6) God had promised Israel to protect them from the sun (Egypt) and the moon (Babylon) but they abandoned Him. That is why they were taken into captivity by the moon (Babylon) and continue to receive threats even to this day. The world history cannot be completed without the Bible. That is why the history is actually His Story. Without knowing this, one cannot solve the problem by seeing the current situation only with the knowledge of the world. Without knowing the Bible, one cannot solve it.

3. Mt. Sinai is presumably located towards the southern part of the Sinai Peninsula. The exact location of Mt. Sinai is unknown but according to the exodus of the Israelites we assume that it is part of Mt. Horeb. God did not lead the Israelites to Canaan but instead to Mt. Sinai.

4. Mt. Hermon as in the 'dews of Hermon' (Psalm 133:3) is located on the right upper side of Lake Galilee. The snow that melts from this mountain streams down to Lake Galilee.

5. On the east side of Lake Galilee is Bashan known as the 'Koran' plateau nowadays. The highlands of Koran are extremely cold whereas the Jordan valley is hot. Therefore, a frequent storm was inevitable in Lake Galilee because temperature differences was too high. This was the reason why the storm occurred in the days of Jesus when He quiets down the storm. The name of Galilee means "the turning of wheels" which gives us an impression how strong a storm was in that region. Lake Galilee is a big lake-11km in width and 22km in length. People in the region called it a 'sea' because of its size. The water of Lake Galilee is crystal blue, very beautiful and even mystical. From this lake, thousands of tons of clear water flow into the Jordan River each day.

6. The water current is very rapid in Jordan River due to the large difference of elevation from the ground. The direct distance of the Jordan River is only 100km but because of its curve streaming, it is approximately 300km in waterway. The stream of the Jordan River flows into the Dead Sea.

7. The Dead Sea is situated at its lowest level in the world that

there is no place to stream further. This trapped water evaporates into salt water which makes it impossible to have any life in it. Lake Galilee is also known for its abundance of variety of fish. You must recall that Peter was a fisherman before meeting Jesus. The fish that swam along the Jordan River suddenly face the salty water forcing them to jump up making it easy to catch fish without any effort. It has been said that salt marinated fishes were exported to Rome from this region during the Roman period. If one were to go on a pilgrimage trip to the Holy Land, they sell 'Peter's fish' even today.

These beautiful lakes and the Jordan River in the Promised Land (Canaan) had no meaning to the people actually living in the land. The only thing left for them to do was fishing in the lake of Galilee. Because of the steep valleys and the lack of technology at the time, it was impossible for them to consider farming by pumping up the clear water from the lake because of the steep valleys.

What's the Difference Between Thoughts and Confession?

"If we say that we have fellowship with Him and yet walk in the darkness, we lie and do not practice the truth;" (1 John 1:6) "The one who says he is in the light and yet hates his brother is in the darkness until now." (1 John 2:9)

No matter how much you remind yourself that 'hating others is wrong' you hate the person next to you without realizing it. Why? It is because thoughts do not have salvation.

Faith is confession. You will experience salvation when you acknowledge what you have understood with your lips and confess it from your sincere heart. " ... and with the mouth he confesses, resulting in salvation." (Romans 10:10) " ... the words that I have spoken to you are spirit and are life." (John 6:63) Spoken words become the channel of spirit and when confessions are made through our lips. That's when the spirit starts to work. It is at that time the Holy Spirit works within you and delivers the love of Christ, enabling you to overcome hatred. 'Let us hold fast our confession ... therefore let us draw near with confidence to the throne of grace.' (Hebrews 4:14-16) Having faith to confess will allow you to go near to God's throne of grace with confidence. "How blessed is the man ... he meditates day and night." (Psalm 1:1-2) In Hebrew language it means 'confession of the Law.' What this means is that the Jews do not just meditate and pray they continuously confess through their lips. One Hebrew scholar said that a Jew will never pray silently. They confess through their lips as well as singing praises. Confession is a short cut to experience the Holy Spirit as we lead our religious life.

. . .

Not that we are adequate in ourselves to consider anything as coming from ourselves, but our adequacy is from God, who also made us adequate as servants of a new covenant, not of the letter but of the Spirit; for the letter kills, but the Spirit gives life. But if the ministry of death, in letters engraved on stones, came with glory, so that the sons of Israel could not look intently at the face of Moses because of the glory of his face, fading as it was, how will the ministry of the Spirit fail to be even more with glory?

2 Corinthians 3:5-8

UNDERSTANDING THE GEOGRAPHY AND CLIMATE OF CANAAN OPENING YOUR EYES TO THE BIBLE

Once you understand the climate of the land of Canaan, it will be very clear to you why God made the people of Israel live there.

Climate of the Land of Canaan

What kind of a place is Canaan? Let's draw the map once again. (Practice drawing the map so that you could do it in 30 seconds.) Look at the Mediterranean Sea. The Promised Land is situated in the territory between Lake Galilee, Jordan River and the Mediterranean Sea. Right above Lake Galilee is a small town called Dan. If one were to ask from which point to which belong to Israel, the answer would be from Dan to Beersheba. "All Israel from Dan even to Beersheba knew that Samuel was confirmed as a prophet of the Lord." (1 Samuel 3:20) In order to arrive at the Promised Land, the Israelites had a long way to go. First, they had to cross the Nile River out of Egypt, cross the Red Sea and go through Mt. Sinai and then after the journey in the wilderness and cross the Jordan River to finally arrive at the Promised Land.

An Impossible Place to Live Without the Pillars of Cloud

There are vast differences of temperature in the climate of Israel. It is hot during the day reaching 40 degrees C/104 F and at night it falls to a freezing minus 10 degrees. Those who have visited the Holy Land may already know what I'm trying to explain.

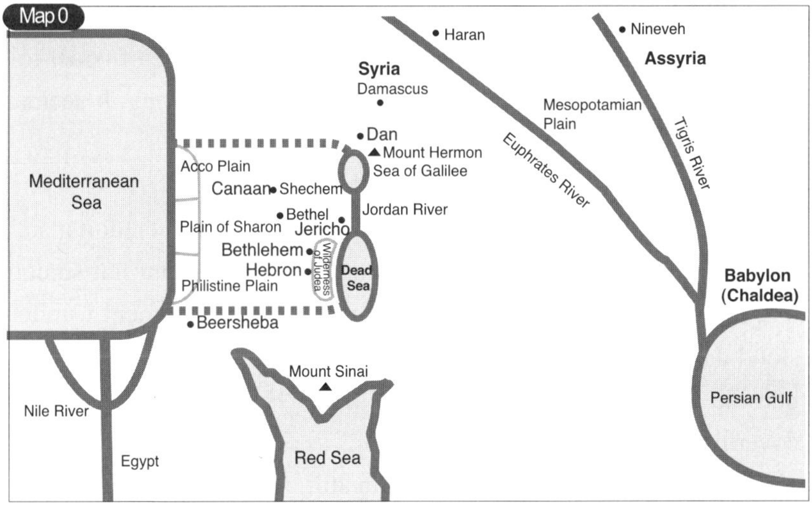

Land of Canaan Why did God refer Canaan as the Promised Land? Geographical knowledge of Canaan will open your eyes to the Bible.

You can walk around in shorts and a T-shirt during the day but once the sun goes down you find yourself going back to your lodging to put on heavier clothing. Due to vast differences in temperature in the land, God guided and protected them throughout their journey in the wilderness by "pillar of cloud by day to lead them on the way, and in a pillar of fire by night." (Exodus 13:21).

What does it mean by guiding them through the pillar of cloud by day? In order to reach Jericho from Jerusalem, one has to pass the wilderness of Judah. Judah is a desert located next to the Dead Sea. When I visited the Holy Land, the tour guide, who happened to be an evangelist, commented that I must 'experience' the wilderness school so we got into a jeep and headed towards the wilderness of Judah. We arrived at the wilderness where Jesus fasted and started to walk. The sizzling heat of 104F penetrated down into my straw hat making it impossible to walk! Within 10 minutes, my whole body was soaking wet with perspiration. The quenching thirst was unbearable that it felt like I would collapse at any minute. I then realized at that moment the outcries of the Israelites. Pleading for water in their journey in the wilderness. I was walking with a water bottle but still thirsty. To imagine the pain and sufferings of over 2 million people of Israel following Moses into the wilderness was just mind boggling. It seemed only natural for them to cry out and complain.

This land was such a place. Shortly after, the wilderness school evangelist said to me, "Please wait and stand still." When doing so, I saw a cloud passing by. It was for about 2-3 minutes but felt so cool that it was unbelievable. I felt rejuvenated. At that moment I understood the passage about God's guidance of the 'pillar of cloud' which became alive to me right there and then. "He spread a cloud for a covering, And fire to illumine by night." (Psalm 105:39)

The pillar of cloud does not remain still. According to the book of Numbers, it records that the pillar of cloud went ahead of the Israelites and whenever the pillar of cloud stopped, whether it was for one month, one year or few years, the people followed and moved accordingly. It meant that they were under God's full protection. Guidance through pillars of cloud by day and fire by night was strictly God's infinite timing and grace.

Someone asked me, "I understand about the pillar of cloud but pillar of fire? Is it possible to stand against the cold?" The assumption is that the pillar of fire was not necessarily to block the cold since the temperature of this area at night is approximately 10 degrees and even though it might have some chill in the air it would not have any significant impact in walking if one wore an overcoat of some sort. So the interpretation of the pillar of fire is that the people of Israel were guided during the night as well. It was as if God was protecting His people in the same manner as a hen would protect her chicks under her wing. This was the way God cared for the people of Israel in the midst of their surroundings.

A Land That Required Rain from God

God spoke through Moses as He led the people of Israel to Canaan, "' For the land, into which you are entering to possess it, is not like the land of Egypt from which you came, where you used to sow your seed and water it with your foot like a vegetable garden. But the land into which you are about to cross to possess it, a land of hills and valleys, drinks water from the rain of heaven." (Deuteronomy. 11:10-11)

Think now using your common sense. Is there such a land that does not absorb water? What does it mean by "land that drinks water from the rain of heaven"?

It meant that the people of Israel were able to live only with rain. Without rain from God, it was impossible to survive in this land. So therefore, they were left with no other alternatives but to rely on heaven. This was God's providence to the people of Israel.

Israel has two seasons: dry and wet. Spring and autumn lasts only a month. Spring falls in the month of April and autumn in October. In Korea, when spring rain comes we know that summer is approaching; and more down pours of rain in the summer. But the weather in Israel is the opposite from us. The dry season begins in springtime where trees and the grounds start to dry up. During the peak of the dry season, all the trees and crops are withered away by May through September. Nothing grows at this time. Then in October and well into November, God sends rain which is referred to as the 'early rain.' The 'late rain' comes down in March. The level of farm produce depended on these early and late rains. This is the way people survived in those days.

Without God's interference, they could not sow the dry land. The early rain was sent appropriately enabling them to scatter the seeds on the moistened land. Even if they sowed in the fall, without the 'late' rain sent by God, harvesting in March would be impossible. The late rain had to come in order for the grains to husk. If the heaven's gate was closed, there would be no harvest. Through the early and late rain, God wanted His people to focus only on Him. That is why Prophets Amos and Isaiah and many other prophets mentioned that if God did not send the appropriate early and late rains then it was a plague.

On the other hand, the Nile River was in Egypt. The Nile River is approximately 600 km in length, making it the main source of water for Egypt. Even during the famine periods, the area was not affected due to its abundance of water. By means of having irrigation supply, water was easily accessible. Therefore, vegetations were plentiful and water was more than enough to supply the entire land of Egypt.

A colleague of mine who used to work as an ambassador in Egypt advised me that it did not rain there making it a 'fantasy' wonderland for golfers! Rain was scarce that it only rained once or twice a year. Even if it did rain, it would be a matter of minutes before it ended. So imagine, how would it be possible to do any farming in such a land? But the people in Egypt had nothing to worry about-because of the Nile River. People could easily live by their own efforts due to the abundance of water supply from the Nile River. Humanism that mankind is the origin of creation was developed in Egypt. Therefore, God told the Israelites the land they're about to possess would be 'different from Egypt.'

A Place Blocked in All Four Directions

Canaan is really an unusual place because of the Mediterranean. The Mediterranean Sea is beautiful and perfect for swimming. When I was stationed in Geneva, I remember spending my vacation in the beach resort of Nice. I felt like a movie star. Lying underneath the parasol with sunglasses and all. It was splendid. But when I visited the capital of Israel, Tel Aviv, the sight of Mediterranean from there was no comparison to the beaches of Nice. It was awesome. We would automatically think of tourism and what great exposure it would bring but that is according to today's standard. The Mediterranean Sea had no significant use for the people of Israel because of the sand shores. It may have been perfect for sun bathing and swimming but without a harbor it was meaningless at that time.

For this reason, there is no mention of any character sailing on the waters of the Mediterranean Sea heading towards Europe throughout the Old Testament. The only person who sailed out on a boat was Jonah. When Jonah was asked by God to go and evangelize in Nineveh, capital of Assyria, he tried to escape and got on a boat. He thought God would not exist if he sailed out of Canaan on a small boat and almost died in the stomach of a 'big' fish. The mention of 'eastern sea' refers to the Dead Sea. The Mediterranean Sea that Jonah tried to escape is mentioned as the 'Great Sea' in the Bible. Other than this incident, there is no record of sea in the Bible. Lake Galilee is referred to as the 'sea' due to the size but it was actually a lake. Basically God had purposely situated the people of Israel so that they could not go anywhere.

In other words, the land was completely blocked in all directions where escape was impossible. Egypt was located on the bottom and Assyria (Aram) on the top; on the right side of the Jordan River were the tribes of Ammon, Moab and Edom and towards the west was the Mediterranean Sea blocking all four corners. The message was loud and clear: affirming that God was in charge. Only when they trust in God does the land become milk and honey. Without the grace of God, there was no way the people of Israel could sustain their lives.

The Lowest Place in the World

The geographical regions of Israel run roughly north to south, parallel to the coast. Inland, the coastal plain gives way to low hills, then the main central highland forms the 'backbone' of the whole country. If you were to divide the highlands in three parts: the top would the plains of Acco, next the plains of Sharon and last the plains of Palestine. The region of Acco was where vegetation was plentiful whereas Sharon was known for abundance of flowers. That is why there is a hymn song entitled, <Jesus, Rose of Sharon> For information sake, when Jesus spoke "look at the lily blossoms in the field, a flower more beautiful than the glory of Solomon" (Luke 12:27) is not what we think it is but actually the flower of Sharon. It is a beautiful red flower called 'Anemone' found in the plains of Sharon. The expression used by Jesus was that the blossoming of these red flowers was more beautiful than the jewels of King Solomon. The plains of Palestine were known for barley and some claim that it was the first place where beer was produced.

Starting from the coast of the Mediterranean Sea the water level gets lower as you go in deeper towards the sea. It is formed in sand with small parts being plains and the rest are mountains. In other words, majority of the territories are mountains and valleys. Probably that is the reason why the land is called the Galilean mountains as God spoke "The land into which you are about to cross to possess it, a land of hills and valleys ... " (Deuteronomy 11:11)

An interesting observation is that the mountainous part of Samaria continues and as it approaches the Jordan River, the configuration of the land suddenly descends. The same effect happens with the wilderness of Judea as it approaches the Jordan River, the land sinks below. The mountainous part becomes steep valleys and the reason is because of the structure of Lake Galilee and the Dead Sea. All rivers of the world are indicated as certain meters above sea level in geographical maps. Sea level is to prove how high it is above the land whether it is above the sea or below. Apparently, Lake Galilee, Jordan River and the Dead Sea where the holy land is located are all below sea level. Lake Galilee flows 212m below land; the Dead Sea flows 400m below land. The Jordan River rises close to the foot of Mt. Hermon and flows south, descending drastically by the time it reaches the Dead Sea. The Jordan River appears in the geographical map but it actually runs underneath the ground making it the lowest place on earth, at its deepest, more than 800m/2,600ft. below sea level. Based on this fact, there was a person who mentioned that Jesus Christ came into the world at the lowest level both physically and geographically. Due to its low level, the mountainous part of the territory start to form into valleys as it approaches the Jordan River. The valley is a deep trough, created by geological faults in this unstable area. It has a hot and humid climate all its own as you go 200m below land.

In Deuteronomy 11:12, "a land for which the Lord your God cares." The word 'cares' means counsel (advice) in the Old Testament. It also means taking care of and protected with the eyes of the Lord your God are always on it. The land where God protects and cares by sending the early and late rain appropriately, depending on the season, is surely a blessed land.

The Word of God vs. Knowledge of Man

Now that God was controlling the people through rain, the people start to dig cisterns as big as a football field. This was designed to conserve every drop of water during the rainy season and utilize it when there's no rain. The result of collaboration of human wisdom and method. God was not happy with this. Prophet Jeremiah cried out to the people right before the fall of the southern kingdom of Judah, "For my people have committed two evils: They have forsaken Me, The fountain of living waters and To hew for themselves cisterns, Broken cisterns, That can hold no water." (Jeremiah 2:13) This meant that no matter what human thoughts may be, this method would not sustain their lives. The people of Israel had committed a great sin--challenging God.

At times during Bible studies, I am asked questions like: "How foolish the Israelites were! Throughout the whole Bible, it is repeated constantly that if you obey the Word of God you will be blessed; and if you leave God and worship Baal, God will curse you and you will be judged. Why in the world did they not obey in the first place? What's so great about the Baal idolatry? I can't seem to understand these people."

Be aware! This is our description. The people of Israel battled fiercely for survival. Namely, whether to live according to their knowledge or by the Word of God. The dilemma between the invisible God who sends rain to the land or the Baal who is visible and gives pleasure through lewd activities was the ultimate challenge. The problem is that it is so much easier to live according to our own knowledge. The fact of the matter is that the people of Israel abandoned God, the fountain of living waters, for Baal many times over.

Baal is an idol that was strictly created by man according to their own needs and knowledge.

The cistern that the people of Israel dug was the idolatry of Baal based on the constant friction and conflict between human's knowledge and desire to do it on their own and the word of God. In Galatians 5:16-17, it says, "the flesh sets its desire against the Spirit, and the Spirit against the flesh; for these are in opposition to one another, so that you may not do the things that you please." Whatever you feel in the heart is the desire of the flesh. The Word of God is the flesh of the Spirit. Through the history of Israel, the flesh of the Spirit is clearly shown to us how difficult it is to follow the Word of God.

THE OVERVIEW OF THE ENTIRE BIBLE

Story of the Old Testament: The Coming of the Messiah

What is the summary of the 39 books of the Old Testament? God created mankind as His love object and made the Garden of Eden to fulfill His world on this earth. The story begins with God's creation in chapters 1 and 2 of Genesis and about the fall of man in chapter 3. This is vital for understanding much of the Bible, for it explains that the human race is out of relationship with God and the whole of creation has been affected by that break of relationship. Basically the theme of the Old Testament is about the fallen humankind where corruption enters into the world and as a result God's Kingdom disappears. The story then folds into the restoration of God's Kingdom through Israel and God's fulfillment of His promise that the Messiah Jesus Christ is to come to the world becomes the main focal message. The Old Testament exists for the purpose of explaining the coming of the Messiah and the son of God, Jesus. Let's find out how it is prophesized in the Old Testament and is revealed in the New Testament.

"And I will put enmity between you and the woman, And between your seed and her seed; He shall bruise you on the head, And you shall bruise him on the heel."(Genesis 3:15)

These were the words spoken by God cursing the serpent after Adam and Eve ate from the forbidden tree. It was a curse to the serpent but a blessing of promise to mankind. The prophecy of the coming of Christ through the descendant of a woman to crush Satan's power was being prophesied. That is why Genesis 3:15 is known as the 'gospel of Eden.' This was the first proclamation of the gospel by God after the fall. The entire content of the Old Testament is the process of God's fulfillment of His promise given in Genesis that Jesus the Messiah will be sent to crush the head of the serpent. The symbolic references to Jesus can be verified through several books in the Old Testament.

- Exodus: The blood of the young lamb on Passover and the ways of offerings in the tabernacle are previews of the redemption of the cross.
- Leviticus: Offerings through the redemption of blood symbolizes Jesus.
- Number: Salvation is symbolized to those who looked at the bronze serpent.
- Deuteronomy: All the blessing and curse are physically fulfilled by Jesus.
- Joshua: The leader in guiding to the Promised Land refers to Jesus.
- Judges: The only true judge is the coming Christ Jesus.
- 1 & 2 Samuel / 1 & 2 Kings: King of God's Kingdom comes through the descendants of David.

As you come to the prophecies, the conclusion of the Old

Testament doesn't stop at the coming of Christ but through the crucifixion and resurrection. It testifies about the Holy Spirit that is to come to us. "Moreover, I will give you a new heart and put a new spirit within you; and I will remove the heart of stone from your flesh and give you a heart of flesh. And I will put My Spirit within you and cause you to walk in My statutes, and you will be careful to observe My ordinances." (Ezekiel 36:26-27). Through the resurrection of our Lord, the Holy Spirit will be sent to us to melt our hardened hearts, enabling us to obey the Word of God.

Story of the New Testament: The Messiah that Came

Then, what is the storyline of the New Testament? The gospel begins with the fulfillment of the law through the prophets (Old Testament). The Messiah had come according to the covenant of Abraham and David which is proclaimed as an opening in Matthew 1:1, "The genealogy of Jesus Christ, the son of David, the son of Abraham." The image and love of the invisible Father God is now being unfolded in the New Testament by the birth of Jesus and His 3-year ministry. Through the cross of redemption, resurrection and ascension, the Holy Spirit was sent to earth resulting churches to be born and enabling all nations to become disciples to carry out the mission work. This is the storyline of the history of the New Testament (four gospels including the book of Acts).

What is the main message that God is trying to tell us through the New Testament? In short, it is showing us the image of Jesus and for us to become like Him. What kind of image was Jesus in the New Testament in the first place? Sadducees questioned Jesus, "What is the greatest commandment in the Law?" This question is the same as "If you were to summarize the Old Testament in one word, what is it?" Jesus responded, "First, you shall love your Lord your God with all your heart, soul and mind. Second, you shall love your neighbor as yourself." (Matthew 22:37-39) There is no one on this earth who loved God with all heart, soul and mind as much as Jesus. By loving neighbors more than Himself, He suffered and died on the cross for all sinners of the world showing His love and complete obedience to God. The message in the New Testament is loud and clear. Jesus is our role model (Romans 8:29) and we must change our lifestyle to become like Him.

Overcoming Self

If you were to summarize the 66 books of the Bible, it would be "the process of self denial" and "emptying self." In other words, throwing away our old self and changing into the image of Jesus. Jesus spoke to His disciples, "If anyone wishes to come after Me, let him deny himself, and take up his cross, and follow Me." (Matthew 16:24) All the miracles and good deed that Jesus performed was for the sake of His merciful and compassionate love towards the people and only to glorify the Father. Certainly not for His own profit or reputation. After feeding the 5,000 men, Jesus quietly went up the mountain to pray alone leaving the outcries of the crowds behind. He knelt down in front of the Father instead. He lowered Himself even to death, denying Himself. This is our ultimate goal for us to become like Jesus!

If you were to tell the people of the world to deny themselves and carry their own cross on a daily basis, some may reply "I've already emptied myself." Surprisingly enough, in spite of saying such remark, unfortunately, it is our human nature to become greedier than ever. It's almost impossible to 'empty' ourselves without any cause. The only way to do so is through love. Only love has the power to overcome us. That is why His eternal love has come to us in the form of the Holy Spirit and with the help of power of the Holy Spirit, we can overcome the world and deny ourselves so that we may become like Christ. This is the message of the Bible to us.

The Bible begins with the story of creation of the heaven and earth with God's Word in Genesis 1 and ends the story with creating a 'new' heaven and earth in Revelation 12. For the purpose of creating the new heaven and earth, the cross of redemption is a mandate procedure. If you were to realize that the creation of the world that appears in Genesis 1 is merely a stage decoration primarily to fulfill the cross of redemption; and that it is a prelude to the 2nd coming of Christ to give us the new heaven and earth then the joy and sorrow of the visible things of the world becomes less significant. Through daily prayers and the Word, we must focus on our efforts in experiencing the existence and love of our God so with that power we're able to throw away the old 'self' and reveal the likeness of Jesus through our daily lives. This is the reason why believers must read and learn the Bible to reflect each day.

What is God's Righteousness?

Abraham was the first person in mankind who overcame himself by sacrificing his only son Isaac that he had at the age of 100 as a burnt offering to God. God chose Abraham to make this man the father of many nations and in course of time benefit for the whole world. It is impossible to share the grace received while holding on to your 'things.' The true purpose of Israel being 'chosen' was to spread the grace with other foreign countries but instead they pursued their own interest which resulted in destruction in the end.

Jesus said, "Seek first His kingdom and His righteousness; and all these things shall be added to you." (Matthew 6:33) In other words, if you were to seek God's ways, things you need, eat or drink will all be taken care of. The definition of 'righteousness of God' has nothing to do with moral or promotion of virtue. It is well explained in Amos 5:24, "Let justice roll down like waters And righteousness like an ever - flowing stream." God's righteousness means the grace and blessing received must be shared with those who are less fortunate than us. Sharing with people in need, sick or poor neighbors like a flowing stream. Water was used as a parable for God's grace since it flows from high to low.

We must first empty ourselves in order to receive God's grace. By doing so, that's when God fills you up with His grace. Without surrendering our freewill, the grace of God cannot reach us. We must first should be successful in receiving by making every efforts in letting go of the things that belong to us. This is because we cannot give unless we receive. God's righteousness is for us to receive His grace first and then be redemptive towards others.

Grace and redemption are the righteousness of God's Kingdom. Redemption means to carry other peoples' burden. As tough as it may be, we must sacrifice ourselves for others which means we lose out at times. This is what redemption is all about. We must be able to open the doorway of blessings for others with the grace received from the gospel.

God gave the people of Israel Lake Galilee and the Dead Sea in order to make them understand what God's Kingdom and righteousness was all about. This is really a special audio visual education material. Mt. Hermon is located right above Lake Galilee. And the melted snow of clear waters stream down from Mt. Hermon to Lake Galilee and three tributaries end up in Lake Hule. Lake Hule is 2 meters below sea level whereas the Lake Galilee is 212 meter making the water pressure forceful due to the differences in elevation. Tremendous amount of water is received in Lake Galilee and streams approximately 60,000 tons of water. Just like the righteousness of God, the waters of life stream downwards. The work of grace and redemption is shown through Lake Galilee.

Lake Galilee receives the clear water which flows downwards while a stream rises up from the bottom simultaneously. The stream of grace rises up when we pray also. We must be able to cleanse away the evil thoughts with the Word first and then filter out the deposits of sin, fault and hurt through prayers. The Holy Spirit moves our hearts, making us acknowledge the Word through our lips and we then feel the stream of grace rising up from within.

'Blessed are those who mourn, for they will be comforted.' Without complete mourning, you cannot be cleansed thoroughly nor can you have the heart of Jesus. Receive the clean water and let it flow; and believe that there is life in a rooting stream when you pray. Our surrounding becomes beautiful when we sanctify ourselves first and flow our living waters downwards. And this is one of the reasons why the surrounding of Lake Galilee is beautiful.

Alternatively, what is the Dead Sea telling us? It literally means 'dead' sea. The Dead Sea receives the water of life. It only receives and cannot give. Attending all kinds of revival seminars, bible studies or listening to sermon tapes become meaningless when you keep receiving only. It is the same as being 'dead.' Concentrating and accumulating your own blessings to yourself without sharing produces bad roots. I must emphasize the importance of the 'flow' of grace you have received. Otherwise, you will slowly die spiritually. How can one expect a beautiful environment when the roadway of blessing is blocked? The place where Jesus got tempted and where David ran away in the wilderness of Judah was next to the Dead Sea. We must realize the wilderness next to us becomes a desert if we hold on to our own blessing and grace.

We find those who pray diligently, study the Bible and even have the ability to pray in tongue. But what's missing is lack of friends around them. No interaction. These type of people are the ones who firmly hold on to the wonderful gifts from God entirely to themselves. A gift is a great blessing from God but if you insist upon your own righteousness instead, people will start to distance you eventually.

We are truly blessed. For that reason, we must yearn for the gift of the Holy Spirit. Even though we may not have much, but if we utilize God's gift, and the more we use it the more He fills it up in us. God's righteousness is when you serve and do the works of God through the Holy Spirit. This is the righteousness in God's Kingdom.

THE OLD TESTAMENT IS A SEGMENT OF A DRAMA

If it is difficult to read the Bible in sequence, then try to focus and grasp the flow of the history of the Bible as if reading a story. Using this method, we willl first form the backbone historically. So when reading the Bible you will experience the works of the living God.

The Story of God the Creator of the World-The Bible

At around 100 A.D., the representatives of Jewish Rabbis gathered in Yamnia. The purpose of this meeting was to decide up to which books to be included in the Bible. The result was the 39 books of the Old Testament that we have today.

The 39 books of the Old Testament are divided into three parts: history, poetry and prophecy. History: 17 books, Psalms: 5 books and Prophecy: 17 books. In particular, the history is the root of the Old Testament. In a way, the history is fixed as a beam whereas psalms and prophecies are left hanging to show us the providence of God. For easy reference, just think that psalms and prophecies are supplements to the book of history.

The History-17 Books

The books of history include Genesis, Exodus, Leviticus, Numbers, Deuteronomy, Joshua, Judges, Ruth, 1 & 2 Samuel, 1 & 2 Chronicles, 1 & 2 Kings, Ezra, Nehemiah and Esther. One thing we must not get confused here is that Ezra, Nehemiah and Esther are not prophets even though they are included in the history. The Five Books of Moses are the shadow of the Law.

The 'law and the prophets' in the Old Testament reflect the 17 history books and 17 books of prophecy. The Jews categorized their scriptures into three sections, the Torah (Law of Moses) and from Joshua

[Chart 1] Period Classification of the Old Testament

Period Classification	The History (17 Books)		Psalms (5 Books)	Prophecy (17 Books)
	Mainstream	Non-Mainstream		
1. Period of Creation	Genesis Chap. 1-11			
2. Period of the Patriarchs	Genesis Chap.12-50		Job	
3. Period of Exodus	Exodus, Numbers	Leviticus,Deuteronomy		
4. Period of Conquest	Joshua			
5. Period of Judges	Judges	Ruth		
6. Period of United Kingdom	1and2 Samuel 1 Kings 1-11	1 Chronicles	Psalms, Proverbs Ecclesiastes, Song of Solomon	
7. Division of Kingdom	1 Kings 12-22 2 Kings	2 Chronicles		Isaiah, Jeremiah, Lamentations, Hosea, Joel, Amos, Obadiah, Jonah, Micah, Nahum, Habakkuk, Zephaniah,
8. Period of Exile				Daniel, Ezekiel
9. Return from Exile	Ezra, Nehemiah	Esther		Haggai, Zachariah, Malachi
10. Period of Silence				

to Esther as the Former Prophets and the rest as the Latter Prophets.

The Mainstream of the Old Testament, Dividing the Old Testament Period

There is a thread running through the 17 books of History and 11 of it is the actual mainstream of the Old Testament, which is categorized into 10 periods. [See Chart 1] The remaining 6 books are supplementary and can be read later on aside from the main 11 books. It is important to read the 11 books first so that you have a perspective idea of the flow and structure of the Bible.

The book of Genesis contains the longest era in the Bible. It contains the (1) Period of Creation and (2) Period of the Patriarchs. Once finished with Genesis, you can easily continue to read Exodus which covers the exodus and the training of faith in Mt. Sinai. The storyline continues to the (3) Period of Exodus and the Journey in the Wilderness. Next is Numbers which is a travelogue of Israel's journey. The book of Leviticus is in the midst of exodus and the wilderness period but since it is not the mainstream put it aside for now. It is not to say that this book is unimportant, in fact, it is very important but in order to form the backbone we're focusing on the continuation of the storyline.

The next book is Deuteronomy which contains a restatement and reaffirmation of the Sinai covenant. Again, since it is a supplement to Exodus and Numbers just as Leviticus, we will put it aside. It is an exposition of the law and the structure of it is very similar to that of a contemporary treaty. The land and God's covenant with His people are the great themes of Deuteronomy. The word "Deuteronomy" in Chinese characters translates into "solving God's command."

Numbers covers the history of Israel; the period of desert wandering in the Sinai peninsula and ends on the eve of entry into the Promised Land to the (4) Period of Conquest and connects to Joshua to lead the new generation home.

Then the (5) Period of the Judges begins. Judges paints a rather different picture of the ongoing struggle emphasizing the importance of keeping faith with God. A story of a righteous woman during this period is Ruth. This book is also going to be set aside.

The (6) Period of the United Kingdom begins and through 1 & 2 Samuel, it explains how David's dynasty is formed. This kingdom lasts from 1 Kings 1-11 until the division at King Solomon's time. God spoke, "your land will be taken away and will be given to your servant" (1 Kings 11:11) as Solomon mismanages and breaks the covenant with God. Finally the kingdom splits into two during Solomon's reign. The identical storyline of this comes out in 1 Chronicles so we're going to put this aside again.

Now, the (7) Period of the Divided Kingdom is described from 1 Kings 12 until the end of 2 Kings. Except the story of Solomon appearing in the first part of 1 Kings in the Period of United Kingdom, the narration focuses on the story of Judah during the divided kingdom in 1 & 2 Kings. Note that 1 & 2 Chronicles is a supplement that covers mainly Southern Judah during this period.

It is very difficult to read 1& 2 Kings. It starts off with, "In the seventeenth year of Pekah the son of Remaliah, Ahaz the son of Jotham, king of Judah, became king." (2 Kings 16:1) While mentioning the divided kingdom, it states both kings from different kingdoms simultaneously. We have a hard time figuring out who's who between Israel and Judah, the reign of the king in the other kingdom, which gives us another headache while unraveling the chronology of the kings. In a historical sense, we nowadays use the terms, 'northern Israel' or 'southern Judah,' but the Bible does not record them like that. So you start to get confused when Judah is mentioned after knowing the fact that Israel existed before Judah.

In addition, the Bible does not explain chronologically about the 1st or 2nd generation. For instance, King Jeroboam is mentioned numerously in 1 Kings. Here King Jeroboam is the 1st king of Israel and the latter Jeroboam is the 2nd generation. When prophets Amos and Hosea were proclaiming the word of God, the Bible does not indicate exactly which generation it is referring to. Also, it is written in the Bible that when David fled to the Philistines, King Achish was suspicious of him at first but the second time he treated him well. We must understand here that it wasn't the same person. It was actually King Achish II. This is one of the reasons why we must have a bible teacher to teach us properly.

After concluding that 1 & 2 Kings was too difficult to read, I decided to separate the kings of Israel and Judah. Later I will explain how kings of Israel strayed further and further from the law and the worship of God; and which kings of Judah tried to recover the worship of God and which kings dirtied themselves in Baal idolatry. This way you will have a clear distinction between the history of Israel and Judah through 1 & 2 Kings. We will also find out how the country collapsed. In other words, 1 & 2 Kings is a somber story which focuses on sin.

The writer of this book(s) is assumed to be Jeremiah and the book(s) of Chronicles assumed to be written by Ezra. Upon return from exile, Ezra wanted to inform the Jews of their identities and origin. 'Why did we spend 70 years of our lives in exile? Who are we?' All their grandfathers had died by the time they returned to their homeland. So Ezra emphasized to the people that they were descendants of David and the direct descendants of Adam whom God created. Ezra encourages the small restored community to believe they truly are the inheritors of God's promise to King David and of a lasting dynasty. This supplemental book delivers the message that Messiah will come through the lineage of David.

The sounds of praises and worship to God ends as the kingdom is now divided. It was at this time God sends prophets to the land. This is strictly the grace of God. There are 12 books of prophecy including Isaiah relating to the period of division, although there are only 11 prophets. Jeremiah wrote two books (Jeremiah and Lamentations). We know that 12 books out of the 17 books of prophecy came out during the period of division. In other words, without combining the prophecy and history together it cannot be interpreted properly.

After the division period follows the (8) Period of Exile. Ultimately, Israel ignores the prophecy of the prophets and get scattered according to the Word of God. "There will be judgment of God. You will be scattered to the ends of the earth." (Jeremiah 34:17) They go into exile. Even then, gracious God sends prophets to them. The prophets during the period of exile are also taken away as prisoners. They are Daniel and Ezekiel. These two prophets live in exile along with the people of Israel and deliver the Word of God: "I have not forsaken you. But Israel said, 'The Lord has forsaken me, And the Lord has forgotten me.' Can a woman forget her nursing child, And have no compassion on the son of her womb? Even these may forget, but I will not forget you." (Isaiah 49:14-15) It seemed like the end of all hopes during their exile but God is telling them there is hope. They appear like dry bones in a deep valley, but through Ezekiel's vision with the breath of God's spirit, their bodies come alive and Israel becomes a great army. (Ezekiel 37)

The (9) Period of Exile begins. According to the prophecy of Jeremiah, the exiled Jews return to Jerusalem in 70 years. That is why God never once gave up on Israel. Ezra and Nehemiah played the roles in rebuilding the temple, restoring the God's law and recovering the Word of God. Esther was a Jewish girl who ended up marrying King Xerxes and became a queen. A plot to kill all the Jews is stirred up by a wicked man. She kept her alien identity from the king and was now the only hope of the Jews. She had the courageous attitude of "If I die, I die" (Esther 4:16) and confronts the king. As a result, the Jews were saved. Since the book of Esther is not the mainstream we will put it aside as we have done previously.

The prophets during the period of return are Haggai, Zechariah and Malachi. Haggai and Zechariah worked on rebuilding the temple and the wall upon their return from exile whereas Malachi came 80 years later (B.C. 400). He brought God's message to the downcast people who have grown careless and had increasingly casual attitudes to worship, called people's attention to set things right. From Malachi until the coming of Christ is referred as the (10) Period of Silence because the Word of God had stopped. We have now learned the mainstream of the Old Testament from Genesis and the links of the 11 books. I recommend my readers to read according to this sequence, namely, because you will see the whole picture of the Old Testament. Once you grasp the structure and the flow, the rest becomes easier to read. We're going to focus on the mainstream and put factual points as we go along the 39 books of the Old Testament.

Psalms_5 Books

The five books of Psalms contain hymns which are inserted in the middle of the Old Testament: Job, Psalms, Proverbs, Ecclesiastes, Song of Solomon and are all worship praises to God. Some may raise a question "why is the book of Job included in this category?" but the Jews interpreted it as poetry, a poetic drama about suffering and praising God. Think of it as a rhythmic recitation of poetry. It is 'hymns' assembled to praise God which starts from the book of Job. Job was a righteous man during the period of patriarchs. His encounter with God made him reach to a new level of faith where he praised God's excellence and authority.

The book of Psalms starts after Exodus until the Period of United Kingdom. It contains praises of Moses given to God after Exodus, passing through the Period of Conquest & Judges and the hymns of David and Solomon. Among the total of 150 psalms, approximately 80 of them were written by David so we call it the "psalms of David." You will be able meditate each month by reading 5 psalms each day. Here is what you should do: You multiply the day of the month you decide to read the Psalms by 5 and add 1. That particular psalm will be your starting point and continue to read 5 psalms each day. For example: If the day you decide to read is October 9th then you start reading from Psalms 46 through 50. If you happen to miss a day, you may skip to the next following psalms according to the day.

Solomon wrote the Proverbs, Ecclesiastes and Song of Solomon. Proverbs is the book of wise teachings based on reverence for God and obedience to His laws. The book of Proverbs has 31 chapters so I recommend reading it one chapter a day.

The theme of Ecclesiastes observes life around and draws the logical conclusions. It is a reflective confession of his own experience in life, giving advice to be always mindful of God while young, never waiting until becoming old, and to fear God. His constructive advice is focused onto the unbelievers of God. Song of Solomon is a compilation of God's love for Israel expressed in a series of lyric poems on the theme of love between man and woman.

Prophecy_17 Books

There are 17 books of prophecy consisting of Isaiah, Jeremiah, Lamentations, Ezekiel, Daniel, Hosea, Joel, Amos, Obadiah, Jonah, Micah, Nahum, Habakkuk, Haggai, Zechariah to up to Malachi.

After David's kingdom, praises toward God no longer existed because of the period where chaos was inevitable after the division of the kingdom and the destruction. This meant that hymns and praises to God completely vanished in Israel. Taking advantage of this, Satan starts to stir the hearts of the flesh and make people focus on earthly and desirable things of the world. We will soon learn how Satan worked through the history of Israel.

Since people stopped praising God, prophets were sent to proclaim His Word. And so the book of prophecy enters the scene. When praises stopped, the Word of God started to come down to earth. The prophets were sent during the period of exile and return. God's primary message was, "It is not late yet. Return to Me." Upon their return, the people of Israel were encouraged through Haggai,

Zechariah and Malachi and the work of recovery began.

I emphasize once again that the main focus is to grasp the mainstream. This mainstream is to be inserted deeply into your mind, not just as a concept because only then the Bible becomes alive. You will hear the breath of our living God; you will feel His love; and finally, you will understand the works of God.

Channel Between God and Man, The Word

God Gave Three Channels to Man :

First, channel with another person. As we live, we come across people that we connect with and those we don't. We are happy when we communicate well especially through exchange of hearts.

Second, channel with our natural environment. God has given us the environment to overcome it and be fruitful, multiply and fill the earth. We eat animals, vegetables and consume calcium from minerals from the earth. Through good digestive and excretion systems, we become a healthy person.

Third, channel with God. We humans need to connect well with one another as well as with nature. But most importantly, we must connect with God. A person who connects well with God is what swe call 'faith.' On the other hand, disconnection with God is what we call 'sin.'

The way to God can be confirmed through the way in which God created the universe.

You can locate the position of mankind by examining the structure of the universe. God made the heaven and the earth when creating the universe. The earth contains mineral and the main representative of it is dirt and water. The universe was formless, void and dark before creation and the Spirit of God was moving over the surface of the waters. (Genesis 1:2) And with His Word, light came down and He started to fill the waters with fish in the seas and birds in the sky. Vegetations and trees were made on earth and animals followed thereafter. There are minerals, vegetations and animals on this earth. In this manner, God created the universe scientifically.

Characteristic of Things that Exist on Earth

First, everything that exists on this earth attributes to change. Minerals start to change according to time and temperature and there is a purpose for it. All existences that God created change for the ones existing above them. The reason for the minerals to change is for the vegetation roots to sprout and grow from the earth. By these changes, the mineral plays a supporting role for the vegetation to survive its life. The vegetation start to change as time goes by. A tiny mustard seed grows into a plant and eventually turns into a tree. All seeded vegetables such as tomatoes, grapes, cabbages, and grain like rice become food. Eventually vegetables change to become food for animals, the higher existence above the vegetation. Minerals supply energy to the vegetation and vegetation in return, supplies energy to the animals. Vegetation responds according to its environment. The leaves of a tree acclimates to the cold climate producing time needles whereas in a hot climate the leaves becomes broadened.

Animals change as they move. A puppy becomes a big dog as it moves around; a chick hatched from an egg moves around all day long picking up food and grows into a full grown chicken, eventually supplying energy to humans that are the higher beings above them.

Second, the commonality of all existence on earth is that they are made of dirt and visible. They do not last forever and have its limit.

Third, all creation on earth respond to light. Not only do we repond physically but we have been created so that our spirit comes alive when we receive the Word of Light.

Characteristic of the Things that Exist in Heaven

First, every existence in heaven is of spirit which clearly distinguishes them from any existence on the earth. It has no bodily forms whatsoever, so it is invisible. For this reason some people declare that they don't believe in God because they can't see God. God is Spirit so one cannot see God. God is a ruling Spirit whereas angel is a serving spirit and Satan, the fallen spirit. Humans also have spirit.

[Chart 2] Structure of the Universe

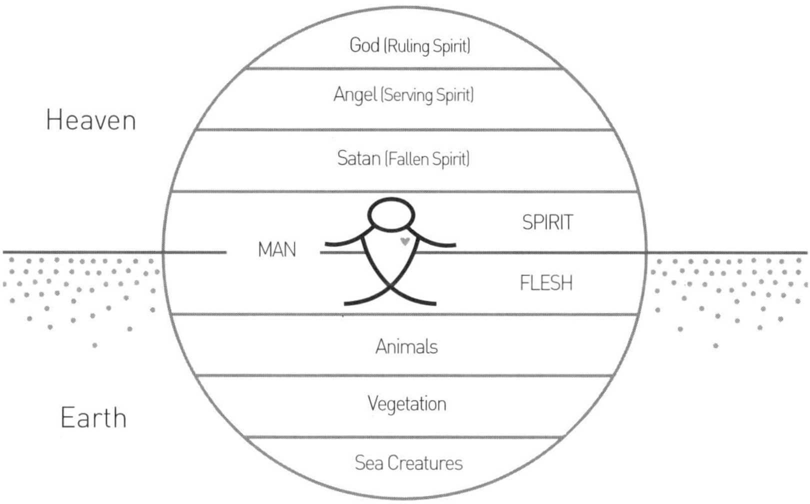

Second, every existence in heaven is of spirit, so it does not change with time whereas things of the earth changes. We refer to things that don't change as 'eternal.' God is eternal. The serving angels of God exist forever as long as God exists. As for Satan, at the approval of God, it will continue to work as the one having authority over the world and snatch away the blessings of God from humankind until the 2nd coming of Christ on judgment day.

We are the linking channel that connects both the heaven and earth. When time comes, those who believe in Jesus, will shake off the dirt and go to God's Kingdom. Heaven is where there are no sufferings, worries or troubles but just eternal joy. The Holy Spirit comes into our heart to change us so that we may enjoy the eternal heaven while living on this earth. This process is what is referred to as the process of sanctification, leading to godliness or Christlike.

Third, spiritual existence inevitably speaks. The serving angels deliver the Word of God to people on earth. Satan, the fallen angel in the Garden of Eden, tempted Eve with words. Humans also have spirits so that is why we speak. The spirits are delivered when we speak. Actual words spoken are the ways and channels for spirits to travel. Faith comes from hearing; and hearing is the Word of God.

A person who has received the gospel with 'Amen' and the Holy Spirit abiding is what we call a 'believer.' "It is the Spirit who gives life; the flesh profits nothing; the words that I have spoken to you are spirit and are life." (John 6:63) God has created man out of dust but we have been given a channel the Word as a mediator for us to communicate with Him in spirit.

Our faith grows as we start to hold on to the Word of God and be aware of God's connection to us. As you realize it more, the hope of sharing God's love with others will fill your heart transforming you to experience new encounters at a higher level.

. . .

Do not worry then, saying, 'What will we eat?' or 'What will we drink?' or 'What will we wear for clothing?' "For the Gentiles eagerly seek all these things; for your heavenly Father knows that you need all these things." But seek first His kingdom and His righteousness, and all these things will be added to you.

Matthew 6:31-33

PERIOD OF CREATION AND PERIOD OF THE PATRIARCHS

Genesis 1-11, Genesis 12-50

Among the 10 periods from the Old Testament, we will select a few major incidents from the Period of Creation and the Period of the Patriarchs in order to form a backbone. In Genesis, it contains the story of the marvelous creation of mankind and the universe, sin and suffering and God's Kingdom. It is extremely important to understand the beginning of God's creation. Primarily because if there are questionable issues about Genesis it would be difficult to believe many parts of the Bible. One of the reasons why this book puts emphasis is that it covers two periods among the entire 10 periods of the Old Testament.

PERIOD OF CREATION_Genesis 1-11

The period of creation can be divided into four parts: creation (Genesis 1-2), fall of mankind (Genesis 3-5) judgment of the flood (Genesis 6-9) and the folly of Babel (Genesis 10-11).

God's Creation_Genesis 1-2

The beginning of all things starts in Genesis 1:1, "In the beginning God created the heavens and the earth." Then in verse 2, it tells us about the state of the world before the creation, "the earth was formless, void and dark." The earth in order yet and it was empty and dark. Then the creation begins. "Let there be light; and there was light" (Genesis 1:3). Through the Word of God, God fills up the space. He fills disorder with order and darkness with light. Imagine a movie screen: a black screen suddenly lights up with the Word of God from heave and the he marvelous creation takes place. The curtain is raised and everything unfolds like a great drama. The wonder and richness of creation from formlessness to teeming life takes place! God brings order out of chaos. The creation has begun with the Word of God coming into the world. The Word which we cannot see starts to unveil itself through creation.

God not only created with His Word but all creation was in His control as well. It's written in Hebrews 1:3 that "He upholds all things by the word of His power." For example, let's say a building has been constructed. Many of us think that the building is solid because of the impact of the cement. But that is not so. It is God who holds all things together. God made everything there is: all things that we see, eat, drink, wear and seek. He made visible things with His invisible Word. It is in God's power and His Word that all things are possible. God is proclaimed as the Creator as well as the Sovereign of the world and of everything therein.

Fall of Mankind_Genesis 3-5

The prologue moves swiftly from the world God created to the world that we have. God's good creation has been progressively soured as a result of the sin of human who turned away from the Creator and ignored His warnings (Genesis 3). The fall of mankind in the Garden of Eden occurs when a fatal choice of eating the prohibited fruit from the tree of good and evil results Adam and Eve to leave the garden forever. Spiritual confrontation has begun in the world ever since men were thrown out of the garden.

The offerings of Cain and Abel explain how it derived from humanly and sinful world and its progression. Sadly enough, the story of the world begins with Adam and Eve's first son, Cain, the murderer. Cain kills his younger brother Abel out of jealousy. He sets out eastward from the garden and builds a city called Enoch taken after his own son's name. This is the beginning of civilization. Lamech was the so-called the 1st king of this first country.

The important fact in the period of creation is the 'civilized country.' The genealogy of the Bible always begins from the worldly tribes and then the tribes of God's people next. This sequence is consistent throughout the entire Bible. Even in the beginning of creation, the earth is mentioned first, described as being void, formless and dark.

Judgment of the Flood_Genesis 6-9

God could not leave Cain's descendants and his successors alone in the beginnings of civilized life. The human race, lost in violence and corruption is bringing destruction upon itself so God judges them through the flood. The mixed marriages between the sons of God and the daughters of the world were the cause. On this note, even though God's Kingdom was yet to begin, we know that the descendants of Cain and those worshiping God existed at the time. "Mixed marriage" means God's people losing their purity and godliness to the world. The Bible says, "Then the Lord saw that the wickedness of man was great on the earth, and that every intent of the thoughts of his heart was only evil continually." (Genesis 6:5)

God created mankind as His love partner to become His image but the thoughts of men were wicked and evil from early on. After the fall of mankind, the sin from Adam and Eve has been passed on and left them to sin. It says in the Bible that God was sorry that He had made man on the earth. In grief, He decided to sweep them away by flood. Humankind sinned from the beginning but God interferes in the world and acts in judgment.

In the 1st judgment, not everything was lost. Against the background of judgment, enters God's saving act. God destroys everything except Noah and his family. In the Bible, these people are referred as "remnants." When God acts in judgment, there is always a residue (waste) left behind and this is called "slump." Slump comes out in the book of prophets and a 'bud' sprouts out in the end. This is God's amazing providence and reason why He does not wipe everything out. This is also a key element in understanding the flow of the Bible.

The Folly of the Tower of Babel_Genesis 10-11

Sadly even the righteous man in his time and his children (remnants) sin. They build a tower of Babel which was in all likelihood a multistoried temple tower and inscribed their names on it describing it as "the building whose top is in heaven." In other words, they were encouraging one another to become god. Humankind's challenge to God continues on. "How you have fallen from heaven, O star of the morning, son of the dawn! You have been cut down to the earth, You who have weakened the nations! But you said in your heart, I will ascend to heaven; I will raise my throne above the stars of God, And I will sit on the mount of assembly In the recesses of the north." (Isaiah 14:12-14) The word "you" refers to humankind. This is the fallen angel becoming Satan.

How did God act in the judgment the first time? Everything was wiped out through the flood. God descended to earth and acted in mercy and with sovereignty, making an unconditional promise of the rainbow never to judge humanity with another flood. That is why God did not blot them out but instead divided the nation by language and scattered them abroad.

Now that you have read about judgement, at the mention of Old Testament the only thing that comes to your mind is the 'scary' God. But know this, God is love and mercy. The story of God's love in recovering His Kingdom starts from Genesis 12. Now within this chapter, the B.C. and A.D. takes place.

PERIOD OF THE TRIBES_Genesis 12-50

Through the tower of Babel, people continue to expand the world without God and sinful desires keep increasing. Now we know that at this point there was no hope in this world since Genesis. God makes us understand from the beginning, "Why God must rule over the earth? Why God's Kingdom was necessary?"

When worldly people gather, they challenge and become rebellious towards God but when God's people gather, a church is formed. It becomes God's Kingdom. Through the descendants of Abraham, God promises to fulfill the three key elements of His world. This is God's greatest principle of salvation. Note the related verses: "Go forth from your country, And from your relatives And from your father's house, To the land which I will show you; (promise of land) And I will make you a great nation, And I will bless you, And make your name great; And so you shall be a blessing; (promise of people). And I will bless those who bless you, And the one who curses you I will curse. And in you all the families of the earth shall be blessed(promise of sovereignty)." (Genesis 12:1-3) The emphasis shifts from having no hope to God's great purpose in redeeming the world and mending broken relationships.

Map 1

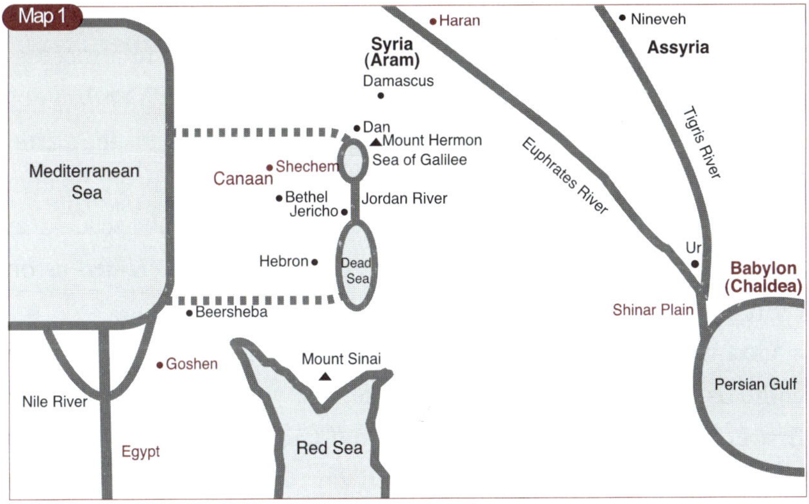

Period of Creation We have no idea where the Garden of Eden is located. There are some who claim that it was in the land of Haran and in today's world, President Bush had once requested a $12 million fund from Congress for the search project for Garden of Eden. But we must understand that the garden is a symbolic place. Garden of Eden is unknown to everyone. Many claim that it is based on Euphrates River since it originated from Eden but we must realize that the river is mentioned in different locations so assumptions must be avoided. Geographical names start in chapter 11 of Genesis. Let's try to locate plains of Shinar where the tower of Babel used to be.

God's Interest

The period of the tribes starts from chapter 12 through 50. It is the period of God of Abraham, Isaac and Jacob. The main underlying concept of the period of the tribes is actually the declaration of God's Kingdom. This is the opening of God's plan while it has yet to be built, this marks the beginning of the process. God was sending a message by saying, "You may have thought there's no hope in the world where constant suffering and judgment follow but that's not true. There is hope. And this hope is My kingdom. I am going to change it around."

Why did God create man from the dust on earth and not with heavenly spirit? It is because blessings come from heaven and the earth receives it. (Note: Chart 2) For example, let's say your child has gone to

Harvard University. People greet you by saying, "What a blessing indeed!" And if your daughter happened to get married to a successful man, "Your family receives so much blessing, What's your secret?" Where do you feel the actual blessings? It's on the earth. That is why we have been created on this earth. When we receive blessings physically on earth, we give praise and thanks to God in spirit. We feel joy and happiness. For this reason, God created us on earth.

God wants to give His world to human beings, whom He created with His love. He wants us to overrule His world on this earth. God first created the earth (Genesis 1) and the Garden of Eden (Genesis 2)-which is His world. The hope that God gave us is to create a kingdom on this earth and rule over it while praising Him and to live forever in His Kingdom after we die. Therefore, wherever God exists "it is heaven even though it may be in a tent or in a palace." Then why is not heaven on this earth? God's Kingdom has to be formed together with other people on this earth. An important command has been to us. And it is up to us to follow through.

Proclamation of God's Kingdom_Genesis 12:1-3

God calls upon one man to proclaim His Kingdom, Abraham. (Genesis 12) When God meets a person, His Kingdom opens. Abraham was called from Ur of the Chaldeans which is another name for Babylon. (Genesis 12:1-3) God had called Abraham from the actual place of judgment, the city of Ur in Babylon, where people had built the tower of Babel.

God did not call Abraham because he had strong faith, strong religious background or a graduate from a reputable college. Abraham's father, Terah, was an idol maker and his son, a businessman. His father moved the family from Ur to Haran in Syria and it is there where God called Abraham at the age of 75. It is assumed that

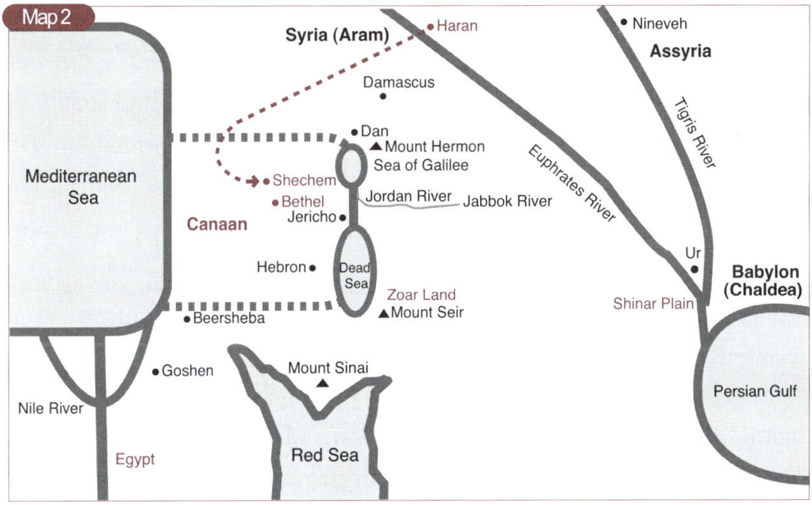

Period of the Patriarchs God called Abraham from the scene of tower of Babel and gives the new beginning(the beginning of Kingdom of God, beginning of salvation), who becomes the seed of the Israelites and raises him as a father of faith.

Abraham went about doing business traveling with donkey caravans here and there. He responded obediently when he was called by God to leave his homeland. (Hebrews 11:8) He sets out on his journey following the guidance of God and this was the beginning of the constuction process of God's Kingdom.

Those who have met God in the Bible are the ones who have heard the voice of God. Since God is invisible, we must be able to hear His voice. God gives Abraham a promise first that through his descendants a nation will rise. By this promise, God has a missionary purpose in bringing up His world through Abraham. God interferes in Abraham's life in various ways by saying, "go here, go there, throw this and that away, give up Ishmael," etc. Abraham waited 25 years for the birth of his heir at the age of 100, but giving up his son was the ultimate test. At God's command to offer his son as a sacrifice, he obeyed. When he offered his son to God, that's when God started to fill Abraham with His blessings. He becomes the ancestor of faith and through him, the seed of faith spreads. Abraham's promise continues for three generations up to Isaac and Jacob. God's covenant was pivotal to the promise of salvation, both to Abraham's descendents and to all the nations a process in building God's Kingdom.

Do you think God chose Jacob because of his good nature? No. He deceived his father who was old and almost blind as well as his brother, successfully snatching away the blessing of his birthright. Afraid his brother might kill him, Jacob goes into exile and finally exhausted falls asleep in the darkness with his head on a stone. In a moment of unutterable loneliness. God meets him. He hears the voice of God, "I am the Lord, the God of your father Abraham and the God of Isaac; the land on which you lie, I will give it to you and to your descendants." (Genesis 28:13) -repeating the promise made to Abraham and Isaac adding a personal guarantee: "I shall be with you to protect you and I will not leave you until I bring you back." (Genesis 28:15) And this promise of Emmanuel is faithfully fulfilled.

The actual fulfillment of God's promise takes place many hundreds of years later. In order to fulfill His promise how many children did God give to Abraham? It was only one and two sons to Isaac. The same promise was given to the third generation. This is the process of making God's people which means that it takes a long time to achieve it. Only at the 3rd generation, 12 sons are given to Jacob who becomes the 12 tribes of Israel. God's people spread as countless as the stars of heaven, like sands of the ocean through these 12 tribes. The work of God's Kingdom was in the process through three generations which is the story of the period of the tribes.

The story of Joseph comes out in the latter part of Genesis. Strangely enough, Joseph's name is missing when we mention God of Abraham, Isaac and Jacob. It is because God revealed himself only to these three people. Joseph did not receive this promise but instead faith was passed down to him. Hebrew people are known to receive religious training from their mothers. Probably Rachel, whom Jacob loved so much, must have inherited the good faith to Joseph. Even though he didn't meet God directly but having received the great

Knowledge Search 1

God's Interference and Fairness

I am frequently asked questions during my Bible study seminar. "Of all nations, God chose Israel as His chosen people and then orders to strike down the tribes of cannanites regardless whether human or animal. Do you think God is fair? "

We must understand that it was God's judgment of the lewd and lustful sins of the 7 tribes. They were destroyed for a reason. As it is clearly shown through Abraham's blessing the heart of God is towards every nation and that is why He sent his only begotten Son to the world. (John 3:16) God's love is universal that He brought His love out of nothing and did not limit it to Israel or the ones at church. He loves all people in the world! Make no mistake that God did not 'choose' Israel out of many other nations. If so, then surely it would not be fair. The most important fact is that God personally 'created' Israel. The procedural making of God's Kingdom was through the collaboration of people of Israel in order to share blessings throughout the world. Israel was chosen for the purpose to save all mankind. This is the important part. Often times, I receive remarks like "It would have been great if God chose Korea as His chosen people!" We must actually be thankful that we were not! Look at the people of Israel and see how they have been torn apart even though they received blessings along the way.

faith from the God of Abraham, Isaac and Jacob, he was able to play a supporting role in accomplishing the promise.

But then again, his 'supporting' role does not properly acknowledge the significance of him because his life resembles so much of Jesus' life. Enduring the sufferings and hardships, he succeeded in overcoming the seduction and held on to his inner resources toward

God. He eventually reaches to a high position as Pharaoh's right-hand man, the governor of all Egypt. At every stage of chapters 12-50, God is present. Not simply presupposed but constantly and actively at work through the lives of people. It explains in detail how the foundation work of God's Kingdom took place and explains also the background of how the people of Israel entered Egypt.

. . .

"For God so loved the world, that He gave His only begotten Son, that whoever believes in Him shall not perish, but have eternal life." For God did not send the Son into the world to judge the world, but that the world might be saved through Him. "He who believes in Him is not judged; he who does not believe has been judged already, because he has not believed in the name of the only begotten Son of God.

John 3:16-18

EXODUS; PERIOD OF THE WILDERNESS; PERIOD OF CONQUEST AND PERIOD OF THE JUDGES

Exodus / Numbers

Today we are going to build the backbone of the Exodus and the Period of the Wilderness; continue on shaping it with the Period of Conquest and the Period of the Judges.

EXODUS AND PERIOD OF THE WILDERNESS_Exodus

We will focus on four themes in this chapter: the exodus from Egypt; training in Mt. Sinai; Kadesh Barnea test and life in the wilderness.

The Exodus

In the time of famine, Joseph, who was now the governor of Egypt, permitted his father Jacob and his brothers and families (approx. 70 members) to move to Egypt. They settled in Goshen and were given the duties to take care of Pharaoh's livestock. Their life in Egypt started out in a privileged status but it didn't last long. Things started to change after a new pharaoh's enthronement who did not know Joseph. The increasing number of Israelites and their abilities made Pharaoh feel uneasy so he decides to make

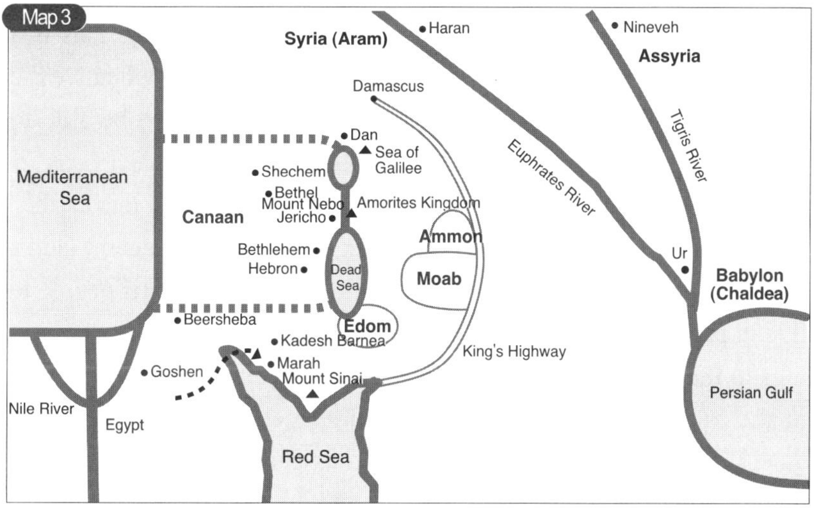

The Exodus and Period of the Wilderness The people of Israel were treated well at first as the family of the governor in Egypt but in the end they became slaves. God took them out of Egypt and lead them to Canaan.

them slaves. This is the beginning of slavery for 400 years for the people of Israel. When the people of Israel first entered Egypt, there were 70 but now the existence of them were great in numbers. Two million--like the stars of heaven and sands of the ocean. A great labor force was imposed on them to dig out mud and make the bricks for building the new city. Just imagine the sufferings they must have endured.

Their cries were heard by God. It was a miraculous intervention by God, in response to the cries of his enslaved people. A leader named Moses was sent to deliver them out of Egypt, ending their 430 years of slavery. The 'Exodus' (exit) gives the book its name. Exodus shows God's salvation and freedom. Exodus must have a starting point 'from' with a destination 'to.' From Egypt to a distinctive destination, Canaan, the Promised Land. God keeps His promise to Abraham by bringing them out.

Egypt symbolizes the world. The world of desires, ambition and sin. This is a place where you become slaves of desires and sin. God saved us from here, the world and guided us along a clear path. The

Canaan that we must enter has a land in the entrance way. This is a very important point. Our purpose is not to go to heaven when we die but to fulfill the heaven on this earth only then will we be able to enter into His eternal kingdom.

The problem is "how can we fulfill God's Kingdom on this earth?" The idea of God was to make such a world through Abraham. God's special favor was to be shown not only to Abraham and His people to live in prosperity but to "become the source and the founder of blessings to many nations to come." This is the key message of the period of the tribes and the reason why Israel was chosen. Therefore, God gave the Word to Israel and used them as channels of blessing ultimately spreading the Word to Gentiles and the world.

Threader: The disciples asked Jesus to teach them how to pray and the prayer that was taught was, "Your kingdom come, Your will be done." (Matthew 6:10) The invisible God's Kingdom must first be fulfilled in our heart so that we become the channels of blessing. It is our calling and mission to evangelize and to spread God's Kingdom and His blessings to our neighbors and to the entire world.

We must understand this story not simply as an event in the distant past but as something significant to us all today. Coming out of the world is impossible with our own strength. God wants to save us and is asking us to come out from the worldly desires and sin but we cannot escape or run away from it on our own. Without God's help, it's impossible. Only when God sees your faith, will you be saved.

After exodus, there was a place where the Israelites ended up. It was the wilderness. After going through this process they entered the Promised Land. Even after entering Canaan, the work continues on in making God's Kingdom. Just the fact that you've entered the land doesn't mean that it becomes God's Kingdom automatically. There's work to be done. There is a sequence of process in order to enter Canaan which is to overcome the wilderness. There's no water, no grass, no food, no clothing--nothing is available in the wilderness. Without God, there's no way to survive in the wilderness. Food was manna from heaven, water was given only upon the command of God by striking the rock. It was essentially God's act of governance. Obviously this was suffering to them. The suffering in the wilderness where there is nothing is actually the beginning of blessing.

While I was stationed in China, I underwent surgery for my stomach cancer and experienced the living God while going through chemotherapy treatments. I went through the bottom pit of death and pain but this was when I held on to the Word of God with all my might. And God poured His Almighty gift to me to teach the Word at that time. Without any memorization, Bible verses began to staple into my heart by looking at it only couple of times. "I will write My Word in your heart." (Jeremiah 31:33)

Suffering is the beginning of blessing. If you hold on to Jesus, you will be able to overcome the wilderness. The important thing is whether you complain or obey during your life in the wilderness. The minute upon their exodus, the people of Israel became God's citizen. An amazing change of identity take place when you are saved by believing in Jesus. God's people, God's children--what a remarkable change is this?! Now that our identity has been changed, our inner self must be transformed as well. God's Kingdom can be accomplished only after changes take place in our inner self. Once you are changed, you are compelled to deliver the Word and that's when you experience the power.

Training in Mt. Sinai

It only takes approximately 14 days to go to the land of Canaan from Egypt. But God makes the people of Israel cross the Red Sea and leads them to the lower southern part of the Sinai Peninsula towards Mt. Sinai. One year of training took place in Mt. Sinai. They were not trained to become skillful warriors to conquer the seven tribes in Canaan but instead received the gift of God's law summed up in the Ten Commandments and detailed regulations for sacrifice and worship, centered on the Tabernacle. This religious training was the purpose and essence of their Exodus.

The book of Exodus is regarded as the most important part of the Old Testament for the people of Israel. Primarily because it contains God's work of deliverance from sin and power of death and guide them into the land of milk and honey. There was no other nation who received the law from God except Israel. And it was God's providence that through the people of Israel that His Word and blessing would be spread to the Gentiles and to many nations.

The highlight of the law is the Ten Commandments. In chapter 20, the instruction of God's agreement with His people is explained setting forth a basic ethical application to all people in all ages. In the beginning, God spoke the words of life now God speaks the words for living. Therefore, we must abide by the code of laws given by God. God has given the Ten Commandments to not only to the people of Israel but to all of us! Based on this standard, we must be able to bear fruit from this seed (God's Word). This seed in the O.T. is the Ten Commandments whereas in the N.T. , it is the Sermon (a new standard) on the Mount given by Jesus. The important fact is that the people of Israel were slow to accept the Word of God and consequently persistent sinfulness recurred during the 40 years of wandering in the wilderness and even after entering Canaan they failed to obey. God's covenant of blessings and curses of 'if you obey ... and if you don't ... is the key message in the book of Deuteronomy. It implies a second law-giving and it is an 'exposition' of the law. It is a crossroad between blessing and curse and is addressed throughout the Old Testament which applies to the New Testament as well.

This crossroad is such a well known fact to even youngsters but why is it so difficult to keep? Just like popular lyrics that goes, "I know that I shouldn't but I do" - the reality check is that this is the way we are. Knowing that Israel was not capable of obeying the law, it was God's compassion to give general instructions about worship in the Tabernacle. Otherwise they would have all died in the wilderness one way or the other.

What does the Tabernacle represent? It symbolizes the grace of Christ's blood on the cross. The offerings were made through the blood of animals in the Old Testament period since Jesus had not come yet. Humans are bound to sin and how do we know this? Sinning means that you have broken away from the Word of God. We must understand the relationship between the Law and the Tabernacle in the book of Exodus. Both aspects must be equally emphasized otherwise God's grace cannot be revealed. We must hold on to both the grace of the blood on the cross and the Word of the Law together. This also applies to the relationship of the Word and Prayer just like a twin wagon. The training in Mt. Sinai was exactly for this purpose.

When the Tabernacle was finished, God signified His satisfaction by the cloud, the visible token of God's presence, which rested above the Tent, and the place was filled with the dazzling light of God's glory. The Exodus chapter ends by saying, "Throughout all their journeys, the cloud of the Lord was on the tabernacle by day, and there was fire in it by night, in the sight of all the house of Israel." (Exodus 40:38) This is the presence of the Holy Spirit. This same Holy Spirit has come into our hearts to those who believe in Jesus. The pillar of cloud and fire represents the guidance of the Holy Spirit and it can now be felt through the five senses of the body. The people of Israel left Mt. Sinai and God led them to the place called Kadesh Barnea.

Test in Kadesh Barnea

God wants to test the people of Israel whether their faith is strong enough after receiving one year training in Mt. Sinai and sends them out to view the land of Canaan from Kadesh Barnea. In other words, God was checking to see whether Israel was worthy enough to fulfill

God's Kingdom in the Promised Land after giving them the Word (Law) and the Tabernacle. Joshua was one of the 12 spies to reconnoiter the land. He and Caleb alone had the faith and courage to recommend to move forward while the remaining 10 made a big fuss with tales of giants and grasshoppers. "Only do not rebel against the Lord; and do not fear the people of the land, for they shall be our prey. Their protection has been removed from them, and the Lord is with us; do not fear them." (Numbers 14:9)

Ignoring Joshua and Caleb's advice, the people of Israel started to grumble. "All the sons of Israel grumbled against Moses and Aaron; and the whole congregation said to them, 'Would that we had died in the land of Egypt! Or would that we had died in this wilderness!' 'And why is the LORD bringing us into this land, to fall by the sword? Our wives and our little ones will become plunder; would it not be better for us to return to Egypt?' So they said to one another, 'Let us appoint a leader and return to Egypt.'" (Numbers 14:2-4) They even wanted to stone Joshua and Caleb for not agreeing with them. In conclusion, the test in Kadesh Barnea failed miserably.

Life in the Wilderness

God punishes the people of Israel for the consequence of their failure by calculating a day of spying as one year and making them wander in the wilderness for 40 years. After the test in Kadesh, the last work done by Moses was conquering east of Jordan. God told Moses that he cannot enter the Promised Land because he failed to honor God. Even after learning this 'deadly' news, he obeys God and leads the people of Israel into the wilderness. Through Moses, east of Jordan is conquered and through his successor, Joshua, the conquest of Canaan begins.

The 1st generation of Israel that left Egypt all died in the wilderness due to their lack of faith and trust. Only their children, the 2nd generation, reached the Promised Land with Joshua after 38 years of wandering in the wilderness. This leads us into the period of conquest

THE PERIOD OF CONQUEST_Joshua

"Moses was very humble, more than any man who was on the face of the earth" (Numbers 12:3) he symbolized a great leadership but in the end, but he failed to enter the land of Canaan. It was his servant and successor Joshua who led the people of Israel to the land of Canaan.

Threader: Joshua is a Hebrew name (the Old Testament is written in Hebrew and the New Testament in Greek). Joshua in Greek is Jesus so Jesus is Joshua in the Old Testament. What did Joshua do? It is said that around the time Jesus was born, because of the great anticipation of the Messiah, many names were given as Jesus. "I am the way, and the truth, and the life; no one comes to the Father, but through Me." (John 14:6) Just as Jesus, Joshua led the nation to God's Kingdom.

The conquest of Canaan begins with the crossing of the Jordan River along with the conquest of Jericho. Jericho is located in between the Jordan River and the Dead Sea. The book of Joshua also shows us the conquering process of the seven tribes of Canaanites.

The theme of Joshua is the 'power of worship' and the victory of the holy war through worship. The seven tribes of Canaanites were extremely lewd. Defeat for the Canaanites during the conquest of the land was for God's judgment on these people whose religion and culture had become thoroughly corrupt. While reading the book of Joshua, there's a part about Joshua giving worship when he comes face-to-face with a man who described himself as "Commander of the Lord's army" (Joshua 5:14). He was sent by God. God was at the head of the army and Israel knew it as the Ark of God's presence led

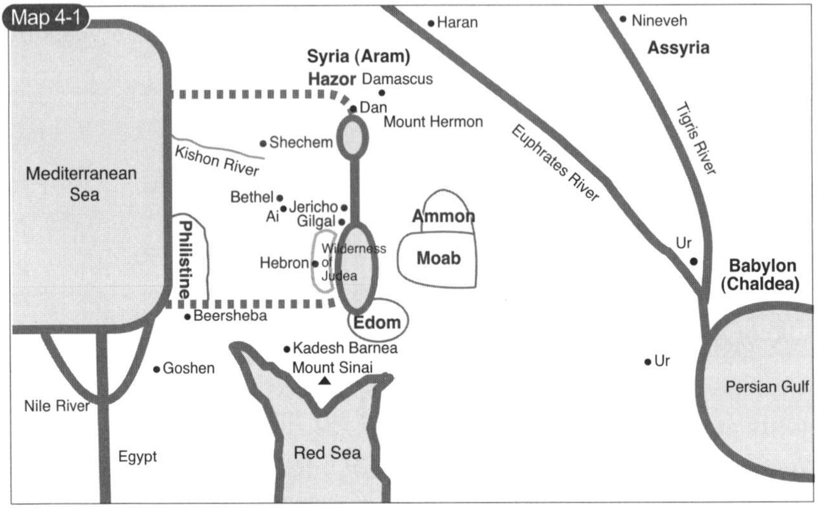

The Period of Conquest The people of Israel receives distribution of the land in Canaan as their own through the victory of worship. The work of fulfilling God's Kingdom begins.

the force into victory. After Joshua successfully conquers the land of Canaan, the 12 tribes of Israel receive distribution of land for their own use.

We are going through the same 'holy war' in this world. Knowing that the world is filled with filth, corruption, plots and trickery everywhere God is calling His servant, a true Israel (one who has fulfilled God's Kingdom in his heart) to become the channel of His blessing so that His Kingdom can be expanded through them. This is the calling of the believers. The important part is that it is not you who fight the war of the evil power; you should let the 'commander of the Lord's army' work for you. "Battle is not yours but God's." (2 Chronicles 20:15) From this, if you fight on your own, you will fall.

God's plan of leading His people into victory of conquest was to distribute the land of Canaan to the 12 tribes of Israel so that they could raise a God worshipping community. But after the distribution of the land, the period of the judges unfolds a sinful period distancing further away from God's will.

Conquest is Partial

As you read, Judges 1 and 2 it feels like you're continuously reading the book of Joshua. The reason for it is because the conquest has not completed yet. The people of Israel were not equipped with weapons or horses and yet they marched on their feet to fight the battles. This was possible only because the 'commander of the Lord's army' fought ahead of them. They failed to take over the Canaanites or the tribes of Philistines who were positioned in the southeastern part of the Mediterranean.

The people of Philistines are Europeans. They were thrown out from the Crete Island of Mediterranean and wanted to settle in Egypt originally but failed. Instead, this tribe took over the partial land of Canaan which occurred around the same time of Joshua's conquest of Canaan but no one can confirm this exactly. However, the land of Philistines still existed and there were still a number of territories in Canaan that were not conquered by the people of Israel when Joshua divided the lands for the 12 tribes of Israel. Eventually the Israelites took over Philistines and completely claimed it as their own land.

But in the period of Romans after the death of Jesus, around A.D. 70, the Jews rebel against the Romans but at the leadership of General Titus the Roman armies raze Israel into ruins destroying Jerusalem and its temple. Israel was in ruins at this point. As a result, people of Israel were scattered throughout the world. This event is referred as the 'Diaspora.' General Titus realizing that such a small number of Jews had actually resisted the great Roman Empire gives the land its name: Philistines as the land of the Gentile tribes. The underlying meaning of Palestine contains oppression and hatred of Israel. That is why the Jews get agitated whenever Palestine is men-

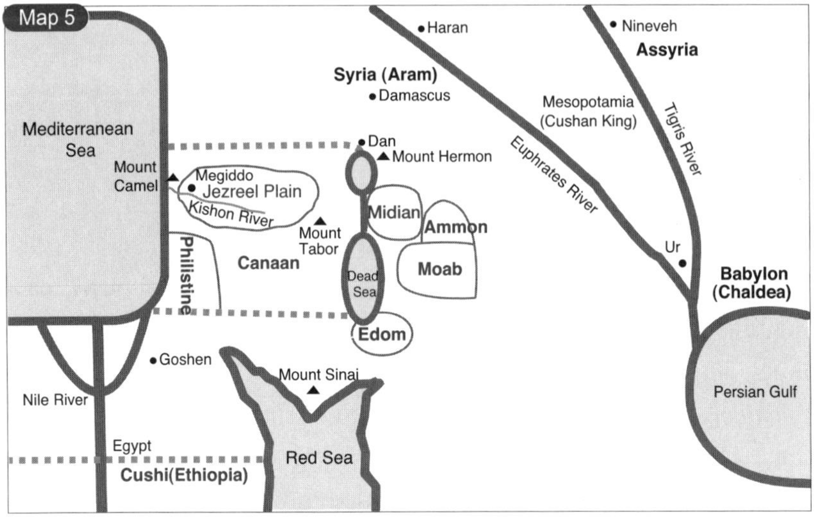

The Period of the Judges The people of Israel had not yet completely conquered the land of Canaan and repeatedly continued to sin. God had prepared various foreign tribes in the outskirts of Canaan to use them as tools to punish the Israelites.

tioned. Even today PLO (Palestine Liberation Organization) raises a problem.

What does this 'incomplete' conquest mean to us? As the Messiah was prophesied in the Old Testament, by the coming of Jesus Christ and His Helper (Holy Spirit) the word of "Which is His body, the fulness of Him who fills all in all" (Ephesians 1:23) is fulfilled. What this means is a church that is filled with Jesus where believers receive fullness of the Holy Spirit. We must clearly understand that without the Holy Spirit, it is impossible to achieve the complete conquest. The Israelites were able to conquer the land with the support of the Lord's commander but they failed to create God's Kingdom. That is why the conquest in the days of Joshua was partially completed. This also applies to us. Our body is also partially conquered as believers of Jesus until the Holy Spirit fills our heart. For this reason, it is important for us to experience (baptism) the Holy Spirit. Jesus said to Nicodemus, "Unless one is born of water and the Spirit, he cannot enter into the kingdom of God." (John 3:5) We must pray in order to receive the baptism of the Holy Spirit.

A judge undertook the various roles of a king, a high priest and a prophet. However, there was a distinctive difference in a king's role. For instance, a king would act as a commander-in-chief if there was a battle and once it ended, would return back as a judge to administer justice. They delivered tribe or nation from the enemy's oppression, winning their laurels in active service. This was somewhat a unique role because normally a king would have his own reserve army under command. Instead, after a battle is ended, the anointed judge would return to his original position and this also applied to the 12 tribes. What this meant was that the assembled armies were dismantled after finishing their job. This was according to God's instruction because He did not want to appoint a king. Reason being the Promised Land given to Abraham, Isaac and Jacob was God's Kingdom.

What are the three basic elements of a nation given to Abraham? Territory, people and sovereignty. During the period of slavery in Egypt, people of Israel multiplied like the stars of the heaven and sands of the ocean in their numbers, totaling 2 million people. Through Joshua's conquest of Canaan, I and was given to them. All was given to the Israelites except a king because sovereignty belonged to God. God's Kingdom is not a worldly kingdom. God is the only king and His kingdom is what God wanted to create in the world. But unfortunately, an inevitable situation arose leaving no choice but to appoint a judge which is the beginning of the book of Judges. God trained the Israelites in Mt. Sinai. The Ten Commandments and the Tabernacle were given to them to create a God worshipping community.

Reaching the end of his life, Joshua assembled the elders of Shechem and renewed the covenant sworn there after their first victory in the land. A loyal pledge by saying, "If serving the Lord seems undesirable to you, then choose for yourselves today whom you will serve: whether the gods which your fore fathers served which were beyond the River, or the gods of the Amorites in whose land you are living; but as for me and my house, we will serve the Lord." (Joshua 24:15) This is such an important verse. He did not say, "since you're in this land, you must worship the Lord" but instead he used the word 'choose.' This is what God has given us--the absolute freewill of choice.

God has driven out great and powerful nations for the Israelites in the Promised Land. Now the ultimate choice lies upon them-whether the land is to become God's Kingdom or that of a foreign (Gentile) world. The authority of the world belongs to the one with physical power (winning battles with swords) and proclaims that he is now king, 'I am king so obey me.' However, God is love and would never force us to obey Him. God's way is to fill us with His love so that in return we choose at our own 100% freewill to follow Him.

It is a miracle for us to believe in Jesus. Jesus said, "Therefore I make known to you, that no one speaking by the Spirit of God says, 'Jesus is accursed'; and no one can say, 'Jesus is Lord,' except by the Holy Spirit." (1 Corinthians 12:3) This is the grace of God. Without the work of the Holy Spirit, it is impossible for us to believe in God. The Holy Spirit fills your heart when you hear and believe the Word of God. "So then, my beloved, just as you have always obeyed, not as in my presence only, but now much more in my absence, work out your salvation with fear and trembling; for it is God who is at work in you, both to will and to work for His good pleasure." (Philippians 2:12-13) It is by the grace of God that we believe. Those who still resist and run away, at times God uses other methods of force to bring you back. This force is our blessing and the works of God which resembles the Exodus.

The 400 years of the period of Judges was a difficult and unsettled time. The human scene in Judges is disturbing because of the sins committed by the Israelites. The definition of 'sin' is the disobedience of God's law. The reason why God gave the Israelites the Law was for them to know what sin was. However, even though the

Israelites were aware that they were moving away from the Law, they did not realize that they were committing sin. Therefore, God uses the tribes of Gentiles to punish the Israelites. Egypt was on the south and Aram (Assyria) on the north of Israel, surrounded by various tribes throughout the eastern part of the Jordan River, Israel was attacked through the tribes of Ammonites, Moabites, Edomnites, Midianites, Canaanites and the Philistine.

There is a reason why God created us in flesh. When we are hit physically, we feel pain. If we didn't have flesh, we cannot feel pain. We must realize that more than 90% of pain comes from our sin. At times, our faith is tested in order to strengthen us just like Job but majority of our pain is caused because we have chosen sin instead of God. Left in a crossroad of God's Word or the world, the Israelites chose the world. They suffered. When it hurt then they cried out to God for help. That is why suffering is a beginning of a blessing.

Link of Suffering

'Judges' were the anointed ones of God's Spirit. The leaders of Israel did not become leaders due to their strength or abilities but by the anointment of the Holy Spirit. "The Lord was with Gideon" (Judges 6:34) means the Holy Spirit was with him. "The Spirit of the Lord came upon Jephthah." (Judges 11:29) "You shall receive power when the Holy Spirit has come upon you." (Acts 1:8) Those who receive the Holy Spirit will receive God's power, authority and charisma. By God's deliverance of the 'judges,' battles were won and all was peaceful for 40 years--for 80 years. (Judges 3:30; 5:31) Then the old patterns of humans start to surface even those who know God. That tells us one thing: If things are too good, humans start to sin again.

Judges were like 'one time use only' which meant that their sons do not inherit the roles of their fathers. It was not up to the judge to select a successor. Rather than serving God as their king, the life of the Israelites started to deteriorate by living according to their own standards which brought them suffering and punishment. Crying for deliverance and salvation from God was the repeated patterns that continued throughout the period of the Judges. Israel's disobedience is summarized in Judges 21:25: "In those days there was no king in Israel; everyone did what was right in his own eyes." In summary, the content of the story of Judges is:

(sin → punishment → cry out → deliverance (judges) → sin and this continued on for 400 years of the judges.)

During the latter part of this period, a unification of the Philistines begins. Samson (who was the last judge during this period) was anointed with God's spirit which gave him physical strength and power. His role was to block the Philistines because they were about to take over Canaan, God's Promised Land. But due to his fleshly weaknesses, Samson gave himself up to Delilah, the harlot, and fails to fulfill his duty. This prompts the curtain call for the period of the judges and becomes an opportunity for God to raise a king for Israel.

. . .

I thank my God in all my remembrance of you, always offering prayer with joy in my every prayer for you all, in view of your participation in the gospel from the first day until now. For I am confident of this very thing, that He who began a good work in you will perfect it until the day of Christ Jesus.

Philippians 1:3-6

FROM THE PERIOD OF UNITED MONARCHY TO THE PERIOD OF SILENCE

1 & 2 Samuel, 1 & 2 Kings, Ezra, Nehemiah

Today we are going to build the backbone of the Period of United Monarchy, Divided Kingdom, the Period of Exile, Return of Exile and the Period of Silence.

PERIOD OF THE UNITED MONARCHY_1 & 2 Samuel

King Saul and David

As the threat by the Philistines became stronger, the more Israelites clamorously requested for a king. A king was given to them by God and therefore, the era of kingship began. The period of this monarchy, a story of how David's kingdom is raised, is written in the books of 1 & 2 Samuel.

1 Samuel introduces Israel's greatest king, David, and what sort of ordeals he goes through before he becomes a king. David spent 13 years as a fugitive, escaping from Saul's sword. He must have prayed each morning thanking God for keeping him alive. Just imagine how frightening it must have been to run away for 13 years from a powerful king and his army.

During his turbulent period, David held on to only God. One of David's confessions was, "Lord is my rock and my fortress and my deliverer, My God, my rock, in whom I take refuge; My shield

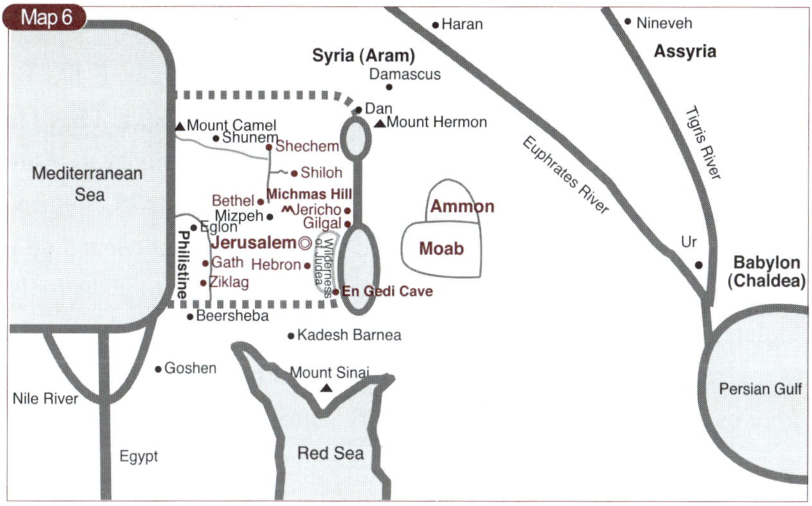

Period of United Monarchy Upon hearing the Israelites, request for a physical king, God raised King Saul and King David. From this point on, the Period of the United Monarchy begins.

and the horn of my salvation, my stronghold." (Psalms 18:2) We must realize that suffering is a blessing. Without suffering, it is impossible for humans to kneel in front of God. The book of Samuel contains how God raises David through his suffering. God prophesied the coming Messiah was to be born as the descendant of David who will endure suffering and become a king.

The book of 2 Samuel records the highlights of David's reign. First, over the territory of Judah, and finally over the entire nation of Israel. From the chapters, a clear distinction between the faiths of Saul and David are revealed. Saul also believed in God and tried his best to trust in God but his faith was primarily a religion of Shamanism which is based on conditions and 'asking' whereas David's faith was based on worship and the temple.

Not only Saul but the people of Israel misunderstood God as a god of war. The god they wanted was a god who helped them win battles, a comforter and a peacemaker when they needed it. Even though they mentioned 'God' in reality they just needed a 'servant with great power.'

The religion of Shamanism is focused on self interest. It has no interest in the god you believe in. In other words, one does not have to do anything for the god you believe in. At times when you try to evangelize someone, you hear such remarks like, "You are correct. We need a god to believe in so that when we are in trouble we can depend on it and be comforted." That is the reason why humans love to make idols. Idolatry is made when something is expected to meet your needs. Moreover, conveniently enough, it does not expect anything in return from us. However our God says, "Purify yourself; do not commit adultery; do not steal, etc." Normally the reactions from these commands would be, "No. Just leave us alone and don't ask anything in return. Just fight for us and send us manna from heaven when we need it." These types of attitudes are what we call religion of Shamanism.

In Saul's case, even though he relied and trusted God in his own way, the ultimate drawback for him was that he refused to obey the Word of God. Love is only complete when you reveal it through your character (mind, soul and action). We must recognize that just thinking of God or feeling joy in our heart does not necessarily equal love. Love is complete only when you act in obedience.

Alternatively, David's faith was based on worship and the temple. The faith and prayer theme of David was, "One thing I have asked from the Lord, that I shall seek: That I may dwell in the house of the Lord all the days of my life, To behold the beauty of the Lord, And to meditate in His temple." (Psalms 27:4) How was it possible for David to have such faith? Living as a fugitive for 13 years and escaping from Saul allowed him to focus on God completely which resulted faith. There was nothing David wanted from God when he became a king. David said to Nathan, the prophet, "See now, I dwell in a house of cedar, but the ark of God dwells within tent curtains." (2 Samuel 7:2) He longed to build the temple of God so that he could outpour his love for God each day. He realized that God loved him so much and his only wish was to love Him back.

Upon hearing David's wish, God promises to build him a house, a dynasty which will be 'forever.' (2 Samuel 7:16) This becomes God's promise with David that runs right through the rest of the Old Testament until the promise is fulfilled at the coming of Christ. This is God's way of giving blessing. Faith is believing in God's promise. By giving up our desires for the righteousness of God's Kingdom (His existence), great blessings will be poured upon us in return.

God created the human race by dust and gave blessings to overrule all creation. "God blessed them; and God said to them, 'Be fruitful and multiply, and fill the earth, and subdue it; and rule over the fish of the sea and over the birds of the sky, and over every living thing that moves on the earth.'" (Genesis 1:28) Why do you think God said, "Do not worry what to eat, drink, and wear but to seek His righteousness and kingdom"? (Matthew 6:31-33) People believing in God do not need to worry about what to eat or wear because these things will be automatically given to those who focus on God's Kingdom and His righteousness. This is the formula of God's blessing.

Divided Kingdom and Wasted Blessing

A stable united kingdom ends with total collapse because of Solomon's sin. Solomon's zeal for God was diminished in his latter years as his pagan wives turned his heart away from worshipping God wholeheartedly. As a result, the king with the divided heart left a divided kingdom behind. The book of 1 Kings (chapters 1-11) records about the United Kingdom under Solomon but in general, 1 & 2 Kings clearly focuses on the divided kingdom. The storyline of the divided kingdom is recorded in 1 & 2 Chronicles as well.

Solomon was the son of David and was raised in good faith by his mother, Bathsheba. After giving 1,000 burnt offerings, God appeared to Solomon in a dream offering a gift of his choice. (1 Kings 3:5) What did he ask for? He asked for wisdom to rule his people justly. It is the choice of a man whose heart was put right before God. God granted all the wealth, glory and fame in addition to the wisdom that Solomon asked, and his kingdom enjoyed great prosperity that never had occurred in the country before. He had all the wealth and glory in the world.

But Solomon confesses in Ecclesiastes 1:2, "Vanity of vanities! All is vanity." What he is saying is that despite of having everything, the end result is just vanity. Nothing can fill your heart even if you have everything so Solomon is telling us, "Remember your Creator in the days of your youth." The downfall of Solomon begins when foreign wives bring foreign gods with them turning him away from worshipping God to idols. He was given warnings by the prophet but refused to listen. As a result, God said, "I will surely tear the kingdom from you, and will give it to your servant." (1 Kings 11:11)

Solomon gave grace and wisdom to others through Proverbs, Ecclesiastes and Song of Solomon but unfortunately, on a personal level, he became a great failure. The difference between Solomon's faith and his father David's was obviously so big "One thing I have asked from the Lord, that I shall seek: That I may dwell in the house of the Lord all the days of my life" (Psalms 27:4) The bottom line is that if you seek earthly things, it will be given to you by God, but such possession and glory becomes meaningless in the end.

THE PERIOD OF THE DIVIDED KINGDOM_1 & 2 Kings

Jeroboam's Way and David's Way

The author of 1 & 2 Kings is unknown although Jewish tradition ascribes the work to the prophet Jeremiah. It exposes the sins of the Northern and Southern Israel to deliver the message that if they had repented God would have saved them. The theme is the story of the kings but in reality, it is God's urgent voice to Israel through the prophets. An important element in this story is the activities of the prophets and the historical stories of the kings. Notable prophets like Elijah and Elisha who appear in 1 Kings did not author any books of prophecy, whereas 17 prophesy books in the Old Testament were authored by other prophets appearing in 2 Kings. So when we look at the entire picture of the Bible later on, we must know both the prophecy books and the history books.

Ezra, who is supposed to be the author of Chronicles, teaches and encourages Israel to go back to their roots. Reminding them that they are God's chosen people and the descendants of Abraham and David. The main message of Ezra was restoration of temple and reassertion of the distinctive identity of Israel and her faith. For this specific reason, David's sin with Bathsheba or the sins of Solomon are not recorded in this book. We will touch base with the activities of kings of Judah and get a clear picture through 1 & 2 Kings by focusing on the divided kingdom.

The books of 1 & 2 Kings provide a prophetically oriented evaluation of the spiritual and moral causes that led the two kingdoms to the political and economical demise. It also emphasizes that the decline and collapse of the two kingdoms occurred due to the disobedient attitudes of the rulers and people, failing to heed the warnings of God's messengers. There were two ways to distinguish the faith of kings of both kingdoms: Jeroboam's way or David's way.

After the kingdom splits into two, Jeroboam became the first king of Israel. He was one of Solomon's servant, the lowest level in today's term, head of the mining forced labor. He came from the tribes of Benjamin. Ten tribes of the northern Israel were given to him by God whereas southern Israel (tribes of Judah) was kept intact, centered at Jerusalem where David's promise is to be fulfilled. Compared to the northern Israel, the land of Judah was lacking in every aspect. Nevertheless, this is where Jesus is born. When

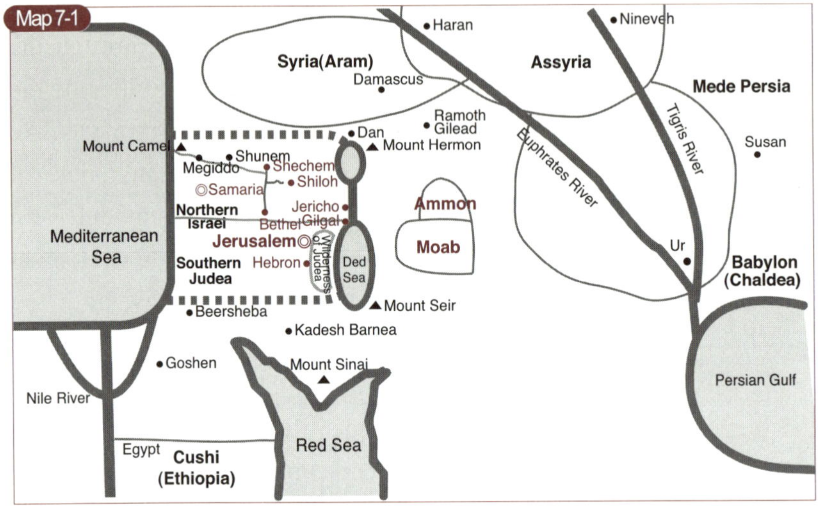

Period of Divided Monarchy Jeroboam's way of Northern Israel who worshipped idols and David's way of Southern Judah who worshipped God, resembles our own identities.

Jeroboam became the 1st king of Israel, the capital was not Samaria yet but a small village called "Deerusara." It becomes the capital during the reign of Northern Israel's 7th king, Omri. There were many battles between the two divided kingdoms since God used both kingdoms as the tools to punish each other.

Methods Produced by Man -Jeroboam's Way

The people of Israel visited Jerusalem during the pilgrimage feasts because of God's temple and the city of David. Therefore, from Jeroboam's point of view, this was not a pleasant sight. He started to worry. 'Who am I? I am a king and yet my servants and my people leave me behind to go to Jerusalem. What will become of my kingdom? I realize that the 12 tribes came from Jacob; and God changed the name of Jacob to Israel. Israel exists because of God.'

Just like Saul, Jeroboam also knew that he needed God but at the same time he wanted a god that would only serve him like a powerful servant from the Aladdin lamp. Eventually he creates an unlawful priesthood and makes bull/calves for the people to worship. We can assume thoughts like, 'Temple in Jerusalem is no big deal. We can make our own' was in the heart of Jeroboam.

The people of the Northern Israel believed God existed in the temple they had built. They created two new sanctuaries for the northern kingdom. One temple with golden calves in Bethel under Shechem and another one in Dan near Lake Galilee. Not only golden calves were created but offerings of the blood of the lamb were conducted by high priest as well. His reasoning was that there was no reason why God should not exist if the same methods were used. Before sacrifices were offered on behalf of the people, the high priest would wear a special robe according to the rituals and put hands on the head of the lamb indicating the transfer of the sin from human. Then the throat was slit to draw blood and the body was burnt as an offering while blood was being spread.

Idolatry worship was encouraged and as time went by, Israelite's worship became more and more degenerate. At the same time they put their efforts in keeping God's Word, the Five Books of Moses. The Five Books were called the Five Books of Samaria (Torah) and the method was the same. They taught the Word and the high priest delivered the Word in front of the temple. But then again, this was not God's promise but a method made by humans. The kings that followed the path of Jeroboam were referred to as worshipping in 'Jeroboam's way.'

Threader: Approximately 1,000 years after the division of the Northern Israel and Judah (B.C. 920), if you read John 4, Jesus goes to Galilee from Jerusalem where he meets a woman of Samaria near a well. The woman asks Jesus, "Our fathers worshiped in this mountain, and you people say that in Jerusalem is the place where men ought to worship so which one is true?"(John 4:20) Jesus replied, "Neither···God is spirit, and those who worship Him must worship in spirit and truth." (John 4:21-24) Jesus was revealing that He was the Son of God and the temple of God's love that came to earth in flesh. (John 2:19-21) Jesus emphasizes that there is no importance of the physical temple in Jerusalem anymore; what is important is to give worship to God in Spirit and in Word.

As mentioned before, David's way was a religion of worship. "One thing I have asked from the Lord, that I shall seek: That I may dwell in the house of the Lord all the days of my life, To behold the beauty of the Lord." (Psalms 27:4) This is exactly the words of Jesus relating that God is spirit. The reason David was blessed by God was because he gave worship in spirit and truth. God judged the faith of the kings of Israel according to which path they followed whether it was David's way or Jeroboam's way. This applies to us today as well. A church was rightfully purchased by the blood of Christ. However, the problematic situations that exist around us today resulted from the existence of 'non-basis' of church teachings and worship methods devised by man just like walking the same path as Jeroboam.

The Activities of the Kings of Israel and Judah

There were 19 kings in Israel and all of them worshipped idols or walked in the ways of Jeroboam. From Israel's 1st king to Jeroboam, until the collapse of the country, we can conclude that the 10 tribes of Israel did not believe in God properly. The history of the Northern Israel ends in B.C. 722. 19 kings ruled approximately for 200 years and on average, one king governed only 10 years or so, but this is only a calculative approach because in reality, in the case of the Northern Israel's king, being in throne for 10 years was regarded as a 'long' time. There were kings that only lasted a month, 3 months or 6 months. Never a dull moment of peace. Something was always going on--schemes and murders. In summary, the vital fact is that from the beginning to the end, Israel compromised their belief and trust in God by taking up with other faiths.

The kingdom of Judah based on the inheritance of David's root lasted for 350 years. In other words, they lasted 134 years longer than the Northern Israel. Similar to the Northern Kingdom, the common problem of Baal idolatry was deeply rooted in Judah as well. But among the kings of Judah, there were 'good' kings such as Hezekiah and Josiah who performed religious reformation and worship reformation. It is said that because of these two kings, 134 years of blessing were extended to Judah.

But we must realize that the reason why blessings were extended this long was because of God's promise to David. As written in 2 Samuel 7:16, "Your house and your kingdom shall endure before Me forever; your throne shall be established forever." Because of this promise to David, God did not punish Solomon even though he sinned but waited until the next generation before dividing the kingdom into two. God kept His promise with David. Another reason God protected Judah was because the Messiah was to come in the lineage of David's root.

The Destruction of the Kingdom and a New Promise of the Holy Spirit

Hezekiah and Josiah's religious reforms were not enough to change the hearts of the people of Israel. Prophet Jeremiah was given a preview of the nation's destruction and devastation that was about to fall on Judah which filled him with unspeakable horror. Jeremiah who is often known as the weeping prophet warns of the coming disaster and appealed in vain to the nation to turn back to God but everyone turned deaf on him. Ultimately, Judah falls by the Babylonian army, is looted and utterly destroyed. The puppet king Zedekiah to whom God gave many warnings through Jeremiah and other prophets ignored them all. Finally, he witnessed his sons being slaughtered in front of him; his eyes were pulled out, bound in chains and brought to Babylon.

At the nation's darkest hour, Jeremiah delivers a remarkable message of hope which is God's new covenant. When it looks like a total extinction, God promised His people (the whole nation-northern and southern kingdom) a future. "'Behold, days are coming' declares the Lord, 'when I will make a new covenant with the house of Israel and with the house of Judah, not like the covenant which I made with their fathers in the day I took them by the hand to bring them out of the land of Egypt, My covenant which they broke, although I was a husband to them,' declares the Lord. 'But this is the covenant which I will make with the house of Israel after those days,' declares the Lord, 'I will put My law within them, and on their heart I will write it; and I will be their God, and they shall be My people.'" (Jeremiah 31:31-33)

They will be saved and restored. This new covenant will replace the old one that was made at Sinai, which they have broken. This time God will remake them from within, giving them the power to do His will. Make no mistake here. God is not giving us another new commandment because the new covenant can easily be interpreted as the New Testament. Jesus clearly said, "I did not come to destroy the Law but to complete it." (Matthew 5:17) This new covenant is a promise from God that through the Holy Spirit, the power and motivation will be poured into our heart so that we can keep the Word of God. It is the Holy Spirit's work through Christ to 'write God's law' on the hearts of all believers.

It is the Holy Spirit that protects us, gives grace and delivers all things from the Father God. The way the Holy Spirit can work is by opening the channel through our lips when we testify and confess the Word. "That is the Spirit of truth, whom the world cannot receive, because it does not behold Him or know Him, but you know Him because He abides with you, and will be in you." (John 14:17) "It is the Spirit who gives life." (John 6:63) Only when you pray will you be able to feel the overflowing invisible love of God. You feel His character when the Spirit of Christ is in you. By feeling His character and love, you start to gradually change into His image without you realizing it. "And goes to bed at night and gets up by day, and the seed sprouts up and grows. How, he himself does not know." (Mark 4:27)

The Action Fields of Prophets and the Period of the Divided Kingdom

In order to outcast Ahab's dynasty in Northern Israel, Elijah and Elisha were sent to perform miracles and signs to reveal God's presence to the people of Israel. (The activities of these two prophets are highlighted in the book of 1 & 2 Kings). On the other hand, the day of the Lord was proclaimed through Amos and Hosea. The relationship between God and Israel was vividly portrayed in prophet Hosea's own marriage. A husband (God) who shows enduring love for his unfaithful wife (Israel) cries out; "It is still not late so return."

There were many prophets sent to Judah because of David's promise. Prophet Isaiah began his ministry during the reigns of Ahaz (12th king) and Hezekiah (13th king). It is known that he was slaughtered and died as a martyr by the evil King Manasseh (14th king). Ahaz and Manasseh were the most evil kings of Judah. They enjoyed power, money, sex and worshipped Baal idols. Many Baal temples were built all over the place, encouraging people to worship the idols. As if that wasn't enough, they even built a 'green hall' where people smoked pot (narcotics) and involved in sexual activities and prostitution in the open area in broad daylight. In response to Israel's corrupted lifestyle, Isaiah was sent by God to proclaim the birth of the Messiah and raised a man of faith like Hezekiah to defend Israel against Assyria. During Hezekiah's reign, prophet Micah was also sent to assist the (good) king. Through these two prophets, the birth of the Messiah was proclaimed and in Micah's case, the prophecy of the

Messiah was made in more detail - i.e., birth in Jerusalem.

Prophet Jeremiah comes into the scene when Judah was about to collapse during the period of the 16th king, Josiah who was active in religious reformation. There were not many activities during Josiah and the 17th king Ahaz, but Jeremiah confronts with Judah's 18th evil king, Jehoiakim. During Jehoiakim's reign, God not only sent Jeremiah but Habakkuk as well.

The time period when the prophet Joel was active is not known explicitly, but God's message he proclaimed is clear. He spoke of the Holy Spirit by saying 'don't tear your clothes but your heart' "It will come about after this That I will pour out My Spirit on all mankind; And your sons and daughters will prophesy, Your old men will dream dreams, Your young men will see visions." (Joel 2:28) This is referred as the 'Certificate of Holy Spirit of the Old Testament.'

Prophet Zephaniah prophesied in the reign of King Josiah of Judah about the time Jeremiah's ministry began. His message was that God will save the faithful few. "The Lord your God is in your midst, A victorious warrior. He will exult over you with joy, He will be quiet in His love, He will rejoice over you with shouts of joy." (Zephaniah 3:17)

Zephaniah emphasized on the blessings that will come upon the survivors and remnants. To those who hold on to God and keep their temple religion in spite of their previous Baal worshipping conduct.

As we can see from this period, God revealed His love in various ways by sending many prophets to delay His judgment as long as possible. In order to fully understand the prophecy, one must know the framework of historical aspects related to the period of the divided kingdom.

PERIOD OF EXILE_Ezekiel and Daniel

We get a glimpse of the actual circumstances during the period of exile through Ezekiel and Daniel since there is no separate book related to it. It looks like the end of all hopes for Israel, but God creates a new hope for them through Ezekiel by the remarkable Holy Spirit. "I will give you a new heart and put a new spirit within you; and I will remove the heart of stone from your flesh and give you a heart of flesh." (Ezekiel 36:26) In the midst of destruction and exile, a 'new' promise is given and it is revealed openly that the Holy Spirit will be sent to us upon the death of the Messiah and His resurrection. And the total transformation of a 'new heart' is realized only 'in Christ.'

PERIOD OF RETURN FROM EXILE _Ezra and Nehemiah

The historical books relating to the period of return from exile are Ezra and Nehemiah where the exiled Jews return and rebuild the walls of Jerusalem, their Temple and re-establish their own worship and God's law.

During 70 years of captivity in Babylon, God used the army of Cyrus of Persia to overthrow the Babylonian Empire. This was the beginning of the war between Iran and Iraq that started 2,500 years ago. According to Jeremiah's prophecy, the Jews were to return to homeland in 70 years to restore the temple and the city of Jerusalem. This was needed as a preparation for Jesus' coming that will take place in about 500-600 years later but the king of Babylon didn't budge. So God used Cyrus, king of Persia, as an instrument to strike Iraq. "I will take the hand of Cyrus and subdue Babylon first and open the gates for you." (Isaiah 45:1-5) War belongs to God. The city of Jerusalem is a symbol of holiness and salvation. The Jews returned to Jerusalem for the very purpose of preparing the road for Jesus to come from the root of David.

Threader: When Jesus was talking about the 2nd coming, disciples asked, "Lord, is it at this time You are restoring the kingdom to Israel?" This question was asked by the disciple right before the ascension of Jesus in the book of Acts. Jesus replied, "It is not for you to know ... but you shall receive power when the Holy Spirit has come upon you; ... " (Acts 1:7-8) What is the main focus of Jesus? He's saying that through the cross and resurrection, if He does not go to Father, the Holy Spirit cannot come to us. That is why Jesus said, "Don't be interested in the restoration of Israel's authority but concentrate whether you receive the Holy Spirit so that you may become My witnesses both in Jerusalem and in all Judah and Samaria and even to the remotest part of the earth." After the exile period, it was God's providence to fulfill His promise with David (2 Samuel 7:8-16) by restoring Jerusalem. During the latter part of His ministry, Jesus enters into the city and carries the cross and resurrects to fulfill Father's promise.

In a panoramic sense, through the Period of the Judges, the United Kingdom and the Divided Kingdom, the message was loud and clear. Who is the 'true judge?' and 'true king' of Israel? The mindset of the people of Israel 'Awaiting of the Messiah' was being instilled.

Threader: God's overruling providence was for the people of Israel to realize who the real king was and for them to wait for the Messiah; Jesus, a true King, who came to earth. The King showed His love during His three years of ministry through His life. He died on the cross and sent the Holy Spirit as He had promised. When the Holy Spirit works. His characters is transferred into us and we feel His overflowing love. As a result, we start to change into a new person and the work in progress of God's Kingdom takes over.

The establishment of God's Kingdom in our heart began from Genesis 12 through the lengthy history of Israel. But now the work of recovery is taking place by the gift of the Holy Spirit through us and through churches. This is the conclusion of God's promise in the Old Testament.

PERIOD OF SILENCE

Upon Israel's return from exile, they rebuilt the temple, the walls and recovered the Law. They waited for the coming Messiah. But 100 years went by and no sign of the Messiah. Then they started to slack off on their worship (offering). The last prophet was sent by God and through Malachi the message of "recovering the worship" was proclaimed. Then there were no words from God for 400 years which is referred to as the 'period of silence.' But then again, it was revealed already through Daniel how God was going to spend 400 years in preparation to send the Messiah to earth.

The period of silence is a link between the Old Testament and the New Testament which makes it easier to read the Bible in two sequel parts just like a major drama series stirring your interest further.

Who am 'I'?

Who is the real 'me'? Majority of us think that whatever we own is ours. My body, house, wealth, children, etc. But is that true?

We think what we have is ours because all of them have been achieved by our efforts. However, according to the Bible, even our body itself is not ours. God made us from dust. Surprisingly, a recent medical experimental report it revealed that 99% of the genetic factors between a human and a mouse are identical. In other words, what makes us human is about 1% difference. That is why a mouse has the closest genetic factor with respect to a human being. When we come across a person who's not worthy of a human being, we frequently find ourselves labeling that person as a mouse which, in fact, is not far from truth after all.

Is the experience that I sense with my physical body is what 'I' am? We normally think that what we touch with our hands, scent with our nose, hear with our ears and taste with our mouth is really what 'we' are. But the feeling of human five senses is just a result of our bodily contact with our environmental circumstances. Basically whatever environment it may be is not 'you'.

The only difference between a human and a mouse is whether it has a spirit or not. If one were to have only flesh but no spirit, then you are not different from a mouse or any other animal so there is nothing to boast about. A human 'thinks' so he claims himself as a 'self-being' but the major difference between a mouse and a human is the fact that we are created like a vessel to put spirit in it. A person is formed differently depending on which spirit is inside of him/her-whether it is God's Spirit or Satan's spirit. "Blessed be the God and Father of our Lord Jesus Christ, who has blessed us with every spiritual blessing in the heavenly places in Christ, just as He chose us in

Him before the foundation of the world, that we should be holy and blameless before Him. In love He predestined us to adoption as sons through Jesus Christ to Himself, according to the kind intention of His will." (Ephesians 1:3-5) Apostle Paul used the plural term 'us,' and not the singular term 'me.' With this in mind, God loved both Rachel and Leah equally even though Jacob loved only Rachel. They were both blessed. God also showed love and mercy to Leah and comforted her by opening her womb to give more sons. It is God who gives us blessings and pours His love and protection over us. We have been predestined and chosen in Christ and it is He who blesses us. Therefore, there is no salvation when there is only 'me.' Full understanding of the importance of 'us' is extremely essential. We must be able to go deep inside the concept of 'us.' Otherwise, if we remain and focus only on 'me,' that is hell. Satan works vigorously inside of those who continue to focus on self-oriented behavior.

Why are we learning the history of Israel for? After the exodus, the tabernacle was built first, then the temple, and the true temple from heaven was Jesus. Upon crucifixion, Jesus resurrected and became the head of a church. Ultimately, the final process of salvation is through the church. Our resurrected Lord is the head of the church and we (believers) are His body. Through our gathering together, 'we' are formed in Christ and this is the reason why Jesus said that He will be in the midst of where two or more people gather to pray. (Matthew 18:20)

Clearly, salvation must not be limited only to you. For instance, as a married couple, if one of you has received Jesus and your partner has not, then you must pray for your partner. There is no excuse for any comments like, "I'm praying but my spouse is still resisting so there is not much I can do." Even though it may appear as a dead end, one must do whatever possible so that both partners can walk in the same path. The emphasis of salvation is on 'us' and not 'me' alone. The Word of God is power itself in our lives. The Word of God is not mere words of speech but should be our lifestyle. Often times we find people evangelizing whenever they get a chance but bear no fruit. The problem lies on the lifestyle of a Christian who apparently is not any better than the unbelievers. That is the ultimate drawback. Let us consider a wife is saved before the husband and he is an unbeliever who tries to solve his problems in his own way by drinking. For example, a non-believing husband deals problems in his own way by drinking but fails in the end. In the meantime, the husband witnesses his wife who handle problems in a peaceful manner. He also senses there is something 'different' about her ways. The joy that gushes out from within because of her experience of 'paradise' in her heart. That paricular 'difference' will lead him to realize what he is missing and eventually prompt him to want to believe in God.

Obviously, you can also experience the Holy Spirit when you pray alone but go to church and pray together with others. By doing so, that is the time you become a part of 'us' in Christ. You will experience the work of the Holy Spirit. As we become 'us' in Christ, our Lord comes into our hearts so that we can live in Christ and become like Him. Once we're successful in achieving this, the Lord who has predestined and chosen us will start to open up our future in Christ. We must experience the 'paradise' and joy in our heart. Those who do not know this 'joy' will say things like "you have so much stuff going on already" or "why do you need to go to church so early in the morning?!"

. . .

God created man in His own image, in the image of God He created him; male and female He created them. God blessed them; and God said to them, "Be fruitful and multiply, and fill the earth, and subdue it; and rule over the fish of the sea and over the birds of the sky and over every living thing that moves on the earth."

Genesis 1:27-28

BEGINNING OF MANKIND, CREATION OF HEAVEN AND EARTH

Genesis 1-2

We have divided the Old Testament into 10 periods. From this point on, we will start to add more detailed 'flesh' as we move forward. The period of creation lies in Genesis 1-11 which contains: First, God's creation (beginning of mankind), second, fall of mankind (sin and beginning of suffering), third, the flood (beginning of judgment) and fourth, tower of Babel (beginning of separation).

Creation Work of Division by God the Trinity

"In the beginning God created the heavens and the earth." (Genesis 1:1) What kind of person is God? "Let Us make man in Our image, according to Our likeness." (Genesis 1:26) Note that God expresses Himself as 'Us'- plural - indicating the Trinity of God. A similar terminology is mentioned in the New Testament in John 1:1-2, "In the beginning was the Word, and the Word was with God, and the Word was God."

If one were to interpret it based on Hellenism (logical and reasoning of accuracy), it does not make sense at all. To say that the same being was with one another does not make sense. And in John 1:3, "All things came into being by Him, and apart from Him nothing came into being that has come into being." What this means is that all things in the world were created by God. We also realize that the word 'word' such as the one in John 1:3 is not the same kind of words that we speak but that it means an existence of someone. "And the Word became flesh, and dwelt among us, and we beheld His glory, glory as of the only begotten from the Father." (John 1:14) The Word is the only begotten Son, Jesus Christ. In the beginning, there was a Son and this Son was with God and He is like God - forming a Trinity of God. 'All things came into being through Him' which means that Jesus Christ was the Creator. That is why the Trinity of God never has conflicts with one another. The order of creation was under the cooperative work of God the Trinity.

It is amazing how the Bible explains the cooperative work of God the Trinity. Father God is referred to us as 'Love' itself and the Son as the Word of God and the Holy Spirit of God is referred to us as the 'Helper.' Let's see now how God the Trinity fulfills the history of creation.

The Son of God, the Main Character and the Word

Among the Trinity of God, the principal player of the creation is the Word of God, Jesus. This is actually proven in many passages throughout the Bible. "In these last days has spoken to us in His Son, whom He appointed heir of all things, through whom also He made the world." (Hebrews 1:2) "In whom we have redemption, the forgiveness of sins. And He is the image of the invisible God, the firstborn of all creation. For by Him all things were created, both in the heavens and on earth, visible and invisible, whether thrones or dominions or rulers or authorities - all things have been created by Him and for Him." (Colossians 1:14-16)

"The Father loves the Son, and has given all things into His hand." (John 3:35) Although Jesus existed in the form of God, He returned all the highest glory to Father God and emptied and humbled Himself by becoming obedient to the point of death. (Philippians 2:6-8) For this reason, Father God exalted Jesus and bestowed upon Him to create all things so that He would receive the highest glory from His creation (mankind) to fill His emptied heart with the joy of love. The Trinity of

God created humankind as His object to love but more specifically, we have been created by the Son (Jesus) for His sake. All creation was made for the Son to receive the highest glory, not for Himself but to return to the Father. (John 5:19-20)

Jesus prayed to the Father, "I have manifested Your name to the men whom You gave Me out of the world; they were Yours and You gave them to Me, and they have kept Your Word." (John 17:6) The phrase "whom You gave me out of the world" means those who have received Jesus and became the children of God. It was Father God that made them to come out but it was through Jesus that they are transformed. Pay attention that Jesus did not praise Himself but instead completely humbled Himself by saying "whom You gave them to Me."

Then why did Jesus die for us when He actually created us? Upon seeing the sinful spiritual power of Satan interfering with His children, He came down personally in flesh to the darkness of the world. Mothers would do practically anything to save their children whether it is jumping into the water or fire since love has already been poured to the unborn child in her womb. So upon birth the infant is watched closely and the mother is prepared to risk her life to save the child from any threat or danger. For that same reason Jesus was able to die for us because He was our Creator. How can one express or fathom the love of God into words?

Faith means believing the unforeseen without experimental verification. (Hebrews 11:1) Here the word 'unforeseen' indicates our spiritual state. Even though we exist in the present time, our spiritual aspect has already existed in Christ before creation. For instance, I was born through my biological mother on April 19, 1949 but my spiritual state has already existed in Christ 1,000, 10,000 years before creation. In this same manner, Jesus has predestined us even before creation. "Just as He chose us in Him before the foundation of the world ..." (Ephesians 1:4) His love has been poured to me in my mother's womb and He is watching over me ever since I was physically born into this world. We have been chosen in Christ before the creation of the world. The Bible clearly indicates how God led His chosen people into the promised land and how His eyes were glued on to them day and night giving warnings and protection. Therefore, the Creator is our Lord Christ. One of the lyrics from a praise song, "My Lord of my life, praises given day and night leaves my heart yearning for more." Jesus predestined us even before the creation of the world. Not only were we born through our biological parents but He also created animals, vegetation and sea creatures for our well being as well.

Father God, the Director of the Creation

The director of the creation is Father God and Jesus is His main actor. Father God had the master plan and prepared all the supplies that were necessary for the creation. That is why Jesus referred all things were done by the Father and returned all glory to God. "...the Son can do nothing unless Father shows it to me." (John 5:19) When a film is made we normally don't remember the name of the director but definitely know who the main actor is in the movie. However, the main actor has one person that he can't treat casually and that is the director. Once a movie is made, it is customary to mention the name of the director rather than the main actor. The movie is introduced as a director's film, not as the actor's film. With this concept in mind, Jesus was the main character in the creation but it was the Father God who created the world.

God the Holy Spirit Who Supports the Son

The Holy Spirit of God plays the supporting role. All the works of the Father have been transmitted to the Son by the Holy Spirit. Just like in a movie scenario, Holy Spirit plays a role that supports the main actor according to the script prepared by the director. A supporting role is not as prominent as the main actor but plays a significant part in assisting the main character.

How come the Holy Spirit knows all the script of Father God? "For to us God revealed them through the Spirit; for the Spirit searches all things, even the depths of God." (1 Corinthians 2:10) Before the creation "The earth was formless and void, and darkness was over the surface of the deep; and the Spirit of God was moving over the surface of the waters." (Genesis 1:2) This means the Spirit of God was waiting (referring to God's existence) for the Word of Jesus to speak. 'Let there be.' For instance, when the Word of Jesus spoke, "Let there be birds in the air" (Genesis 1:20) then the Spirit of God was waiting above the waters and would notify Father God of His plan, i.e., the description. The energy in the Word itself makes things physically appear from null. "For to us God revealed them through the Spirit; for the Spirit searches all things, even the depths of God. For who among men knows the thoughts of a man except the spirit of the man, which is in him? Even so the thoughts of God no one knows except the Spirit of God." (1 Corinthians 2:10-11) The Holy Spirit only works according to the Word, the Son of God.

Creation through the Word

What was the state of the earth before the Word of God came down? The earth was formless, void and dark. (Genesis 1:2) What was the state of the earth before the Light of God came down? It was formless, void and dark. God started to fill the formless (confusion), emptiness (void) and darkness of the earth.

In the book of Job, God raises questions: "Where were you when I laid the foundation of the earth! Tell Me, if you have understanding, Who set its measurements? Since you know. Or Who stretched the line on it? ... who enclosed the sea with doors, When, bursting forth ... ?" (Job 38:4-5, 8)

Through the work of God's creation, we come to realize that 'Gospel' means 'acknowledging the Word of God with our lips and confessing it, which should subsequently follow.' The way to find the truth in Buddhism is to meditate with your mind. Conclusion of a monk after 3 years of meditation was 'life is null.' Why? A human's mind is made out of dust so no matter how you utilize wisdom there is no salvation. "In Him was life, and the life was the light of men." (John 1:4) There is light in the Word so until the Word comes into the mind of men, the earth remains to be formless, void and dark.

The wisdom of mankind is the enemy of the Word of God. (Galatians 5:17) The wisdom that becomes an opposing foe of God is what we call 'philosophy.' It is impossible to understand the Word of God with philosophical approach or knowledge. The only method to understand life is through the Word of God and without the awakening of the Holy Spirit, one cannot understand the Word either.

Everything was created by God's saying "Let there be." According to the scientists, fundamental existence of any material in the world is through the combination of forced impact of 'energy' which is explained in a formula of energy combined $E=mc^2$. History of creation can never occur without energy. For instance, a seed from the earth sprout and branches out into the form of a tree is possible because of the impact of energy.

If one would ask a scientist, "Where did the energy come from?" they are unable to fully explain the origin of it. So majority of them conclude with mutual statements like "the energy existed from the beginning" or "we don't know where it came from." This is the so-called theory of 'big bang.' It states that without the impact from outer energy to the DNA of dirt, it cannot be activated. A form of material is established only through contact. They claim that the creation took place through an energy flying from an unknown place which caused a great impact resulting particles into a tiniest level which is referred to as "quirk." For example, if one were to examine a molecule closely, there is an atom which consists of a neutron and proton which is the quirk. A neutron is formed with the combination of several quirks together which then form an atom. However, these neutrons alone cannot stick together without the help of the outer energy. Then the same question arises, "where did this energy come from?" and their responses were "we don't know."

But the Bible tells us exactly where this energy came from. "The Word of God is living and active and sharper than any two-edged sword, and piercing as far as the division of soul and spirit, of both joints and marrow ..." (Hebrews 4:12) The most important aspect of creation is that the word of God is alive and active. If we were to look up 'active' in the Greek language-it is referred to as 'energy.'

In other words, the Word of God is a living energy and whenever the Word came down the earth was filled. " 'Let the waters teem with swarms of living creatures, and let birds fly above the earth in the open expanse of the heavens.' And God created the great sea monsters, and every living creature that moves, with which the waters swarmed after their kind, and every winged bird after its kind; and God saw that it was good." (Genesis 1:20-21) He started to fill the earth with delightful visual creations such as the trees and flowers, by separating organic and inorganic elements of the dirt and also filling it with two-legged animals, four-legged animals (us) and all living creatures after their kind. How majestic is this? How remarkable!

Whenever the power of the energy of the Word came down, particles started to form. Not only things were filled on earth by the Word of God but all creation was controlled by God. "By the Word of His power, He upholds all things." (Hebrews 1:3) He sustains everything with His powerful Word. God has the power to fill all things, visible and invisible. God provided manna and quails from heaven to the people of Israel during their journey in the wilderness. This was to let them understand, through their life, that all things come from God.

The Sequence of the Creation

Creation of Time_1st Day

"Then God said, 'Let there be light'; and there was light." (Genesis 1:3) The first scene of God's creation was putting the disorder (formless) into order, filling up the place (void) and bringing light into darkness. (Genesis 1:2)

God's creation can be divided into two segments: formless and void. How did God resolve these two problems? First, there was a problem of disorder but God did not grant order to disorder until the 3rd day. On the 1st day, light was created and by separating the light and darkness order was installed. The Bible reflects this as "God called the light day, and the darkness He called night. And there was evening and there was morning, one day." (Genesis 1:5) The energy of the Word came upon the light and darkness, separating day and night. The other creation that took place at this time was "evening and morning, one day." God's redemptive work of mankind begins within the 'time' that He created with His Word.

God works within the timeframe that He created. But normally, we find people saying things like, "I don't have time for Bible study" or "I don't have time to pray." We must remember that time was created by the Word of God. We must get it straight. It's not that we don't have time for Bible study because time gets created once you hold on to the Word. The important thing is that we must not let go of the Word and spend time for it during our busy affairs. There are no excuses in saying that we don't have time in front of God because time itself belongs to God.

Creation of Expanse of Life_2nd Day

"Then God said, 'Let there be an expanse in the midst of the waters, and let it separate the waters from the waters.'" (Genesis 1:6) God created the expanse on the 2nd day. With the energy in the living Word of God, the waters were divided into two by the works of the

Knowledge Search 2

In the 'beginning' from Genesis 1:1 and John 1:1- Would this the same time period?

"In the beginning God created the heavens and the earth" in Genesis 1:1 and "In the beginning was the Word" in John 1:1 may appear the same but it is not the same time period. The 'beginning' that comes out in the book of John predates Genesis. It is because Jesus is the Word and the Creator of the creation. The word 'beginning' in the book of John refers to the time before creation--in other words, it indicates 'before eternity.'

Holy Spirit. By doing this, the waters were separated into the one below the expanse and the other above the expanse. God called the expanse above as heaven and the expanse below as seas. By creating an expanse God granted order to the formless universe.

We are created to live under the limitation of time that God created. But God is different because He is spirit. Our life totally depends on time and space given to us and the only way to go beyond and overcome these boundaries is through spirit. Normally we think the time and space that we visually see rules over us entirely and don't think much of it. Little do we know that all the problems occurring in this given space can only be resolved through Spirit. "Be anxious for nothing, but in everything by prayer and supplication with thanksgiving let your requests be made known to God. And the peace of God, which surpasses all comprehension, shall guard your hearts and your minds in Christ Jesus." (Philippians 4:6-7) God is telling us through the creation that when His powerful Word and the comfort of the Holy Spirit is upon our heart then all problems that are confronted in the time and space will be overcome and resolved. The reason being it is God who created our life in this space.

Knowledge Search 3

What are the waters above the heavens?

We know that the waters below are seas but what about the waters above? It is written in the Bible that all the fountains of the great deep burst open and the floodgates of heaven opened and covered the earth during the judgment of the flood during Noah's time. The water expanse above was used in the flood. According to scientists the longevity of mankind was shortened due to the ecological adaptation after the flood incident.

Creation of Forms-3rd Day

"Then God said, 'Let the waters below the heavens be gathered into one place, and let the dry land appear', and it was so."(Genesis 1:9) On the 3rd day, God created shapes and forms. A land that was underneath the water surfaced when God gathered the water to one side with the energy of the Word. He divided the water and the earth.

God created beautiful things such as vegetation, plants and trees of every kind at this time. The Jewish people still believe to this day that God's creation began from bringing things up from water which explains their concept of the baptism. They believe that God is in heaven and Satan is underneath the waters. Their definition of baptism is saving those who have been under the water below. Nowadays, baptism has become simplified in the Presbyterian churches as sprinkling of water by pastors whereas the Baptist churches continue to put the person into the water and bring up for the baptism ceremony.

Creation of Filling the Void-4th, 5th and 6th Days

From the 4th to the 6th day, the creation of filling the void took place. "Then God said, 'Let there be lights in the expanse of the heavens to separate the day from the night ... let them be for lights in

Knowledge Search 4

Is the light of the sun different from the light of the Word?

If you look at the sequence of God's creation, the light of the Word came down first. In other words, light did not come out because of the sun. This means that the light we see was created on the 4th day but the true light of God's word already existed before then.

When Saul was on his way to Damascus to persecute people who believed in Jesus, he was met with a sudden light from heaven that flashed around him in broad daylight. (Acts 9:3) This was the light from God-a light that came down with God's Word. So understand this correctly that it was not the 'sun' but the 'light' of God.

the expanse of the heavens to give light on the earth, and it was so. And God made the two great lights, the greater light to govern the day, and the lesser light to govern the night; He made the stars also."(Genesis 1:14-16) A form of control was necessary for the light and darkness so God created the sun and the moon on the 4th day. By the energy of God's Word, the sun, moon and the stars were made to fill the void. Namely, the sun, moon and the stars to rule over the light and darkness (of time).

This earth is rotating every 24 hours even now. Imagine now, the earth is on air as well as the sun. How is it possible this sizzling sun that is constantly exploding within itself, pumping high level of heat, is not falling on to the earth? The Bible clearly indicates that God is holding on to the earth and the sun. (Hebrews 1:3) This fundamental principle is that of Newton's universal gravitation. The pulling force not only applies to the ground but also to the sun. In order for the sun not to fall, God also made the sun and the moon with the same pulling force upon each other. Other planets like Mars, Mercury, Jupiter, Venus and Saturn were made for the moon as well as many other unnamed galaxies. The amazing universe was created with the Word of God, a result of the ultra speed of light that passed on for thousands and thousands of years! It is the power of God's Word that upholds all things.

On the 5th day, God filled the expanse with living creatures of the sea and every bird of its kind. "Then God said, 'Let the waters teem with swarms of living creatures, and let birds fly above the earth in the open expanse of the heavens.' " (Genesis 1:20)

On the 6th day, God created all the living animals. "Then God said, 'Let the earth bring forth living creatures after their kind: cattle and creeping things and beasts of the earth after their kind.' " (Genesis 1:24) And finally, man was made last. God took care of all the disorder and filled up the void first and then made man on this earth. We must realize that God created all things (birds, sea creatures, vegetations, trees and animals) on earth for 'us.'

Creation of Man

God created man differently from any existing animals. The main purpose of God in creating man was for His own love target (object). Human is the only one that can connect heaven and earth. Heaven is a place uniting in one spirit and the earth is formed with the power of the Word. Man who is linked to both heaven and earth must praise and glorify the invisible God forever.

The unique characteristics of humankind are as follows:

First, man has been created in the image of God. We are the object of God's love and have become His vessels to contain His spirit. (1 Corinthians 6:19) Man was made from dust on the ground and as God's breath was breathed into the man's nostrils, man became a 'living being.' Some Bible has translated it as 'living spirit.'

Whether one believes in Jesus or not, this is the scene where man is receiving the spirit. It is why animals move according to their instincts whereas humans move according to their thoughts. Person who steals or prays are alike because they are acting according to their spiritual activity. People who have faith obey and move according to the Word of God. The grace of the Holy Spirit and the Word dwells in our heart as a result of our actions. Those who steal are moving according to Satan's spirit, tempting you to fill in the void with other belongings. Therefore, we must realize that our life is the constant movement of our actions and process of accumulating the Holy Spirit within us.

The true reality of the spiritual war is whether you are moving according to the spirit of the world, the spirit of Satan or moving according to the Word of God. We must be able to broaden the existence of the Holy Spirit within us by moving according to the Word. Through this process we are walking the path of becoming true Christians. Ultimately becoming like Jesus which in fact is the process of sanctification as well as filling our hearts with the Holy Spirit.

Second, God has given humankind the ability to become like His character, the ability to 'Love.' The love of man is called 'Philia.' Upon resurrection, Jesus met Peter in the Lake of Galilee and asked him, "Do you love me more than anyone else?" Rather than a straight forward answer, he shifts the judgment to Jesus and responded, "Lord, you know that I love you." (John 21:16) Peter had blurted out in confidence that he would also die if Jesus died but found himself betraying his own words when confronted at the most crucial moment. He was admitting his own weakness at this moment. Peter knew that he was capable of only 'philia' type of love and realized that he would never reach God's Agape love. We must admit that we cannot become like Jesus. However, we have been given the power to love like Jesus because we have been created in His image. With that in mind, God has given us family as our fundamental unit of love.

Third, God has given us complete freewill. Among all creations in the world (both heaven and earth), visible or invisible, a special element has been given solely to us, which is the complete freewill. Because of this freewill, the temptation of Satan in the Garden of Eden asking 'to eat from the tree of good and evil' was allowed. This incident clearly shows the complete freewill given to us by God. To decide whether to listen to the temptation or to follow God's command-whether to choose the narrow gate or the wide gate, the freedom of choice has been given to us by God. Even when Adam failed to overcome the temptation, God did not block him but instead waited patiently with tears in His eyes. God waits patiently in His own time for His loving children to return to the Father's arm at their own freewill. So freewill is a tremendous privilege and at the same time, a dangerous option. Depending on how you utilize your freewill, it's either becoming like Christ or becoming like Satan.

Fourth, God has provided man with a helper. 'Helper' in Hebrew is 'Ezer' which means 'a spiritual helper.' If a person is alone, one becomes self-centered and ends up being trapped in the spirit of Satan. So God created Eve for Adam. The Bible does not indicate the time frame after creation of Eve, but we must assume that there was a lapse of time in between when God created Eve and when God gave her to Adam as his helper. Adam accepted Eve as his love partner and confessed that she was "Now bone of my bones, And flesh of my flesh." (Genesis 2:23) At the moment when he confessed, Adam had overcome 'himself' (self) by receiving Eve as his loving wife in his heart.

But unfortunately, there is no record of Eve saying the same thing as Adam, "bone of my bone, flesh of my flesh" which plays a significant role in the fall of mankind. As a spiritual helper to Adam, Eve did everything that was good for Adam because she loved him. Before Eve had the time to receive Adam as her complete love partner in her heart, Satan captured that moment and tempted her to 'eat from the tree of the good and evil.'

God's command not to eat from the tree of good and evil was only given to Adam in the Garden of Eden and this command was given before Eve's creation. Adam delivered the same message to Eve, "From the fruit of the trees of the garden we may eat; but from the fruit of the tree which is in the middle of the garden, God has said, 'You shall not eat from it or touch it, lest you die." (Genesis 3:2-3) But in spite of this warning, the temptation of Satan sounded sweet in Eve's ears. She ate the fruit of the good and evil and then gave it to Adam. The problem was that Adam could not reject Eve since he had already confessed his love for her as 'bone of my bones and flesh of my flesh.' If you love someone you automatically obey. Sadly, Eve was not able to fulfill her role as his helper as she had fallen to Satan. Ultimately, a woman was created for Adam so that his 'self' would be overcome but instead, the woman ended up becoming a servant of self-serving Satan.

That is why Jesus came in the seed of a woman as our true helper. Let us understand that we would never have been saved from our sins eternally if Jesus did not come into our heart in His Spirit to help us.

Creation of Angels

God created all things for man and He also created angels.

A story about King of Tyre comes out in the book of Ezekiel which in fact is referring to the fallen angel. " Son of man, take up a lamentation over the king of Tyre, and say to him, 'Thus says the Lord God, You had the seal of perfection, Full of wisdom and perfect in beauty. You were in Eden, the garden of God.'"(Ezekiel 28:12-13) The 'king of Tyre' is the spirit of Tyre, a partner of the Baal idol, Asherah who tormented the people of Israel throughout the Old Testament. This Asherah idolatry was the spirit of Tyre of Canaan.

The Garden of Eden is described in all kinds of precious stones like ruby, topaz, diamond, beryl, onyx, jasper, lapis lazuli, turquoise, and the emerald. "And the gold, the workmanship of your settings and sockets, Was in you. On the day that you were created They were prepared." (Ezekiel 28:13) From this verse, we realize that the angel was created in order to give praise to God. At first, the angel was the "The anointed cherub" (Ezekiel 28:14) which means it was the guardian angel. This was the angel who chased out mankind from the Garden of Eden after the fall. Then, the two cherubim of angels were stationed over the ark with their wings wide opened with the flaming sword to guard the way to the tree of life. The Bible does not record exactly when this guardian angel was created but the important fact is that they were created before the creation of man. In Job 38:4-7, "Where were you when I laid the foundation of the earth! ... When the morning stars sang together, And all the sons of God shouted for joy?" The accurate translation of 'morning stars' and 'sons of God' is 'angels.' It is clear that the angels existed before the foundation of the earth since they gave praise to God. The key point to understand is that the angels had fallen before the creation of the earth.

The roles of the angel are as follows:

First is to give worship to God. Angels giving praise and worshipping in front of the temple of God can be seen in the book of Revelation (Revelation 5:11) and in Isaiah (Isaiah 6).

Second, they practice good virtue among all creations. In the book of Daniel, Archangel Michael defeats the enemies and performs the good works of God. Even in real life, we refer to people as 'angels' when they conduct good deeds.

There are many other roles of angels. "Are they not all ministering spirits, sent out to render service for the sake of those who will inherit salvation?" (Hebrews 1:14) Each one of us is assigned with a helping angel. So, therefore, when we pray through the inspiration of the Holy Spirit, the ruling spirit receives our prayer and materializes it. This is what many people refer as 'miracle.' Angels are eternal without any rewards of any sort. Their role is to just serve and work.

But the angels had fallen even before the foundation of the earth was established. The fallen angel is well explained in Ezekiel 28. The fallen angel was a complete beauty but became proud and was chased out of the Garden of Eden. 'Your heart was lifted up because of your beauty' and going back to king of Tyre, "By the abundance of your trade you became proud and were internally filled with violence, and you sinned; therefore, even though you served God in His garden you have cast yourself out from the mountain of God." (Ezekiel 28:16-17)

The angel, the messenger of God, became god while serving on behalf of His power and authority. "Son of man, say to the leader of Tyre, 'Thus says the Lord God, 'Because your heart is lifted up And you have said, 'I am a god, I sit in the seat of gods, in the heart of the seas'; Yet you are a man and not God, Although you make your heart like the heart of God.'" (Ezekiel 28:2) This is the reason why people fall into the trap of challenging God constantly -- trying to become like god. "How you have fallen from heaven, O star of the morning, son of the dawn! You have been cut down to the earth, You who have weakened the nations! But you said in your heart, I will ascend to heaven; I will raise my throne above the stars of God, And I will sit on the mount of assembly In the recesses of the north. I will ascend above the heights of the clouds; I will make myself like the Most High." (Isaiah 14:12-14) The bottom line is: it is 'me' wanting to become God.

God's plan was to assign the people of Israel to carry out the works of angels. Worship, praise, deliver God's Word and to be healed and comforted by the Word while the angels of God were to serve and protect them (Hebrews 1:14), but unfortunately, they failed. The work that was originally appointed to Israel has now been transferred over to us through church; we are the church, the body of Jesus, and He is the head of the church upon His resurrection. For this reason, as believers of God and those who have received His calling must give worship, praise and deliver His Word, giving comfort and healing to others. When we carry out these acts, that is when we become the most precious living creatures on this earth by doing the virtue of a good deed and by receiving great blessings from God in return. Unfortunately, just as the angels had fallen due to their beauty and virtue, the importance of 'me' being accentuated, many people who received God's calling and gift have also fallen and became the servants of Satan.

Spirit of Satan

The Bible says the body of a person who has received God's spirit is the "Temple of the Holy Spirit." (1 Corinthians 6:19) The other spirit that comes into our body is the spirit of Satan. We must clearly understand the spirit of Satan. Majority of us are living under the spell of Satan's spirit out of ignorance or disregard without realizing our life will be in ruins in the end. As mentioned, the good angel (Lucifer) that was created before mankind had fallen from heaven and became Satan because of his arrogance of wanting to become higher than God.

The characteristics of the spirit of Satan are as follows:

First, the spirit of Satan emphasizes on 'self.' Majority of Christians think they do not have the spirit of Satan. But the spirit of Satan is nothing special. If you are 'full' of yourself with regard to appearance, ability, brain, behavior, etc., that results from the very control of Satan's spirit. That is probably why when we try to evangelize to unbelievers, they respond by saying, "I'd rather believe in my fist and myself." This kind of attitude is all stirred by Satan's spirit making you to focus on you and yourself only.

Second, the spirit of Satan makes you to focus on the things of the world that are all perishable. Once you follow Satan's spirit, your basic instinct becomes just like an animal--eat, drink and multiply. Once a person reaches its level of financial success, his/her interest turns into animalistic ways which is given by the spirit of Satan. In today's world, many of us worship money, expanding their wealth and reputation; gradually becoming a slave of your own environment and instincts. Satan tries to make us pursue things of the earthly world and live with basic instincts but David confessed, "To Thee, O Lord, I lift up my soul. O my God, in Thee I trust, Do not let me be ashamed; Do not let my enemies exult over me." (Psalms 25:1-2) David chose at his own freewill to lift up his soul while Satan is trying to do the opposite. He was capable of doing this only because he was a man of prayers. There is nothing that can deter our lives from the animalistic instincts other than the Word of God.

Third, the spirit of Satan makes you fill up your own needs. Is it possible to think of others when you're starving, sick, going through hardships and falsely accused? This is exactly what Satan wants you to feel so that you would only focus on yourself--no one else but you, even to the point where you take away what belong to others in order to fill your needs. The meaning of 'eros' is filling up your own needs as well as sexuality. Satan's goal is to make you focus on yourself and block you from thinking of others, leading you to destructive relationships.

Prophet Hosea frequently compared the lustful desires of men with a hot furnace. During the reigning period of King Jeroboam II, Northern Israel was very prosperous. Rejecting God and the complete adoption of pagan religious practices brought a moral landslide. While they were building new palaces, the people committed detestable and sinful acts at the same time. Prophet Hosea pleaded towards the people of Israel that their state of lust was hot as an oven and also that it was like a dough sizzling on a red hot furnace. Following bodily desires results in animalistic instincts which may appear as if you are enjoying your life in the world but in the end, it is the shortcut to hell.

Many people think that once you die, it's the end. Some think that a certain sensor called 'soul' disappears once the flesh is gone (the soul represents the 'outer' person that is characterized by thought, feeling, and behavior). In other words, they think that their thoughts and everything disappears once a person dies. People think that a soul is attached to the flesh. We say 'soul' not 'soul flesh' because the soul (or the outer person) is attached to the spirit (or the inner person). Therefore, even though a person returns to dust, the soul is not a sensor that just disappears, but is like a diskette where all things that were captured through the sensor while living in the world has been stored, both spiritual and fleshly things. A soul remains even after the flesh decays away. In addition, even after the flesh is gone, a person who has lived according to the Satan's spirit still has the lifelong fleshly desires. Since there is nowhere to relieve those burning desires because God has thrown away the flesh, the fleshly lust remains unresolved and therefore, the eternal torture begins. This is 'hell' and is the reason why it has been expressed as the burning lake of fire.

Fourth, the spirit of Satan tempts you to eat from the tree of good and evil. God commanded Adam and Eve not to eat the forbidden fruit in the Garden of Eden. God also warned them that it would be a sin if otherwise. Eating the forbidden fruit implies the thought that whatever you think is good is all correct. In other words, you become the standard of all the judgments. By the fall of Adam and Eve, we are all living our lives eating from the tree of good and evil. Everything is in accordance with our thoughts what we think is right which is also the same message in Judges 21:25. The 400 years of history of the judges were all a vicious cycle of sins from the start to the end. The sinful history during the period of judges concludes with a reason by saying "In those days there was no king in Israel." God did not give a king to Israel because God was king to them. God had ruled over them directly but they refused to accept God as king. This is the good and the evil, "Everyone did what was right in his own eyes." It is a sin when we think and act in the way we want and the result of sin is death.

A training of yielding for others is necessary in order to overcome greed and desires. Obviously you must also win over it with the Word and training of prayers. You must start to taste casualties or losses in your daily life in order to overcome Satan's temptation. I believe the tipping culture in America is a remarkable way to receive God's blessing, because it is one way to yield for others. Having worked in six different countries in five continents, I have found that the U.S. is the only country that has a tipping system. It does not exist in Europe, Australia or New Zealand - only in America. When God first sent the Puritans to this country, they shared their blessings with one another rather than keeping it to themselves and initiated tithing to the ones that were in need. This was a biblically righteous act of God and a blessing from God. I believe that one of the reasons why Americans are blessed is because they have adapted this tipping system into their lifestyle so that after eating at a restaurant, people automatically give 10% of the meal cost for the ones in need. What an automatic training is this! Through this kind of training, God has given us wisdom to overcome the power of Satan.

Reasons Why Satan's Activities are Permitted

God does not oppose and fight with Satan. Satan is nothing but a creature created by the invisible Almighty God, the Creator. Satan has been cut off from receiving any love from God and there is a reason why it has not been destroyed. God spoke of Job's character, "For there is no one like him on the earth, a blameless and upright man, fearing God and turning away from evil." (Job 1:8) Upon hearing this Satan replied, "Does Job fear God for nothing? Have You not made a hedge about him and his house and all that he has, on every side? You have blessed his house and all that he has, on every side? You have blessed the work of his hands, and his possessions have increased in the land." (Job 1:10) The word 'hedge' here means the hedge of angels, just like the guardian angels protecting us when we pray. Satan asked God whether he might test Job and God allowed it. (Job 1:11) Then Satan started doing his work.

Why do you think God approved of Satan? The reason is simple. As humans are made of dust, we can only distinguish the good and evil through physical experiences. For instance, 'bright' can only be known when you experience darkness. A person who has not crossed a dark tunnel will not know brightness. Only through the experience of darkness, one can be thankful for the light when you get a glimpse of it. We appreciate 'good' through experiencing the 'bad' in the world and it is why everything is relative.

Through Satan's tests, all the wealth, children, and servants of Job are wiped out. In the end, even his wife curses and runs away. What Job went through was unspeakable and it was a tremendous tragedy in real life. We also experience many hardships through our lives but we must realize that there is an amazing blessing, joy and fulfillment behind the sufferings.

Satan controls and has the authority of the spirit of the world which is darkness, pursuit of evil doings. God had given this authority to Satan. Adam and Eve were thrown out from the Garden of Eden after sinning which symbolizes that they have entered into the Satan's authority. Again, this was permitted by God as if to say, 'give whatever pain or suffering to the person' but realize that God is not forsaking the person. It is God's work of redemption and work of salvation.

Through the trials and tribulations of poverty, solitude, illness, pain and suffering, God is telling us to experience His peace and love by choosing Him. The freedom to choose belongs to us. Through tough and difficult times, we can experience God's blessings and it enables us to reverse our feeling toward God to be eternally thankful and praise Him.

The entire book of Job is trying to explain this concept to us. Job held on to his faith towards God to the end in spite of the terrible sufferings he went through. Not once did he blame God instead he endured and awakened to God's blessings that were to come through suffering. In the end, he received double blessings in every way, children, wealth, servants and much more than he had before. It was the trial of love that God allowed. Those who have sinned were made to go through the process of this trial of love, but not left alone-Jesus is with them, who's sitting next to the throne praying in grief. And whoever endures and overcomes, He will make us a "Pillar in the temple of My God." (Revelation 3:12) Just as the Word says, we must go through this test and overcome it with faith in God.

This process is like an example to make us realize that once we overcome our flesh, the eternal kingdom and hell really exist. We actually experience heaven and hell on this earth. We are being trained through this process of life to understand God's loving-kindness and mercy so that we may give thanks and praise to Him. When you believe in God's promise and hold on to His Word in faith and pray, the shadow of hell vanishes and you start to feel His kingdom on this earth. The kingdom of heaven is not a place you go when you die. Heaven and hell starts from this earth. God has already allowed us to have a glimpse of heaven and hell here on earth. Through Jesus Christ, the Word and through the guidance of the Holy Spirit, we enjoy the kingdom of heaven on this earth. We can definitely live our lives with great joy and deep gratitude.

Satan only works in the boundary that has been allowed by God and the time limit is until the 2nd coming of Christ. God has promised in the book of Revelations that Satan will be thrown into the lake of fire for eternity. There will definitely be the last Judgment Day.

PROCLAMATION OF THE FIRST GOSPEL AFTER THE FALL

Genesis 3-11

The spiritual war begins in Genesis: whether to follow God's command or to eat from the tree of good and evil; whether to choose God or to fill our lust. Simultaneously, the work of God's salvation begins by covering the flaws of mankind with leather clothes.

FALL OF MANKIND_Genesis 3-4

Original Blessing

Whenever the word 'fall' is mentioned, we think of the original sin and the tree of the good and evil. But we must realize that God had already blessed us even before the fall of mankind. In other words, an 'original blessing' existed prior to the original sin.

Let us first find out about the original blessing. After creating Adam and Eve, God said, "Be fruitful and multiply, and fill the earth, and subdue it; and rule over the fish of the sea and over the birds of the sky, and over every living thing that moves on the earth." (Genesis 1:28, cultural command of God) God gave abundant blessings to mankind for them to govern all creation on earth. We have the right to rule over all things.

It appears that the Garden of Eden was a fascinating place. It was surrounded with all kinds of jewels that we know such as diamond, ruby, topaz, emerald, jasper, lapis lazuli, sapphire, turquoise, beryl, onyx, etc. But the environment of the Garden of Eden has folded due to the original sin. God started His work of redemption after the fall of mankind and recovered the original blessing through Jesus Christ by resolving the original sin. "I pray that in all respects you may prosper and be in good health, just as your soul prospers." (3 John 1:2) What this means is that the original blessing God gave us is that not only do we receive blessings spiritually, but as we are blessed spiritually, it influences everything else so the prosperity and health is given to us as well.

In our modern churches today, there are two extreme concepts regarding the blessing. First is the excessive interest in the world based on the fascination of health and prosperity, such as 'if you believe in Jesus, you will receive blessing regardless of any.' Main interests are basically children, family, health, business, and prosperity. When our soul prospers, blessings of environment follows automatically. Unfortunately, however, many are only interested in the environmental blessings. This is totally reversed which is the religion of Shamanism (fascination of the world).

The other concept is the idea that since Jesus has given me salvation, I will move to a remote place and wait for the 2nd coming of Christ rather than dealing with the ongoing conflicts of the world. These extreme devout measures are actually running away from the world. We must not run away from the world because our work is to "Go and make disciples of all the nations and teach them to observe all of God's commands." (Matthew 28:19-20)

Obviously, both concepts have problems. "Blessed be the God and Father of our Lord Jesus Christ, who has blessed us with every spiritual blessing in the heavenly places in Christ." (Ephesians 1:3) All heavenly spiritual blessings come through the Word of God. Blessings come through worship, the Word and through our confession of prayers.

The Fruit of the Good and Evil

What is the original sin Adam and Eve committed? They disobeyed God's command and ate the forbidden fruit.

In Korea, a heretic Presbyterian group led by Tae Sun Park actually regarded a peach as the 'fruit of good and evil' that he wiped out the fields of peach trees and turned it into a religious ground. It is wrong to think that the tree of good and evil is actually the 'fruit' from the tree. The essence of the tree of good and evil is that we become the main force in distinguishing and judging what is good and evil. We have been created as God's love partner and received complete freewill. God gave us the authority to rule over all creation and the earth. Just like a breakwater between the ocean and the land, the barrier that we, as God's creation, must not go over. The meaning of God's command, 'do not eat,' is a clear indication of drawing the line that we must not cross.

The First Result after Eating the Forbidden Fruit-Becoming The Master of Your Own Life

Often times, we hear remarks like, "It's my life and nobody lives it for me." We must understand it correctly that God has given us complete freewill with the Word saying, "For you were called to freedom, brethren; only do not turn your freedom into an opportunity for the flesh." (Galatians 5:13) But what has happened is that we live according to our standards and making our own judgments of good and evil. In other words, we are practically eating from the tree of good and evil on a daily basis.

Due to our own standard and judgment of good and evil, our lives are led to destruction in the end. The message is the same: "Destruction and misery are in their paths, and the path of peace have they not known." (Romans 3:16-18) Therefore, "If you are living according to the flesh, you must die; but if by the Spirit you are putting to death the deeds of the body, you will live." (Romans 8:13) "According to the flesh" means controlling your own life.

Jesus said, "Come to Me, all who are weary and heavy-laden, and I will give you rest." (Matthew 11:28) Why does it state 'weary and heavy-laden'? The reason is because making our own life decisions from good and bad makes us weary and burdensome. That is why Jesus is calling so that He could give us rest. "Take My yoke upon you, and learn from Me, for I am gentle and humble in heart; and you shall find rest for your souls. For My yoke is easy, and My load is light." (Matthew 11:29-30) What does this mean? God wants us to make commitment at our own freewill and let down our own yoke and trust Him so that He could lead us into the restful and good path. There's no force or whatsoever involved here.

Normally, we, humans, think that freedom is when we're free from a yoke entirely. If one were to wear a real yoke then you become a real prisoner and a slave in this world. However, if we do not bear the yoke of Jesus, we wear the yoke of the world. God is saying, 'From now on with all My love I will make you blameless, holy and transform you so that you will become as the same character as Me.' It becomes a blessing to us once we give our yoke to the Lord. But if you eat the fruit of good and evil upon Satan's temptation, then you become your own master and basically throwing away the yoke of Jesus.

The Second Result after Eating the Forbidden Fruit-Rejection of Grace

Satan makes you to reject God's grace. "Why do I need God when it's my life and I can do whatever I please?" The people in the world say things like, "I will not give nor ask anything for free. I don't need anyone's help. I work hard so that's enough." In Asian culture, not accepting for free is regarded as a noble attribute. On the other hand, however, the Bible tells us to continuously share with others. We regard sharing as a sign of love but the important thing is that in order to give, we must succeed in receiving first. If you cannot receive you cannot give. It would be absolutely impossible to give to others with a mindset of 'It's my hard earned money.' Only when you have the heart of 'the money that I have right now has come from the grace of God.' will open your heart. Just like Job's confession, it is God who gives everything so what reason is there for not being able to give?

All creations cannot exist without receiving the love from our Creator, God. Satan has fallen out from God's love so the supply of love has been cut off. Since Satan does not own anything, it needs to take away so that is why Satan is referred as a thief and the one who robs. (John 10:10) Everything disappears, evaporates, and dies once the spirit of Satan works.

When Satan tempted Eve, she was asked to pick the fruit and eat it. It was not picked for her. What this means is that Satan cannot 'give' because it cannot 'supply.' Even in the wilderness when Satan tempted Jesus, the devil said, "If You are the Son of God, command that these stones become bread." (Matthew 4:3) Here again, the Satan did not make the bread and asked Jesus to eat it.

As prophet Isaiah had lamented, each one of us have no choice but to go separate ways. We are basically living according to our own ways. "All of us like sheep have gone astray, Each of us has turned to his own way." (Isaiah 53:6) Having lived in New Zealand, I have seen many sheep. They are literally blind and when you see them from a distance, they appear quite nice but up close they are actually ugly animals especially their eyes. Their slanted small eyes are blurry, making them difficult to identify anything. Probably that's why they go astray but then again, their ears are very sensitive. Therefore, the sheep recognize their owner's voice. Jesus spoke numerously regarding ears. Those who have ears will listen" indicating that we cannot follow Him with our eyes but only those who have ears will listen (eating the Word of Life) and follow Him.

Beginning of Sin_Genesis 3

The Stages of the Fall

"When the woman saw that the tree was good for food, and that it was a delight to the eyes, and that the tree was desirable to make one wise, she took from its fruit and ate; and she gave also to her husband with her, and he ate." (Genesis 3:6) Satan tempts us by visible things first and then by words. As a matter of fact, this is exactly the same sequence how we are tempted. If you do not guard yourself with the Word (the sword of the Holy Spirit), the words of Satan repeats itself in you, making you think about it, the more convincing it becomes. As a result, your desires increases. The minute you feel the desire, the forceful entry of so-called 'tank of desire' takes over prompting you to react in action. This is the process of falling.

Without faith and the sword of the Holy Spirit which is the Word of God, there is no way we can win over Satan's temptation. Apostle John also said, "All that is in the world, the lust of the flesh and the lust of the eyes and the boastful pride of life, is not from the Father, but is from the world." (1 John 2:16) All the lust of the world can be satisfied with money so that is why the world moves around by the energy and power of it.

The only place that moves the opposite of this is the church. A church moves according to the energy of the Word so only at church it is possible to let go of money. Only at church, the hard-earned money, the reward of your sweat and long working hours, becomes less important. Putting aside your worldly pride is only possible at the church. This is why after the Nero Empire, the kings and the power of the world persecuted churches but they have all perished in the end while the church remains forever. The church can win over the world because it moves by the energy of the Word.

Apostle Paul said, "Love of money is a root of all sorts of evil." (1 Timothy 6:10) 1 Timothy is a letter written by Apostle Paul, who was working in the area of Ephesians, laments to Timothy about the members of the first church where many of them passionately believed in Jesus but turned away from their faith by following money. This applies to us today as well.

The original sin of Adam has been inherited to us. For this reason, we continuously commit sins of our own on top of it. Therefore, in order to resolve this problem of sin, Jesus Christ came to us as the 2nd Adam. The first thing Jesus did was to receive baptism in the Jordan River by John the Baptist. Shortly thereafter, led by the Holy Spirit, Jesus faces the devil's temptation in the wilderness of Judah. This test was for the purpose of resolving the sin of the 1st Adam which was critical before starting His ministry.

The Result of the Fall - Curse

First of all, the serpent had to sustain its life by eating dust forever. "Cursed are you more than all cattle, And more than every beast of the field; On your belly shall you go, And dust shall you eat All the days of your life." (Genesis 3:14) Our bodies and animals are made from dust. The living boundaries for Satan are also dust. When Jesus was about to cast out the demons of the two men who were demon possessed near the graveyard, the demons asked to be sent into the herd of swine. Satan is like a crying lion constantly following the footsteps of humans because it cannot survive without a body or dust. Literally they live eating the dust by crawling on their belly forever. Therefore, Jesus said 'you will live if you overcome your physical actions in Spirit.'

As a result of sin, woman has been cursed with the pain of childbirth as well as lifelong worries related to children. In order to survive the curse of man was lifetime sweat and labor. After the fall, the Garden of Eden was now changed into a place of survival in the midst of suffering.

The Beginning of the Work of Redemption

The Beginning of Redemptive Work After the Fall

_Proclamation of the Gospel of Eden.

The remarkable aspect of God's salvation is that it began at the scene of the fall. "And I will put enmity Between you and the woman, And between your seed and her seed; He shall bruise you on the head, And

Knowledge Search 5

Three Test Topics of Jesus

The three tests of Jesus was to resolve the fall of Adam which resulted from eating the forbidden fruit (desires of flesh: appetite / desires of sight: delightful / boasting present life: attractive).

First temptation: Satan asked Jesus who had fasted for 40 days to 'command the stones to become bread and eat it (fleshly desires).' Jesus wins over Satan's temptation with the Word, "It is written, Man shall not live on bread alone, but on every word that proceeds out of the mouth of God." (Deuteronomy 8:3)

Second Temptation: After showing the entire world and glory, Satan asks Jesus, 'worship me then all the worldly glories that you see will be given to you (visual desires).' Jesus spoke, "Begone, Satan! For it is written 'You shall worship the Lord your God, and serve Him only.'" (Matthew 4:10)

Third temptation: Satan had Jesus stand on the pinnacle of the temple and said, "Throw yourself down; for it is written, 'He will give His angels charge concerning you'; and 'On their hands they will bear You up, lest You strike Your foot against a stone.'" (Matthew 4:6) The temptation was towards the boastfulness of the present life prohibiting Jesus to carry the cross but instead be acknowledged and glorified as the Messiah. But the Lord Jesus proclaimed that He came into the world in the lowest manner and that only through the cross will He become the Messiah.

Jesus won over all the temptations and through this victory the inherited original sin was resolved and ultimately it opened the door of salvation for us.

you shall bruise him on the heel." (Genesis 3:15) The Messiah who was to come through the woman's body will bruise the head of Satan is the first gospel given to mankind (also referred to as the 'gospel of the Garden of Eden.')

The name "Eve" means the mother of the living. Eve became the mother of the living even though she failed to support Adam spiritually as his wife and made him fall at Satan's temptation. In Revelation 1:18, Jesus spoke to John who was in the island called Patmos, "I am the living One; and I was dead" speaking of His death on the cross and resurrection. Thus, Eve as the mother of the living became the mother of the Messiah.

Clothed Them in Leather

After sinning, Adam and Eve realized they were naked and sewed fig leaves together to cover themselves. Yet, covering a mistake with something visible is not possible.

God clothed them with garments of skin (leather) to cover their flaws. "For the life of the flesh is in the blood, and without shedding of the blood a sin cannot be forgiven." (Leviticus 17:11) Without shedding of blood there is no forgiveness. Similar message is written in Hebrews 9:22, "And according to the Law, one may almost say, all things are cleansed with blood, and without shedding of blood there is no forgiveness." The reason is because there is life in blood. That is why God began the work of redemption from the scene of sin by shedding the blood of the little lamb, Jesus. God showed His merciful love towards Adam and Eve by clothing them with garments of skin. In a way Eve became the first fashion model of all mankind in the Garden of Eden from changing her outfit from a fig leaf to leather.

Thrown out from the Garden of Eden

Throwing the sinners out from the Garden was the true blessing and grace of the redemptive work. Actually, throwing Adam and Eve out from the Garden was a blessing in disguise from God. Otherwise, there would not have been a chance for them to find God again. This was the beginning of God's redemptive work.

After being thrown out, the sins start to amplify as they enter into the world. Basically sin gives birth to sins. After the fall of Adam and Eve, the amplification of the sin is shown through the murder committed by their son, Cain.

The result of sin is death. Therefore, after being thrown out from the Garden, Adam and Eve endured great sufferings and through it they reached out for help. This is God's way of reaching out to His loved ones just as the father of the prodigal son, who remembers the love of his father and voluntarily returns to the arms of his loving father in the end. (Luke 15:20)

The Beginning of the Spiritual War

Offerings of Cain and Abel

The first spiritual war begins with the offerings of Cain and Abel. "By faith Abel offered to God a better sacrifice than Cain, through which he obtained the testimony that he was righteous, God testifying about his gifts, and through faith, though he is dead, he still speaks." (Hebrews 11:4) By faith, Abel offered to God firstlings of his flock of sheep which God accepted gladly whereas Cain's offering of the fruit of the ground was rejected. What was the problem here? Both Cain, the farmer, and Abel, the shepherd gave from each of their respective background but what went wrong? The Bible says it was not what Abel offered, but his faith which made his gift acceptable.

Cain's bitter resentment shows a very different spirit from that of Abel. God said to Cain, "Why are you angry? And why has your countenance fallen?" (Genesis 4:6-7) What this means is that Cain was already filled with anger and evil heart. Why? By faith, Abel gave a firstling of his sheep as an offering. Where do you think this faith came from? God had cursed Adam in the Garden of Eden and clothed him with leather skin. It has been shown clearly to Adam and Eve that "Without blood there is no forgiveness." (Leviticus 17:11) Obviously, Cain and Abel must have heard the Word of God through their parents. Upon learning this,

Abel believed his father's word and gave his offering in faith by shedding the blood of the lamb. By the blood of the lamb, he was confessing, 'I am a sinner. My parents have disobeyed Your Word and that makes me a sinner as well. Please forgive our sins.' The offering itself was given in faith, confessing that he was a sinner.

On the other hand, Cain's offering was crops from his field. It doesn't mean the offering from the land was bad but that it was an offering of a Gentile. The problem of this type of offering lies in a concept of 'exchange of gifts.' Basically, it means 'I have given the works of my sweat and labor to the Creator so you must give something back to me as well.' Cain had fallen into the trap of a religion of Shamanism.

Once a person gives something out of their own effort, most likely, there is a purpose behind it which is basically focused on 'Me.' God refers this attitude as a sin. All God wants from us is our confession of faith by admitting, "I am a worthless sinner. I cannot be forgiven of my sins without Your grace." A precious prayer seeking God's love and grace is by confessing that you are the descendent of a sinner.

Abel's Death and Birth of Seth

Cain kills his brother Abel. Not only does Adam and Eve fall in the beautiful Garden of Eden that God gave by eating the forbidden fruit but their first son kills his brother Abel, who confessed that he was the sinner in front of God. We see the redemptive work by God in giving Seth and his descendants to Adam and Eve. The bloodshed of Abel and redemption of Seth can also be interpreted as a shadow of Jesus Christ.

The Bible lists the family trees (genealogies) of Seth referring to the sons of God. The first son of Seth, Enosh, becomes the first man to give worship to God ever since the first creation of man in the Garden of Eden. And from his bloodline, Enoch is born. Enoch becomes the father of Methuselah at the age of 65; and he walked with God all the days of his life until he was brought up by God. The son of Enoch, Methuselah also walked with God and the Bible records him as the person who lived the longest until 969 years old. From his family line came the righteous man, Noah. The genealogy of Seth records the sons of God up to Noah, the righteous man.

City of Cain

After being driven out of the Garden, Cain heads towards the east of Eden and settles in the land of Nod. He builds a city of Enoch after the name of his son. (Let's not confuse the name of Enoch, latter descendant of Seth, who walked with God.)

This shows us that the first thing people do when they gather is to create civilization as well as making living arrangements on their own basically taking control of all the consequences of life without God. What this means is that you are allowing no one else but yourself to become the master of your own life.

On the other hand, look at the life of Abraham. Patriarchs like Abraham, Isaac and Jacob did not build a city but instead led their lives as nomads even though God gave them the Promised Land. Living in tents indicates that they were not permanently residing at one place but rather like sojourners focusing only in the city of Jerusalem that God was to build and manage. (Hebrews 11:9-10)

The Start of World Civilization

The beginning of the 'world' starts from Cain's descendant, Lamech, who becomes the originator of ancient culture. It appears Lamech must have been a warrior and had several wives. Apparently, Lamech must have been wounded by a boy who tried to strike him with a spear for some unknown grudge so he kills the boy heartlessly and brags about it and wrote the 'song of Lamech's sword.' By having several wives, the custom of polygamy begins and the sinful nature of mankind increases through Lamech.

In addition, his two sons plays a major role in both culture and civilization. His first son, Jubal becomes the ancestor of music (lyre and pipe); and Tubal-cain becomes the first inventor of weapons in the mankind's history. The world originates from this point on. Once men started to make weapons, the concept of the strong against the weak began to lead the battlefields. In other words, the more people are killed, the more chance to become a leader.

The development of both culture and civilization may have brought convenience and prosperity to human but in the end it brought negative results. The descendants of Cain continued fostering culture and civilization whereas the descendant of Seth. God's people like Enosh who was the first to worship God, and Enoch, who walked with God, Methuselah and Noah historically were at spiritual war with them.

JUDGMENT OF THE FLOOD_Genesis 6-9

Mixed Marriages_Period of Conscience

The key element of the corruption began when mixed marriages took place. The descendants of Seth who worshipped God marrying the daughters of Cain's descendants, smitten by the beauty of their flesh. The Bible indicates the Holy Spirit that was with Enoch, Methuselah and Enosh left their descendants which meant that God decided to pass judgment upon them.

The sins of mankind were so great and overflowing to a point where God grieved that He had created mankind. Every thought and plan of men was evil, therefore, judgment was inevitable. "The heart is more deceitful than all else." (Jeremiah 17:9) This explains why God passed judgment of the flood.

All creation moves according to God's purpose. But as for humans, God has given us freewill to choose, whether to move according to God's Spirit or to move according to the spirit of the world. The decision made is our responsibility. The human race, lost in violence and corruption, is bringing destruction upon itself and only an act of judgment will rid the world of sin.

It was a period of conscience until the flood because there was no standard of the Word of God before God gave the commandments to Moses. So everything was left to the conscience of people. Without the Word of God, the conscience of humankind changes according to time and space, therefore, it is inevitable that our hearts get deceitful and dirty.

Burst of the Expanse

Against a background of judgment, God's saving act of Noah, 'who found favor in the eyes of the Lord,' the only good man of his time and the one human being who lived in fellowship with God, made him survive while the rest was wiped out. God had a detailed rescue plan. He provided a safe place and a refuge. The eight of them: Noah, his wife and his three sons, Shem, Ham and Japheth and their wives became the remnants.

Upon God's command, Noah obeyed and built the ark for 120 years. There was a purpose in giving this lengthy time. God had waited patiently and allowed 120 years for the people to repent and return before the judgment of the flood.

When Noah reached the age of 600, God finally decided to wipe out the land by pouring rain for forty days. We must refer back to the days of creation, namely the 2nd day where there was a division of the upper and lower waters of the expanse. The flood came from the waters from the upper expanse as it is described in Genesis 7:11 "The fountains of the great deep burst open, and the floodgates of the sky were opened." Even the waters from the ground were gushed out that everything on earth was covered with water completely.

Through God's Word of energy, an expanse was created, however, through sin the flood reversed the world back to formless, void and emptiness. Without His Word and energy, the problem of formless cannot be resolved. We must understand that the energy of the Word moves only when we pray and confess the Word freeing us from bondage; filling us with peace and experiencing the opening of the heaven gates within our heart. The more you are burdened with the problems and obstacles in life, the more you should yearn for the Word; study the Word; kneel down and repent to the grace of the Word; and pray. Then you will experience the gates of heaven opening up inside of your heart where a small stream of light, the light of God and the light of life, will shine upon you and your problems will be lifted.

Noah's ark floated on water for 7 months. He had to wait for 4 months for the water to dry up. A raven was sent out first and then a dove. The dove brought a freshly picked olive leaf back in her beak and they realized only then that the water was dried up from the earth. This tells us that that they were inside the ark for about a year and the only remnants left behind through the judgment.

God's Grace after the Flood

Noah and his family members came out of the ark after the flood. It is necessary for us to draw a map because the history of mankind begins after the flood. To reiterate the drawings of the Old Testament map, let's first draw a bread and fork with a chicken leg beside it. And underneath it the pig's feet with the head of a cobra showing a tongue sticking out. The ark was stationed in Mt. Ararat, the upper part of River Tigris which is now the mountain in Turkey.

Re-Affirmation of the Blessing of Eden

God made a promise to Noah's family after the flood which was actually re-affirming the first promise given in the Garden of Eden. "God blessed them; and God said to them, 'Be fruitful and multiply, and fill the earth, and subdue it; and rule over the fish of the sea and over the birds of the sky, and over every living thing that moves on the earth.'" (Genesis 1:28) This is the same blessing given to Adam and Eve.

It was from this point on that they were allowed to eat meat. From the time of creation and the flood, the people were vegetarians but starting from Noah's family, they were given the blessing to eat meat from hereon until produce from farming was available.

It took almost 4 months for the water to dry up since the world had been under water completely for a year. What must have crossed the minds of Noah and his family members when they finally came out of the ark? What food was available for them to eat? It would have been impossible for them to consider farming because of the length of the time the earth was covered with water. There was no vegetation of any sort. The only food available was the animals that were inside of the ark. The rapid breeding that took place inside the ark enabled them to eat meat from this point on. The appropriate time that God helps is His grace and mercy. From this point, the animals begin to fear man. (Genesis 9:2)

The First Law is Given

It was God's grace to chase Cain out from the Garden of Eden after he murdered Abel. Now, after the judgment of the flood, God gives a definite law about killing and thus, the punishment follows whoever commits murder. (Genesis 9:6) The reason is that man was created in the image of God, and so whoever kills a man would be the same as killing God. Among the 10 commandments given to Moses, the 6th commandment of 'do not kill' was first declared to mankind through Noah after the flood, marking the first law of God given to us at Noah's time.

The first police enforcement and ruling of judgment was established at this point in time. So the period after the flood can be referred to as the 'period of human government.' The justice of human laws was introduced from this period. For instance, the police catches the murderer, brings him to court and judgment is passed.

Covenant of the Rainbow is Given-Genesis 9:11-16

A covenant of the rainbow was given to Noah's family by God. This was a promise by God that He would no longer judge people until the 2nd coming of Christ. Knowing the hearts of human were corrupt and that it would be impossible to wipe out each time, God decides to delay His judgment for all sinners until the last day.

Threader: The parables of the wheat and tares in Matthew 13 are referring to the covenant of the rainbow.

Noah's Sin

First Produce Not Offered

In spite of receiving God's grace of the covenant of the rainbow, unfortunately, Noah committed a sin. The earth was ready for farming when it had dried up. The first produce of farming was harvested but it was not offered to God. The Bible repeatedly emphasizes the offering of the first fruit throughout the entire Bible.

If you happen to go to Israel, you will come across many Jews praying in front of the wailing wall, wearing a black clothing, a black matchbox-like thing on their foreheads and with a similar packet around their arms and swaying their arms while they pray. Incidentally, they are following the instructions according to the words of Deuteronomy. "You shall bind them as a sign on your hand and they shall be as frontals on your forehead." (Deuteronomy 6:8) Even though the temple or the country do not exist any longer, they continue to carry out the rituals according to what is written in the Bible. Inside the little packet contains the Word of God that is written in small letters. Out of mere curiosity, I bought one and looked inside. Obviously, it included other passages, but the majority of them had a similar message, which was "to offer your first produce to God." It shows us how important the Jews regard the offering of the first fruit.

Unfortunately, Noah did not offer his first produce to God but instead made wine and drank from it. Then he got drunk and naked. He gave away his freewill to Satan and sinned. (Genesis 9:20-21)

"There is none righteous, not even one." (Romans 3:10) This is so true.

Canaan's Homosexuality

Noah's sin was his nakedness. One might think, "Why is it a sin when he gets drunk by himself? And besides what does it matter whether he is naked or not?" However, the Bible clearly tells us that it is a sin. The following are the reasons.

Ham, father of Canaan, saw the nakedness of his father and told his two brothers. He gets cursed by this act. Noah had three sons, Shem, Ham and Japheth. Why is it that the Bible refers Ham as the father of Canaan while the other two sons are called by their names? Here's the answer. Who is Canaan in the first place? He is the youngest son of Ham. Never, not even once, is the name of Ham mentioned, but instead, he is referred as the father of Canaan. It is strange that he, the youngest, is rather referred as the father of Canaan, when there is the oldest son, Cush. It is because Canaan had committed a sinful sexual act.

Waking up, Noah was extremely upset and cursed at Ham realizing that he had told his brothers of his nakedness. Then a more severe curse is passed towards Canaan, a curse to become the lowest level of servants and also to serve his brothers as well. Why? The word 'nakedness' in Hebrew means acts of homosexuality.

Let us organize this sinful scene once again. Noah who did not offer his first produce to God fell drunk and gave up his freewill to Satan. At that time, his grandson Canaan went in and committed a strange sexual act. Coincidently, his father Ham happened to notice this and was greatly alarmed so went out and told his brothers. Upon hearing from Ham what had happened, both Shem and Japheth took a garment and walked backwards to cover the nakedness of their father.

Among the three brothers, Noah gave great blessings to Shem and Japheth. But a great curse was given to Ham and his descendants. After being cursed, Canaan moves away from Mt. Ararat and is the first one

Is It a Sin for Christians to Drink Wine?

In the past, I had absolutely no guilt at all and thought it was perfectly fine to drink liquor while believingin Jesus. I found comfort and justified by the verse in Ephesians 5:18 since it did not mention anything about not drinking as long as you don't get drunk.

However, there is a problem when drinking liquor. Normally if you drink, your appetite increases as well as your sexual desires. You're opening the doors of vulnerability and eventually fall into the trap of Satan's plan where the flesh overpowers your diminishing ability of self control.

What does 'getting drunk' mean? The important fact is that making a decision to drink means that you are surrendering your own freewill to Satan. Once your freewill is surrendered your body is led wherever Satan leads you. For instance, you start to get violent or commit adultery with another woman, etc. Then the next morning, when you wake up, you say "I don't remember a thing." It is because you have surrendered your freewill to Satan voluntarily making you unable to remember. Unless the Holy Spirit comes into us and recovers the stolen freewill, we're out of control.

So that is why the messages are "That is (Holy Spirit) the Spirit of truth" (John 14:17); "The truth shall make you free" (John 8:32) and "Do not get drunk with wine, for that is dissipation, but be filled with the Spirit." (Ephesians 5:18) Faith is all about determination and commitment. Let us not forget that getting drunk with alcohol only collects rottenness. "Wine betrays the haughty man, So that he does not stay at home. He enlarges his appetite like Sheol, And he is like death, never satisfied. He also gathers to himself all nations And collects to himself all peoples." (Habakkuk 2:5) to settle in the land of Canaan. The land where the seven tribes of Canaan lived is the actual land where the people of Israel were to conquer later on. God had commanded all living beings to be wiped out from this land. Why such a command? Because the Canaanites became the worst tribe of all ever since, the sinful sexual act was committed in Mt. Ararat where Baal idolatry (group sex) was openly introduced and was worshipped as a god in the world. The worship of Baal would have easily trickled down to the people of Israel so in order to prevent them from adapting immoral sexual activities they were to be wiped out beforehand. The most vulnerable point for humans is the physical temptations.

The Canaanites worshipped not only the Baal but also the Asherah, the partner of Baal. The Baal idol was made from bronze whereas the Asherah was shaped like a pillar carved in wood. The Asherah idol was shaped as a woman especially emphasizing on the breasts and buttocks that by rubbing it lustful thoughts were triggered. During the divided kingdom period, Queen Athalia and the wife of King Ahab, Isabelle, were the ones who worshipped Asherah idolatry. We are to assume that homosexuality rooted from here.

The sin of Noah after the flood has been passed down to the mankind. Therefore, by right, there is no one righteous on this earth. Noah was saved not because he was a righteous man but because it was the grace of God that he found a favor in the eyes of the Lord.

After Noah gave the blessings, he gave praise to Shem, "Blessed be the Lord, The God of Shem." (Genesis 9:26) Shem had covered his father's naked body with a garment but it wasn't for that reason that Noah blessed him. Noah knew that Shem had served God ordinarily so it was natural for him to praise God of Shem. Then both Japheth and Shem were blessed. "May God enlarge Japheth, And let him dwell in the tents of Shem." (Genesis 9:27) Blessings of territorial enlargement as well as spiritual blessings were given to Japheth.

The nations of the Biblical world are all traced back to Noah's three sons, Shem, Ham and Japheth. Shem is the spiritual firstborn of Noah. We can see that the Bible records the genealogy of sinners first and then God's people next.

The first son of Noah, Ham, becomes the ancestor of the blacks. The first son of Ham is Cush who is now known as the Ethiopians. Cush is located in the lower part of the Nile River in Egypt near the Red Sea. Canaan was the first to settle in the land of Canaan after being cursed out from the Mt. Ararat and then followed by Cush who settled in Ethiopia. The Bible indicates that the second son of Ham, Mizraim, became the ancestor of the Egyptians. The country next to Egypt is Libya where the third son, Put, became the ancestor. Lastly, the youngest son, Canaan became the ancestor of the Canaanites.

Japheth is now known as the Caucasians. According to the Bible, Japheth followed the strips of the Mediterranean Sea while eventually heading towards Europe. It appears that they are the ancestor of the Europeans. Japheth received the blessings of prosperity and territory from God. This is fulfilled over the years -- ruling of the Greek and the Roman Empire; the 19th century ruling of the Great Britain, and the dominating power of America are all which originated from the blessings of Noah. Japheth was to dwell in the tents of Shem and from Shem, the Hebrews came and ultimately, the Gospel was spread throughout the world through the descendant of Abraham, the source of blessings of all nations, Jesus Christ came forth.

Shem is an Asian but more precisely a Middle Easterner. The Bible talks about the 3rd son of Shem, Arpackshad and his grandson, Eber who becomes the ancestor of the Hebrews, known also as Israelites. Through Eber, Terah was born and through Terah, Abraham at last. 'Eber' is the same as the name 'Hebrew' Even though it is not mentioned in the Bible, it is believed that the Sumerian horses came from Shem. The Sumerian tribes were in the vicinity of Babylon and were chased out eastward by Nimrod and were destroyed in eastern Asia. Based on this fact, we are to assume that the Far Eastern people might have been from the Sumerian tribes. As Asians, we all belong to the tribes of Shem. Now through these three nations spread out after the flood, the genealogy of mankind has finally entered into the world.

Threader: The evangelical journey of Apostle Paul started from the church of Antioch and then to Asia Minor in the region of Galatia. The spirit of God blocked Paul whenever he wanted to continue his missionary trip to Asia. A vision appeared to Paul, a Macedonian man standing and appealing, saying "Come over to Macedonia and help us." (Acts 16:9) As a result, through Paul's 2nd missionary trip, the gospel was proclaimed in Europe where the church of Philippi was established and many more. We see the fulfillment of Japheth's dwelling in the tent of Shem. The Europeans received the gospel after the Galatia (Asia Minor) and circled around the world with it and finally reached Korea via America.

Progress of Civilization of Mankind

The Bible indicates that the tower was built on the plain of Shinar (=Sumer, ancient Babylonia in southern Mesopotamia), kingdom of Nimrod. The plain of Shinar was in the region of the meeting point of the Euphrates and the Tigris. Nimrod is the youngest son of Cush who is Ham's first son. Nimrod didn't go far after coming down from Mt. Ararat and settled in the lower part of Mesopotamia in Shinar.

The book of Genesis records him as the first hunter at the time. (Genesis 10:8-9) What kind of hunter do you think he was? He hunted people. He is the descendant of Cain being the first master hand in opening the doors of weapon and evil ways. Later on, Nimrod being the leader overthrows Assyria and Syria and forms the kingdom of Babylon. In all likelihood, the main player of building the tower of Babel is Nimrod. The people lived strictly according to their efforts in the flat plains of Mesopotamia and eventually humanism start to develop and progresses into civilization of mankind.

Among the civilization of mankind, the geometric skill of Babylon was extremely impressive that the approach of metes and bounds (originating from a dot line structure brick) were utilized in making bricks and mortar since no stones were available on the flat plains. The Tower of Babel was in all likelihood a multi-storied temple-tower or ziggurat, similar to those developed in Babylonia in the 3rd millennium BC. It was feasible theoretically, but their intention was to build the pyramid-like tower with "Its top in the heaven." (Genesis 11:4) The tower was built to satisfy the people's vanity: "Let us make a name for ourselves." (Genesis 11:4) These people were trying to approach God on their own self-serving terms. That is why humans start to challenge God once they get together.

Do you think the tower would reach heaven? Human minds think it can but it cannot. God knew the heart of men and their intention and probably said, "Nothing but evil thoughts are in the heart of people." Therefore, God intervened to prevent the builders of Babel from taking the power and glory that belongs only to Him. "The whole earth used the same language and the same words." (Genesis 11:1) The language of the builders was confused so they could no longer communicate with one another. In their frustration, they abandoned the project. The prideful builders were scattered abroad. Humankind's misguided efforts at self-glorification brought confusion and frustration and their dispersion throughout the world. The different languages began from this point on.

Threader: But there was a time when all languages became one-at the time of Jesus with His Word. At the end of the Old Testament after the prophet Malachi came, the Word of God had vanished for BC 400 years on this earth. Why do you think there was this silence period? During that time, God did an amazing thing. One of the works He did during the silence period was He had prepared the Greek to spread the Word throughout the world through the Messiah.

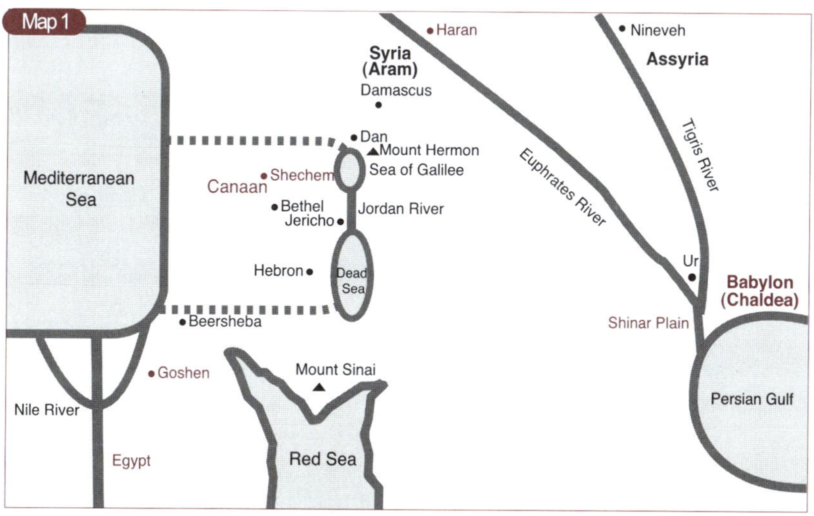

Period of Creation People treason God and build a tower of Babel on the plain in Shinar to make a name for themselves. This place became the scene of the judgment.

Greek was the common language used and through Apostle Paul who was fluent in Greek the remarkable history was unfolded by his teaching that spread throughout the world. As God prepared the Greek to spread the gospel in the past, now English is the world's language of today.

After scattering the sinners, God meets one person. God's redemptive plan now focuses on the family and descendants of one individual, Abraham. In order to send the Messiah, Jesus Christ, to this earth, a preparation of a community who worships only God is being made; a selected and distinctive nation is being prepared.

God calls, not a nation or tribe, but a man named Abraham in his ancestral city of Babylon, the place of the Tower of Babel. "Go forth from your country, And from your relatives And from your father's house, To the land which I will show you." (Genesis 12:1) Chaldeans is another name for Babylon. Note that God called one man, one soul, not when people were gathered together but when they were scattered away. This opens the period of the God of Abraham, God of Isaac and God of Jacob, he faithful patriarchs.

The Lord Who Gives Grace to the Murderer

The Bible talks about the descendant of Cain, who was a murderer. We must realize that God had shown mercy even towards Cain. Cain pleaded to God by saying, "My punishment is too great to bear! You have driven me this day from the face of the ground; and I will be a wanderer on the earth and whoever finds me will kill me" (Genesis 4:13-14)

When Cain struck his brother Abel with a rock killing him, God called out to Cain, 'Where is Abel your brother?' He protested by saying, 'I don't know. Am I my brother's keeper or what?' Even to the person with this kind of character, God shows mercy and grace. "Don't worry, you won't die. Whoever kills Cain, vengeance will be taken on him sevenfold." (Note: Genesis 4:15) God even gave a sign so that he would be protected from whomever he meets.

I receive inquiries from people raising questions such as: "Based on the story, there's supposed to be only Adam, Eve and Cain. I don't understand why Cain was afraid of being killed by someone in the first place? Does that mean that there were other people living at the time?" after reading this verse.

We must understand that the concept of Hebrews is different from our concept today which is based on Greek minds. We constantly try to understand the Bible in a logical, intellectual, and radical way but that is why it leaves us with many puzzles and confusion in the end. After Cain killed his brother Abel, there was no one living at the time while he was running away. According to a psychologist, if a person commits murder, the first thing that comes into the mind is fear of being killed by someone. With this in mind, what Cain felt was the result of a killer's psychological fear of death. Along this line, when God said that 'whomever kills Cain will be punished sevenfold' was not because there were other people living but to emphasize the fact that he would live strictly by the grace of God.

God gives mercy and grace to murderers as well. God does not punish nor destroy us because of our failure and sin. Even though Cain was driven away, God did not kill him but instead gave grace and even a 'sign' to protect him. God's love and patience in giving a chance to a person, even to those who sinned, to recover is clearly revealed here.

There are two characters in the Bible who betray Jesus. Judas Iscariot sold off Jesus and the other, Peter, whom he acknowledged that Jesus loved him the most, cursed and denied Jesus three times. However, their ending results are totally different. One's life changes drastically according to which choice is made after a crime.

Judas Iscariot's guilty conscience led him to despair to the point of death and eventually he committed suicide. But what happened to Peter? He repented. In spite of his enormous guilt of denying Jesus three times, he believed in Jesus and knew of His love more than anyone else and held on to Jesus' love and repented. Upon resurrection, Jesus meets Peter in Lake Galilee and recovers his denial and curse, by asking Peter the same question, "Simon, son of John, do you love me more than these?" (John 21:15) three times and receiving the same responses from him, "Lord, You know that I love You." From this example, we know how drastically a life can be shifted depending on the choices we make after we sin.

In the Old Testament, King David was regarded as the man after God's heart. And even throughout the history of the kings, each king was judged whether they walked in the path of David or in the path of Jeroboam. But even David committed a major sin, adultery and murder. The result of his sin was running away from his own son's conspiracy and sword in tears, fleeing from the palace in Jerusalem barefooted in the middle of the night. A man named Shimei cursed and threw stones at David and then the commander of David's army said, "Shall I kill him?" David responded, "No, leave him alone and let him curse, for the Lord has told him" (Note: 2 Samuel 16:10) and repents to God. David is a classic example of showing us how to repent.

We can easily commit sin momentarily. But do not despair and never take your own life. When we repent and return to God, merciful God holds and raises us again. We must focus only in Jesus no matter what circumstances we find ourselves in.

ABRAHAM, ANCESTOR OF FAITH

Genesis 12-23

After scattering the people, God calls upon one person, Abraham. The period of the patriarchs starts from this point on. Why do you think God called Abraham? We are now going to find out how Abraham becomes the ancestor of faith by tracing his life.

Of All People, Why Abraham?

God called upon Abraham to become the ancestor of the nation of Israel. With full authority God specifically called one person to fulfill the works of His providence on this earth. 'God's full authority of selecting' is referred to as 'predestined.' The word 'predestined' is frequently explained as "God already predestined believers and unbelievers of Jesus." Even though it is my opinion, I think this is a wrong interpretation. If so, the command of Jesus to evangelize to the ends of the earth would then have no bearing or whatsoever.

"Blessed be the God and Father of our Lord Jesus Christ, who has blessed us with every spiritual blessing in the heavenly places in Christ, just as He chose us in Him before the foundation of the world, that we should be holy and blameless before Him. In love He predestined us to adoption as sons through Jesus Christ to Himself, according to the kind intention of His will." (Ephesians 1:3-5)

We have been chosen by God before the foundation of the world in Christ. He chose us to receive spiritual blessings of heaven to be holy and blameless before Him so that we could become like the image of Jesus. In other words, there are many characters in the Bible who are specifically called to expand the world of God. Clearly, God has not predestined anyone to go to hell and waits for them there.

To Spread the Blessing of God

There was a concept of being 'chosen' by God for the people of Israel. They regarded themselves as special and a holy nation without realizing that God had chosen them so that they may fulfill their responsibilities in sharing the blessings they received to every nation and Gentiles of the world. But Israel's attempt to fulfill their responsibilities ended with many conspicuous failures, primarily because of their pride of being 'chosen' (elitism). They boasted themselves and treated the Gentiles like the dogs.

But God clearly said "All the earth is Mine" (Exodus 19:5) in Mt. Sinai through the covenant with the people of Israel. "For God so loved the world, that He gave His only begotten Son" (John 3:16) God loved the world, every country and every person. It is not only you whom God loves, but everyone in the world. God predestined us to be His loved ones even before creation. We must become His witnesses even to the remotest part of the earth. (Acts 1:8) With the grace and blessings we have received first from God, it is our great commission to make disciples of all the nations. (Matthew 28:19)

Then you would ask, "What kind of 'predestination' is that?" When God created humankind, we were given freedom of choice and the 'predestination' should be understood under that boundary. God has provided all kinds of circumstances for us to make constant decision in our lives. This is the real nature of the predestined theory. God has given each individual specific decisions to make and He is waiting, "I stand at the door and knock; if anyone hears My voice and opens the door, I will come in to him, and will dine with him, and he with Me." (Revelation 3:20) God never forces anything on us. He only knocks and it is up to us whether to open the door or not. God wants us to choose on our own freewill which is a privilege and a blessing. "Whoever believes in Him should not perish, but have eternal life." (John 3:16)

Due to the Mentalities of Hebraism (Dependency to God)

It was under God's sovereignty that Abraham was called to become the ancestor of faith but the possibility of him being raised up as a Hebrew (for him to become an ancestor of faith) might have been another element for God in choosing him. There is a considerable difference between the mentalities of Hellenism (Greek) and Hebraism (Hebrews).

First, the mentality of Hebraism is God-centered-meaning Hebrews are passive (attentive to emotions/feelings). Hebrews were able to follow God without any resistance because of their passiveness. Their attitude was, 'Since God is the center of the universe, we just need to follow Him.' On the other hand, the minds of Hellenism are self-oriented and focused on self - efficiency. That is why unbelievers say things like, "We must open our store early so that we can earn more. Why do we have to go to the church's early prayer sessions?" Alternatively, believers have attitudes of "God is our center of the universe. It is God who gives all things so let us focus on God first." What a great difference in attitudes!

Second, the mentality of Hebraism are: not only are they God-oriented but also relationship oriented. As we know, the Old Testament is written in Hebrew and the New Testament in Greek. However, the bulk of it was written by the Hebrews so their mentalities are clearly reflected. For instance, when you read the Bible, it does not mention a 'name' only. Rather, it always elaborates who the person is related to, for example, Andrew, the brother of Peter, or Isaac the son of Abraham, or so and so brother, etc. The person is never mentioned by itself. Why? It is because a kingdom cannot be created alone. Alter natively this means that it senseless to believe in Jesus all to yourself.

We must all become 'us in Christ' altogether.

God sacrificed His Son; resurrected and raised Him high to become the head of the church for us. Fundamentally, salvation begins from an individual's soul (salvation by His acknowledgement) one by one because Jesus comes into our heart as His Spirit, the Holy Spirit. As salvation has been given to us by believing in Jesus, we must go through training in the church community to become blameless snd holy as God's children. "In whom the whole building, being fitted together is growing into a holy temple in the Lord." (Ephesians 2:21) Salvation comes through the church. After the church is restored then we are saved when we become 'us' in Christ.

For that reason relationship with 'others' are very important to us. "You shall love the Lord your God with all your heart, and with all your soul and with all your mind." (Matthew 22:37) We must first align our relationships with God and His ways. Then, the next would be, "You shall love your neighbor as yourself." (Matthew 22:39) With God's peace within us, we must humble ourselves for others and steadily progress to change our life so that we may truly become one in Christ. Only then will we be able to experience His 'kingdom' within us.

Third, the mentality of Hebraism is experience-oriented. This is exactly where the majority of people of today with mentalities of Hellenism have conflicts with. The Bible is difficult to prove scientifically or logically since it involves complicated emotions and experiences. "In the beginning God created the heavens and the earth." (Genesis 1:1) "The virgin shall be with child." (Matthew 1:23) "And what is the surpassing greatness of His power toward us who believe. These are in accordance with the working of the strength of His might which He brought about in Christ, when He raised Him from the dead, and seated Him at His right hand in the heavenly places." (Ephesians 1:19-20) How can one explain creation, a virgin with a child, and resurrection in a logical manner? The emphasis of Hellenism mindsets is cool-headed rationale and logic. Simply put, if it is not logical it does not make sense.

Often times we find many things in the Bible that does not make sense. It is because our underlying knowledge and education are all based on Hellenism. But one thing positive is that the Bible is clearly oriented along the lines of experiences and feelings. One of the reasons why churches today have lost its energy of vitality is because the Word of God has been approached analytically or theologically. The gospel is not a theory, philosophy or even theology. It is strictly an experience. In plain words, you just believe in Jesus when He brings you into His Light through the blood of the cross while you were wandering around in the midst of darkness of the world. Once you feel His existence within you, His love is overwhelming! When you pray and give praise, shedding tears of joy in public won't matter! Without having this kind of experience or feelings, you may analyze or understand the Bible in your head but have a hard time believing it.

That is why Apostle Paul told the church members of Corinth, "For the letter kills, but the Spirit gives life." (2 Corinthians 3:6) As written, letter kills but the Spirit gives life. Spirit has nothing to do with logic or rationality. Rationality belongs to the worldly knowledge. Apostle Paul said that worldly knowledge is elementary knowledge and referred to it as a faith of an infant.

We have five senses just as animals do. Animals remain at the level of beasts with their five senses but as human we are different. We have what we call the '6th sense.' As for the Hebrews, they lived according to their '7th sense' which are the Word of God and the thoughts of God. The reason why it is difficult for us to pray is because we pray with our 5th or 6th sense. We get frustrated for not receiving any answers in spite of our prayers. True prayers are done with the 7th sense that is through the movement of the Holy Spirit.

Covenant with Abraham-A Promise to Make God's Kingdom

The following are the promises given to Abraham. (The 3 key elements of a country.)

First, the land starting from Hazor of Egypt all the way to Euphrates was to be given. (Territory)

Second, many descendants as countless as the stars of heaven and the sands of the seashore were to be given. (Nation)

Third, a promise of 'Immanuel' (God's presence) was given. (Ruler)

God repeats His promises in Genesis 12, 13, 15 and 17 until Abraham genuinely believes it.

The promise of Immanuel is "I will bless those who bless you, And the one who curses you I will curse." (Genesis 12:3) Basically it meant that God was going to be on Abraham's side. This promise was more specifically emphasized in Jacob's time, "I am with you, and will keep you wherever you go, and will bring you back to this land; for I will not leave you until I have done what I have promised you." (Genesis 28:15) How amazing is this! God's promise to Abraham was ultimately proclaiming that He had a missionary purpose in building His land and the nation forming God's Kingdom.

Through the incident of the Tower of Babel, language was divided and people were scattered and after the judgment of the flood, people experienced desperation and confusion (aka Babel) leaving them with no more hope in the world. However, God is proclaiming, 'There is, in fact, a true hope in the world.' He is proclaiming His world will be accomplished through Abraham. Israel was chosen to become a nation where God directly got involved and managed to make them a community who worships only God so that they may become the source of blessing, spreading their blessings throughout the world.

Threader: In fact, Jesus Christ, the Messiah was sent to earth through the covenant of Abraham. It was God's plan in choosing Israel to become the founder of nations and the source of blessings through Abraham and in reality, Jesus Christ did become the source of blessings to all nations. After the resurrection of Jesus, the 12 disciples prayed in the attic room and received the Holy Spirit; and from this point on, they risked their lives in becoming the witnesses of Jesus and traveled throughout the world to spread the news. Apostle Paul was also the descendant of Abraham. Today, as believers of God, our role is to become the source of blessings to all nations as well.

Life of Abraham

The life of Abraham was a process of surrendering his self-serving life to God which was already predestined in God's plan and training. "Go forth from your country ... To the land which I will show you." (Genesis 12:1) Abraham obeyed to this summon. "By faith Abraham, when he was called, obeyed by going out to a place which he was to receive for an inheritance; and he went out, not knowing where he was going." (Hebrews 11:8) First, there was the command and upon Abraham's obedience the presence of God's promise was with him.

I remember receiving so much grace when a missionary introduced the contents of a prayer by Missionary Underwood. This young man in his 20s, who graduated from Harvard University, came to a foreign land, Korea, on his mission trip. He wanted to spread the Word to people but at that time, men were not easily approachable. Even worse, women were moving outside in carriages so that it was difficult to meet them face to face. One late afternoon, almost at sunset, he stood in front of a big intersection in Korea and lamented in prayers claiming that the 'hearts of Korea' could not be contacted. He continued to pray: "I will obey; and through my humble obedience, I know that the Lord will start to work. I know that one day, I will rejoice in tears when they realize that we are all one in spirit."

The prayers (obedience) of Underwood changed our nation. I recall my tears of joy after realizing that we are indeed one in spirit in

Christ-worshiping and praising the Lord together. That is why the Bible tells us that "we are a temple raised through the foundation of such faithful prophets and teachers." (Ephesians 2:20)

God Who Meets Abraham

God called Abraham in the land of Haran and told him to leave. Since he was 75 years old at the time, we can assume that Abraham must have lived in Haran for many years. When God commanded Abraham to leave his 'home,' it meant for him to leave his parents, relatives, friends, lifestyle and habits behind. All the things that he was familiar with and accustomed to were to be thrown aside to follow God. It was a command to change his lifestyle completely. Besides, to set forth to a place where he's not familiar with at all was a rough journey ahead indeed. There were no signs or the final destination or whatsoever, but Abraham just followed wherever God lead him. Without tremendous conviction, one cannot easily move but Abraham obeyed.

Abraham traveled with donkey caravans through the land as far as to the oak of Moreh in the site of Shechem. When he arrived at Moreh, the other dwellers, the Canaanites, were living in the land already. (Genesis 12:6) They must have exchanged looks with one another wondering who they were. God promises Abraham the land that was occupied by other dwellers was going to be his. He believed that 'with the grace of God, the land was going to be given to him' and as an acknowledgement, he built an altar. In other words, he gave worship to God. It is natural to give worship when you receive God's grace. Worship is when we acknowledge God to praise Him for his sovereignty and mercy. It is at this point the 'quality' is created.

The current name of Shechem is 'Nabulus.' After entering the Promised Land, he continued living as a nomad moving here and there. It is said that he traveled towards the south and finally reached Egypt. There he put down his tent to live because of a severe famine. The minute he arrived in the promised land, he was faced with a

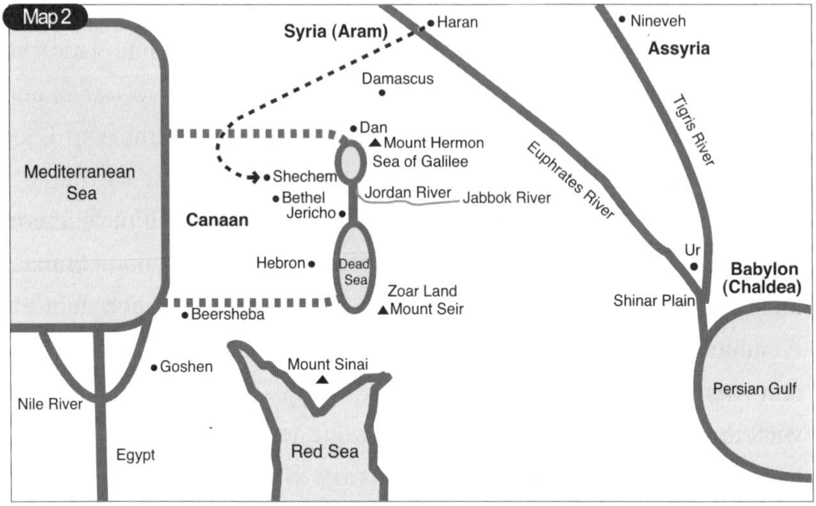

Period of the Patriarchs-Abraham At God's command, Abraham left Haran and worshipped Him in Shechem. Abraham goes down to Egypt due to the famine.

famine so he quickly changed his direction towards Egypt.

Lesson Learned from Egypt

The land of Egypt was a resourceful place to live, primarily because of the Nile. It was a place where one could easily live as long as one worked. "Now there was a famine in the land; so Abram went down to Egypt to sojourn there, for the famine was severe in the land."(Genesis 12:10) Hunger due to the famine drove Abraham into Egypt. Under the stress of fear and insecurity, this man of faith defends himself with a dangerous half-truth which puts God's whole plan at risk. It was a natural move for him to be influenced by the environment because he had not yet achieved total conviction of faith.

Upon arrival in Egypt, Abraham was confronted with an unexpected ordeal of losing his wife Sarah to Pharaoh. He thinks of a scheme pretending his wife Sarah to be his sister and finally the Egyptian soldiers bring his wife to Pharaoh because of her beauty and to please him. In return, Abraham was given all kinds of riches such as sheep, donkeys, camels and servants. Now, when Pharaoh was about to sleep with Sarah, God intervened with plagues in his house. After realizing that the plagues were caused because of Abraham's wife, Pharaoh promptly sent her back to Abraham and they were ignominiously deported from Egypt. From this incident, Abraham learned that a plague follows when he moves away from God's promised land. There was a purpose in God's chosen people--for them to fulfill God's master plan.

The Bible records many plagues that were encountered by those who left the promised land. For instance, Lot was destroyed completely when he moved away to Zoar where Sodom and Gomorrah were. Upon Jacob's return to Haran, Esau (Jacob's brother) had left home in Hebron for Mt. Zale, an area below the Dead Sea and eventually became a tribe of the Gentiles. Also in the book of Ruth, Naomi's family leaves Bethel and moves to Moab because of a severe famine. There she loses her husband and two sons, which resulted in three widows in one family household. Another example is Jonah. God commanded him to go to Nineveh to spread the Word of God but he resisted. Instead, he got on a boat in Joppa to take off towards the Mediterranean Sea thinking that he could get away from God. In his mind, he thought God only existed in the promised land but he ended up in the belly of a 'big' fish.

It was God's plan to give the promised land to the 'chosen' people of Israel in order to create His world on this earth. The 'Promised Land' that is mentioned in the Old Testament is now the 'church' after Jesus came to this world. This is the reason why we must not leave a church, otherwise you're disconnecting yourself from receiving blessings from God.

The lesson Abraham learned from Egypt was that he must not leave the promised land. The promise of God was actually happening in his own life. Just as the promise of Immanuel, he realized that God was with him in Egypt. Even though his wife was taken away to Pharaoh, it was God's grace that she returned unharmed.

Separation with Lot_Genesis 13

After realizing his mistake in Egypt, Abraham builds another altar to God between Bethel and Ai. At this time, God tells Abraham 'Now it's time to let go of your dependency towards Lot so separate with him.' Increasing flocks and herds precipitate the last break in family ties. There was an argument between the herdsmen of Abraham's livestock and Lot's making it difficult to sustain their relationship. It was inevitable for them to say farewells.

Here again, let's briefly talk about the theory of 'pre-destiny.' It is strictly up to us which environment we choose. This is a natural process how God guides us in all given circumstances. That is why the Bible teaches us to be "thankful in all things." (1 Thessalonians 5:18) Abraham proposes to his nephew Lot that it would be best to go separate ways by saying, "If you choose to go to the right, I will go left; and if you to the left then I will go to the right." (Genesis 13:9) Lot is given the first choice by his uncle and selects the fertile pasture of the Jordan Valley. (This area is to be assumed where Sodom and Gomorrah existed.)

Lot had no interest in God's promised land. Farming would be productive with such abundant waters so he decided to take upon his own life from this point on. But be aware that if you think you can hold on to the things you claim to be yours-it will all be taken away. Lot's choice of the land was already predestined to be taken away which came true in the end.

War of the Northern Kings_Genesis 14

In Abraham's day, although a semi-nomadic living style was common, there were also people settled in villages which were ruled over by local 'sheiks' who in turn were often vassals of more powerful kings. The overlords of the five Dead Sea towns came from a distance; from Elam, Babylonia (Shinar), and Anatolia (King Tidal). These northern kings became allies to the valley of Siddim (Dead Sea), confiscated and conquered all the neighboring regions, capturing the kings of Sodom and Gomorrah. Since Lot was living in Sodom, obviously

Knowledge Search 7

Who is Melchizedek, King of Salem?

Melchizedek is mentioned in Hebrews chapters 5~7 but who is he exactly? Melchizedek, the king of Salem, greeted Abraham with bread and wine when Abrahams returned from victory. Then Abraham gave a tenth (tithe) of all to Melchizedek. This is a very important and an amazing event. Abraham who had risked his own life for others just like Jesus received a promise of 'I will be with you' from Melchizedek. A similar incident is portrayed by Jesus towards the disciples at the last supper. "He who eats My flesh and drinks My blood abides in Me, and I in him." (John 6:56) The reaffirmation of God's promise was given to Abraham through Melchizedek. The ability to risk his life for others had gained this honor.

Abraham offered tithes to Melchizedek. Tithing in the Old Testament period was given to the tribes of the Levi. As the ancestor of the tribes of Levi, why did Abraham offered tithes to Melchizedek? It was because Melchizedek blessed Abraham for his redemptive action for Lot.

The name of Melchizedek is mentioned as 'king of Salem.' Salem means peace (shalom) which is interpreted as the "King of righteousness, king of peace." (Hebrews 7:1-7) Who is this person? Without a father, without a mother, without genealogy, having neither beginning of the days, nor the end of life, but made like the Son of God, he remains as a priest perpetually. He is Jesus. "Where Jesus has entered as a forerunner for us, having become a high priest forever according to the order of Melchizedek." (Hebrews 6:20)

"Your father Abraham rejoiced to see My day, and he saw it and was glad." (John 8:56) Jesus clearly states that 'He was Melchizedek.' Then the Pharisees and the scribes retorts to

Jesus, "You are not yet fifty years old, and have You seen Abraham?" (John 8:57) Jesus replied, "Truly, truly, I say to you, before Abraham was born, I am." (John 8:58) This is clearly the truth. "In the beginning was the Word, and the Word was with God, and the Word was God." (John 1:1) Jesus who was with God in the beginning was telling them that 'I existed before Abraham who rejoiced to see My day, and he saw it and was glad.' In other words, He was explaining that He was Melchizedek.

God appeared in many different ways, such as a person or along with angels in the Old Testament period. For instance, God appeared as a person in front of Abraham before the judgment of Sodom and Gomorrah, or like the angel appearing to tell the news of the birth of Isaac. Quite naturally we accept God appearing as an angel but have strange attitudes towards Jesus who appeared momentarily during the Old Testament period. The author of Hebrews tells us, "Concerning him we have much to say, and it is hard to explain, since your faith is like an infant and that it has not grown enough to digest solid food." (Hebrews 5:11) Basically the author is saying that there are many things to talk about Melchizedek but since our faith is not mature yet that he will refrain from explaining that it was actually Jesus.

all of his possessions were also confiscated and were taken into captivity.

When Abraham heard that his nephew had been taken captive, he sets out to rescue him with 318 'home' trained men and went in pursuit as far as Dan and Damascus. Speed of pursuit and a surprise attack gave Abraham victory bringing back all the confiscated goods. Not only was God with him but upon his return from the defeat,

Melchizedek, king of Salem greeted him and brought out bread and wine. Then Abraham offered him with tithes. Risking his life to save Lot was an act of redemption and that's when he comes to face to face with Melchizedek (Jesus), the king of righteousness and the king of Salem.

After that incident, Abraham settled in Hebron. Hebron was an extremely barren land. However, this is an important place in the Old Testament period which becomes the foundation ground for Abraham, Isaac and Jacob. This is also the place where David becomes the king of Judah after being a fugitive for 13 years from the sword of King Saul. In addition, at the same token, Caleb inherits this land after conquering the land of Canaan along with Joshua.

Reassurance of God's Promise_Genesis 15

After rejecting all the treasures offered by the king of Sodom and Gomorrah, Abraham returned to his dwelling tent in Hebron. Then suddenly, he felt uneasy because in the back of his mind he was afraid that the northern kings might retaliate against him. That is when God appeared and reassured him by saying, "I am a shield to you; Your reward shall be very great." (Genesis 15:1)

But then Abraham expresses his discontent to God. "Ten years have passed since you promised and I am still childless, what reward are you talking about?" Abraham's age was already 85. Realistically, he was getting old and his wife had already passed her menopausal stage. In such a situation, thinking that God promised him a great nation was something beyond his imagination. The only person that he could think of becoming his heir was his loyal servant, Eliezer. God then leads Abraham outside of the tent and have him look at the stars in heaven and reassures him that he will have descendants as much as the countless stars above.

God reaffirmed two promises:

First, promise of a nation.

"Your descendants will be like those countless stars in

heaven."(Genesis 15:5) The Bible records that he believed it. "And He reckoned it to him as righteousness." (Genesis 15:6). This is the 'justified salvation.' Abraham was complaining about God's blessing but God makes him believe the blessing of descendants after bringing him out of the tent. Then God justifies Abraham to be righteous even though he was not. Being 'justified as righteous' means that we are linked into the tree of life of Christ without being aware of it. Faith comes from hearing the Word of God and hearing comes from God. So when the Word of God comes into our mind, it becomes faith.

Satan uses the same pattern. Worldly thoughts are the temptation of Satan. The more we listen to the world, the more desires we accumulate. The things of the world such as TV, newspaper, and stories of the world penetrate into our mind and it turns into our faith and desires. Desires are like the powerful tanks that lead to destruction.

We move according to our consciousness whether we are led spiritually or physically. The decision is up to each individual, to choose God's Word or Satan's word. In faith, we must be able choose the Word of God. Through our own freewill and determination, we must eat the tree of life whenever time permits us.

Satan puts idolatry into our hearts, things that are associated with the world; false images such as worries, despair and anxiety. "Are you able to extend an hour of your life by worries?" Jesus said. (Matthew 6:27.)

"Casting all your anxiety upon Him, because He cares for you." (1 Peter 5:7) The best way to get rid of our worries and despair is to trust in the Lord and surrender ourselves to Him completely. Through the guidance of the Holy Spirit, we must receive the Word and pray. Then we will feel God's presence and experience great strength from within our heart. By His presence, we are filled with the Creator Himself who fills all creation so worries and fears are wiped away and replaced with joy and comfort.

Second, promise of the land. (Genesis 15:7)

God again gives reassurance to Abraham that he will be given a great piece of land from Hazor, Egypt as far as up to Euphrates. For the first time, Abraham requests a proof from God that he would actually possess it. Just as God had shown him the stars of heaven, a quick course of visual education was presented to him. He is instructed to get a heifer, a goat, a ram and divide it. A flaming torch passed between the pieces that were cut in half symbolizing His presence. Abraham was again moved and touched by God.

Abraham was some sort of a caravan merchant and in those days any kind of contract was made not by signatures but by cutting an animal in half and then have the business partner walk through the blood of the animal. The significance of this method was to prove that if the contract was not kept then he would be killed just like the animal that was cut into half. This was an enormous act of promise. In Korea, people casually say things like, "if I don't keep this promise I will burn my hands" or "if I don't keep this promise I will change my family name, but these remarks are only verbal words. On the other hand, the Middle Eastern tradition of keeping a promise in such a method was significant and serious.

For Abraham, it was a huge step forward in understanding that his God was present, powerful, living and able to move around with him. His religious experience convinced him that God knew him, cared about him personally and acted in his life with power and purpose. He believed that God would protect him and his descendants in order to fulfill God's promise and purpose. His concept of God represents a boggling mind, leaping forward in revelation. The promise of the land was to be fulfilled 400 years later; through the fourth generation after serving the Gentiles. The Bible says, "The sins of the tribes of the Amorites were not yet filled"(Genesis 15:16) We must understand that when God promised the land to Abraham, the seven tribes of Canaanites were already living there which meant that the land would be given after they were demolished. Again, the emphasis is that God does not 'destroy' for no obvious reason. The Amorites were the major tribes among the Canaanites and once their sins were filled for the judgment, God commanded them to be wiped out completely. "Let no breathing soul be left unkilled." (Joshua 10:40)

People frequently raises questions like: "If you're saying that God created mankind to be His love partner and also created us in His image, why then is He passing on the judgments? If God is merciful, why doesn't He send all people to His kingdom regardless of whether they are sinners or righteous ones?" God is trying to illustrate to us that there is an eternal heaven and hell by giving us foreshadow of heaven and hell in our daily lives. But the most important point to remember is that it is not God who sends the people to hell but themselves who have rejected the eternal life.

Whoever received the Word and Jesus Christ as their Lord God goes to heaven. People with the spirit of God and who live according to it go to heaven. On the other hand, people who refuse to receive the eternal life of God will end up in hell because of their rejection of God's grace. It is with our own freewill to choose either to go to heaven or hell. The choice is ours. "Therefore, they are without excuse." (Romans 1:20) We cannot blame anyone for where we end up with and the Bible confirms it.

In conclusion, the Amorites receives God's judgment. Remember the formula of redemption-a sacrifice is behind a blessing but clearly God wants to save all people - "All men to be saved" (1 Timothy 2:4) Let us not misunderstand that only selected people are saved but that God wants to save 'all' people. That is why we have the role to spread the gospel to the ends of the world.

Abraham's Mistake-The Birth of Ishmael_Genesis 16

Abraham believed the promise of God that an heir would be given to him but his wife thought otherwise. Sarah devises her own way of making God's promise come true. Childless herself, she falls back on custom, giving her slave girl, Hagar, to Abraham and she bores him a son, Ishmael. But human emotions in such a situation are complex. Because of the child, Hagar had an advantage and became insolent, with smugness of showing her looks and actions down towards Sarah.

Sarah could not take it anymore and with Abraham's approval, she responds severely by chasing Hagar out of her household. Hagar was in the long desert road when an angel of the Lord found her and called her by name, "Why are you here?" "I was chased out because of a harsh treatment from my mistress." "Go back to your mistress. God loves you. The child that you bore was given by the grace of God." The angel told her to go back to her mistress, and she obeyed.

The encounter must have been a profound spiritual experience for Hagar. The name, 'Ishmael' means 'one who has received the grace of God.' God wants to save all mankind regardless of race or reli-

Knowledge Search 8

Comparison of Judaism, Islam and Christianity

	Judaism	Islam	Christian
Target of Faith	Jehovah / Yahweh	Allah	Trinity of God
Scripture	Old Testament, Five Books of Moses	Koran	66 Books of the Bible
Theory on Salvation	The Law	Inshalla (It is God's will)	By faith in the Gospel
Geographical Backgroun	Jerusalem	Jerusalem and Mecca	Jerusalem

1. Problem with Judaism

"Those who receive Jesus and believe in Him has been given the privilege to become God's children." Therefore, without the Trinity of God, there is no salvation. The Jews rejected Jesus and ended up killing Him on the account of defiling the divinity. One cannot fulfill salvation through the law.

2. Problem with Islam

There is no salvation when a religion has no repentance. The word “Inshalla” (meaning ‘God’s will’) is frequently spoken in the Islamic religion. For instance, when a person bumps into another person while walking on a street it is ‘Inshalla’; a person is killed in a car accident, it is ‘Inshalla.’ Everything is directed to ‘God’s will’ taking the fault or sin off from themselves. Truthfully even among Christians, we also find people who have this kind of ‘Inshalla’ mentality. Before reborned in Christ, while attending church I also thought “whatever I did wrong was God’s will because He had made me like this.” But what a dangerous thought!

Mohammed was a Saudi caravan merchant who married a wealthy widow who was 7 years older than him. With the support of her wealth, he was able to travel to various parts of Arab countries and started to gather all kinds of cultures including religious materials.

First of all, Mohammed emphasizes on Ishmael to be the firstborn of Abraham. Moreover, he also claims that it was Ishmael, not Isaac who was offered in Mt. Moriah. If you go to Jerusalem today, there is a place called Temple of Rock (Mosque). The Islam believes that it symbolizes the ‘gold rock’ as the actual rock where Abraham offered his firstborn son, Ishmael, in Mt. Moriah. They believe Ishmael to be the firstborn and claim “why is Isaac carrying forth the tradition, not Ishmael?” For this reason they are rejecting the Jews.

There is another big temple next to the Temple of Rock which is called “Al Aksa Temple.They are said to believe that Jesus came down from heaven and stood next to Mohammed on that spot claiming that Mohammed is the true prophet. They also claim that Jesus is not the Son of God but rather He is another prophet like Mohammed.

gion. (1 Timothy 2:4) God promised Hagar that a great nation was going to be given to Ishmael and blessed him. The promise given to Ishmael was the 12 kingdoms later on. There are more than 12 Arabic countries today which is a clear indication of how God blessed them as well.

But what has resulted out of that one mistake of Abraham? God blessed Ishmael when he was born and told him to go 'settle in the eastern part of Canaan' which is Saudi Arabia today. Approximately in A.D. 7, Mohammed, the founder of the Islam religion, came about in Saudi Arabia. The original plan of making a worshiping community through Abraham has gone astray by the sufferings caused by the descendants of Ishmael. The impact and result of one mistake is this great.

The Judgment of Sodom and Gomorrah_Genesis 18:16-19

God appeared to Abraham along with two angels as a man and promised him the birth of Isaac while the two angels left earlier for the judgment of Sodom and Gomorrah. Alone with Abraham, God spoke "Since Abraham will surely become a great and mighty nation, and in him all the nations of the earth will be blessed?" (Genesis 18:18) and "The outcry of Sodom and Gomorrah is indeed great, and their sin is exceedingly grave." (Genesis 18:20) God informs Abraham of the judgment of Sodom and Gomorrah. This is when Abraham starts his intercessory prayer for his nephew Lot who was living in Sodom. "God, indeed You have decided to wipe them away and there's not much I can do. But my nephew Lot is there so I can't let you sweep him away."

Being a skillful businessman, the famous dialogue with God takes place. "If there are 50 righteous men, I will not pass judgment." So Abraham negotiates the number down to 45, 40, 35 ... and finally asks God, "Will you not pass judgment if there were only 10 righteous men?" God answers that He would not destroy the city if 10 righteous men were found. Sadly, there was none and the cities and their evil inhabitants were destroyed.

Instead, God heard Abraham's intercessory prayer and saved Lot and his two daughters. The doom of Sodom and Gomorrah began. The two angels arrived at Lot's house to alert him and his family to flee. However, then again, Lot was not a righteous man. Through Abraham's request, he was acknowledged by God to be justified as righteous. His two sons-in-law took the whole thing casually, stayed behind and died in the midst of the destruction of the city. Upon seeing that the city was swept by fire from heaven, the two angels grasped the hands of Lot and his family to rush them to escape. The angels commanded them not to look back but to run for their lives to the highest mountain. Lot cried out in desperation that he wasn't going to make it and pleaded a closer place called Zoar. They agreed because there was no time to spare. While running away from the burning city towards Zoar, Lot's wife turned into a pillar of salt by looking back at the city where they used to live and thinking of the belongings left behind when she was told not to do so. No one survived except Lot and his two daughters.

After the judgment, they were supposed to go to the promised land for it was the only safe place for them but they had no interest nor had any idea. Due to their lack of understanding, the first story of immorality appears in the Bible. After their escape, Lot was afraid to stay in Zoar and ended up living in a cave with his two daughters. There were no men around them so in order to continue their bloodline, the eldest daughter came up with an idea. She made her father drunk by giving him wine and slept with him; her sister followed the same method. As a result, descendants were born and they became the tribes of Ammonites and Moabites. The Ammonites eventually settle in the eastward of the Jordan River whereas the Moabites settle on the right side of the Dead Sea.

Later, both tribes play a wicked role in blocking the people of Israel during the exodus while crossing the Jordan River from the wilderness. Not only that, we also witness their interference towards the Israelites during the period of the judges and the divided kingdom era. Even though Abraham saved his nephew Lot through his intercessory prayer Lot did not have faith, therefore, acted immorally and eventually interfered with God's chosen people.

Various tribes experience the living power of God through the ten plagues during exodus and they are referred as the 'assembly of Israel' in the book of Exodus. The only tribes eliminated from 'the assembly of Israel' were the Ammonites and the Moabites.

Birth of Isaac_Genesis 17

At last, God appeared to Abraham when he was at the age of 99. Before announcing the birth of Isaac, God first commands circumcision. Circumcision was the first law given at Abraham's time. It was the outward sign by cutting the flesh of the foreskin of the male's penis when the infant was eight days old. In Abraham's case, he was already 99 years old but God commands every male including Abraham and servants to be circumcised. What does this circumcision symbolize? The law given to Moses was written on a stone tablet and was carried around, placed inside of the ark whereas the circumcision was the law written on the physical body reminding them that they were the God's chosen people. It also signified a special relationship with God; not simply a mark of ownership, but also the sign of obedience to God on the part of His people.

Threader: The people of Israel were extremely proud of their status of being the 'chosen people.' That is why David passed a remark towards Goliath by saying, 'who is this uncircumcised Philistine, that he should taunt the armies of the living God?' The Gentiles were treated like dogs due to the fact that they were uncircumcised in those days. By this sign of circumcision, God distinguished His people from the rest. In the time of the New Testament, the emphasis was made on the circumcision itself to those who do not believe in Jesus so Apostle Paul pointed out that salvation is not given just because one is circumcised. "Rend your heart and not your garments. Now return to the Lord your God" (Joel 2:13) indicating that one must be circumcised in the heart.

God gives a more detailed promise. Before, the promise was much broader, "Descendants will be given to you as countless as the stars of the heaven; like the sand of a sea shore." But this time God promises Abraham a son and even gives him a name. Not only does God name the child but He promises the same covenant with Abraham will be, established with his son as well. "Sarah your wife shall bear you a son, and you shall call his name Isaac; and I will establish My covenant with him for an everlasting covenant for his descendants after him." (Genesis 17:19)

This was a significant promise indeed.

However, Abraham, our ancestor of faith, laughed in disbelief. The book of Romans indicates Abraham's reaction as "He contemplated his body as dead even though he was alive ... " (Romans 4:19) meaning in his mind it was impossible for him to perform any physical relationship with his wife and therefore, laughed in disbelief as a result.

At each interval in the process in which God transforms Abraham through his life long journey, his level of faith elevates each time. Overcoming himself, risking his life to save Lot and intercessory prayers were all such processes, and each step in the whole process was orchestrated by God so that he may trust in God completely-bringing him to the point where he earns his name as ancestor of faith. For 24 years, Abraham was guided by God and yet, he laughed at God's prophecy of a son. Not only did Abraham laugh but Sarah who was outside the tent laughed as well. She couldn't believe she could have a child since her menstrual period had ended long ago. This tells us how difficult it is to believe in God's promise when we are of flesh.

Though at its peak, Abraham might have laughed in disbelief but a year later, faithful God fulfills His promise and Isaac is born to Abraham at the age of 100. God fulfilled His creation. What an overwhelming joy it must have been for the elderly couple whose bodies were almost near death to bear a son!

Becoming an Ancestor of Faith_Genesis 22

Isaac had grown and became a young man. Abraham's ultimate test of faith was stretched by the command to sacrifice his son as a burnt offering to God. To offer Isaac as a burnt offering meant Abraham to poke a knife into his son's neck to drain the blood out and then to cut him into pieces and burn him in the fire. It was an unbelievable request. However, it is written in the Bible that he obeyed. Abraham believed in God, the Creator. "Who gives life to the dead and calls into being that which does not exist." (Romans 4:17) He believed that life and death are in the hands of God. This was Abraham's faith at its peak and through his obedience, he became our ancestor of faith.

At the moment Abraham was about to strike his son, God had already prepared a lamb for the burnt offering. The message of this incident was for all the mankind to understand the pain of God the Father who let His only begotten Son die 2000 years ago. Abraham earned his reward as the ancestor of faith by his obedience and through his descendants prepared for the path for the coming of Jesus Christ as reflected in the genealogy of Christ. "The book of the genealogy of Jesus Christ, the son of David, the son of Abraham." (Matthew 1:1) This incident is the shadow of the redemptive cross of offering Jesus' life.

The blessing of longevity was given to Abraham by God but unfortunately, the ending was rather negative. After the death of his wife Sarah, he also had many sons with his other wife, Keturah and lived until 175 years. We have learned that the Ammonites came from the descendants from Ishmael and through the sons of Keturah, the Midianites. The sons of his concubines all turned out to become intruders in hassling Isaac and his descendants.

Threader: As always, the ending is the problem. Just as in Solomon's case, when he asked for wisdom, he received abundant blessings from God including longevity which he didn't ask for; but at the old age, he got corrupted. King Hezekiah who appears in the book of Kings falls into the same category. He prayed when he was near death and God extended his life by 15 years but then again, in the end, he became proud and swayed further away from God. Therefore, rather than praying for longevity, it would be wise to live just as God permits us.

The Characteristics of the Patriarchs

People Who Threw Away Their Personal Pursuits in order to Follow God

God calls upon one person and trains him to surrender his "self" in order to create Israel - a shadow of God's Kingdom. This is the training process of the patriarchs.

Abraham

Abraham was not a man of great faith in the beginning. His father, Terah, was an ordinary man making a living by carving idols, an idol maker. How did Abraham become the ancestor of faith? He went through vigorous training of surrendering 'self' for 25 years.

First, Abraham left his home. The place where God called Abraham was not Ur in Chaldeans but Haran. When he was 75 years old, God commanded Abraham to leave his home. "Go forth from your country, And from your relatives And from your father's house, To the land which I will show you." (Genesis 12:1) Imagine leaving behind not only your family but also your possessions, friends, relatives and all the things you relied and depended on for 75 years. Abraham obeyed and his migration began by leaving home without knowing that he was to enter the land of Canaan. The first thing he did was giving up his possessions.

Second, Abraham had to be separated from his nephew Lot. When he left Haran, he took his nephew along with him. He relied on his nephew as his companion, to talk, discuss or receive support from him during the long journey. But God wanted him to let go of his dependency towards Lot. Abraham obeyed.

Third, Abraham disowned Ishmael, a son that was born through Hagar, the bond servant of his wife. This would have been the most difficult thing to do since Ishmael was his son that he had at an old age although he obtained through his servant. However, Abraham sends away both Hagar and Ishmael who was 14 years old at the time to the wilderness. God was training Abraham to completely let go of everything that he depended on.

Fourth, Abraham even gave up his son Isaac, a son that he had at his tender age of 100. This was his one and only son! Needless to say, to kill his precious son as a burnt offering was more like killing himself but God commanded Abraham to shed the blood of his son. This signifies the climax of his 25 years of training, starting from his calling at the age of 75 through the age of 100. The maturity of Abraham's faith was proven by giving up his one and only loving son, Isaac. We must understand that people of faith are being constructed through tough training such as giving up what you love; giving up what you depend on; giving up what you desire, etc. Denying and surrendering yourself is the message of Jesus; "If anyone wishes to come after Me, let him deny himself, and take up his cross, and follow Me." (Matthew 16:24) Once Abraham was able to deny and ultimately sacrifice his loving son, he earned his name as an ancestor of faith.

Isaac

The son of Abraham is a person who threw away his thoughts completely. He was totally obedient towards his father. Never once did he question or challenge his father. His life was like that of Jesus. "The words that I say to you I do not speak on My own initiative, but the Father abiding in Me does His works." (John 14:10) Whatever Jesus did or spoke came from the Father. To which degree was Isaac obedient? Normally a young man can put aside his opinion on certain things but when it comes to marriage, it's a different story. It is not easy to tolerate another's opinion when it comes to choosing a wife. But then, Isaac gave all authority to his father even selecting his own wife. Abraham's servant leaves for Haran to find a bride for Isaac. He was in the fields meditating when he met his bride, Rebekah. His obedience reached to its peak when he quietly gave up himself for his father's offering. Even though his activity was not elaborated among the patriarchs, he is known as the ancestor of obedience, playing a significant role as a stepping stone of God's promise. Isaac is given the same promise as that given to Abraham and to his son, Jacob.

Jacob

The meaning of 'Jacob' is a person who cheats. His name carried the meaning of deception. Jacob was a very possessive and a greedy man which made him ignorant of others. He succeeded in extracting his brother's birthright and even tricked his father to bless him and ran away to his uncle, Laban. There, he his match since the uncle was known as the master of trickery. He worked diligently under Laban's deception and endured 20 years of training. His endurance and patience was commendable. For that reason, he receives great blessings of wealth from God in the end.

While visiting his son Joseph who had become the prime minister of Egypt, he confessed in front of Pharaoh in Egypt and said, 'my years of sojourning are 130 years; and I have led a tough life.' He was the man who tricked not only his brother but also his father and ran away after stealing his uncle's seal. When he came to Egypt, he was in a despicable state because he had lost everything from the severe famine. If his youngest son Joseph had not invited him and his other brothers to Egypt, they would have all starved to death. To make things worse, his only daughter Dinah was raped by Shechem, a chief of the Hivites, in between. Now, this was a man who tried to 'hold on' to everything he possessed and lived a harsh life. He was literally a pauper in the end. Realizing that "I am nothing," Jacob finally knelt down in Beersheba in front of an altar he had built and asked God, "Is it alright for me to leave the promised land to go to Egypt? This shows us that Jacob completely surrendered to God by laying down all his greed and ambition. Even a scheming rogue like Jacob has his place in establishing God's will, and can be changed in the end by an encounter with the divine God. The process of God's 'training' is shown to us through the lives of the ancestors of faith.

Joseph

The four generations of the patriarchs who dominated were Abraham, Isaac, Jacob and Joseph. But Joseph's name is not mentioned when referring to the God of Abraham, Isaac and Jacob and the reason is that God's promise was directly given only to those three people. Joseph was the 11th son of Jacob and played the supporting role in fulfilling the promise of God.

People Who Filled Up the Gap Between Promise and Reality By Faith

The promise that God gave to Abraham, Isaac and Jacob was great but there is a significant difference between God's promise and reality itself. "All these died in faith, without receiving the promises" (Hebrews 11:13) They died in faith without seeing their promises being fulfilled. Abraham was told to leave his home town to the land where God will show him. There was no mention about 'settling down at a certain place.' Departing to an unknown place was an act of faith and actually, he went around in circles because God had not specifically indicated where he should go. When his wife died he did not have any land for his wife's burial site. Even though reality was different, Abraham believed in God's promise. "Faith is the assurance of things hoped for, the conviction of things not seen." (Hebrews 11:1) The fulfillment of God's promise of giving the land from Hazor to the Euphrates to Abraham was accomplished during the King Solomon's period.

The patriarchs 'filled up' the gap between the promise and reality by faith and overcame the boundaries of time. "By faith he lived as an alien in the land of promise." (Hebrews 11:9) They lived as foreigners in their own promised land until God really gave it to them. Rather than dwelling at one place, they traveled here and there and finally settled in Hebron. "For he was looking for the city which has foundations, whose architect and builder is God." (Hebrews 11:10) They visualized the city but did not build it on their own. Instead, they welcomed it from a distance until God was ready to build it. This city was fulfilled 1,000 years later by David-the city of Zion.

Jesus spoke to Apostle John, "Because you have kept the word of My perseverance, I also will keep you from the hour of testing, that hour which is about to come upon the whole world, to test those who dwell upon the earth." (Revelation 3:10) "He who overcomes, I will make him a pillar in the temple of My God, and he will not go out from it anymore; and I will write upon him the name of My God, and the name of the city of My God, the new Jerusalem, which comes down out of heaven from My God, and My new name." (Revelation 3:12) It is God's promise that a 'new' Jerusalem will be given to those who keep the Word of God to the very end.

We must understand that the idea of God's special selection of individuals carries with it two subsidiary features: promise and responsibility. The Lord God's special favor was to be shown not only to Abraham and his family but to all people through him. However, God's promises to Abraham were not just for the selfish enjoyment of a chosen few. Those promises were to be used with responsibility so that others might share in the benefits. Right at the heart of God's choice of Israel, it is made clear that God has a missionary purpose. Holding on to the promise that was to be fulfilled in 1000 years or 500 years later and accepting it in your heart is what is called 'faith' in the Bible.

ISAAC'S OBEDIENCE, JACOB'S REPENTANCE, JOSEPH'S BLESSING

Genesis 22-50

Isaac plays a role of a stepping stone in delivering the blessings of Abraham to Jacob. Jacob pays his dues as his life turns turbulent in exchange for his greed in receiving the blessing of a firstborn. But it was through his son, Joseph who delivered the nation that he ultimately became the blessing in becoming the ancestor of faith.

Isaac, a Stepping Stone

Isaac showed complete obedience. There was no resistance or whatsoever at his father's request in fulfilling God's will. What a remarkable obedience! As a result, he received a great blessing.

Realizing that Abraham was about to offer his son as a burnt offering, God interfered and provided him a goat instead. At this point, God reconfirms His promise with Abraham after witnessing his faith of action and blesses him that a nation will be raised through his descendants and become the source of blessings of all nations. "By Myself I have sworn, declares the Lord, because you have done this thing, and have not withheld your son, your only son, indeed I will greatly bless you, and I will greatly multiply your seed as the stars of the heavens, and as the sand which is on the seashore; and your seed shall possess the gate of their enemies. 'And in your seed all the nations of the earth shall be blessed, because you have obeyed My voice.'" (Genesis 22:16-18)

Isaac settled in Gerar and as a farmer he had to dig a lot of wells. In those days, water was precious so digging wells was significantly important. There was a famine in the land and he decided to go down to Egypt but God appeared to him and reassured the same covenant that was given to Abraham. The primary role of Isaac was a stepping stone to pass on Abraham's promise to the next generation Jacob.

Jacob, a Cheater_Genesis 25-50

Why was Jacob Born as a Second Child?

The book of Genesis is a lengthy one containing 50 chapters but from chapter 25 to the end, it covers the life of Jacob. It is because Jacob eventually becomes Israel. The latter part .of the story of Joseph is primarily to complete the story of Jacob. Therefore, Joseph is merely a supporting character in the entire picture.

Among the characters in the Bible, Jacob represents as a man with strong self-reliant personality astute and always concerned with advancing his position. God said to Rebecca that in "Two nations are in your womb."(Genesis 25:23) which, in fact, became true.

As the second of a pair of twins, he evidently struggled much during the pregnancy, since he emerged from the womb with a firm hold on the heel of his first-born brother Esau. Even before birth, he cheated so he earned the name 'Jacob' which means deception. When one grabs the ankle of an opponent in wrestling in the Middle East, it is regarded as a penalty because you fall when someone grabs your ankle no matter how strong you may be.

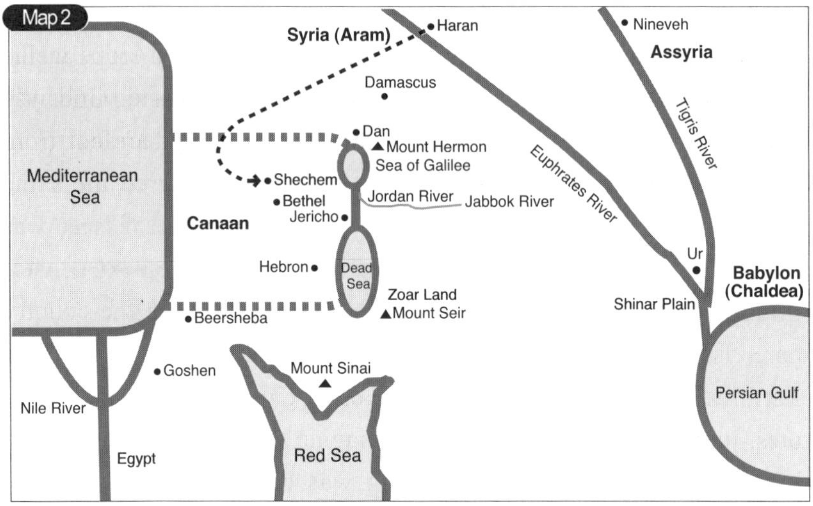

Period of the Patriarchs-Jacob Bethel is the place where Jacob dreamt the ladder of the angels; the River Jabbok is where Jacob encountered a wresting bout with an angel. Shechem is the place where the rape incident of Dinah took place. The Bible indicates as if one was going 'upwards' from Bethel to Shechem but geographically it is downwards. The reason is because Bethel is a highland.

Honoring his name, Jacob appeared from the start as a typical con-man and was determined to do anything in order to achieve his desires. Jacob succeeded in extracting his brother's birthright from the hungry and exhausted Esau who surrendered his birthright in exchange for a bowl of food. He was a master at trickery. It was a custom for the Hebrews that the first-born receive double amount of inheritance. Jacob succeeded not only at snatching away his brother's blessing but also tricked his father Isaac for his blessing.

The content of father Isaac's blessing was about prosperity and the right in receiving brotherly service. (Genesis 27:27-29) The purpose of God is at work with, not just through the extraordinary faithfulness of Abraham, but through the devious areas of self-interest and personal ambition of Jacob. The blessing is Jacob's, as God always intended but at a heavy price.

Knowing his brother Esau was ready to kill him, his shrewd mother claimed that he should marry a Hebrew sent him off to her brother in Haran. So Jacob runs away from Abraham's homeland (Hebron) to Paddan-Aram at night.

God of Bethel_Genesis 28

As darkness falls in the land of Bethel, in a moment of unutterable loneliness and fatigue, Jacob took one of the stones, put it under his head as his pillow and fell asleep out of exhaustion. He had a dream of a ladder set on the earth and its top reaching to heaven with angels going up and down. God was standing above it and said, "I am the Lord, the God of your father Abraham and the God of Isaac" (Genesis 28:13) and repeated the promise made to Abraham and Isaac.

Imagine now, Jacob was in the midst of running away from his brother, afraid that he would be killed. As a comparison, God used indirect form of speech to Abraham: 'I will bless those who bless you, and the one who curses you I will curse' whereas God gave a personal guarantee of promise to Jacob: "I am with you, and will keep you wherever you go, and will bring you back to this land; for I will not leave you until I have done what I have promised you." (Genesis 28:15)

Scarcely daring to believe, he wakes up and says, "'Surely the Lord is in this place, and I did not know it.' And he was afraid and said, 'How awesome is this place! This is none other than the house of God.'" (Genesis 28:16-17) And named the place 'Bethel,' ('Beth' means place and 'El' is God) claiming that 'this is the house of God and the gate of heaven.' He also responds with a promise of his own by saying 'if God will be with me and keep me on this journey that I take, and give me food to eat and garments to wear, and I return to my father's house in safety, then the Lord will be my God. This stone, which I have set up as a pillar, will be God's house, and of all that You give me I will surely give a tenth to You' and poured oil on its top.

The oil that he poured was olive oil. It was precious at the time since it was used in multiple ways, a key element in making food and also used for lighting (torch light) at night. Even now in Israel, there are people who live only on olive oil. It was also utilized as 'money' in those days. (One could exchange anything with olive oil.)

Pouring oil over the stone was a tremendous act of faith. He had no idea how long his journey was going to be and yet, he gave up the 'precious' oil for God. He was able to do it with God's grace and his faith in God's promise.

For the first time in his life, Jacob met God directly but his request was conditional and he promised that he would serve God as long as food and clothing were provided during his journey. Despite his deceptive actions of stealing the blessings of prosperity and service from his brother Esau, it was God's plan to utilize the blessings to raise His world by switching it to Abraham's promise.

Uncle Laban, an Incredible Boss_Genesis 29-31

Jacob left Bethel with a happy heart being assured that God was going to take care of him all the way and headed towards Paddan-Aram.

He meets a woman of his dream, Rachel, near a well in the outskirt of Haran. He is mesmerized by her beauty and is led to her father,

Knowledge Search 9

How does the Jewish Religion Interpret Jacob's Ladder?

Jacob dreamed angels of God going up and down on the ladder and received a new name, 'Israel.' Jacob's ladder is extremely important in the Jewish religion. It is what they focus only in the gospel. If you were to go on a pilgrimage trip to the Holy Land in Israel, there are monuments of a ladder in the cities and parks wherever you go. The rabbis interpreted the Jacob's ladder as the 'gate of heaven' and taught that without God's Law, one cannot receive salvation nor go to heaven. They believed it firmly until

Jesus came. And for this reason, they had conflicts with Jesus.

Such teachings of the rabbis were so strong that even the 12 apostles also thought that the Israelites had to be circumcised since there would be no salvation without Israel. For this reason, Apostle Paul wrote the book of Galatians upon his return his 1st missionary trip. He writes that salvation is not through the Law but by faith in believing in Jesus Christ.

Do you remember the scene where Philip, one of the disciples of Jesus, brings Nathanael to Jesus? (John 1:47-51) While he was approaching, Jesus spoke of the man, "Here is a true Israelite, in whom there is nothing false." In contrast, Nathanael was startled and asked, "How do you know me?" Jesus replied, "Even before Philip brought you to me I saw you underneath the fig tree." At the time, Nathanael was going through some conflicts in his mind because he had been taught from young that the only way to go to heaven was through Jacob's ladder and now this man was saying that 'He is the way, the truth and life and that no one can go to God's Kingdom without going through him.' But at the persistence of his friend, Philip, that Jesus was the Messiah, he followed him and witnessed what was being taught. Jesus already knew the heart of Nathanael and said that He had seen him underneath the fig tree. Upon hearing this, Nathanael declared and confessed his faith by saying, 'Rabbi! You are the Son of God; You are the King of Israel.' He was able to confess in this manner because the prophecy throughout the Old Testament was about the coming Messiah to be the King of Israel. Upon hearing this Jesus said to Nathanael, 'You believe as I told you I saw you under the fig tree. You shall see greater things than that. It is not through Jacob's ladder but through Me that will lead you to His world since I am the way, the truth and life.'

Laban. Laban was the brother of his mother Rebecca who had tearfully blessed him when he left Haran. Upon seeing his own sister's son who was all grown up, Laban was overwhelmed and held Jacob in his arm and wept. But how long do you think this feeling would last? Unfortunately, human beings cannot help but hurting one another. Probably the uncle treated him warmly for about a month but as time went by, the hospitality started to wear off and situation started to shift drastically.

"Hey you! Do you expect to bum around and live for free? You better work."

"Yes, uncle. I will."

Jacob goes into contract with his uncle Laban. Actually, this contract was quite a challenge. Even more dramatic than the old movie called, "The Gunfight at the OK Coral." Why? We know that Jacob was a con-man but he had finally met his match. His uncle Laban was reputed to be a master of trickery in the Middle East at the time. This situation tells us that if you trick someone, God provides someone more skillful. Jacob spent 20 years working under his deceiving uncle.

The condition of the first 7 year contract was that upon completion, Rachel, the woman who captured his heart, would become his wife. He worked diligently longing for Rachel to become his wife (Genesis 29:20) and finally the day had arrived for his wedding night. The sly father-in-law substitutes his oldest daughter Leah to Jacob's tent instead of Rachel. This was truly an unforgivable act of deceit! Besides, just imagine how Jacob must have felt the frustration and anger. He broke down in agony not realizing that it was God's providence in showing him that whatever you do returns back in the same manner. He should also have reflected how his brother Esau must have felt when he tricked him.

This was God's way of training him and in fact, it was only the beginning. Jacob was a character who was obsessed in clinging on to his own ways but God was always ahead of him to challenge him throughout his life.

The next day, Jacob protested against his uncle in disbelief.

"How can you do this to me?"

His uncle's reply, however, was non-apologetic and instead explained, "It is our custom here that the younger sister cannot get married first when the eldest sister is unmarried."

Jacob was left speechless. By right, he should have been informed earlier but then again-this is the method a con man uses. Another 7-year contract was made for the sake of Rachel. He had no other choice but to follow Laban's way which meant that he obeyed his 'boss' completely. This was all possible because of his love for Rachel.

In total, Jacob endured working for 14 years for his crooked uncle but they were not wasted. He grows in substance, knowledge and his success in shepherding ensures that he is now someone to be reckoned with. Out of greed, Laban starts to exploit Jacob but in the end, he gets tricked by his nephew in a big way. The lesson here is that one gets tricked by his own method. After extending another 7year term, Laban realizes that it was too long a wait so he marries off Rachel to Jacob. It was God's providence that two sisters end up as wives of Jacob even though it was through the trickery of his uncle. But this was in accordance to fulfill God's promise to Abraham to give descendants as much as the stars of heaven and sands of the seashore.

Through Jacob, 12 sons were born to him with the compelling competition between two women. The constant discord between his two wives and his own favoritism towards Rachel, however, sow the seeds of a family feud. By God's work of opening and closing of the wombs, these two women gave birth to the 12 tribes of Israel.

Since his uncle constantly broke the promises and exploited his labor without paying him, Jacob left very uneasy as his family grew bigger. After 14 years, Jacob said to his uncle, "My family is growing and I also need possessions for my household. You have not kept your promises so far and it's about the time that you give some wealth to me now."

The uncle had not much to say at that point and 14 years later, a new 6-year contract was made strictly for the sake of wealth. God's blessing was in this contract, and appeared concretely in a dream. "Let me pass through your entire flock today, removing from there every speckled and spotted sheep, and every black one among the lambs, and the spotted and speckled among the goats; and such shall be my wages." (Genesis 30:32) This is what we call the formula of 'inheritance' today. The methods of inheritance have developed remarkably in today's world, but 3000 years ago, there was none. Realistically, what would be the percentage of having striped or spotted flocks? Probably one or two at most out of 1,000.

At Jacob's proposal, the uncle must have thought "Gee... all along I thought he was smart but I suppose he's not. There's more to gain than lose." So Laban agrees. God's blessing to Jacob was by revealing the formula of inheritance to him. Jacob was tending the flocks near the Euphrates River and he thought animals' seeing the rods during gestation would affect the unborn lambs. In fact, he owed his flocks to the overruling God and to the practice of selective breeding which was revealed in the dream. The deal was that the final count of the spotted and speckled flocks would be Jacob's. So Jacob came up with a special specimen: taking fresh rods of poplar, almond and plane trees and peeled white stripes in them, exposing the white part which was in the rods and set them in the gutters, in the watering troughs where the flocks came to drink. The flocks mated by the rods brought forth striped, speckled, and spotted animals. God knew that Jacob did not have a chance to win over his uncle and gave blessings to Jacob because he had endured his circumstances for 14 years. The channel of God's blessings of prosperity is opened when we serve and humbly obey our superiors - like Jacob. In order to receive God's blessing of prosperity, we must serve and humbly obey our superiors just like Jacob had done. God blesses us when the spirit of Satan of ‘self’ dies.

Six years have passed by and ultimately, Jacob has kept the stronger flock to himself while giving the feebler ones to Laban and becomes exceedingly prosperous. Then Jacob heard the words of Laban’s sons saying, “Jacob has taken away all that was our father’s and has made himself wealthy; and look, there’s nothing out there in the field except striped, speckled and spotted flocks. Jacob also started to notice the change in Laban’s attitude. Jacob could have rightfully stood in front of his uncle claiming that a contract was a contract, and therefore, he had done nothing wrong. Then again, however, since he has been cheated by Laban over the years, he decides to leave secretly for Canaan with his two wives, servants and large flocks including camels and donkeys.

A ‘teraphim’ is a household idol in the Middle Eastern countries. It is like a ‘seal’ representing a symbolic ownership of possession of wealth in a modern sense. After learning that her father had wrongfully tricked Jacob, Rachel steals the ‘teraphim’ from her father before fleeing. Laban pursues after Jacob and finally catches up with him. His first words to Jacob were, “Why did you flee secretly with my daughters and grandsons without saying a proper farewell?” Jacob replied, “Uncle, think about how you have not kept your promises for the last 20 years. If I had told you that I was going to leave you wouldn’t have approved of it, so that’s why I left secretly.” “That’s fine but where’s my teraphim? Give it back to me.” Jacob did not know that Rachel had stolen it. In the meantime, Laban was searching like a madman but Rachel had put it in the camel’s saddle and sat on it. She excused herself to her father by saying that she was having her menstruation and was unable to come down. He left without finding it.

God of Peniel_Genesis 32-33

Jacob certainly had a turbulent life. After accumulating great wealth and returning homeward bound, he is again confronted with the most critical junction of his life. The meeting between the two brothers is inevitable. He recalls the revenge of his brother Esau 20 years ago which meant that he could easily lose everything including safety of his family overnight not to mention his own life. To protect himself among others, he sends off messengers to find out whether his brother had forgiven him or not. The news that Esau is coming at speed with 400 men strikes terror into Jacob. It was a matter of life or death situation.

Out of fear, Jacob finally recalls God of Bethel and prays and confesses his fear and asks for help. "O God of my father Abraham and God of my father Isaac, O Lord, who didst say to me, 'Return to your country and to your relatives, and I will prosper you,' I am unworthy of all the lovingkindness and of all the faithfulness which Thou hast-shown to Thy servant; for with my staff only I crossed this Jordan, and now I have become two companies. 'Deliver me, I pray, from the hand of my brother, from the hand of Esau; for I fear him, lest he come and attack me, the mothers with the children.'" (Genesis 32:9-11)

After praying to God, reiterating Abraham's promise, Jacob was doubtful of God's answer. This happens frequently to us also. When we pray, we gets doubtful sometimes. There was an incident in a village long time ago where church members prayed for a drinking place (bar) to be struck down by lightning. Then sure enough, a lightning struck down and burnt the place into ashes. The owner who was an unbeliever found out about the prayers of the church members and sued them. The response from the church members was "I cannot imagine such a thing would really happen." Just like them, Jacob had no faith.

Jacob comes up with a plan. He divided the people and flocks and herds into two groups thinking if one group gets attacked at least the other group would escape. "If Esau comes to the one company and attacks it, then the company which is left will escape." (Genesis 32:8) He divided the children among Leah, Rachel and maidservants putting 4 sons from the two maidservants in the front; and placing the 7 sons and one daughter from Leah and Rachel in the rear. After ensuring all his possessions were safely across the river, he remained on the other side.

He was alone and sleepless in a place near the Jabbok River when a man wrestled with him until daybreak. (Genesis 32:24) At the time, a wrestler in the Middle East was normally a thief. Rather than sticking a knife to a person and demanding possessions, it was common to confiscate by wrestling and having them surrender their possessions.

What state was Jacob in? It was life or death for him. Jacob's lifetime struggle against God culminates in this strange wrestling bout. He is neither the first nor the last. In some crisis, he is the first one to pick a fight with God, then at last, he holds on to God with new faith. This nightlong struggle marks the turning point for Jacob. At first, he demands not the man's name as we might expect but his blessing before he let the wrestler go, realizing he was the God's servant. But when the stranger has given the blessing, Jacob limps as he walks up from the water into the rising sunshine. The encounter has wounded him and he is frail, as we have never seen him before. At the same time, he is greater than he was before, for now he has a new name, Israel, because he has 'struggled with God and with men' and prevailed. For once, Jacob is awed, "I have seen God face to face and have survived." The name Israel is actually two Hebrew words combined - 'Isra' means 'to fight' and 'El' means 'God' and by putting them together, it means the 'one who prevailed by struggling with God.' What does the 'one who prevails by struggling with God' mean? It is just like a loving father saying to his child, "You have won over me." It was God's promise that Jacob was His child. Then Jacob calls the place 'Peniel' after struggling with God. 'Peniel' means that one has not died even after seeing God.

The encounter with Esau goes well since he too has prospered. Jacob said to his brother, "I see your face as one sees the face of God."(Genesis 33:10) After meeting God, the long 20 years of broken relationship with his brother Esau ended with an emotional reconciliation.

The Shechem Incident_Genesis 34

The two brothers who embraced, though from out of respect rather than from affection, eventually departed to different ways. Contrary to his promise that he would build an altar in Bethel upon his safe return to his homeland, instead Jacob arrives in the city of Shechem. He purchases a plot of land to pitch his tent and settles there. (Genesis 33:19) He had completely forgotten about God of Bethel since once again devious areas of self interest and personal ambition have taken over now as his wealth has increased.

Then again, another threatening event was waiting for him so that he would call upon God - the rape incident in Shechem. The son of Hamor, Shechem (one of the Canaan tribes) falls in love with Dinah, the only daughter of Jacob and rapes her. Brothers of Dinah were filled with grief and anger when they heard the news. They had no interest in what Shechem had to say.

"Even though I have raped her, I really love her so please give me your permission to marry her. Then I will give up my god and serve your God instead."

Ultimately, Simeon and Levi (Jacob's 2nd and 3rd son) deceives Shechem.

"If you really want to marry our sister and serve our God then you must carry out circumcision."

Obviously, this was a scheme for revenge. While all the males in town were lying in bed to recover from circumcision, Simeon and Levi attacked the unsuspicious town in revenge, killing every male including Hamor and Shechem. Seizing flocks, herds and everything else that belonged to the city; looting all their wealth, women, children and even all who were in the houses. The terrible vengeance exacted by Dinah's brothers for the insult to their sister shows the need for the law to limit revenge.

Upon hearing this horrible news, Jacob was greatly disappointed and scolded his sons that their behavior was wrong, resulting the bloodshed of revenge. "You have brought trouble on me, by making me odious among the inhabitants of the land, among the Canaanites and the Perizzitesand my men being few in number, they will gather together against me and attack me" (Genesis 34:30) His sons' reply was, "We had no choice. It's our one and only sister and we can't let her be treated like a prostitute." At that point, Jacob feared that without God's interception, there was no way for them to survive this ordeal.

God said to Jacob, "Arise, go up to Bethel, and live there; and make an altar there to God, who appeared to you when you fled from your brother Esau." (Genesis 35:1) Geographically, if you were to look at a map, Bethel is downward from Shechem but in the Bible it says to 'go up' because of its high altitude (plateau).

Threader: Jerusalem is the same way. From any region, it is said that one would 'go up' to Jerusalem. Not only was it an important place but also the fact that Jerusalem/Bethel was a plateau.

Jacob moves to Bethel, the place of his original, long-neglected dream. "Let us arise and go up to Bethel; and I will make an altar there to God, who answered me in the day of my distress, and has been with me wherever I have gone." (Note Genesis 35:3) There, his status as patriarch is completed with a further appearance by God. The promises to Abraham and Isaac are now firmly established on him. Jacob tells his household to get rid of foreign gods and jewels and purify themselves. And they buried everything beneath the oak tree near Shechem. Then Jacob finally kneels down to God and confesses, "I now realize that whatever I had and owned was all worthless."

Jacob's 12 Sons; Birth of the 12 Tribes of Israel

After experiencing God's grace, Jacob builds an altar in Bethel and returns to Hebron. On the way, his wife Rachel dies while giving birth to his 12th son, the most beloved one, Benjamin, in Jerusalem.

Upon his arrival in Hebron, Esau voluntarily leaves home to Mt.

Knowledge Search 10

The 12 Sons of Jacob are not the 12 Tribes of Israel

It is true that the 12 sons of Jacob were the foundations of the 12 tribes of Israel but not all of them became the 12 tribes. This is evidenced in Jacob's prayer of blessing in Genesis 49.

Simeon and Levi were cursed because of drawing their swords in the massacre of Shechem. Though Simeon inherits land, in a matter of time, the Philistines take it over. On the other hand, the Levi's is stripped entirely from inheriting any land and instead, were made as the nation's priests. Therefore, the Levi's are omitted from the tribes and even though they appear from time to time they are referred to as the Levites rather the tribes of Levis. (Strictly speaking, they are not tribes.)

Joseph also does not have a tribe. Joseph was to receive Jacob's firstborn blessing but instead his two sons, Ephraim and Manasseh received it. In a sense, we can conclude that Joseph had actually received his double inheritance (blessing of the firstborn) through his sons. Ephraim and Manasseh replace Levi and Joseph and complete the formation of the 12 tribes of Israel. Focusing on the 12 tribes marks the beginning of God's work of salvation - making Israel a God worshipping community.

Zale where he used to go hunting. This mountain appeared like red clay as was Esau's bodily hair. His nickname carried the meaning of 'reddish' and there he became the ancestor of Edom.

The story of Joseph unfolds from hereon, making it appear as if the story of Jacob ends when it is not.

Joseph Who Fulfills God's Dream

The story of Joseph begins from Genesis chapter 37 but we must understand it as an extension of a story developed so far. Joseph portrays a supporting role in the entire picture.

The Bible mentions God as the 'God of Abraham, Isaac and Jacob.' This testifies that the blessing, salvation and love of God surpass time and continue on to the generations coming afterwards-meaning that God's love is not toward one particular individual but to the generations. God is 'our' God.

The reason why Joseph's name is not mentioned when referring to 'God of Abraham, Isaac and Jacob' is because God did not give the covenant of Abraham to Joseph. That is why we refer Joseph as a supporting character. Joseph's role was to make sure God's promise was fulfilled successfully and he played a significant part as a supporting character to accomplish a bigger scale of God's plan.

There's no lack of recognition of Joseph's role because many biblical scholars praise him for living the 'life of Jesus in the Old Testament period.' From the beginning to the end, Joseph's life journey was filled with sufferings. In the midst of hardships, he focused on and trusted in the Lord, overcoming all obstacles and ultimately, received God's blessing as a result.

Joseph's adolescent period was not an easy one. He was favored by his father and when he was given a multi-colored tunic by the father, his brothers became jealous and were full of hatred. As a result, he was treated like an outcast from his own brothers who referred him as a 'dreamer boy.'

In one of his dreams, he dreamt that the sun and the moon and eleven stars were bowing down to him (Genesis 37:9) and quite naturally, his brothers were more furious than ever because they knew that the eleven stars were referring to them. Even his own father scolded Joseph because the sun and the moon meant the parents.

Originally, the brothers wanted to kill Joseph but changed their mind and sold Joseph off to caravan merchants heading towards Egypt. Joseph spends his youth in misery, as a slave to Potiphar, the captain of Pharaoh's bodyguards. While Joseph was living in the household of Potiphar, his wife tried to seduce Joseph. Being young and full of energy, Joseph refused the temptation of lust by the name of Jehovah. The people of Israel believed in the name of God Jehovah only. Actually, Joseph could have led a comfortable life if he were to accept the temptation from Potiphar's wife but he refused to do so because he did not want to smear the precious name of God.

Threader: Another person who experienced victory by regarding God's name as precious is David. The young David volunteered to fight against a Philistine champion, Goliath and King Saul responded in awe, 'How could you fight when you are still a very young kid?' Then David confesses his faith, 'I am a shepherd and was tending my father's sheep when a lion came and took a lamb from the flock. I went out after him and attacked the lion and rescued the lamb from his mouth. Then he rose up against me but I seized him by his beard and struck him and killed him. I trust that my God will deliver me!' Surely, the people of faith are such as this entrusting God's name as Most High resulting in a power to them.

Joseph ends up in a prison cell after Potiphar's wife accuses him falsely. There, he interprets a dream for the Pharaoh's wine steward (butler in a modern sense) and the king's baker. As the interpretation of the baker's dream was realized, the baker died within three days whereas the cupbearer, to whom Joseph said, 'You will be released and be restored to your duty once again. Please keep me in mind and get me out of here' was reappointed to his position. Joseph was 28 at the time and, unfortunately, the wine steward completely forgot about him once he was released.

Two years later, the wine steward remembers Joseph when Pharaoh was frustrated for not having anyone to interpret his dream. Joseph not only proves that he is able to explain God's message, but also comes up with a clear cut plan of action. He interprets that there will be seven years of abundance in the land of Egypt and after that, seven years of severe famine would come. Pharaoh appoints Joseph as a governor of entire Egypt. We must understand here that Joseph did not become such a high official of Egypt just because he interpreted dreams well but rather because his faith in God empowered him to overcome the seven years of famine.

According to the law of Egypt at the time, a person had to be at an age of 30 at least in order to become a ruler. What this means is that it was God's plan that the wine steward's memory was deliberately forgotten about Joseph for it was not yet his time. Even if Joseph had been released from prison earlier, he could not have been made a ruler. At the age of 30, he was released from prison.

Finally, Joseph, as a governor meets his family. Now the famine was spread over in Egypt as predicted and the people from everywhere came to Egypt to buy grain from Joseph. Joseph's brothers were among them for famine was also in Canaan. The scene of Joseph's generous forgiveness of his brothers' wrong doing to him shows a real understanding of the way how God controls human's destiny: "God sent me before you to preserve for you a remnant in the earth, and to keep you alive by a great deliverance. Now, therefore, it was not you who sent me here, but God!" (Genesis 45:7-8) Joseph is clearly a man of deep feeling, moved by tears of sorrow and joy-he forgives his brothers and then hugs Benjamin.

Families of Jacob Moves to Egypt_Genesis 46-47

As the story of Joseph ends Jacob comes into the scene. At the invitation of Joseph, Jacob's household set out for Egypt. As Jacob sets out for Egypt he builds an altar in Beersheba and worships God. God had finally changed Jacob into a 'new' person from 130 years of self-absorbed, greedy and deceitful man.

This was the very first time he built an altar voluntarily and knelt down to worship God. In the past, he gave sacrifices to God out of desperation. For the first time for no other reason he knelt down to God and asked, "God, is it alright for me to leave this land?" His grandfather, Abraham had almost lost his wife when he left the promised land for Egypt; his father, Isaac was stopped when he set out for Egypt because of famine; and now it was his turn.

He receives God's reassuring promise that He will accompany them and bring them back as a nation. "Do not be afraid to go down to Egypt for I will be with you." (Note: Genesis 46:1-4)

Along with his 70 members of his family, Jacob leaves for Egypt. By the time Jacob left for Egypt, he was very confident in spite of his overall poor appearance. He even took his hand and put on the king Pharaoh's head, blessing him. The only person who could actually put a hand on a person's head at the time was either a king or the high priest. Then this old man dared to bless the king, so Pharaoh asked, "How old are you?" (Note Genesis 47:8)

Jacob responded, "I have lived 130 years and led a tough life. The turbulent years have made me look like a pauper but I carry God as a treasure within me so that is why I can bless you." This is a true confession of faith. "It may not be gold or silver but with what I have I give to you" (Acts 3:6) was what he was saying. As Christians, we must realize that even though the exterior of us may be bleak a precious treasure is within us. Eventually, the descendents of Jacob serve foreign gods for 400 years in Egypt and expanded their population as much as the stars of heaven and sands of the sea shore-reaching to almost 2 million, forming a great nation. God had brought in Jacob's family into Egypt to raise His nation.

Why was the Book of Genesis Written?

In order to help our religious life, it is extremely important to understand the book of Genesis. Among the Five Books (Genesis, Exodus, Leviticus, Number, Deuteronomy), the book of Exodus is the most significant and important one for the Hebrews (Jews). They have witnessed God's remarkable work of salvation through Exodus; the Ten Commandments in Mt. Sinai; the Tabernacle and the way Israelites were guided through the pillars of cloud and fire. The book of Exodus is emphasized to Jews because of all the amazing events that were happened to them are recorded in this book. As for Christians, however, the book of Genesis is extremely important since the beginning of all creation is explained in this book. (See Day 7)

Why do you think the book of Genesis was written? The Israelites who left Egypt and lived in the wilderness reflected back and had questions: "Why did we spend 400 years in Egypt and why did we leave? Why did we end up as slaves for 400 years in a foreign country, Israel?" Moses explains all their questions. While explaining the reason for their slavery, he couldn't leave out Joseph's story, who became the governor and by mentioning Joseph he couldn't help but tell Jacob's story, his 12 sons; and then while explaining about God's covenant, he couldn't help but tell them about the God of Abraham, Isaac and Jacob; and while explaining about Abraham's calling, the incident of Tower of Babel had to be mentioned. While doing so the background of God's creation had to be explained-therefore, the book of Genesis inevitably became a must.

Correction of Consciousness

Being in flesh, we easily get upset when we find ourselves taken advantage of. Not only that, there are occasions where hostility arises when a person doesn't agree with one another even at church premises. The grace you received during worship service is all wiped out when you come face-to-face with the person whom you've had conflicts with. That is our true nature.

Jesus said "Love your enemies, and pray for those who persecute you." (Matthew 5:44) How can you pray for someone who persecutes you? Consider it lucky if you did not curse with your mouth.

God is just and does not distinguish the good and evil but shines the light equally to both. God is totally different from us. God is fair and just.

When you hate a person you may think that it is 'you' who hate. But spiritually, it is the opposite. In fact, it is your spirit that is affected and bounded by the other person's spirit. This is the 'hell' that you are experiencing.

For instance, we go to a doctor when we get sick; we eat when we're hungry but the food we eat is through the labor of farmers. In this manner, God's spiritual blessings come through the Word of God and are delivered to us through the preacher. So, basically, all blessings come through people. In this sense, if you happen to dislike a person, it means that you're actually blocking the path of blessings that is coming to you.

That is why Apostle Paul emphasized on love and not to hate anyone. "If we say that we have fellowship with Him and yet walk in the darkness, we lie and do not practice the truth." (1 John 1:6) "The one who says he is in the light and yet hates his brother is in the darkness until now." (1 John 2:9) Hatred in the heart is the same as lying to God according to these two verses.

The Bible tells us that there is fear in darkness and punishment in fear. In other words, without realizing it, darkness takes over our heart once hatred fills inside. There is nothing but love to cast away fear. "There is no fear in love; but perfect love casts out fear, because fear involves punishment, and the one who fears is not perfected in love." (1 John 4:18)

How can we fix the feeling of hatred? Some may say, "is it really necessary to fix the feeling of hatred?" and I believe the important explanation is this. Do you think that all the accumulated anger in our conscious will be erased the minute you die as you go to heaven? Unfortunately, that is not the case. The minute we die, the accumulated consciousness during our life span comes along with us.

Jesus said, "I am the way, and the truth, and the life." (John 14:6) What this means is that we will never experience 'paradise' if Jesus does not come into our heart to change our consciousness. Without Jesus, anger in our hearts will never disappear. Without Jesus, we cannot go to His kingdom.

Jesus tells us "To be alert and pray at all times." (Luke 21:36) Apostle Paul's confession must be taken into consideration very sensitively. "I find then the principle that evil is present in me, the one who wishes to do good" (Romans 7:21) After that confession, he concludes by saying, 'Only in Jesus Christ will I overcome' which means that because of these two existing laws, it makes him to realize his sin. Therefore, for non-believers, there exists only one law which is the law of flesh, whereas for Christians, there are two laws which trigger us in guidance to life from death. We are able to repent through the light of Jesus. Through prayers the darkness of death is shifted to life and our consciousness gets corrected when we act according to the Word.

Knowledge and memorization of the Word of God is not enough. We must first correct our awareness and through this, our actions must be changed correspondingly. We cannot call ourselves

Christians when there is no change of action in our lifestyles. We admit that it is tough to live according to God's standard. But when we put our efforts in it, the Holy Spirit helps us become more aware of our actions and gradually changes our consciousness. It is extremely difficult but we must rely on the Holy Spirit on a daily basis and confess our sins. Through repentance, our life will be led to obedience and when this is performed, God will then transform us. Please remember this fact that without this practice in our lives, we cannot enter into God's Kingdom. I urge you to break away from the misconception that the heaven's gate will be opened with a big 'bang' just because you believe in Jesus.

Even the ancestors of faith lived as they pleased in following their flesh and 'self' serving ways until God interfered into their lives. But after meeting God and receiving His promise of fulfilling His world through their descendants, they also went through the process of correcting their consciousness through the Word of God (the law of the Holy Spirit). They surrendered their 'self.' Just as Joseph had forgiven his brothers who had sold him off to Egypt, God's Kingdom can only be fulfilled when one overcomes the world.

. . .

But Peter said, "I do not possess silver and gold, but what I do have I give to you: In the name of Jesus Christ the Nazarene - walk!" And seizing him by the right hand, he raised him up; and immediately his feet and his ankles were strengthened. With a leap he stood upright and began to walk; and he entered the temple with them, walking and leaping and praising God. And all the people saw him walking and praising God; and they were taking note of him as being the one who used to sit at the Beautiful Gate of the temple to beg alms, and they were filled with wonder and amazement at what had happened to him.

Acts 3:6-10

LEAVING BEHIND THE MEAT CARRIAGE OF EGYPT

Exodus 1-18

We are now in the book of Exodus but the important thing is that there is more to it - "Exodus and the Period of the Wilderness." At Joseph's invitation, Jacob and his 70-family members arrived in Egypt. Let us find out how the people of Israel became slaves in Egypt and why exodus had to happen. The story begins 430 years later after Jacob and his extended family members experience prosperity in the land of Goshen. which is the beginning of the Exodus.

How did the People of Israel End up as Slaves?

Searching the Historical Record of Joseph

When Joseph was a governor of Egypt, Jacob and his household of 70 members left Hebron and settled in Goshen. Being the family members of the governor, they were treated well. Joseph had them in charge of Pharaoh's livestock so life was good for them.

Ironically, Egyptian history does not mention Joseph or the exodus. For that reason, liberal religious scholars claim that Joseph was a beautified story that was made up.

The Egyptians were known for being very proud of themselves among the ancient nations so it was natural for them to record in detail only successful conquers or battles rather than negative events. They deliberately omitted periods of defeat. It has been evidenced that the period from 16th through to 14th century B.C.

approximately 150 years of history of Egypt is missing. The historians researched and found that this gap was the period of defeat by the tribes of Hyksos, the Central Asian tribes living near Afghanistan. They were the first to make chariots and the one Pharaoh used to ride in was made by them. The history of Egypt getting conquered by the Hyksos who used the chariots was not recorded for the reasons stated above.

The Hyksos are from the tribes of Shem. Among Noah's three sons, Shem, Ham and Japheth, Egypt was the tribes of Ham's second son, Mizraim. The Egyptians had dark skin since they were the descendants of Ham. In the land of Africa, the Hyksos, a tribe of Shem from Central Asia attacked and conquered Egypt and took over the pharaoh's place. The Hyksos broke the power of the pharaoh and the Upper and Lower kingdoms were once again united. The nation was at the peak of its military power, ruled by a new dynasty of Hyksos. It was during this period that Joseph was sold off as a slave. We can assume that he was assigned as governor over Egypt possibly because of his Shem heritage.

It is evident in many ways that when Joseph was the governor, the tribe of Hyksos ruled over Egypt. After seven years of prosperity and during the seven years of famine, the people of Egypt bought food from Joseph. Ordinarily, money would be used in exchange for food but the latter part of Genesis indicates that Joseph accepted the land for food. Why would he do that if the land belonged to Pharaoh in the first place? This may be explained by the fact that the rest of Egypt was not yet conquered by the Hyksos even though they had taken over the central government.

The Reason for Downfall of Their Identity

Why was their privileged status stripped away and suddenly they became slaves under the new pharaoh? The Bible explains the situation as “After Joseph’s death, a new king arose over Egypt, who did not know Joseph.” (Exodus 1:8) It was out of the question that a king would not have known Joseph because he was the governor ruling over Egypt. Things have been changed in Egypt.

This 'new king (Pharaoh)' meant that the original owner of Egypt, the tribes of Ham had chased off the tribes of Hyksos. After recovering the position of kingship, the Egyptians discovered the Hebrews (the descendants of Joseph) were completely a 'foreign' (Gentile) tribe.

The population of the Hebrews had drastically increased. When they first arrived in Egypt, they were 70 in number and by the time of exodus, grown men were 600,000 and together with women and children, they added up to approximately 2 million people. The scholars had calculated that in order for the number to increase from 70 to 2 million, approximately 12 children had to be born to each family without any death for 400 years. We get a glimpse of how rapidly the Hebrew people grew in numbers. The existence of such a large alien group in his borderlands for some time made Pharaoh uneasy. He ordered the midwives to kill the infants born to the Hebrew women but their response was "The Hebrew women are so strong that even before we arrive the babies are born." Not only were the women fertile, they were also physically strong. God's promise to Abraham, Isaac and Jacob was fulfilled during their 400 years of slavery by giving them descendants as many as the stars of heaven and the sands of the sea shore.

These people proved to be disciplined, smart and hard working. The Egyptians felt threatened and decided to overturn their status to the slaves. This sudden change results the people of Israel to call out to God. Why? Primarily because of their sufferings. The life of slavery became progressively hard. Pharaoh felt more threatened as time went by and hard labor was among unbearable sufferings inflicted upon them. It even came to a point that they were forced to make bricks to build a new city without giving them proper supplies.

Finding ourselves shifted to a totally different position is our reality as well. Not too long ago, Korea experienced the IMF crisis and many wealthy people were confronted with bankruptcies losing their homes, jobs, reputation and whatever security they had. But we must know one thing, not to get discouraged when our life takes a sudden change. We must realize that a sudden change of environment holds a message that we must call upon God. If the people of Israel were led only to a comfortable life, then exodus would not have occurred. Who needs God when things go well? Farming was flourishing due to the abundance of water from the Nile River and worshipping the 10 different idols at the time in Egypt would have made them live comfortably without feeling any needs for God. There was no reason for them to leave Egypt.

When unexpected suffering or change of event occurs in our lives, we must be thankful knowing that there is God's providence awaiting us. Apostle Paul said, "Be thankful at all times." (1 Thessalonians 5:18) No matter what happens we must be thankful because God's salvation awaits us. Otherwise without sufferings, it would be impossible to exodus from darkness, suffering, sins and the power of death. Therefore, we must remember that God provides unexpected downfall of our status, illness or other methods in our lives to change us.

Moses, the Leader of the Exodus

The cries of the people of Israel reached God. He remembered the promise made to Abraham, Isaac and Jacob. The Israelites were the chosen people. Why? Because God called their forefather Abraham from Ur of the Chaldeans and gave His promise to raise a nation who would worship Him and spread His blessings to other countries of the world. God remembered the promise that was made 430 years ago with Abraham and heard the cries of His people. The time had come to end their slavery and He exiled His people to the land of Canaan.

Before calling out the people of Israel from Egypt, God raised a leader. It was Moses who was raised as a son of the princess of

Pharaoh for 40 years in the palace. We have heard frequently of the story of Moses. How infant Moses was discovered in a watertight basket by the princess who was bathing in the Nile River and raised him like a prince in the royal household. Due to his quick minded sister, his biological mother became the nanny and he was raised under his own mother's supervision.

There was nothing lacking in Moses' life. Then one day, Moses was 40 when he tried to strike his first blow of freedom, which ended in disaster. He saw an Egyptian beating a Hebrew and struck down the Egyptian and was accused as a murderer. He ran away to the wilderness of Midian. From a prince who spent 40 years in the palace, now he leads a life in the wilderness for 40 years. The Bible records that rather than enjoying his life as a prince, he enjoyed the life in the wilderness more with his fellow people sharing sufferings together. (Hebrews 11:24-26)

Threader: This is the same as our Lord, the only begotten Son of God who left His throne to come to earth to save us. A comparison of Moses and Jesus can be found in the Vatican museum in Rome today.

Moses threw his identify as the royal prince and fled to the wilderness where God raised him as the leader of the people of Israel who spent 40 years with them in the wilderness. But before that, he had already spent 40 years in Midian.

Mt. Sinai is a long stretched mountain. The southern part of the Sinai peninsula is called the Mt. Horeb where God meets Moses with an astounding commission: to be His messenger to Pharaoh and lead His people to freedom. No one knew more about the mountains than Moses which rendered him an ideal person to lead the Israelites. At the calling of God, Moses raises one objection after another and each is countered by God. Upon the claim that he was not up to the job and that he was no speaker, God appointed his brother, Aaron, as his spokesperson. This was the first system of a 'spokesman' in mankind history. God then gave Moses a staff. This was to demonstrate God's power with which to convince people that he really has met with

God. This was the kind of magic the people were familiar with-the kind that went with the religion of Egypt. The staff became a serpent when he threw it. His hand became leprous like snow and when he put his hand into his bosom and took it out, his hand was restored again. God raised Moses as the leader and from this point on, he was about to carry the cross of redemption.

There is one and only purpose for the exodus to take place: It was to keep the promise given to Abraham, Isaac and Jacob and it was also time to raise God's Kingdom in the land. The sins of the Amorites were now intolerable and it was time for judgment against them through the people of Israel.

The Meaning of the Ten Plagues

In order to take the Israelites out from Egypt, God sends Moses to Pharaoh and begins a series of judgments which will teach Pharaoh and his people who the Lord is and show them the extent of God's power over all creation. God actually hardens the heart of Pharaoh. But the last plague, the killing of all the firstborns including the one of Pharaoh's finally makes him kneel down and surrender to God. At that point, he even allows the people of Israel to leave Egypt with treasures of gold.

Why didn't God strike the last plague (killing of the firstborn) as first? It is because each object of the 10 plagues symbolizes Egyptian idols. Striking Egypt with all these plagues, God was challenging the saturated idolatries in Egypt.

Threader: In Genesis 12, Abraham was called in the area of Tower of Babel where God destroyed the tower, divided the language and scattered the people. God is in control and His goodness and justice are awesome-and the gods of Egypt are powerless to reverse God's judgments. The magicians may counterfeit but they cannot countermand. Through the 10 plagues, God was demonstrating His absolute control. He distinguished between His people and the Egyptians showing that He was the living true God and Redeemer.

The 1st Plague: Turning the Waters of the Nile into Blood

The Nile River was referred to as the spirit of 'Hophi' which sounds similar to the word 'hope' but it means the spirit of prosperity. The Nile River was the heart of the nation's economy and worship. Its life and blood so it was natural for them to idolize this river as their god. How do you think the Egyptians would have felt when the river which was their source of farming turned into blood? It is said they had worshipped and made offerings in front of the Osiris,their god of the Nile so God showed them that in front of God-the god of the Nile was nothing.

The 2nd Plague: Frogs

The people believed the frogs as a god ("Heket") known as the spirit of birth. It symbolized 'fertility' as well since the pot belly of a frog in Egypt at the time had a lot of eggs in it. Relating to the fertility , the Egyptians worshipped the frogs as a crop producing spirit and by striking the Egypt with the plague of frogs, it brought disgust instead of fruitfulness and was found everywhere throughout the entire land-crawling over their beds and other living places in every household.

My career as an ambassador took me to various countries and certainly not all of them were well developed countries. I recall my days in Africa. At the time I thought people in Africa would be walking around half naked with a tree leaf around their private areas just like Tarzan. But to my surprise upon my arrival, men wore neck ties and women were wearing make-ups and well dressed. Even though their life was less fortunate compared to the Western countries, living in Africa was the same as any other place. The only thing different was that there were lizards in the house. Their bodies were unusually large. They had creepy reddish bumps in them and whenever they were spotted in the room, my wife and children almost always yelled out a scream in terror.

Probably the Egyptians might have felt the same way. Imagine frogs crawling over your face and body while you are sleeping. Leaping over vour dining table and found everywhere. The Egyptians had worshipped frogs as god but do you think they regarded them as god at that point? God showed them that frogs are not to be worshipped as god.

The 3rd Plague: Gnats

The Egyptians idolized golden calves and regarded gnats (Seth)that were living on it to be holy as well. These gnats were all over the Egyptian's entire bodies, making them unbearable.

The 4th Plague: Flies

It is quite unimaginable to think that people served flies as god(Khepra) but they did in the old days in Egypt. Why do you think flies were regarded as spirit? One may find swarm of flies in foul smelling areas and hear the humming sound from them. The ancient people thought the sound that came from the swarm of flies gave a certain sense of mystical effect and assume that it had more power than the invisible God. By sending a swarm of flies, God declared the message once again that this was something not worth idolizing.

Threader: Apparently, the people idolized the swarm of flies even up to the days of Jesus. If you read the New Testament, after Jesus healed the demon-possessed man who was blind and mute, the people gathered around said, "But when the Pharisees heard it, they said, 'This man casts out demons only by Beelzebul the ruler of the demons.'" (Matthew 12:24) The 'Beelzebul' they're referring to is the spirit of the flies. There are many stories relating to worshipping the 'flies' in the Old Testament. (2 Kings 1:2-3)

The 5th Plague: Contagious Disease

This disease was contagious and it struck all the livestock, especially the young calves. God showed Egyptians that the calves they worshipped are not god. The Hindus worship cows and so even today, every car stops when a cow passes by.

Threader: God had directly shown them that calves are not God to be idolized but 400 years of idolatry that settled as a ritual among people did not get easily wiped out. We know this because while Moses fasted for 40 days in Mt. Sinai to receive the Ten Commandments from God, the people who were waiting for him, building a golden calf in the end since there was no live one around. All the while God had shown them that idols are all useless but people continued to make calves their idol again.

What this tells us is that even though we believe in Jesus, it takes us a long time to kick our old habits. We must understand that the habit of sinning within us takes a long time (the process of becoming sanctified) to be corrected.

The 6th Plague: Boils

The boils were eruptive typhus (rashes) that broke out on humans and animals. The 6th plague was a skin infection of boil breaking out with sores and uncontrollable itchiness that would make one crazy. But in those days, the Philistines idolized the boils quite seriously even though it is hard to believe for us now.

Threader: In the book of 1 Samuel, the weak motives of Eli the prophet brings total disaster to the people of Israel resulting in seizure of their Ark by the Philistines. At that time, God's power breaks out from the temple to fall upon the people in(Philistines as) an outbreak of plague (bubonic plague, carried by the rat-flea) and moving the Ark simply spreads the disease. Eventually the Philistines have had enough and realize that God of Israel is responsible for the disasters and return the Ark along with the gold trophy of the boils inside of it. This shows us the level of faith the people had towards this idolatry in those days.

The 7th Plague: Hail and Thunderstorms

The hail and thunderstorms ruin the flax and barley crops in the fields and all their efforts of labor have gone to waste. God was teaching them that whatever efforts they put in, things are not from their efforts alone but from God.

The 8th Plague: Locusts

The wind blows and gust of locusts appear stripping the country bare. This reminds me of a movie scene in Pearl Buck's 'The Good Earth' where locusts rampage the fields of crops in a matter of minutes, turning it into total bareness. Imagine the fear the people must have felt when literally everything was being stripped away by armies of locusts. God was washing out the minds of self-reliance and mentalities of humanism.

Threader: Various names of locust which is the symbol of judgment appear in the prophecy book of Joel.

The 9th Plague: Darkness

The Egyptians idolized the sun as their god (Ra). The religion of the sun also existed in many other countries but Egypt worshipped it above all that the country was recognized as the country of "the Sun and Cobra." It rarely rains in Egypt and even if it does it is like a tropical rain that showers momentarily. All year long the sizzling sun covers the land and this is what they worshipped. You may have seen a picture of a Pyramid and fertility Sphinx with a glaring sun above it-giving you an idea of the hot climate in Egypt.

One can imagine how the Egyptians worshipped the sun by looking at the pyramid. If you look closely at a pyramid, a small hole is designed on the tip so that through the ray of the light from the penetrated sunlight the actual place of the king's mummy is revealed. This was discovered in the early 70's by Swedish scientists when they had to move the pyramid for the construction project of the Aswan Dam. Apparently computerized technology was utilized in calculating the move but still an angle of 1 centimeter was off when they completed it. This proves how advanced the knowledge of geometry and physics was at that time. In any event, God blotted out the sun by covering it with thick darkness teaching them who the real God is.

The 10th Plague: Death to the Firstborn

Now the preliminaries are over and God's warning is about to be finalized. This was an important god that the Egyptians worshipped, even more so than the sun, the Pharaoh. For that reason, God dealt with death to the firstborn sons of Egypt including Pharaoh's own son who was to succeed the throne. The Egyptians were all devastated, including especially Pharaoh. Finally, Pharaoh surrendered but now was too anxious to see the people of Israel go out of Egypt.

This is a day to remember down through the ages; a new feast is instituted and a new religious year begun-the Passover which literally means 'pass over.' A great cry was heard when the death of angel came across Egypt but the angel passed over the houses with the blood on lintel and two doorposts. Of all the Jewish festivals, Passover is the most important one.

Lessons Learned from the 10 Plagues

The important thing to focus is that God sent these 10 plagues to the Egyptians and spared the people of Israel. As Israel's freedom has been purchased by the death of the firstborn of Egypt, two lessons were learned from the plagues.

First lesson: The people of Israel were the chosen nation by God.

Second lesson: A fearful warning was also shown to them that wraths will come if they disobey God.

Threader: How were the people of Israel and the Egyptians distinguished? What does the salvation obtained by smearing the lamb's blood on the doorpost symbolize? It represents the cross of Jesus. We must also realize that our salvation is achieved through the blood of Christ on the cross. It is necessary to reflect the grace of God once again. "You are a chosen race, a royal priesthood, a holy nation, a people for God's own possession, that you may proclaim the excellencies of Him who has called you out of darkness into His marvelous light." (1 Peter 2:9)

In other words, the event of exodus is referred as the salvation of God's justification. It was the grace of God that led the people of Israel to freedom after hearing their outcries of oppressed sufferings under Pharaoh's power. It is God who saves us from Egypt. It is God who delivers us from darkness and death into light.

But it does not stop there. In order to go into the promised land, one must go through the journey in wilderness. It is a journey where there is no water, food, or clothing. Nothing that one can achieve by effort but survival by only worshipping God who provides manna and water. Through this process, people are trained to become humble and sanctified. The book of Exodus reveals this process of transformation through the lives of the people of Israel.

The Path of Exodus

Guided to Mt. Sinai_Exodus 13

God did not direct them to the promised land right away but instead led them to the west of the Sinai peninsula. The way to Mt. Sinai was the road of sufferings. One of the primary reasons of God leading the Israelites to Mt. Sinai was to give them the Word (Law) and to train them for one year according to God's plan so that they may worship only Him as a community. The other reason was that they were not ready to encounter the Philistine army and would have easily returned to Egypt out of fear. (Exodus 13:17)

But the most important reason was to fulfill God's promise with Abraham. In the beginning, God spoke the words of life and now God speaks the words for living. Sending His people into Canaan for the sake of just conquering the land apart from God's promise with

Abraham, Isaac and Jacob was meaningless. Therefore, in order to fulfill God's promise, His people had to become a nation which worships God first. The Israelites were guided towards Mt. Sinai to be trained--the process of becoming sanctified.

This applies to us as well. By faith we have been given salvation by believing in Jesus who brought us out of darkness. But we must realize that this is merely the beginning. From this point on, we must go through the process of becoming like Jesus, the process of sanctification.

Crossing the Red Sea_Exodus 13-14

The first thing that the Israelites experienced during exodus was the division of the Red Sea. Hemmed in between sea and mountains, with waves of the Red Sea before them and Pharaoh's forces at their backs, the Israelites meet their first big test of faith. They panicked, cried out to God and accused Moses for betraying them. They were terrified of drowning since they regarded the bottom of the sea as 'hell.'

"Why did you bring us out here to drown us? We would have been better off if we remained in the land and die there!" In the midst of chaos, Moses as a man of God began an intercessory prayer. This was possible because he had met God and experienced the Holy Spirit.

An intercessory prayer makes God work. Don't be fooled that "God will take care of everything." God works only when we surrender our will and call out to Him. It is because God is love. God provides when we continuously respond and give praise to Him. This is the eternal formula of love in our relationships with God. It is because the joy of love is generated when the relationship is two-way, not one-sided.

God who never sleeps nor tires hears Moses' prayer and divides the waters of the sea by sending the winds from the east so that they can cross the sea safely and then breaking the wall of water rushing down upon Pharaoh's forces. Through this, Israel learns the truth of Moses' words. What does 'dividing the Red Sea by sending the winds from the east' mean? The energy in God's word as mentioned in Genesis 1 made the water evaporate. Just as in the beginning of God's creation, the water was gathered onto one side resulting the dry land to appear and the only difference from Genesis 1 and here was that it occurred by the energy of the prayer given by Moses.

Threader: The Israelites' crossing of the Red Sea signifies a spiritual meaning of passage (salvation) from hell towards light. This act symbolizes the baptism of the water in the New Testament. People receive baptisms as a sign that they believe in Jesus and the ritual symbolizes the deliverance from the darkness of hell.

Bitter Waters of Marah_Exodus 15

Through the crossing of the Red Sea, the people of Israel has gained great confidence in Moses leadership. "When Israel saw the great power which the Lord had used against the Egyptians, the people feared the Lord, and they believed in the Lord and in His servant Moses." (Exodus 14:31) There is an anointment of the Holy Spirit to those who believe in Jesus and do God's work. It is God who anoints us, seals and gives the Spirit in our hearts as a pledge. "Now He who establishes us with you in Christ and anointed us is God." (2 Corinthians 1:21)

God guides the Israelites down the west of the Sinai peninsula in the desert for three days without water nor finding any source of it. People are soon thirsty and hungry and mutinous. They finally arrived at Marah but the water was bitter to drink. It was not long before the complaints and grumblings against Moses started. He didn't react to their complaints. Instead, he was indifferent of the situation and cried out to God on behalf of the people and guided intercessory prayer. If you think about it, Moses could have easily complained in such a situation as well. "God! What are you doing? You're making it tough for me to lead this people." But Moses knew

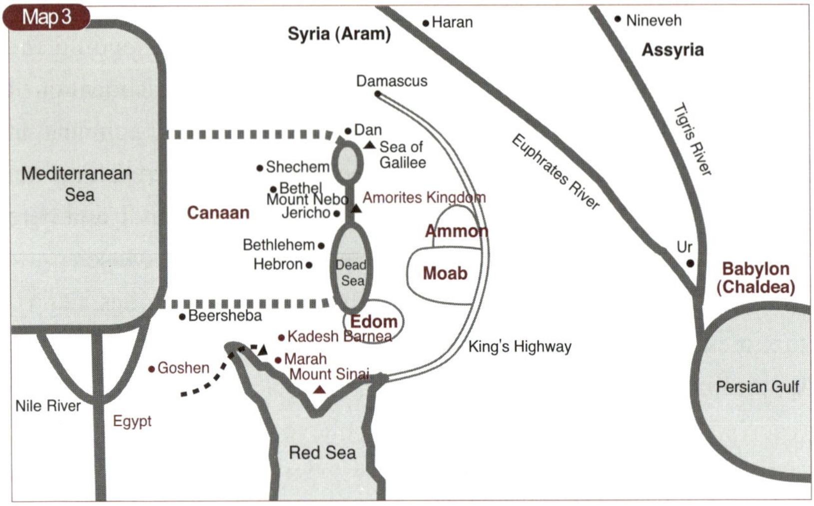

Exodus and the Period of the Wilderness: The base of Philistines is today's Gaza Strip. The Philistine is a city nation consisted of five cities.

better. He trusted that God would not let His people down.

God instructed Moses to throw the tree branch into the water which changed its bitterness into sweetness. The Israelites regained their strength after drinking the sweet water. The salvation was given to 2 million people because of one man, Moses. Such as this, one person is very important. The world can be saved through one person's faith. We must be touched by this fact and be thankful to God. The wilderness may appear bare but it is also a place where tree branches (the cross) that turn bitter waters into sweet ones are hidden.

From Marah to Elim_Exodus 15

After passing through Marah, the Israelites were led to a beautiful oasis of Elim where there were 12 springs and 70 different palm trees.

The thing to be thankful for was that not only are there deserts in the wilderness but oasis as well. What happens to ordinary people when they are confronted with 'bitter' waters, such as bankruptcy, broken relationships, accumulated debts, etc. in their lives? Self pity creeps in and you cry your lungs out behind closed doors. Thoughts of self-pity compound your heart driving you to think that you're the most miserable person in the entire world. But this is the voice of Satan.

Before confronted with hardships, it was Satan who boasts you to think that you're the best of the best in the whole world. But then suddenly one day, the wicked spirit whispers and breaks you apart by making you feel that you're at the bottom of a pit. The sky rocketing praises reaching to the level of heaven and then abruptly falling down to hell is the works of Satan. (Isaiah 14:12-15)

Once we start to feel sorry for ourselves when things get tough triggered by Satan, we tend to blame God. This is what happened to the Israelites. Continuous grumblings were heard. Making comparisons with their lives as slaves in Egypt claiming that at least they had plenty of food and water back then.

We must be sensitive in what God is trying to tell us through various kinds of tests and trials. Instead of complaining, we must pray even more at the time of hardship because after all, it is God who provides alternate situations. This is the promise of the Bible that after bitter waters, oasis follows because only then will we be able to give thanks to God. We must believe that blessings come after sufferings.

Failing to trust in God's promise is disbelief and because of it, you feel victimized and have thoughts like "What is happening to me! After all, I believe in Jesus and devoted myself in church choir and other church activities." There is a reason why God let us go through bitterness before guiding us to the oasis. In order to feel joy, there must be sorrow as well just like one needs to experience bitterness to appreciate sweetness. When unexpected turn of events occur in our lives, we must believe that God is preparing us to give something more valuable so we need to come before God, confessing our faith and praying. Then God will have mercy and will lead us to Elim. Not only is this a promise of blessing that follows after suffering but also a promise of eternal kingdom.

God is in His Kingdom of heaven where it is full of joy, peace and happiness. Just as God promised Abraham a nation and the land, He promised us His kingdom. We must have faith that behind bitter waters are blessings and that His kingdom awaits us. It is not up to us but up to God how and when He guides us to Elim. Apostle Paul confessed that he was led to Elim by becoming a captive of Jesus. With the same concept, we must also be captivated by God. It is not up to our efforts but through the work of the Holy Spirit. "Not that I have already obtained it, or have already become perfect, but I press on in order that I may lay hold of that for which also I was laid hold of by Christ Jesus." (Philippians 3:12)

Moses went through the same hardship as the Israelites and yet he was able to pray because he met God. He met God in the burning bush in Mt. Horeb. A person who meets God believes in His promise. Under no circumstances and no matter how others complained and grumbled, Moses believed in God's promise and led the people of Israel in the wilderness.

The Manna_Exodus 16

The exodus of the Israelites exhibits a similar portrayal of our nation during the Korean War. "They set out from Elim, and all the congregation of the sons of Israel came to the wilderness of Sin, which is between Elim and Sinai, on the fifteenth day of the second month after their departure from the land of Egypt." (Exodus 16:1) The Israelites escaped Egypt with food, clothing, and blankets all bundled together but food supply was emptied after 45 days of exodus.

In a way, the food had lasted for quite some time but the Israelites had no idea where they were heading except the fact that they had escaped from slavery. Once again, now that the food supply was consumed, they started to complain against Moses and God again. "Why did you bring us out here for us to die in hunger?" By right, it was probably a natural reaction that anyone would show under such a harsh condition.

God provided 'manna'(daily bread) by sending them from heaven and used it as a way to teach His people about obedience and daily dependence on Him. Manna was provided just enough to fill them for one day. Just an adequate amount for one day and it was given in the early dawn. They were allowed to collect double amount on the day before the 7th day (Sabbath) of each week but if they collected more than a day's worth out of greed, they found that it was rotten and wasted.

Let us think for a moment of the Lord's Prayer that Jesus taught us. We should seek for the 'daily bread' for today not for multiple days. Many times we complain to God that one year's worth of food or even 10 year's worth of food is not given to us and we find ourselves worrying over it. There would be no reason for us to worry if we were to think only of the daily food. God leads our life, giving us daily bread and filling it appropriately at His own time. Believe in God's word that it will be done.

Water from the Rock_Exodus 17

The Israelites journeyed by stages in the wilderness and they camped at Rephidim at one point. Again, there was no water for the people to drink. The same cycle of grumbling against Moses and testing God started once again. Then being a man of prayer, Moses called out to God and received an answer to strike the rock with his staff. Water flew out from the rock quenching the thirst of the Israelites. (Exodus 17:6)

Threader: Jesus is our solid rock and promises us that "Whoever drinks of the water that I shall give him shall never thirst; but the water that I shall give him shall become in him a well of water springing up to eternal life." (John 4:14) Furthermore,Paul testifies "The Israelites drank the same spiritual drink ; for they drank from the spiritual rock that accompanied them, and that rock was Christ."(1 Corinthians 10:4)

Attack of Amalek_Exodus 17

The people of Israel had barely reached Mt. Sinai when the Amelekites attacked them.

A similar incident such as the attack of the Amelekites occurs in our lives also when we have the passion to hear the word of God. We hesitate to leave home and go to church when it starts to rain. Do not forget that for those who pray can easily overcome and come forward to God in all circumstances.

Joshua (the man who will be Moses' successor) leads a picked force against the Amalekites. He had never fought before but through Moses' prayer with his hands lifted, God showed that it is Him who gives victory. The power of 'intercessory prayer' by Moses, Aaron and Hur took place on the top of the hill with their hands raised. If Moses lowered his hands, the Amalekites became winning in the battle so when Moses' hand grew tired, both Aaron and Hur held his hands up to make it steady until the battle was won. God promised His presence in prayers conducted by more than two people and the remarkable power of intercessory prayer was revealed through this incident.

We can never win a spiritual battle without prayers. This method also applies to our life as well, raising our hands brings victory but lowering it brings defeat.

As God promised, Moses brought God's people to Mt. Sinai, the training ground. Those who have experienced military service might relate to this more realistically because before arriving at the camp, the travel on the train is not bad. On the train, the trainers leave you alone even if you make a lot of noise while drinking beer. The Israelites were in the same boat. On their way to the campground, they complained and grumbled but God left them alone. It was only Moses who wept in tears and prayed to God. And yet, God still listened to and acted upon Moses' prayer, satisfying the Israelites' needs each time.

Finally, the Israelites arrived in Mt. Sinai, a religious training ground. God started the training by giving them the code of the Law and through this religious training, the Israelites were becoming distinguished as a God worshipping nation, a special community and the chosen nation.

Spiritual Search 9

A Prayer that Receives Answer

Pray at Ordinary TImes

Do you pray ordinarily? Do you only pray when you're desperate? Prayers at desperate times are too late according to God. That is why we are reminded to be in Christ (Holy Spirit) and pray at all times. "Rejoice always; pray without ceasing." (1 Thessalonians 5:16-17) As a Christian, we are already saturated with hearing the word 'in Christ.' But we don't pray and yet grumble to God even at the slightest turn of events in the course of our lives. If you do not ask, you will not be given; if you do not seek, you will not find it; if you do not knock, the door will never open.

Pray daily as the Holy Spirit guides you. Prayers will be delivered to our invisible God through the spiritual angels and become activated. The Bible says that angels are the ministering spirits for us. (Hebrews 1:14) The serving angel waits in front of us when we pray. And when the spirit works and fulfills something into reality, it is what we call a 'miracle.'

Those who pray in conviction receive great power. Normally a person who works 5 times harder would only gain 5 but a believer who works for 1 will receive thousands times more through the works of the angels. We must believe that the great force of support team is behind us. Do not worry of your ability. We have God backing us up with His great power.

Praise God When Praying

"Do not worry by saying 'What will we eat? What will we drink? What will we wear for clothing?'" (Matthew 6:31) "But seek first His kingdom and His righteousness; and all these things shall be added to you." (Matthew 6:33)

When we pray we must first seek His presence and His kingdom. We must worship God and praise His name to the highest. We must confess "God! Thank you. Lord! We praise you. We trust in you." Only then will we be able to experience His presence.

Diplomats spend their years living in different countries so naturally their interest lies on which country they will be dispatched next. I have also urges to pray like "please send me to such and such country" time to time. But instead, I pray, "Wherever you send me Lord, I will carry out the works of the salt so that I may change the place where I will stay. Permit me to go to a place where I may be able to do so. Even though it may be a place that I do not fancy but with your guidance I will rejoice you wherever you send me." The reason why I am able to seek God's will is that I have already experienced God's overflowing grace when I did seek His will in the past.

Holding post as the U. S. diplomatic affairs was known to be the fast track for success so it was natural for me to look forward to a higher position afterwards. But due to the shift in the personnel dept. in the new government, I was notified to return to Korea without any assigned position. It was a big blow. But still I thanked God and praised Him as I returned. The hymn song that I favored at the time was, "I Can Hear My Savior Calling ... Where He leads me I will follow" (Hymn #360) (better to have the Hymn title than Hymn number). As I praised God, little did I know that He had plans for me. I received an unexpected request from the Duranno Publishing House to write a book on an early morning prayer. The book entitled "Early Bird Christian" was published in 2004. With this publication, regardless of denominations, I had suddenly become a well known lay believer 'leader.' Numerous requests for assembly meetings throughout the entire country started to pour in. For 6 months, until I was appointed as the New York Consul General, I visited 200 churches and assembled congregations, testified about 'To Awake the Dawn' throughout the region and had the privilege and glory to testify God.

Be Thankful Unconditionally When Confronted with Crisis

Ordinarily, people complain and say "Why have you made me this way?" when they confront a crisis. However, be aware that you will be separated from God once you complain and Satan takes over.

When there is a crisis, we must be thankful regardless of our situation. "Be thankful at all times." (1 Thessalonians 5:18) We must confess to God, "Whatever You do, You are complete."

A popular evangelist king Deacon Ki-Dong Kim when he was bankrupted he prayed, "Lord! Thank you. If I had not been bankrupted, my life would have been very stressful. My body could not have sustained the fatigue that I had accumulated over time. And probably my liver would have deteriorated and I might have died of liver cancer. God, I thank you for stopping all this." Faced with really, everyone started to worry. Survival for their future, children's education and so forth. But the family did not starve nor their children affected. God had led them through. God uses His own method of recovery.

I urge you never to complain even though nothing changes in reality after praying diligently. It is God's plan to lead you to the righteous path so instead be patient and be thankful. You will meet God as He works in the midst of darkness and emptiness. I challenge my readers that you will be able to pray like this when you are confronted with a crisis: "I know that I deserve worse but since you know that I have prayed diligently. I thank you for stopping it here."

"Be anxious for nothing, but in everything by prayer and supplication with thanksgiving let your requests be made known to God. And the peace of God, which surpasses all comprehension, shall guard your hearts and your minds in Christ Jesus." (Philippians 4:6-7) When I was in Geneva in 1991, at a bible study group held by some couples, the leader had asked that we memorize this verse. At the time, the verse was somewhat displeasing to me so I was reluctant to memorize. Why wasn't it written as "With thanksgiving, let our requests be known to God then all problems will be solved" instead of 'the peace of God will guard your hearts and minds.' About 10 years later, through the prayers moved by the Holy Spirit, I awakened to the precious meaning of this verse.

Due to the result of our wrong choices (sin), God makes us go through the tunnel of darkness (suffering) for a period of time. But the important thing is that during this time of suffering, if we pray with thanksgiving without complaints or grumbling then God protects our mind and heart with His peace which is beyond our knowledge. He makes us go through the tunnel of pain safely and resolves our problems without us realizing it. Hallelujah! So when you are in crisis, just be 'thankful' and pray.

RECEIVE THE LAW AT MT. SINAI

Exodus 19-20

God gives the Law to the people of Israel upon their arrival at Mt. Sinai and begins a year long religious training. It is to make Israel a kingdom of priests and raise her as a holy nation so that she may become the source of blessing to the entire world.

GOD'S LAW, THE TEN COMMANDMENTS_Exodus 19-24

The Ten Commandments was Given along with a Calling

The first thing God did was to explain the reason for giving the Law in Mt. Sinai. "Now if you obey me fully and keep my covenant, then out of all nations you will be my treasured possession." (Exodus 19:5) The code of laws rests on the authority of God who graciously saves people and now He summons them to obey out of gratitude all for the purpose of making them a holy nation of priest. "Although the whole earth is mine, you will be a kingdom of priests and a holy nation." (Exodus 19:6)

'Kingdom of priests' means Israel is distinguished from among other nations. God is proclaiming that it was His plan to save the whole world through Israel. Then, what exactly is 'to be distinguished as kingdom of priests' mean?

First, the role of atonement for the sins of people.

They lead a consecrated and redemptive lives on behalf of the people. In other words, they must be able to carry the cross of redemption for others. This is the same streamline of message to us by Apostle Peter that "You are a chosen race, a royal priesthood, a holy nation, a people for God's own possession." (1 Peter 2:9) God's message to the Israelites was for them to carry the burden of others rather than pursuing their own interest.

Second, the role of teaching and spreading the Word of God.

Their primary work was to teach the Word of God in the temple. When God chooses people for a particular work He also equips them to do it. The definition of 'holy' means unworldly. The Gentiles are the ones who seek earthly things rather than invisible heavenly things. They pursue constant competition, self-satisfaction and greed. On the other hand, heavenly people who are a part of the holy nation share God's love with others.

It is a calling when selected as 'kingdom of priest' and 'holy nation.' God had specifically given the Israelites a calling in Mt. Sinai. Unfortunately, they failed in fulfilling their duties as a holy nation and ended up becoming the same as the Gentiles seeking physical and lustful pleasures by worshipping the Baal resulted in a disastrous benchmark in their history. Israel splits into two, the Northern and the Southern Kingdom. Due to Israelites' failure in fulfilling God's duty, Jesus Christ had to come on earth as the 'true' Israel and completed the duty of the high priest and holy nation by dying on the cross.

Threader: Jesus is the chosen tribe, a royal priest, a holy nation and whoever believes in Him are called 'saints.' He calls upon us and gives us a task with a certain role by saying, 'you are the chosen race, a royal priesthood, a holy nation, a people of God's own possession.' It is up to us to carry out the command of God to spread His Word to the ends of the earth because the entire world belongs to Him. "Go therefore and make disciples of all the nations, baptizing them in the name of the Father and the Son and the Holy Spirit."(Matthew 28:19) We must realize that the same message from God to the Israelites is given to us today.

As Christians, we have received God's command through Jesus. A person while giving a testimony said, "We need to perform our duty if we are alive; and if we die, kingdom of heaven is ours." It is so true. We must do all our best to do the work of God while we are still healthy and alive. There can be only one reason when people are healed and receive extended time to live. It is to do God's work.

The Ten Commandments is Love

God first explains the purpose of the Law and then gives the Ten Commandments. The Ten Commandments ends with 'do not's so we assume the list contains all the difficult things to keep.

In addition, we have already gotten a glimpse of God's judgment against the Israelites when they disobeyed, so quite naturally we are burdened with guilt and fear when it comes to the Ten Commandment. What happens if you make trouble while on duty in uniform after completion of a recruit training? You get into a bigger trouble (beaten up). So having all these in mind, we feel greatly burdened when we bring up the Ten Commandments. But be relaxed and assured that it is not the case.

Jesus talks about the two great commandments. A man asked Jesus, "which is the greatest commandment in the Law?" and Jesus responds by saying that there are two. "First is to love the Lord your God with all your heart, soul and mind; and second, love your neighbor as yourself." (Mark 12:30-31) In this sentence, Jesus have actually set the core teachings of the Law. In the same manner, the Ten Commandments can be divided into two parts. First four laws concern people's relationship with God and the rest six are for people's relationships with one another. As Jesus summarized it, the commandments are all about loving God and loving our neighbor. In the book of John, the two summarized commandments become condensed into one. (John 13:34-35) It is 'love.' First is God's love and then neighborly love.

This is spiritually loving God with all your heart, mind and soul which is the same as carrying the 'cross.' Just as in one of the hymn songs, 'each and every day we move towards the highest,' (Hymn #534) (change with the Hymn title) we move towards the third heaven where our Lord is through the Word. Pray everyday because this is what we must do if we love Him.

In order to achieve this, the cross that leads us to God cannot be fulfilled if we remain as we are. This cross represents self denial and it would be impossible to go in front of God without it. Simply put, selfishness (self-centered) comes from Satan. Whenever you move with this self awareness of 'me' we are automatically under the control of the five senses within us which means that we move according to our own benefit and not others. Therefore, without the cross, loving neighbors becomes almost impossible. Without the love of God one cannot expect to care for others. But then again, there are some charitable organizations emphasizing on neighborly love as if it's possible apart from God's love.

Apostle Paul states in the book of Galatians that the two great commandments of God are condensed into one. (Galatians 5:14) Anyone who reveals their love towards others is the one who successfully carried the cross by self denial and focused only in God.

The Ten Commandment for us today is a way of lifestyle and attitude: not simply a set of rules but something we must hold on to in order to become like the image of Christ. We must treat the Commandments like a mirror for reflection of our sins on a daily basis so that we may be able to repent when we sinned. The commandments also serve as our life's indicator, reminding us that even though we are weak in keeping all the Laws there is a way to recover through repentance of our sin.

1st Commandment: You shall have no other gods before Me.

'You shall have no other gods before Me.' What is this? It means to love your God with all your heart, life, will and with respect. It means to focus only on God.

A person with good faith tends to focus on one thing. On the other hand, a person with no faith tends to move around and constantly seek for something else. The need of change is evident to this type of person. They change things frequently such as cars, houses or even wives. What is the next thing they change? Church. They go to church to church, find faults and complain like "this church does not have 'love'; I didn't like the pastor's sermon. A person whose heart is focused on God is persistent in one thing to the end. The actions clearly indicate whether a person have faith or not. "Even though I believe in Jesus I also believe in Buddhism. Shouldn't one have an interest in different things as well? Besides, I find many Christians are narrow-minded and intolerant of other religions." These kinds of attitudes are shown in the people who are scatter-brained. The spirit of Satan stirs your mind to distract and self-justify.

Even among the churchgoers, there are many who are also vague in their attitudes. Majority of them have keen interest in the areas of entertainment and sports which are the two worlds apart from God. Actually they know more about the personal lives of celebrities than about God! Interests and curiosities on these two areas are continuously pumped to us through media, newspaper and people. These are caused by Satan to block us from focusing on God.

We are under the control of Satan who holds the power and authority over the world. Without overcoming this spiritual encircling net, it would be difficult for us to connect with God. Obviously Satan would do anything to stop us from going closer to God. And quite frankly, freeing ourselves from the encircling 'net' of Satan is not easy. It tries to hold us by pumping the 'self-interest' in us so that we move around like animals on earth (seeking earthly things). For instance, what would be the strategy to win when you are surrounded by the enemy in a battlefield? You must put all of your force and effort in that one key area in order to strike out of it.

We have heard of 'fasting assembly meetings' conducted by churches on special occasions. There are many reasons for fasting but what do you think the most important reason is? Some claim that since Jesus suffered on the cross, therefore, we must also suffer in some way in order to get closer to Him. This is a wrong concept. Going through physical suffering as a way to go closer to God is triggered by other (Gentile) gods. In some other cases, people say "Since Jesus fasted for 40 days I'm going to fast for 41 days. It is also absolutely a wrong idea because basically that person wants to compete with God. During the period of Elijah, the prophets of Baal and Elijah tested their gods to see who is the real one. The prophets of Baal cut themselves with swords and lances until blood gushed out since their god failed to respond. This sort of conduct was customary to the unbelievers at that time. The assumption was that they could get closer to the spiritual world by inducing physical harm since sin rooted from fleshly bodies.

Fundamentally, the reason for fasting is to focus inwardly from the scattered thoughts of the outer world. It enables you to shut off all the interests that captured your mind and instead helps you to focus on God. Once fasting begins, nothing interests you anymore and quite naturally the interest in the world start to diminish. We must focus on God.

2nd Commandment:
You shall not make for yourself an idol.

God said, "Do not make an idol or worship one." God also said even the ones, among any creature, that we consider resemble God should not be made into such a form or image.

What is idolatry? Have you seen an idol that was made small? Normally idols or statues are made big in size in order to make it appear superior and to intimate people. When the Israelites camped at Kadesh-Barnea, spies were sent ahead to Canaan and they reported back and said, "They are giants being the descendants of Anak and we are like grasshoppers compared to them." People bow down in front of the idols out of the dominating visual appearance.

God is invisible and a loving Spirit. Since we cannot see God, He does not dominate us outwardly but moves our hearts quietly. This is the difference between the worldly spirit and God. Love is invisible. True love is felt strongly within our heart and gently transforms into inner feelings. For this reason, God does not want us to be overpowered by visual things and tells us not to make an image of idols.

Countless idols have existed since old ancient times. Among all, television and internet are the worst idols of the modern day. Many people have time to watch television dramas but no time to pray or read the Bible. This is our reality of idolatry in the world we live in today.

Idols are false images. The images that travel through television are all originated from humans. Fundamentally, idols stir the craving desires and fleshly ambitions to human mankind so its influence is undeniably strong. The themes of television dramas are based on murder, adultery, immoral conducts, or violence. Primarily these themes project cravings of humans that people secretly desire for themselves, get intrigued and are excited by watching it. Through the dramas, the worldly spirits, consisting of knowledge, money, power, sex, desires, ambition, jealousy, betrayal and murder, travel through our bloodline and smear into our mind and heart. It is impossible to avoid the surroundings of the world but at least we must not get too involved in it. Obviously, there is a need to know the news of the world but we must limit ourselves not to get too absorbed by it.

The two messages are repeatedly mentioned in the Bible. "I am setting before you today a blessing and a curse." (Deuteronomy 11:26) Freewill has been given to us by God and with this freewill, God wants us to choose and decide, whether to serve God or to follow other gods. (Deuteronomy 11:27-28)

The blessing and curse was up to the Israelites depending on whether they worshipped God or followed the foreign god (Baal) that the Canaanites worshipped when they enter the land of Canaan. But then again, it was strictly up to their freewill to make decision. It was not by force but by freewill so that is why Joshua said, "My house will only worship God; and it is up to you to choose." (Joshua 24:15) He didn't say "you must believe." The failure of the Israelites throughout the Old Testament period was instead of God they chose the Baal idolatry which satisfies their fleshly desires, ultimately leading them to destruction.

Threader: What do the two paths represent in the New Testament? It is the small and narrow gates. "Enter by the narrow gate; for the gate is wide, and the way is broad that leads to destruction, and many are those who enter by it. For the gate is small, and the way is narrow that leads to life, and few are those who find it." (Matthew 7:13-14) The other conclusive messages written by Apostle Paul and others in the New Testament refer these two paths as one who follows their fleshly desires and the other who is led by the Holy Spirit. Unfortunately, majority of us still live according to our fleshly needs inspite of our belief so that is why the Bible repeatedly requests us to make the right choice.

Whether knowingly or unknowingly seeking visual things means that we are moving towards the idolatry. We will not be able to comprehend the spiritual world by chasing the worldly things. That is why we are reminded by God to be alert at all times. In order to succeed, we must awake the dawn and train to close (prayer training) our eyes. (Colossians 3:1-2) For believers of God, the minute we open our eyes we must practice to close it.

3rd Commandment: You shall not misuse the name of the Lord your God.

In other words, precious is the name of God. If we suppress our flesh and earthly desires in obedience for God's precious name, He will also regard us as precious and lift us up. Joseph and David have clearly shown the testimonial examples through their lives and actions on how they subdued themselves and honored God's name which resulted in great rewards from God. From an imprisoned slave, Joseph became the prime minister and David became an Israel's king and ultimately, the ancestor of the Messiah, Jesus Christ.

How difficult it must have been for the people of Israel to believe in the invisible God who couldn't be touched or felt at all? They believed only in God's name. The Bible introduces various names for God-Yahweh, Elohim, and Jehovah. When God gave instructions to build a tabernacle, He said "Construct a sanctuary for Me and my name that I may dwell among you." God also spoke to Solomon, "My name will be in the temple you build forever" (1 Kings 9:3).

Threader: This applies to us today. We pray to Father God and heal, cast out evil spirits in the name of Jesus.

4th Commandment: Remember the Sabbath Day by keeping it holy.

God completed the creation in 6 days and gave His blessings on the 7th day. What this means is that God blessed a specific 'time' which can be interpreted as that people who observe it are blessed.

The Israelites observed the Sabbath starting from Friday evening to Saturday evening whereas the Christians today observe it on Sunday since Jesus resurrected on that day. "Now after the Sabbath, as it began to dawn toward the first day of the week," (Matthew 28:1) It was on Sunday early morning that Jesus had risen and entered into the eternal rest. That is why we observe Sunday morning as the Lord's Day. It is important to understand and realize through Jesus' resurrection, we have been given the privilege to enter the eternal rest with Him. Surely, this is an amazing day of grace for us.

The 'eternal rest' means new heaven and earth as recorded in the book of Revelation. (Revelation 21:1) It is the Holy Spirit who transforms us into a new being, casting out the darkness into light and creating the paradise within our hearts. All these are the result of our Lord's resurrection so we must be thankful for this Sabbath and return our gratitude by giving worship.

"Blessed be the God and Father of our Lord Jesus Christ, who has blessed us with every spiritual blessing in the heavenly places in Christ." (Ephesians 1:3) This 'heavenly blessings' comes to us through the Word that comforts, heals and fill our hearts.

The reason why we observe the Lord's Day is to receive the heavenly blessings through the sermons given by pastors at church before going out into the world. We go to church to re-enforce our relationship with God and to prepare ourselves to share the love we received with others(cross of redemption). A true worship is not a service on Sunday at church but our life in the world throughout the week reflecting the loving nature of Jesus. "Present your bodies a living and holy sacrifice." (Romans 12:1)

The other misconception is about the main service on Sunday morning; however, in fact, it is a minor (elementary)service. The mixture of people gathered in one place of worship. Some are just beginners who have just started believing in Jesus; some are overwhelmed with emotional changes and some attend the service without knowing exactly why they are there in the first place-all kinds of people are gathered in one place of worship. Even though the attendees may be large in numbers, the worship service is actually a minor (elementary) one.

Realistically, we must receive the heavenly blessings on a daily basis through the Word and prayers. Why do we restrict ourselves in receiving the heavenly blessings only on Sunday? There is a huge difference between a person who receives blessings daily and someone who receives blessings once a week at the church on Sunday. People are affected differently when they receive the Word of God-some may experience comfort, healing or peace; through our spiritual recovery, we gain strength, confidence and courage in return.

Why not experience God's never failing grace and its impact that He works within you?" Gently and regularly like the late rain wetting the hard grounds? Through Him, our hardened hearts, proudness and self-centeredness get melted away and become a good soil. I urge you to experience it each and every day. I trust that my readers will be challenged and start each day at the break of dawn with prayers before going out to the world.

I urge you to believe in the works of the Almighty God. Once you believe this, you cannot help yourself but attend the 'main' service which is at dawn. Rain or snow, you will wake the dawn in His presence. A 'true' life unfolds for those who seek heavenly blessings, overcoming the visible obstacles of reality. "So let us know, let us press on to know the Lord. His going forth is as certain as the dawn; And He will come to us like the rain, Like the spring rain watering the earth." (Hosea 6:3) A true worship is at dawn. Under no circumstances, if you awake the dawn to seek Him then your tired soul will be restored and rejuvenated with the power of life.

Spirit of God

The most blessed spiritual being that a human can receive is the Spirit of God. Fundamentally, God's spirit is love (1 John 4:8). So in order to know the Spirit of God, we must first understand the principle of God's love which is as follows:

Love Requires a Partner

Love cannot be accomplished alone. There is only one God but in Him is the Trinity of God. We must understand that there was an incident before God's creation of the universe. There was Father God who gave all His love to the Son of God. That is one of the reasons why Jesus numerously confessed in various passages: "All things that are Mine are given by my Father" (John 17:10) and "The Father has given all things to the Son." (John 3:35)

Jesus was equal as the Father God but He emptied Himself to the level of a humble servant and obeyed God even up to His death. "Have this attitude in yourselves which was also in Christ Jesus, who, although He existed in the form of God, did not regard equality with God a thing to be grasped." (Philippians 2:5-6) A beautiful loving relationship between the Father God and the Son of God had taken place before creation. Father God had given everything to His Son and in return, the Son of God gave the highest glory to His Father. Jesus confessed that there was nothing He did on His own even though He was God Himself. The complete love relationship was accomplished in heaven. What state would heaven be if things were different? For instance, what if Jesus challenged His Father by saying, "Father God, let us be equal." But Son of God, Jesus, completely lowered Himself and obeyed His Father even to the degree of death.

The Spirit of God knows best the thoughts of Father. (1 Corinthians

2:11) All the works of the Father is revealed to the Son through the Holy Spirit. This is why Jesus was born through the Holy Spirit and when Jesus was baptized in the Jordan River (the 'inauguration' of the Messiah) the Holy Spirit descended as a dove upon Him. The Holy Spirit also helped Jesus win victory over the temptation of Satan in the wilderness before starting His ministry. This proves that the Son of God cannot carry out His Father's will without the help of the Holy Spirit.

The Trinity of God works independently but because of this 'complete' love among them, they are united as one. Only love is eternal; therefore, God exists eternally for He is love.

Father God said "Why are you returning all the love and glory to Me?" (See John 14:13-15) Since He loved His Son so much, He wanted His Son to experience the same joy of receiving love. Thus, the Father God made His Son create a 'love partner' which is us (believers of Jesus Christ) and gave everything under His power so that Jesus may receive the same glory and praise from His believers just as the Father had received it from His Son, Jesus. This is why we must give glory and praise to Jesus because it completes the cycle of love. The other reason why we have been created is to eternally give praise and glory to God. (Ephesians 1:6)

It is impossible for us to know, understand, touch or feel Father God without going through Jesus. That is why we are called "Christians" those who believe in Christ. Jesus said, "I am the way, and the truth, and the life; no one comes to the Father, but through Me." (John 14:6) This is the principle of the Trinity of God which has been explained already in Genesis.

We must love God with all of our heart, soul and mind and love our neighbors as ourselves. (Matthew 22:37-40) As Christians, we must be able to share with others what we have received. Our challenge is to become like Christ during our days on this earth and since this doesn't happen overnight, we are all in the process of making progress. When we 'give' to others, gratitude is exchanged and this fulfills the cycle of love. While this progress continues, God's love is being expanded and simultaneously, glory is being returned to Jesus. The essence of love is that one must have a partner to share. A solitary person experiences certain level of isolation because he / she has no one to share love.

As the Lord's Prayer that Jesus taught us says, "Thy will be done on earth as it is in heaven" (just as the completed love cycle between Father and Son in heaven before creation), we must also complete the love cycle with others on this earth.

We have been chosen by God even before the creation. (Ephesians 1:4) We humans use our logic and understanding which makes it impossible to comprehend God's existence. Just as it is up to the the potter to make whatever kind of a pot out of clay, we have no right to object to God's decision. God has chosen us and has come into our heart just like an umbilical cord attached to a mother's womb. With that concept in mind we are inside the womb of Jesus. The embryo moves because it is attached to the mother. It is not aware of its surrounding nor survives on its own. The fetus does not know the mother and have no interest on who the mother is but the mother, on the other hand, continues to caress her tummy and pour love towards the unborn baby. Surely this love is one-sided. Our existence is the same with God. Though it may appear that we live on our own but God has predestined us. God is telling us to "Abide in Me." (John 15:4) Without remaining in Christ, we can never exist on our own.

Love Satisfies the Partner

Not only do we need a partner to love but we also need to satisfy them. The world is consumed with nothing but the idea of 'give and take.' But there is one exception - only God gives constantly without requiring anything in return and fills your satisfaction to the max. The Bible mentions the word 'fullness' when referring to Jesus and God the Father.

Then what exactly does God fill you up with? With the heavenly blessings, He fills us inwardly first and then outwardly. "The fullness of Him who fills all in all." (Ephesians 1:23) Just like a parent who fills all the necessary things for a child, God fills all things for us.

It is because God knew us from the beginning even before we were born. "Before I formed you in the womb I knew you." (Jeremiah 1:5) Even before being formed in the womb of our mother, God knew what kind of a person we were going to be, how we were going to live and to what capacity we will be working; even before our birth, we have received privilege to become His children. Therefore, we are told not to worry.

A writer already knows who the main character is going to be before the script is written. Then the story starts to develop around the character. In the same sense, God already knew us so He starts to write His plans according to each individual. Hypothetically, let's say the author creates a story where a young boy from the ghetto is the main character. During the course of the story many different characters appear, some rich and powerful, but they all disappear in the end except the young boy because he is the main character. Since the story evolves around this young boy, he will be kept alive to the very end of the story. Just like the prince and the pauper-from rags to riches as the story gets deeper into the climax, the hardships are overcome by unexpected turn of events. The bottom line is that the main character will never lose its attention from the writer. Just like this, God will protect us to the end.

What is the reason for God to distinguish and raise us? It is because we are to be sanctified and become blameless in front of Him in love. Not only are there blessings but also hurt and pain in our lifetime. As the parable of the prodigal son, through suffering and hardship, we come to realize the love of the Father and it is up to our freewill that we return to God. This is the blessing that God has given us- 'the fact that He knew of us.'

Love is Met from Within

True love is felt from the heart. A husband who goes through verbal abuse or unpleasant treatments at work is able to overcome his frustrations when he thinks of his loving wife. The invisible love conquers over physical surroundings. Love is felt inwardly so that is why God, the Word came in flesh to the world to meet us. Jesus came to shed blood to save us because "Sins cannot be forgiven without the shedding of blood" (Hebrews 9:22) and the other important reason is to meet us in our heart.

The Jews or Muslims believe that God only exists in heaven (third heaven). We cannot see, nor feel or get closer to God. God became a conceptual God and that is why the people of Israel had a hard time believing in God. It was not the time yet to 'meet' God inwardly until the Son of God, the Messiah came into the world in flesh.

The invisible God, who is so great in His existence that we humans feel unapproachable, came to earth in flesh and visibly revealed Himself. The four gospels tell us about God through the life of Jesus. Jesus came into the world in flesh and felt the same hunger and pain as we did. And the ultimate love that Jesus showed us was His crucifixion. He died on the cross for us, completely giving Himself up for us. After His ascension to the throne, He now meets us through the Holy Spirit inside of our heart.

The prophecy that He would meet us in Spirit was already foretold through the prophets of the Old Testament period. "I will give you a new heart and put a new spirit within you; and I will remove the heart of stone from your flesh and give you a heart of flesh. And I will put My Spirit within you and cause you to walk in My statutes, and you will be careful to observe My ordinances." (Ezekiel 36:26-27) Both kingdoms (Northern Israel and Southern Judah) were destroyed and the Israelites were taken into the captivity in Babylon. During the exile, this word was given to prophet Ezekiel which meant that the days of worship through sacrifice were over. In other words, "I know that keeping My Word is not possible with your strength alone and after all, historically, the Israelites failed to obey Me and received judgment due to their idolatry and disobedience. Therefore, I am going to send My Spirit in your heart so that you may obey My Word." New spirit-without receiving the Holy Spirit our hardened hearts will not change.

Love is met intimately within our hearts so that is why we close our eyes when we pray. When we pray and hold on to the Word, the Holy Spirit fills our heart with His love. A person who has experienced God's love (one who has received the power from 'above') will start to 'offer' themselves for Christ. Upon seeing this, the Lord will shed His tears of joy. This is what 'meeting' Him inwardly is all about-in God's words "I am in You; and you in Me." (John 15:5)

. . .

Therefore I urge you, brethren, by the mercies of God, to present your bodies a living and holy sacrifice, acceptable to God, which is your spiritual service of worship. And do not be conformed to this world, but be transformed by the renewing of your mind, so that you may prove what the will of God is, that which is good and acceptable and perfect.

Romans 12:1-2

COVENANT CEREMONY AT MT. SINAI

Exodus 20-40

The reason why God did not lead the Israelites directly into the Promised Land but instead to Mt. Sinai was to make a covenant with them through the Word of God (the Law).

5th-10th Commandments: Love Your Neighbor

Each and every one of the 10 commandments that Moses received from God in Mt. Sinai is all precious. It gives us a clear distinction on how a believer of God must live. "God has told us to become 'salt and light' of the world so how exactly should one live?" If you are wondering about it, the answer to this question is quite simple. Think of the 10 commandments.

There are some who may say "All the commandments are 'do nots' so how is it possible to observe them all?" The reason for God to mention the 'do nots' was because it benefits us. God wants to give grace and fill our life with His love. Besides, we have been given the strength to keep it in the first place. Therefore, we must strive to observe it.

When you cannot think of a prayer topic, say your 10 commandments: "Help me from saying any false testimony against my neighbor; Help me control my temper so that I may not commit murder; Help me not to become envious of others; Help me to feel gratitude of what I have received." The primary reason for us to have these 10 commandments is for us to realize that we are sinners in front of God and for us to come forward to Him. Knowing that we are unable to keep all the commandments, God has opened the way to forgive our sins through the tabernacle.

5th Commandment: Honor your parents.

Among the closest neighbors are your parents and family members. That is why it starts off with family relationships.

Parents are called "Abu" in Hebrew and this word includes everyone above you. By 'honoring parents' in this context it means to respect not only your parents but anyone above you. We are surrounded by people 'above' us and through them, our life starts to unfold. The first is through the family by honoring parents; second is through the work places by honoring our supervisors; and third is through the church, honoring pastors/ministers. All the blessings in our life come through these three channels.

The importance of obeying and honoring our pastors are essential. Otherwise we cannot receive the heavenly spiritual blessings given by God. Let us strive to obey and respect our respective pastors.

At work, there are people who get upset with their supervisors and ignore them completely. Out of outbursts of anger, some say "I just want to beat the hell out of him!" Then, however, what would be the outcome? You will be fired, which means your financial supporting channel will be blocked. We all experience that it is not easy at times to deal with unrealistic and demanding personalities at work. But we need to understand that feelings of resentment and anger towards the colleagues or even the supervisors at work are stirred by Satan. The heavenly Father has given authority to the worldly masters according to the Bible. "Slaves, be obedient to those who are your masters according to the flesh, with fear and trembling, in the sincerity of your heart, as to Christ." (Ephesians 6:5) No matter what position or authority the person may be in, and irrespective of whether he is capable or not, let us be obedient and respectful so that God can bless us by observing His Words. There is no reason to complain to God and say “How come I don’t get a promotion even though I believe in Jesus?”

A customer is a king to a businessperson. If a store owner ill-treated a customer just because he didn’t like the person, what would happen to his business? Not only has he lost a customer but the word of mouth would spread and eventually would bring damage to his business. Even though explosive anger may appear satisfactory to you but it is actually harming you.

This applies to families as well. Most likely, when a child does not obey the parents, his/her future cannot be bright. Think about how much influence the parents have towards the children! Of course, some children will make their own decisions for their future, but for the majority of them, it is the parents who hold the handle of their children’s future. On the other hand, it is the fault of parents if they have troubled their kids. As long as the parents work things out harmoniously, the child will learn precious lessons through their parents no matter how difficult problems the family may face.

Satan’s spirit triggers us to focus on and boast ourselves. So, in order to teach us to deny ourselves, God has provided someone over us in our lives. The channel of blessings will be opened once we obey and give respect to others. “Why did you give me such a tough mother-in-law?” Would it surprise you that the tough mother-in-law is a hidden blessing for you because you are being ‘molded’ inwardly through that particular person? If you do not have anyone that bothers you then you will never be able to ‘deny’ yourself. Therefore, when you are challenged through someone, be thankful to God instead for giving you such a person. The more we learn about God’s way, the more we realize that denying ourselves for the sake of others is actually winning over the spirit of Satan.

Honoring and respecting others who are above us must not be

taken casually. Being obedient towards parents and elders are not a matter of duty but a channel of blessings from God. If you don't respect those above you, your blessings will disappear. The spirit of Satan travels back and forth into our hearts like a crying lion making us to focus on 'me.' It is why it is not easy to respect the person 'above' me. We must win over Satan by giving honor and respect to those above us through the Word of God. God wants us to keep the three channels of blessings to win over Satan and gives us 'honor/respect those above you' as the first commandment relating to loving our neighbor.

6th Commandment: You shall not murder.

God created humans in His image so the one who kills a person is actually challenging God. In other words, it means that whoever commits murder is actually killing God. After Noah's judgment, God commanded, "Whoever sheds man's blood, do not keep him alive."(Note: Genesis 9:6)

Jesus spoke on the Mount, "You have heard that the ancients were told, 'You shall not commit murder' and 'Whoever commits murder shall be liable to the court.' But I say to you that everyone who is angry with his brother shall be guilty before the court; and whoever shall say to his brother, 'Raca,' shall be guilty before the supreme court; and whoever shall say, 'You fool,' shall be guilty enough to go into the fiery hell." (Matthew 5:21-22) We call ourselves Christians and yet how casually and easily we say things like "you stupid fool" to our brothers or sisters. Spitting words out of contempt and anger is regarded as the same as murder.

Why is anger and despising of others regarded the same as murder? Words of anger do not literally murder the flesh but kill the 'inner' person. It kills the character of the other person who hears those words of anger. As Christians, it is important to control our temper and anger at all times.

"With humility of mind let each of you regard one another as more important than himself." (Philippians 2:3) Let's face it. This is not easy. We receive continuous temptations from Satan to bring others down as much as possible and put thoughts of "there's no one smarter or better than me" into our minds boasting our ego to the highest pedestal. Satan has the power and authority over the world so we fail miserably on a daily basis.

After learning that anger is significantly negative, you may decide to stop expressing your anger in the future but, unfortunately, the decision itself is not enough. Awareness quickly disappears and the same old habit comes out again even before you know it. God's judgment on us is being accumulated each time when anger travels out of us. Just imagine the 'hell' that is being accumulated in our heart because of our anger. Being angry with colleagues, friends, or even with the family members or church members are the same as living in hell. Living in such a manner is pretty much like having received judgment already.

Let us not be fooled with the idea that we can control our anger or arrogance. It is only through the help of the Holy Spirit that our hearts can be controlled. Going to church once a week to listen to sermons is not enough to change our character. We must pray earnestly on a daily basis to suppress our anger and show humility towards others. Our character can only be changed through the Holy Spirit and God's love (Romans 5:5). We then can become a person who gives life to others rather than killing the character of others.

7th Commandment: You shall not commit adultery.

Since we are of flesh, we consume things of the earth which is the way our body is maintained. We eat, drink and excrete and basically through this process, we feel satisfaction and joy. In other words 'sensations.' Consuming the products of the earth is a happy activity for us so probably that's why we often exchange the greetings like "let's get together for a meal' to one another. Even one can feel satisfied after a good morning's session in the bathroom. It is how our physical body works. And it is why a person commits adultery. The irony is that where there's food, adultery takes place. On the other hand, the thought of adultery does not arise if a person is hungry. Adultery takes place when you feel 'full' and contented. It is our fleshly desire to have both.

The Bible tells us not to commit adultery. "Every other sin that a man commits is outside the body, but the immoral man sins against his own body. Or do you not know that your body is a temple of the Holy Spirit who is in you, whom you have from God, and that you are not your own? For you have been bought with a price: therefore glorify God in your body.'" (1 Corinthians 6:18-20) Adultery is a sinful act of flesh. Your body is a temple of the Holy Spirit whether you like it or not. It has been bought at the price of the blood of Christ. We must be able to give true worship in body. "Do you not know that the one who joins himself to a harlot is one body with her? For He says, 'The two will become one flesh.'" (1 Corinthians 6:16) Adultery means becoming totally captivated by the spirit of Satan.

What happens if a person continues to commit adultery while believing in Jesus? "Hand this man over to Satan, so that the sinful nature may be destroyed and his spirit saved on the day of the Lord."(1 Corinthians 5:5) What this means is that if a man continues to commit adultery, his/her body would be thrown to Satan. The only thing Satan can do is to destroy our body but the spirit will be judged by God. It is clearly written "If you are living according to the flesh, you must die" (Romans 8:13)

Those who believe in Jesus must realize how great a sin of adultery is and try to sustain our body in holiness. In order to overcome the flesh, we must communicate with the Holy Spirit within us through early morning prayers at all times. Don't be fooled that just spending hours in Bible study would enable your body move. It is only through the prayers that the Holy Spirit works within us, giving us strength to live according to God's way. Jesus also said that lustful heart is also a sin of adultery. The only way to control our heart is also in the Holy Spirit.

8th Commandment: You shall not steal.

God blessed Abraham to become the ancestor of God's chosen people, and this is not an event that simply happened in the distant past but something significant to us all in the present day as well. The idea of God's special choice of individuals carries two subsidiary features with it: promise and responsibility. Blessings received from above must be shared with others. Stealing those belongs to others to fill your needs will prompt God's punishment to your body.

Let's look at Jacob's case. Jacob had prospered in Haran by the grace of God. He left with many possessions and also took the family treasure of his father-in-law with him. What did God do? His life was threatened. As Jacob traveled back to his home territory, he faced with the expected wrath of his brother Esau at the Jabbok River. He almost lost his family members, let alone his possessions.

People steal for various reasons, such as poverty-stricken or out of despenateness. But for whatever the reason is, stealing is taking someone else's belonging away from them to fill your needs. Filling the emptiness of the flesh with the flesh creates problems and the needs will remain unsatisfied because that 'empty' feeling (heart) belongs to God. Then, what must you do when you feel the need? We must look at God. We need to fill our hearts with the Word of God. Jesus said, "Man shall not live on bread alone, but on every word that proceeds out of the mouth of God" (Matthew 4:4) when Satan tempted Him in the wilderness. A 'true' bread is not the literal bread. We must fill our hearts with the Word of God when we are in need and emptiness. All visible things of the world were created with the energy of the Word of God. The Bible clearly tells us that we can live by the Word of God. (Matthew 4:4) Animals die if they are starved for a week whereas humans can still survive without food for 40 days. Even though you may experience hunger physically, if you fill yourself with the Word of God, then amazingly enough, a creation will start to evolve and you will experience 'miracles' of life.

Look at the missionaries. They are the ones who left their home, family and relatives to do the missionary work. In other words, they have left 'themselves' behind back at home so filling their fleshly needs is out of the question. They have surrendered everything. So obviously, they constantly experience hardships and needs. What if they decided to settle the matter on their own? Stealing would be their easy way out but instead they hold on to the Word of God. By doing so, they are met with the works of God and a person comes into the picture to fill their needs. This is what faith is all about. Those who have faith will hold on to the Word of God at the most difficult time.

Stealing is not limited to those who lack things. There are those who have everything and yet continue to steal. Think about the animals. Have you ever seen an animal suffering from indigestion? Animals do not overeat. Even wild animals like lions stop eating when they are full. As for humans, we overeat even when we are full. Plus, animals do not have constant sexual needs unlike humans. They eat in order to fill their hunger and when it's time for mating, they consummate once. But humans are different. In many cases, humans become addicted to sex. This is the difference between the animals and humans. Animals strictly act according to their basic instincts as programmed by God so they live as created and therefore have no sin.

God Himself is the abundance of all things on earth. "The fullness of Him who fills all in all" (Ephesians 1:23). Heaven is abundant whereas the earth is empty and void. God created humans on earth so that we could be filled with His abundance of heaven. His abundance does not necessarily mean materialistic things. God fills our heart through the Word which is what we refer as 'spiritual blessing.' When the spiritual blessing comes into our heart, it gives us joy and peace that the world cannot possibly offer. At that point, you no longer need to steal from others anymore but instead have the heart to share with others. God not only stores us from within but outwardly in flesh as well.

Why do humans constantly crave for more? It is because we have been created in the image of God. It may puzzle you with a question: "Strange, I thought God's image was good." The image of God is definitely good but we must understand clearly what the image of God is. We are created to receive His Spirit under no circumstances but we fail to do so. Instead, we go around to fill our needs by ourselves which results in constant cravings and emptiness no matter what we do or have. It is why it is important to fill our heart with God's spirit. Spiritual emptiness leads us to cravings and needs which create the problem.

9th Commandment: You shall not give false testimony against your neighbor.

This commandment could sound as if one is inside the courthouse but not only is this true, it has another meaning to us. Whenever there's a gathering of people, we end up gossiping and slandering about others. This common practice is done so casually that we don't even blink an eye about it. Gossiping is 'false testimony.' There's a hidden agenda for gossiping. Basically, it is for self gratification and recognition. Even though words are not exchanged the person is proving to others that they are different and better than the other. Putting yourself to a higher position than others is already wrong because we are not perfect. It is not up to us to judge in the first place. Every individual has faults and when we realize about our own flaws, then we must automatically seal our lips.

This is the sinful nature that rooted from the Garden of Eden. The good and evil is the character of sin. The Satan tempted Eve, "If you eat from the tree of the good and evil your eyes will be bright." By eating the fruit of the good and evil, our eyes have become brightened which means that we no longer can see ourselves but rather find faults in others instead. We make decisions about what is good and bad; and when we compare ourselves with others with our standards, we consider ourselves correct and better than them. Therefore, we sin on a daily basis. Jesus said, "A man who has good inside him gives out goodness." (Matthew 12:35) So we must eat from the tree of life (the Word) rather than from the tree of the good and evil. The grace and inspiration of the Word enables us to feel our own flaws. The reflection of our own sins makes us repent so there would be no time to gossip anymore. The problem arises because we end up eating from the tree of the good and evil rather than eating from the Word.

Among the 10 commandments, this is the easiest one for the Christians to break today "Let all bitterness and wrath and anger and clamor and slander be put away from you, along with all malice. And be kind to one another, tender-hearted, forgiving each other, just as God in Christ also has forgiven you." (Ephesians 4:31-32) Just knowing the knowledge of the Word will never change your life. "Lord, have mercy on me. Help me to get rid of all anger, slander, revenge and all things that are evil. Instead, make me to be kind, compassionate and have a forgiving heart even though at times I feel like doing something that I would regret later. Lord, help me to forgive others just as you have forgiven my own sins." This is the way a true Christian must pray. There is no need to boast and say, "I'm a Christian; I believe in Jesus. "All we need to do is to reflect and believe that our sins were forgiven by Christ so if we really believe in Him, we must do the same with others and embrace others when they hurt us.

10th Commandment: You shall not covet your neighbor's belongings.

"You shall not covet your neighbor's house; you shall not covet your neighbor's wife or his male servant or his female servant or his ox or his donkey or anything that belongs to your neighbor." (Exodus 20:17) 'Do not covet' sounds similar to 'Do not steal' but it is slightly different. A person who covets belongings of others is the one who continues to wrongfully desire other person's belongings. You fail to see the grace that has been given to you by God. There is no heart of gratitude. As the saying goes, "grass looks greener on the other side" it is so true in many ways.

Comparison is another form of covetousness. I recall my own personal experience years ago. I was invited to a friend's house and tasted the best 'kimchi.' Rather than stopping at one praises I repeated numerously to my wife and eventually said to her, "why don't you make it the same way?" Obviously my wife was not so pleased with my remark. Along the same line, wives must also refrain themselves from comparing their husbands with others. "How come you're not smart and sophisticated like my friend's husband?" This also applies to the children as well. "Such and such a kid is doing so well in studies and obedient, how come you're not?" These kinds of comments are all under the category of covetousness.

Normally grumblings and complaints follow when you start comparing yourself with others. This is exactly what the Israelites did during the 40 years of their journey in wilderness. The grumblings were endless because they were comparing their situation in the wilderness with their days in Egypt. Even today we find people who claim to be Christians yet complain just like the Israelites. Unfortunately, they are not true Christians.

It is God who provided them daily manna and water from the rock during their journey in the wilderness. As Moses confessed in the book of Deuteronomy (Deuteronomy 29:5) that clothing or shoes were not worn out during the journey and yet they did not trust God who went ahead of them to provide everything necessary. Grumbling begins when one fails to see the blessings given right at the moment. God is always present, not only in the past or in the future but now. For those who are thankful for what God has provided already may feel envious at times but they never dwell on it to become covetous.

The things that we take for granted are monumental. Be thankful to God for today. My heart is filled with thankfulness whenever I enter my home. Even though I lived in an official residence as an Ambassador, I thanked God for allowing me to live in such a place. 'What matters where on earth we dwell? On mountain top or in the dell, in cottage or a mansion fair, where Jesus is 'his Heaven there.' (Hymn 495) If Jesus is in you, then you will be able to give thanks.

We are all in different situations and rightfully so. But then again, there is someone who gets selected to become a governor even though there is a shift in the government just like Daniel. There is someone who is faithful to God even with their authority in hand. There may be a poor person like Lazarus who survives by eating the crumbs of the rich. In the eyes of God, our inner soul is more important than the outer physical being. Whatever situations we may be in, as long as we live with Christ in our hearts, we will be able to feel joy and give thanks to Him.

Various Ordinances for Daily Lifestyle
_Exodus 21-24

Not only did God give the Ten Commandments to the Israelites but He also gave various rules and regulations applicable to their daily lives. The code of laws was necessary for them since they had become an independent nation. We must understand that in the Bible, legal, moral and religious laws are inseparable from each other, showing God's concern for life as a whole. A high view of human life is demonstrated by fixed and limited penalties: one crime, one punishment.

God chose the Israelites to make them become a source of blessing to every nation, so they must have something different from other gentiles. The Laws are further explained in Leviticus and Deuteronomy which is more of a rule that contains a restatement and reaffirmation of the Mt. Sinai covenant.

The law of Israel: the laws for God's people are distinctively different from the law of the world. For instance, ear of grains had to be left remaining on the ground rather than collecting them entirely. This applied to vineyards. Some grapes had to be left unpicked so that the poor people could eat. And a system called 'sabbatical' was set up. The land was entitled to a rest of its own on the 7th year and there was a system that in the 50th year followed by the year of 49 (7 years x 7 years = 49 years), every slaves were to be freed. This system also made business contracts to be expired or returned to the original owner after 50 years.

The Jews succeed in every business they do or no matter where they are because God gave them this kind of law. It is known that the Jewish community exceeds far ahead from any communities in terms of donation. It is because of the law God gave them. Though they may be stingy about how they earn money, they give willingly and generously when it comes to offering and donation because of the compassion for others. The lives of Israelites were different from others and God blessed them. There is a reason why many wealthy people are Jews. It is because God is protecting their lives.

Our life must be different from the worldly people if we believe in Jesus.

Sealing of Covenant_Exodus 24:4-8

The communion ceremony takes place by a special sacrifice, representing them by their representatives in the presence of God. The blood sprinkled on the people and on the altar unites the two parties to the agreement. Dashing half of the blood of sacrifice against the altar signifies that it is through the blood that people can come to the presence of God.

Sin inevitably means death, being cut off from God. But when the penalty for death has been satisfied, the people can be brought to God and established permanently in His presence. In effect, each is swearing to keep it on pain of death. This ceremony symbolizes that the Israelites have now officially become the people of promise signifying that God is to be their guide and partner in their lives. Alternatively, if they break the covenant, God sent out a message that He will punish them in the same manner.

Threader: But who broke this covenant? The people of Israel. There was tremendous bloodshed among the Israelites and in the end, it was not enough so God Himself shed His own blood. God's grace is just awesome!

Once we become God's promised people, our life must be focused on God. God is now our partner of life. We should try to distinguish between heaven and earth rather than good and evil. Life or no life, we must always ask whether our intents are godly or earthly.

For the life of the gentiles as opposed to the God's promised people, things of the world are constantly judged into two categories-good and bad. For instance, "a great product is on sale at the department store which is a great bargain" "that restaurant's food is terrible so and so is a lot better." When your interest dwells on the things of the earth, everything is based on the judgment of the good and the bad. Majority of the people's interest are solely based on earthly things. What does it mean to be focused on God? Let's ask ourselves. When we wake up in the morning, to whom do we communicate first in our heart? Our spiritual diagnosis can easily be detected by no other than ourselves. We must be able to recognize whether we are moving around on this earth with the consciousness of God or of the world.

The Stone Tablet_Exodus 30-34

God commanded Moses to build the Tabernacle and gave a detailed construction layout. Then afterwards, a stone tablet was given to him. When Moses fasted for 40 days, praying in Mt. Sinai, God gave him the two stone tablets of the testimony written by Him. Apparently, the size of the stone tablet is an adverse criticism among the theologians. The Bible clearly indicates that Moses came down with the two stone tablets in his 'hand' so it must have been small in size.

God commanded Moses to go down 'at once.' While the leader was praying and receiving God's command, the people of Israel were committing a great sin in front of God's eyes. They building an idolatry of a golden calf. They were breaking the 2nd commandment: Do not make an idol of any form or worship one. Upon seeing what was happening, Moses threw the tablets and shattered it out of burning anger.

Even though they were trained for a year with the Word, the people of Israel felt nervous and were afraid when their leader was absent for 40 days. They could not possibly believe in the invisible God. This shows us how difficult it is to believe in God, who is Spirit.

Threader: Since people did not believe in the invisible God, God who was the Word came into the world in flesh. Even the disciples of Jesus doubted of His resurrection. When 120 people gathered in the upper room at the Mark's house, the Holy Spirit came upon them and only then the disciples believed that Jesus was the Messiah. "You shall receive power when the Holy Spirit has come upon you; and you shall be My witnesses both in Jerusalem, and in all Judea and Samaria, and even to the remotest part of the earth." (Acts 1:8) According to this Word, the disciples became the witness of Jesus, risking their lives. No matter how much we know the Bible or listened to the Word, the knowledge itself will lead us to make a golden calf. Instead, when we commit to, testify, and confess the Word received- the energy of the Word, the Holy Spirit will work within us. Therefore, we must pray daily.

God killed off approximately 3,000 men who masterminded in building the golden calf. Before the law, the complaining people were left alone in the past, but ever since the covenant of the blood was made with God, people were punished according to the promise. God keeps His promise since He is truthful and faithful.

Originally, God wanted to wipe out everyone including Aaron since he was also the front leader in building the golden calf except Moses. God said, "You may think that you're special being the descendants of Abraham but I can easily replace 2 million people with this stone right here." At that moment, Moses conducts a intercessory prayer 'Lord, if you blot out everyone then the Egyptians will ridicule You by saying "They have exodus from Egypt to serve God but their God has brought them out to kill them." Upon hearing Moses prayer, God only punishes the main leaders in order to keep His promise. God then replaces the two tablets to Moses. We must not forget that the lives of the people of Israel were saved because of the prayer from one faithful man.

The Grace of the Tabernacle_Exodus 25-40

It is almost easy and smooth in reading the chapters of Exodus until we reach chapter 25, from which we start to feel suffocated. The instructions given for the Tabernacle in chapters 25-31 are so detailed that we often find ourselves lost in numbers - all those cubits for widths and heights, etc. But we must understand that this instruction is actually the report of grace given to the people of Israel.

God wanted His people to commit themselves to a life of obedience but He knew that humans had limitations in keeping His Word. It is impossible to feel God with our five senses. "The letter kills, but the Spirit gives life." (2 Corinthians 3:6) If one breaks the law, God's curse and judgment follows but humans cannot keep all the laws.

The amazing grace of God is in the Tabernacle itself. God built the Tabernacle with the intention of primarily saving His people and carrying the values Israelites learned at Mt. Sinai. God did not want to provide the Israelites only a memory to cling to. The Tabernacle represented the truth that the Lord was determined to live among His people and the will of God would govern the whole plan of the great Tent and its construction. The Tabernacle sums up the basic biblical truth about religion: it must conform to the will and nature of God. Time and again the Bible exposes the human's tendency to make religion suit to our own needs and expectations. But if religion does not match up with the will of God, it is ultimately futile. Upon completion, God blessed their handiwork by covering the tent with a cloud (the presence of the Holy Spirit) and filling the sanctuary with the dazzling light of God's glory.

Threader: The Tabernacle of the Old Testament changes into a Temple in the New Testament. A Temple should be understood in light of the incarnation, when God's Son became a human being-

Jesus Christ. Our Lord came to the world in flesh and died on the cross, resurrected and came into our heart as the Holy Spirit. We, as believers of God, are temples now. What an amazing grace and a blessing is this? During the Old Testament period, God met Moses in the mountain and then later came down to His people through the Tabernacle. And now, God is coming directly into our heart. He is approaching closer and closer to us in order to fill our hearts with His love each and every day.

The Tabernacle was built in accordance with God's specific instructions and set up as a portable tent. Since the Israelites had to constantly move from place to place during the years of wandering in the wilderness until they reach the promised land, it was a perfect solution in setting up God's tent in such a way.

There is only one entrance to the Tabernacle. This is the door of salvation for us. Once you enter there is the court, Holy Place and Most Holy Place. But then, why does one go inside the Tabernacle? It is to meet God who is in the Most Holy Place. But many people remain in the courtyard and say "I have received salvation from Jesus after believing in Him. So I will automatically go to heaven. In the meantime, I will continue to live as I have in the past." They have no interest in going further to meet God in the Most Holy Place. "When you come to appear before Me, Who requires of you this trampling of My courts?" (Isaiah 1:12) Through worship we must go inside the Most Holy Place where the presence of God is. That is why there are two sections: the Holy Place and the Most Holy Place.

The Five Stages of Maturity in Faith shown through the Structure of the Tabernacle:

1st Stage: Altar of Burnt Offering-Justification of Salvation.

The first thing you would notice as you enter the court of the Tabernacle is the altar of burnt offering where animal sacrifices were offered, located along the path leading to the Ark. It somewhat reminds you of a barbecue grill. It was used as where live animals' (lamb, goat or cow) blood of the sacrifice was sprinkled on the four horns of the altar and then burnt. The important fact is that the fire used for burnt offerings was not by humanly induced methods such as matches but were ignited by the fire from heaven. In the Old Testament period, the Pentecost was expressed as 'fire' from heaven.

Threader: During the Old Testament period, fire from heaven came down frequently. Gideon prayed to God for signs of power where he asked God to show him a sign so that he would believe that God is alive. So he prepared a young goat and even a pot of broth and placed it under the oak when a 'fire' sprang up from the rock and consumed the meat.

Before believing in Jesus, we enter God's Tent and then stand in front of the altar of the burnt offering and through the blood of Christ, the Holy Spirit comes down from above and into our heart. Jesus said, "No one can say, 'Jesus is Lord,' except by the Holy Spirit." (1 Corinthians 12:3) This is what we refer to as "justification of salvation." It is by the grace of the Holy Spirit that you have been saved, not by your own deeds. This is the 'fire' from heaven.

God consumes the offering once the fire from heaven burns the offering. This is the first stage toward to God.

2nd Stage: Bronze Laver-Repentance.

After the Altar of Burnt Offering is the Bronze Laver. The word laver means to 'cleanse' and it is where the priests would come to wash their hands and feet before entering the Ark of the Covenant. They must be pure to enter the presence of God or else one gets killed. Why did they wash hands and feet? This symbolizes repentance.

Threader: Once you believe in Jesus, the next thing you must do is to repent.

3rd Stage: Table of Showbread - The Word.

In the Holy Place, the Table of Showbread was a stand on which the offerings were placed. Always in God's presence, warm loaves of bread were on the table, symbolizing the bread of life -- the Word.

Threader: The first thing after believing in Jesus is to repent and then receive the Word. We are to 'eat' the bread on a daily basis. Those who do not receive the Word are people who go to church claiming that they have been saved without realizing they are merely stepping on the grounds of the court. The commitment to go in further 'inside' to the Holy Place to meet God is our goal. Normally when we first believe in God, our interest is on the knowledge of the Word since it is important to know the historical facts applied in the Bible. As time goes by, however, our level of faith must progress.

4th Stage: The Golden Lampstand - Oil (the Holy Spirit).

The Golden Lampstand is in the Holy Place opposite to the Table of Showbread. In the lampstand, a wick was lain with one end in the olive oil of the bowl and the other end hanging out, lighted. This lampstand symbolizes the Holy Spirit.

Threader: One must deeply be awakened by the Word of God and receive the Holy Spirit on a daily basis so that we may go forward to God.

5th Stage: Altar of Incense - Prayer.

Right in front of the heavy curtain separating the Holy Place and the Most Holy is the altar of incense.

Threader: According to the book of Revelations, incense symbolizes the prayers of saints (believers). Upon the aroma of prayers guided by the help of the Holy Spirit, one can go into God's presence in the Most Holy Place.

Inside of the Most Holy Place is the Ark of the Covenant where two angels with their wings wide opened are protecting on top of it. This place is referred as 'the throne of Zion', a seat of God's mercy. The high priest brings inside the sacrificed animal's blood and scatters it here. This is the place where God's presence is and where we must go to meet Him.

Thy Kingdom Come

"Thy Kingdom Come"

Jesus taught us the Lord's prayer and said that we must first seek His kingdom in our daily lives. He emphasized that "His kingdom must dwell in our daily lives." (See Matthew 15) His kingdom is not a place where we go after we die but the place that existed before eternity and also exists today. We must pray for His kingdom where God rules and controls. Our problems in this life cannot be resolved without the presence of His kingdom.

The world is an intersection of shadows of heaven and hell - making us realize that there is an actual world of eternity. For example, a shadow of a tree from a neighbor's house covers your garden. Let us imagine that it is a snake curled up in the tree that causes the shadow. "Yuck! There's a shadow of a snake in my garden." And you try to get rid of it by digging up the shadow with a shovel. Will that make it disappear? Digging up the shadow will only make the hell larger. If you really want to get rid of it you must destroy the actual snake in your neighbor's tree. Like this, all things of the world is a shadow.

"Rejoice always; pray without ceasing; in everything give thanks." (1 Thessalonians 5:16-18) In other words, be thankful for all the things that happen in our life whether it's good or bad. When good things happen (promotion in job, your kid got into a reputable college, etc.) in our lives-the shadow of His kingdom is portrayed to us. We must be able to pray "Lord, you have shown great things of the invisible kingdom. I thank you for showing me the shadow to such a sinner and an unworthy person like myself. Glory to You, Lord." The more we give thanks the bigger the shadow of His kingdom shines upon our lives. Being thankful is the best shortcut to His 30, 60, and 100 fold blessings!

As we know, not all good things happen in our lives. There are bad things as well. When we are confronted with negative incidents, we must quickly realize that this is a glimpse of a 'shadow of hell.' We must never complain to God when things are not working out positively. Because no matter how great the suffering may be there is no such thing as eternal suffering. Good things follow after suffering and vice versa. Life on this earth is temporary. Nothing is eternal on earth.

Revealing the shadows of heaven and hell into our lives is God's way of saying that all things on earth are temporary; instead we must look toward the eternal Kingdom. "Knock, and it shall be opened to you." (Matthew 7:7) Prayers seeking His world and righteousness are prayers of seeking God's will. "God, what do you wish to do with me through the shadows of hell?" The Bible says that the best time of our salvation and faith is when we're knocking on the door and investing our time in His world. "Faith is the assurance of things hoped for, the conviction of things not seen." (Hebrews 11:1) A person with faith actually can see the heaven's door and therefore, knocks.

"Your Will be done on Earth as it is in Heaven"

Only when God's Kingdom comes, His will be done on earth as it is in heaven. This is the truth. In the same manner, as the Son of God completed the circle of love with God the Father, He wants us to have the loving relationship with God the Father' as it is in Heaven.' God the Father who is in heaven gave all things to His beloved Son. In reverse, the Son returned all glory to the Father and even died in obedience. Not only has the Son returned all the glory to the Father but He gave all things to His followers. We, in return, give glory to the Son of God, Jesus. This completes the cycle of love.

What must be fulfilled on earth? It is 'God's Kingdom' and 'righteousness of God.' We have learned that righteousness of God means sharing our blessings with others. Once the presence of God's Kingdom is in us, we can then receive the power (love) to share with others who are less fortunate than ourselves. This is one of the reasons why God has prepared many people around us who are in more need than us. When we're sick, there are people sicker than us around us; when we think we are broke, there are more people around us suffering from poverty.

. . .

And He put all things in subjection under His feet, and gave Him as head over all things to the church, which is His body, the fullness of Him who fills all in all.

Ephesians 1:22-23

RESULT OF FAILURE - 40 YEARS IN THE WILDERNESS

Numbers

The book of Numbers got its name from the numberings of the Israelites during their time in the wilderness. The Israelites spent one year of religious training by God in Mt. Sinai. He gave them the Law and also instructed them to build a Tabernacle. The Israelites went through a painful process of testing and maturation in which God taught His people the consequences of rebellious and irresponsible decisions. It was primarily testing of the nation whether they were ready to take possession of the Promised Land in accordance with God's promise to Abraham, Isaac and Jacob. The first test was at Kadesh Barnea (Spies to Jericho). God judged Israel because of their unbelief and disobedience so none of the entire 1st generation survived through the 40 years of wandering.

Test at Kadesh Barnea

Various Incidents of Greed_Numbers 11-12

The people of Israel are led into a village of Barnea near the area of Kadesh. God's divine presence and guidance is evident in the pillar of fire and cloud as the Israelites marched and camped. As mentioned earlier in the book, the sweltering heat goes above 100 degrees during the day in this part of the region which makes it enormously difficult to travel especially on foot! As they traveled in the wilderness, the 12 tribes were divided into 4 groups, 3 tribes each in one group, placing each group in each direction: north, west, south, east, Levites with the Tabernacle in the center. God's guidance in the wilderness was clear and visible in reality.

Cloud by day and fire by night covering the Tent at the center of their camp showed God's presence in their midst. When the cloud was lifted, they moved. Where it settled again, they camped: no movement of the cloud, no movement of the people. Without the cloud blocking the sun, the population of some 2 million people would have all died in the desert. This also means that we also, as spiritual Israelites, cannot take one footstep forward into the world without God's grace and mercy. The Tabernacle was extremely important for the Israelites in the wilderness. It was their life; without it, God's presence and guidance was gone. The pillar of fire and cloud symbolizes the Holy Spirit and the Ark, the Word (Son of God, Jesus).

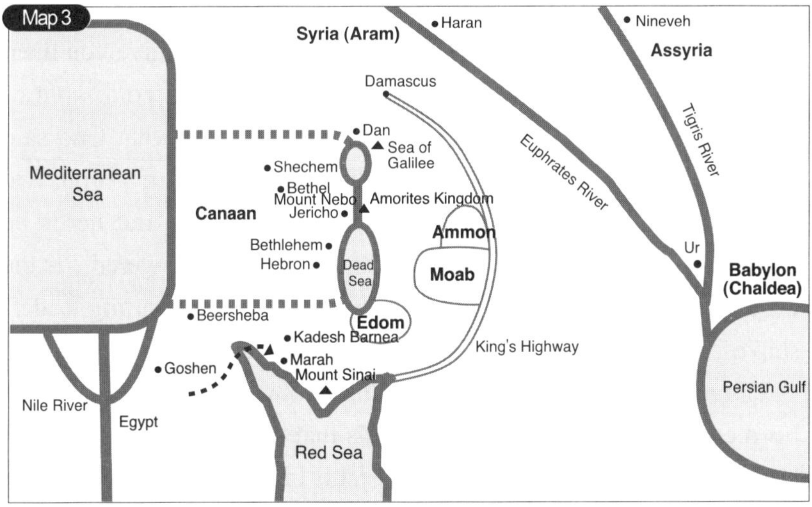

Exodus and the Period of the Wilderness After failing in their test in Kadesh Barnea, the Israelites spent 40 years of wanderings in the wilderness. A thorough religious training is necessary before entering into the Promised Land.

Greed of Meat

God leads the Israelites to Kadesh Barnea to test them whether they trusted and depended on Him. God demonstrated His care for His people through the daily provision of food, manna and water from the rock for people to drink while they camped at Mt. Sinai. When they tried manna for the first time, it was delicious because manna tastes like wafers made with honey. But at this point, they were sick of it because it was all they ate for one entire year. The same monotonous taste made them hard to swallow manna by then for it tasted like sawdust to Israelites. Mouth watering thoughts of meat and vegetables that abounded in Egypt soon produced irresistible cravings. They started to complain and grumble underneath their breath saying, "we were better off as slaves in Egypt. There, at least we ate freely meat, fish, vegetables and all kinds of fruits, etc. Here, there is nothing but manna! What are we doing here? Let's pick a new leader and go back!"

Outcries from people were unbearable even for Moses so it prompted him to plea to God, "Have I given birth to these two million people? Why are you giving me this pain? It is too burdensome for me to handle so just kill me instead." God recognized the exhaustion behind Moses' own complaint and replied, "I will give you meat not for a day, nor week but for a whole month until it comes out of your nostrils!" Moses was not convinced of whether what God said would be done because of the overwhelming amount of people two million of them and said, "Where would the flocks and herds be found in this desert to feed them for a month?" God answered, "Is the Lord's power limited?" His response was to give a supporting leadership of 70 some of the 'spirit' (also means 'wind') to Moses.

The result of this was dramatic. With strong gust of wind from the Lord came along vast amount of quails that flew from the sea falling beside the camp. While the meat was still in their teeth before it was chewed, God struck the ones who were the leaders of the pack that caused this grumble with a severe plague but the rest of the people ate meat for a full month. This incident clearly reveals how weak we are in flesh.

I heard from one of the pastors during a revival gathering in Los Angeles that he had spent almost 18 years in nourishing his congregation and in the midst of reconstructing the church building the IMF crisis occurred in Korea. Immediately thereafter, elders and deacons stormed into the pastor's quarters threatening him and his family members to give back the money they have contributed. The bottom line of this message is that no matter how much you have received the Word, fleshly needs overpower the Word in front of any crisis or emergencies. This shows how weak we are in flesh.

Miriam's Rebellion

Miriam, Moses' sister, becomes the instigator of challenging the leadership. Miriam played a significant role in saving Moses and yet she rebelled against her brother. Moses escaped from death when Miriam put him inside of a basket and successfully floated him in the Nile River. She followed him behind to see who was going to find him. Then, when Pharaoh's princess found Moses, Miriam was the one who introduced his mother to the princess and made her to be the wet nurse for the baby Moses. An enemy originates from someone who is very close to you.

What made her rebel? It appears that Zipporah must have died during the journey to Kadesh Barnea. So Moses had married a Cushite (an Ethiopian) woman among the midst of the people. (Numbers 12:1) Now we must understand that when the people of Israel left Egypt, a mixed multitude also came out with them (see Exodus 12:38) along with flocks and herds. The Israelites and the gentiles who left Egypt along with them were referred as the 'assembly of Israel' after their exodus and most likely this Cushite woman was among them.

Miriam accused Moses that he had married a Gentile when it was prohibited by God. On the surface, it appeared as if the issue was the marriage that was prohibited but the real bone of this contention was not Moses' gentile wife but his position as the leader. Over the years, she must have felt certain frustrations and jealousy towards her brother who was now acting as a leader of almost 2 million people. Truthfully, she might have wanted to say, "How come you're acting like a king when I am also important?!" Her participation during the journey was also important. Her 'self' was being magnified through the works of Satan.

Moses was silent but God's answer is a remarkable tribute to the man. It is God who judges, not us. According to God's command, we are to obey and respect parents and anyone above us. God punished Miriam by giving her leprosy and at the request of Aaron, she was healed through the intercessory prayer of Moses but eventually died in the end. There comes another incident referred to as the 'Korah's rebellion' where God makes use of natural forces (earthquake) to execute judgment by splitting the earth open and swallowing the people alive. We must realize that rebellion against a leader who has been anointed by God results in judgment.

As I travel around the world to teach, I hear many tragic stories such as "an elder who was the key player in removing the pastor of our church passed away in a miserable condition; he had a severe stroke and paralyzed, etc." Rebelling against a leader is a great sin. The claims of many voices are "we had no choice but to criticize the pastor... after all, if he is the anointed one, he should act and live as one but he is not." Once you start to judge a person, there can never be a 'perfect' leader in your eyes.

There is no perfect or righteous man on this earth whether a person is the leader or not. Every one of us are in the process of becoming like Jesus. The only thing that we need to do is to respect and obey God's anointed messenger. For instance, the silverwares used in churches are no different from the ones we use at home but since God has anointed it, we are to treat it holy. Therefore, changing the silverware that is found unholy is meaningless.

If you come across a fault of a leader, refrain yourself from gossiping with others and instead repent and pray. The reason why you see the faults of others is because your eyes were made 'bright' as a result (making own judgment) of eating from the good and evil. (Genesis 3:5) Pray "Lord, how much have I eaten from the good and evil that I even see the faults in the pastor? Why is that I see flaws of others? Help me, Lord so that I stop eating from it." Those who have faith focus on the salvation of the Lord and not the world or 'self.' Once you see the Lord's salvation, the faults of others fade away.

Spies to Canaan_Numbers 13-14

The Failure at Kadesh_Barnea

The failure of the spies is inevitable at this point. It was not God, but people (Israelites) who suggested to send 12 spies ahead to the land of Canaan. When the 12 spies returned, after 40 days since their departure, accomplishing their task, people listened to 10 of them who doomed their path with the story of giants and grasshoppers. "We are not able to go up against the people, for they are too strong for us." (Numbers 13:31) But the two men of faith, Joshua and Caleb's interpretation, which was true and was based on the facts, was different from the other 10. "The land which we passed through to spy out is an exceedingly good land. If the Lord is pleased with us, then He will bring us into this land, and give it to us, a land which flows with milk and honey. Only do not rebel against the Lord; and do not fear the people of the land, for they shall be our prey. Their protection has been removed from them, and the Lord is with us; do not fear them." (Numbers 14:7-9) The congregation wanted to stone Joshua and Caleb. This is the outcome of the believers and non-believers.

Why did the 10 spies fail? They focused only on the visual existence. They had no faith. "Faith is being sure of what we hope for and certain of what we do not see." (Hebrews 11:1) Faith means assuming the unforeseen without experimental verification. With faith, the invisible Word becomes the real image for the Word of God is living and active. (Hebrews 4:12) That is why those who have faith have no fear.

Threader: The army of the Arameans circled the house of Prophet Elisha to capture him. The house was on a hill. So when the Elisha's servant went out in the morning to wash his face, he noticed the surrounded horses and chariots and returned home yelling, "Alas, my master! What shall we do?" Upon hearing this, what do you think Elisha did? He prayed to God to open his servant's eyes that he may see. With Elisha's prayer, the servant's spiritual eyes were opened and he saw the mountain was full of horses and chariots of fire all around the house. Like this, if we believe that God is alive, we must not be afraid of the things we see around us.

The problem with the 10 spies was fear. What that means is that they did not have complete love for God or trust in Him. Love has no fear. Love enables you to do extraordinary things-such as, one easily jumps into the water or fire to save the loved ones. "There is no fear in love; but perfect love casts out fear, because fear involves punishment, and the one who fears is not perfected in love." (1 John 4:18)

Those who are in captivity by Jesus fear nothing; and if you receive the Holy Spirit, you receive the power to become a witness of Jesus wherever you go. "Who shall separate us from the love of Christ? Shall tribulation, or distress, or persecution, or famine, or nakedness, or peril, or sword?" (Romans 8:35) "We have come to know and have believed the love which God has for us. God is love, and the one who abides in love abides in God, and God abides in him." (1 John 4:16)

Those who receive God's spirit will feel His everlasting love. It was this love and faith that the apostles of the first church sustained during their dreadful persecution and torture in the fire. Confessing that God was with them, they were able to see God's Kingdom rather than the actual reality. Stephan was stoned to death and yet he did not utter any foul words. Pain did not disorient him and instead, he saw the Lord next to the throne. This is faith!

The problem arises when we claim that we believe in Jesus and yet do not feel God's love. Because we don't feel God's love, we often act like the 10 spies. Finding ourselves discouraged many times. Why you don't feel God's love? It is because you do not pray. The strong wave of God's love can only be felt when we pray led by the Holy Spirit.

Judgment Due to Lack of Faith

The people of Israel have now revealed that they had no faith. God judges Israel for their unfaithfulness by making them to journey in the wilderness for 40 years by calculating one day of spying as one year so 40 years for 40 days of spying. This is the period where the 1st generation (primarily those over 20 years old at the time of exodus) was slowly dying away. People who listened and followed to the report of the 10 spies all died by the plague sent by God. The life of the stubborn nation that is going down in rumbles is portrayed in this judgment. Only Jacob and Caleb, those who have faith in God, entered the Promised Land.

The principle of God is not for majority but rather for small number of people. God does not raise the hands of a massive group who do not have faith. "For the gate is small, and the way is narrow that leads to life, and few are those who find it." (Matthew 7:14) Small number of people with faith are more important than a big crowd who do not have faith.

The Israelites journeyed around Kadesh Barnea for 38 years. God, and the good land, were all forgotten. With their final destination in front of them, a whole generation of Israel cut itself from all that was promised. Only when the leadership was shifted to Joshua from Moses, the nation started to change.

Korah's Rebellion_Numbers 16-17

After failing in the test at Kadesh Barnea, the Israelites journeyed in the wilderness for 40 years. They continued to grumble and complain throughout the journey from the beginning to the end. Korah, the descendants of the Levites were the first to rebel.

Korah's grievance and that of his company of 250 Levites challenged Moses on the grounds of priesthood. "God has promised His midst among our assembly and yet why do you exalt yourself. We are also Levites so why the monopoly of the priesthood go to Aaron's descendants and not us? Let Korah become high priests as well!"

But the fact is that it was not Moses' doing, it was God's commanding order. So Moses responds, "It is fine with me but is it not enough for the Levites since you already are participating in God's work by skinning the animals for offering? How is it that you regard it as less important and yet seek priesthood? Let's see whether you are capable in taking the role of priesthood or not. You and all your company present yourselves before the Lord tomorrow each bringing fire pans and incense on it and see if the Lord consumes it."

The 250 members of Korah and their families assembled and stood in the doorway of their tents the next morning. Then, the earth was split open and swallowed them. Probably the entire congregation might have perished if God had raised a bigger earthquake but only the alliance of Korah, Dathan and Abiram and their immediate families were killed. They failed to recognize that the calling of priesthood only comes from God.

Only those who are called by God must conduct priesthood - nowadays referred to as pastor which includes the missionaries as well. I have come across people who switched their careers in a drastic way after attending revival movements at church or prayer and/or fasting sessions. They suddenly quit their jobs and start registering in various seminaries in order to become pastors or missionaries. This is surely a dangerous action. One must hear the voice of God. The calling must be loud and clear. Unfortunately, we find many who have decided on their own personal conviction without God's distinctive calling. Surprisingly, it is found that almost 70% of missionaries fail as missionaries. One cannot do God's work with compassion only and cannot succeed in performing their duty or overcome the hardships without God's calling.

There was an elite man who attended my Bible class when I was a deacon in New Zealand. He had graduated from a well known university and was taking his masters at the time. One day he approached me and requested a consultation. "Deacon, I have finally made up my mind." "What decision?" I questioned. "I have decided to give up my studies and instead enroll in a seminary to become a pastor." I then suggested that we pray together and asked him, "Have you received God's calling?" "No, not exactly. I received so much grace after listening to your lectures that I thought it would be great to become a pastor." "Why do you want to become a pastor?" "To become a professor or a scholar is alright but after receiving the Word and grace, I am convinced that I should live a 'holy' life. And besides, I know myself. I love to drink, goof around a lot and once I start working in the society, I know that it would be tough to persuade myself to do otherwise. So if I become a pastor, I am forced to become 'holy' and therefore, my lifestyle will change." My urgent response followed, "Don't ever think about it!" The disappointed young man said, "I thought you would be very happy for me. My pastor at church and many others were happy about my decision. Quite frankly, I wanted your approval more than anything else."

God decided to show why He chose the Levites (Aaron's descendants) among the 12 tribes to the priesthood and instructed each leader from the 12 tribes to place their rod in the Ark. Aaron's rod was among them. The likelihood of sprouting bud on the new rod was more than Aaron's worn out rod but as we find in all biblical miracles, the budding, blossoming and fruiting of Aaron's rod had a very practical point. Everyone could see where God's choice fell. There was no room for dispute. The rod was kept in God's sanctuary as a permanent warning against the rebels.

Trees do not bear fruit for their own sake but for others. Various animals eat it as well as humans once a tree bears fruit. Bearing fruit is primarily for others not for the benefit of oneself-and this is the sacrificial attitude of priesthood. What was the significant message that was shown through the budding of Aaron's rod? It is for us to bear fruit; to surrender ourselves. All the fruit of your efforts and profit must be shared with others. A person who ministers without God's calling cannot atone for others and end up pursuing their own personal needs. That is why God blocked it. One must not go forward hastily without God's calling.

Moses' Sin_Numbers 20

Moses' sin was not from his own mistake. It was strictly according to God that he had sinned. The best part of 38 years has passed since the Israelites journeyed in the wilderness. The hardship was inevitable but each time God showed endless miracles. Starting from the 10 plagues in Egypt, the bitter water turning into sweet water, manna from heaven, water from the rock, overturned the attack of the Amelekites. But nothing seemed to cure the people's grumbles. They were moaning when they first left Egypt. They were still moaning for water again, after all the years of God's provision. One thing we have learned from the Israelites is that miracles have nothing to do with one's faith and salvation.

At this point, the Israelites took it for granted that Moses' striking brought water from the rock. Upon seeing the grumblings of the people, God instructed Moses "Take the rod, and you and your brother Aaron assemble the congregation and speak to the rock before their eyes, that it may yield its water. The rock will bring forth water for the congregation and their animals to drink." (Numbers 20:8)

God had clearly instructed to 'speak' to the rock but what did Moses do? Out of anger and frustration, he struck the rock twice with his rod. Even though water came forth abundantly, God regarded Moses' act as unbelief and sin. 'Must we get water ... ?' as if he and Aaron, not God, brought the water from the rock. How often words spoken in haste are repented! Moses had forgotten that it was God not him who is bringing the water from the rock. Because of this, God said Moses will not lead the people into the land he has so longed to enter. Even the greatest of God's servants, after a long lifetime of trust and obedience, can fall.

With one slip of disobedience, the privilege to enter the Promised Land was forfeited for Moses. "Love is patient, love is kind, and is not jealous ... does not act unbecomingly ... not provoked ..." (1 Corinthians 13:4-5). A lot of times we express anger as if it was righteous - when elders or eldress get upset in the church they often say, "This is a righteous thing to do since we are following God's will." But the real underlying problem is that if one feels righteous over someone then it is wrong. We must control our anger at all times.

What makes Moses a great leader is that even after he was told that he himself would not enter the Promised Land, he completes his job to the end. By obeying God's command to lead His people. Majority of us would have reacted differently, "Since I can't go in, there's no need for me to continue this work. I quit!" That is why Moses stands out as the greatest leader and the Bible says "The man Moses was very humble, more than any man who was on the face of the earth." Moses was indeed a mild, gentle man and there was no one who prayed intercessory prayers as much as him. Moses' leadership in carrying out God's command up to his last breath is truly remarkable and admirable.

Edom Refuses Passage_Numbers 20

The tribes of Edom were situated underneath the Dead Sea. The word "Edom" means reddish and they are the descendants of Esau, Jacob's brother. Biologically, they are actually the brothers of Israel. The Israelites had to go east in order to travel further north to reach the far side of the Dead Sea. But Edom was in the way. The King's Highway (main road) ran directly north from the Gulf of Aqaba to Syria, leaving the Dead Sea to the west. All Middle Eastern traders of every kind traveled through the King's Highway at the time. For obvious reasons, Moses wanted to lead the Israelites through this short cut and so approached Edomites. "Please let us pass through your land. We shall not pass through field or through vineyard; we shall not even drink water from a well. We shall go along the king's highway, not turning to the right or left, until we pass through your territory." (Numbers 20:17) In other words, water being very precious they were not going to touch it. Instead they were going to buy their own drinking water as they pass through. Edom's response was, "You shall not pass through us, lest I come out with the sword against you." (Numbers 20:18) Edom's refusal to let Israel pass involved them in a long detour to south and round.

With all his might, Moses tried to calm approximately 2 million people by taking them to Mt. Hor, northeast of Kadesh Barnea. It was a critical moment for Moses since both Miriam and his spokesperson, Aaron had already died. God had taken away everything that Moses had depended on. Just imagine the state of Moses at the time!

Generation Replacement of the Israelites
_Unbelieving 1st Generation-Faithful 2nd Generation

The Incident of Fiery Snakes_Numbers 21:4-9

A turning point event occurred during the life in the wilderness.

Israelites' complaints have now reached to sky level. "What kind of a leader are you?! Why have you brought us here to die in the desert?" Moses felt hopeless with desperation. Then God sent venomous snakes as a punishment to those who complained; but a remedy was provided. The people had only to look at the bronze snake to be healed.

The Israelites left Mt. Hor and was coming down towards Mt. Sinai. There were many copper mines enabling Moses to make a bronze snake at God's command. Why do you think God instructed them to make a snake? Ever since Exodus, the complaints of the Israelites were endless and their rebellious attitudes were like 'stiff necks' resembling a cobra. Picture a cobra in your head. The erected neck and the eyes facing downwards, it resembles 'me' in all of us. Those with stiff necks must be bitten by the fiery serpent and ultimately receive God's salvation. The bronze snake on the tree symbolizes crucifying our 'self' on the tree. This incident is a shadow of the cross from the New Testament. Jesus reminds Nicodemus of this incident, saying that he too must be lifted up, so that everyone who has faith in Him may have eternal life.

Many of us come to Jesus when we are physically or emotionally wrecked. Let us pray for those who are weak and sick: "Your people are suffering at this time. Let their flesh be broken so that they may meet You Lord." Rather being rejuvenated in flesh through a miracle, it is better for your spirit to be healed through the hardships. This is the true salvation and God's true blessing.

If you rebuke God by saying, "Why are you giving me pain?" Then you are just like the Israelites, complaining stiff necks. This type of person is not worthy to enter His promised land. Let me rephrase this, God will not allow it. When we are broken in flesh, we must pray "Thank you Lord. Through this experience, help me so that I could come forward to You. I confess that I am nothing. Please meet me, Lord. Permit me Your blessing that I may meet You through this suffering."

Conquest of Eastern Part of Jordan

The conquest of Canaan was already initiated during Moses time, prior to Joshua's. It was evident that Moses was not going to enter the Promised Land but he faithfully led the people of Israel and took over the eastern part of the Jordan River.

Moses and the Israelites conquered two countries and attacked the Amorites (who was one of the seven tribes of Canaan) and took over the eastern part of the Jordan River. God also instructed them to go up further to Lake Galilee and take over the land of Bashan as well. Sihon, king of Amorite and Og, king of Bashan were known to be the strongest force at the time. The Amorite King Sihon has conqured the land of Moab and ruled from the Ammon in the south to the Jabbok in the north, from his capital city of Heshbon. Continually heading north, the Israelites defeated Og (north-east of Lake Galilee) at Edrei. This victory had a great impact and was a shock to other tribes in the region.

Threader: The Moabites were located next to the Dead Sea where-as the Ammonites were at the east of the Jordan River. Remember now that these two gentile tribes were the descendants of Lot and his two daughters (whom he had relationship with). And as a result they were excluded in the assembly of Israel. These two tribes combined is now Jordan today. The capital of Jordan is Amman but in the Bible it is written as Ammon. It is now the kingdom of Jordan but in those days, it was two different countries. Bashan is a territory next to Mt. Hermon which is connected to Syria; it is also located on the east side of the Jordan River and is now known as the Plains of Kolan. Being on a highland, it was a strate gically important area where not only one can view the Lake Galilee but also the entire land of Canaan -Palestine at one glance. The land was also fertile. In the book of Amos, the Israelites who had no faith and lazy were expressed as the cows in Bashan which meant that they were fat and lazy that they could roll down the green pastures as cows.

Now the victorious Israelites returned to the camp in the plains of Moab. Balak, king of Moab, with Midianite support, sent for Balaam, the diviner to come and curse his enemies. It was an usual business arrangement for the prophet, in a day when everyone believed in the power of words (especially formal blessings and curses) to influence events. Balaam who wanted to receive considerable money from the king after cursing Israel saddled on a donkey to leave with the leaders of Balak but the donkey wouldn't budge. This was a donkey he had ridden for 20 years! Balaam got upset and started to whip the donkey to move. At that moment, God opened the mouth of the donkey.

"Master, why are you hitting me? As you know you had ridden me all your life to this day and never once did I object to your commands. But I am sorry I cannot move because the angel of the Lord is standing in the way with a sword in his hand so what am I suppose to do?" (See: Numbers 22:22-28)

Then the Lord opened the eyes of Balaam for him to see the angel with the sword in his hand. At this point, Balaam wanted to turn back but the angel of the Lord said, "Go with the men, but you shall speak only the word which I shall tell you."(Numbers 22:35) Upon arrival, Balaam was brought up to the high places of Baal and in front of the seven bulls and seven rams, he started to prophesize rather than cursing Israel, he blessed them instead. "God is not a man, that He should lie, Nor a son of man, that He should repent; Has He said, and will He Not do it? Or has He spoken, and will He not make it good? Behold, I have received a command to bless; When He has blessed, then I cannot revoke it. He has not observed misfortune in Jacob; Nor has He seen trouble in Israel; The Lord his God is with him, And the shout of a king is among them. God brings them out of Egypt, He is for them like the horns of the wild ox." (Numbers 23: 19-22)

Three times they went through the same ritual; three times Balaam blessed Israel, only increasing Balak's anger. The fourth oracle tops all predicting a victorious future king who would defeat all Israel's enemies. God's purpose seems to impress Balaam that no matter how Balak works on him, the prophet would stick to the truth. This was the way in which God struck the Moabites. On the other hand, the

Ammonites were not destroyed but were scattered. The reason for it will be revealed shortly. Moses' life was almost over, as he looked out over the Promised Land. Joshua, his right-hand man was God's choice of successor. He was not invested with the authority to lead the nation in Moses' place. He started off with conquering the Canaan; the division of the land between the 12 tribes took place later on. Down the line, Joshua died and the period of the Judges unfolded. Throughout the 40 years of the period of the judges, God used the Amorites as a whipping lash against Israel whenever they sinned. This was one of the reasons why God left the Amorites intact.

Division of the Land East of Jordan_Numbers 32

As a result of conquering Ammon and Bashan, vast amount of livestock were confiscated. Change of mind seep through rather than taking trouble of moving the livestock to the Promised Land, they wanted to settle. So they requested to Moses division of the land amongst them. The tribes of Reuben and Gad want to settle in the good grazing lands east of the Jordan. Their request was granted, but only on condition that they help in the conquest of Canaan first. So they worked out a practical plan to enable the fighting force to leave the livestock and their dependents behind, safe and secure. Part of the tribe of Manasseh conquered Gilead, and Moses gave them this land for their own.

After distributing the tribes east of Jordan, God raised Moses in Mt. Nebo opposite of the Jordan River. Mt. Nebo is 1,700 meter above sea level and Jordan River is a valley that travels 200-300 meters below earth level; Jericho is 400 meter below sea level so if one goes up to Mt. Nebo-the entire land of Canaan can be viewed. This was where God spoke to Moses. "You cannot go in the Promised Land." After seeing how beautiful the land was, Moses asked God, "Is there any way I could go in?" The answer was no. What an unsympathetic God! After coming down from the mountain, Moses wrote the 'famous' Deuteronomy (repetition of the law) and died afterwards. Through the book of Deuteronomy, he reminded the Israelites of their history. All that God had done for them throughout their 40 years of journey in the wilderness, and the laws they had to continue to obey as God's chosen people. He also summarized God's laws, including the Ten Commandments. One subject that Moses pervaded in the whole book of Deuteronomy is the loving relationship of the Lord with His people and that of the people toward the Lord as their sovereign God. Moses obeyed God until his death. He may not have entered the Promised Land but God took him to a better place.

What does the book of Deuteronomy teach us?

First, it explains whether to follow God at our own freewill or to worship idol. The book of Deuteronomy not only explains in detail of the Law but clearly shows the two crossroads of blessing and curse.

Second, it is a record of the Israelites journey in wilderness after the exodus. It raises the fact that throughout their 40 years of journey in wilderness, it was God who fed and led His people. How great is the grace of God!

We must realize the same message applies to us as we walk in the wilderness of the world today. "You have repeatedly acted out and betrayed me during your journey in wilderness. But as your Jehovah, I do not speak casually; I do not regret, nor remember the faults of Jacob. I turn away from your rebellious acts. I will forgive you whenever the high priest brings the blood of the offering lamb inside the Holy Place."

Through the exodus and the long journey of the Israelites in wilderness until their entry to the Promised Land, we must hear the patient, loving voice of God, His overruling providence in keeping the promise to the ancestors of faith (Abraham's covenant).

The Difference between an Angel and Satan

It is quite simple to distinguish the difference between an Angel and Satan. Satan is proud so wants to control everything under him all the time whereas the angel only wants to serve unconditionally. This is the difference between the two.

Why do couples fight? Why do political parties fight? It is because one wants to rule over the other party. Unfortunately, this also applies to churches as well. In some instances, raising voices in committee meetings inside the church can mean only one thing. A strong desire to control over the other which comes from the spirit of Satan.

Jesus said, "I have not come to be served, but to serve, and to give His life a ransom for many." (Matthew 20:28) He showed His disciples an example of what he meant in this verse by kneeling down to wash their feet at the last supper before carrying the cross. We are all in the process of learning to 'serve' which is the cross of redemption.

While praying, we must focus on the cross and go towards 'the highest place each and every day.' Those who have reached the third heaven and met God must come down to serve. Coming 'down' is referred as carrying the cross of redemption. A person who only keeps going 'up' without carrying the cross of redemption creates a problem.

"Since I have brought you to church and made you believe in Jesus, you must only listen to me now." "Since I have healed you, you take my orders from now on." There are people who pass this kind of controlling remarks out of possessive attitudes. Rather than serving in humility and with the love of Christ and His blood they are putting themselves high on a pedestal and it causes the problem. With God-given gift, some people heal many others and as time goes by they end up thinking that it was their own ability. If a person prays in tongue and receives the gift of prophecy then it becomes more dramatic.

The church of Corinth was where Apostle Paul worked during his 2nd missionary trip. The works of the Holy Spirit was so powerful that majority of the people in the church of Corinth prayed in tongue. They performed their services and praises in tongue and when someone spoke in tongue, those who received the gift of prophecy would stand to interpret. This was the way it was conducted in that order. Since the works of the Holy Spirit was so powerful, the church members were free to utilize their spiritual gifts during this period. But it created problems among the spiritually gifted members. Probably all the problems that we face in churches today actually originated from the church of Corinth in spite of the powerful spiritual gifts they had received. Elders were suing each other; some were committing adulteries; or bragging that they had received the spiritual gift and so forth. For this reason, Apostle Paul wrote in detail regarding spiritual gifts in 1 Corinthians 12-14 explaining how one should be cautious about it.

In this connection, Jesus also said "You will know them by their fruits." (Matthew 7:20) There are many spiritually super-powered people around us as well as false prophets. We must not judge by their powers or abilities but rather focus on their fruits (actions). A spiritually gifted person can easily be detected whether the Spirit is from God or Satan by looking at the fruit. The fruits of the Holy Spirit are "love, joy, peace, patience, kindness, goodness, faithfulness, gentleness, self-control." (Galatians 5:22-23) Control, arrogance, and pride cannot be found in the fruit of the Holy Spirit. We must realize that the devil also has the powers of prayer in tongue and prophecy. It is difficult to differentiate between the powers of the Holy Spirit and magic because of the similar outcome. It is why the only way to distinguish the Holy Spirit and Satan is by examining its outcome according to its 'fruit.'

It is important for us to pray and train ourselves diligently so that we may be able to bear fruit-which will enable us to carry the cross of redemption. The cross itself is suffering, suppressing your desires and needs. Simply put, arriving in the position of glory is only possible through the cross and for those who have reached the level of glory by faith-they must come down and carry the redemptive cross. As Christians we must bring the attitude of service into reality. It may seem difficult and burdensome but without practicing it, you cannot call yourself a true believer of Jesus who has saved you and chose you.

. . .

Love is patient, love is kind and is not jealous; love does not brag and is not arrogant, does not act unbecomingly; it does not seek its own, is not provoked, does not take into account a wrong suffered, does not rejoice in unrighteousness, but rejoices with the truth; bears all things, believes all things, hopes all things, endures all things.

1 Corinthians 13:4-7

WAR BELONGS TO GOD

Joshua 1-6

Conquering the seven tribes of Canaan was strictly under God's hands. It was more of a spiritual war than a war only fighting with the weapons and God was the key to the people's success under Joshua. The spiritual war that takes place on earth cannot be won with human's intellect or ability but through worship. God clearly shows His grace and power, which enable us win the spiritual war on earth, to the Israelites through the book of Joshua.

Joshua, the New Leader_Joshua 1

A new leader Joshua was raised by God. The name Joshua in Hebrew is Yeshua, equivalent to the name 'Jesus' and it means 'the one who will lead to heaven.' Joshua was Moses' right-hand man as well as a companion during the exodus and the time of wondering in the desert. Why do you think Joshua was chosen as a leader? He was a man of prayer. God raises a person who is always aligned with Him.

Joshua was with Moses when he prayed in the early dawn inside the tent and remained there praying even after Moses left. "When Moses returned to the camp, his servant Joshua, the son of Nun, a young man, would not depart from the tent." (Exodus 33:11) God instructed Moses that Joshua was a man of Spirit and that he should anoint him before all the congregations. (Numbers 27:18-20)

So basically the formal commission to lead the nation came directly from God as Moses' life drew to a close.

After being chosen as the new leader God spoke to Joshua, "As I was with Moses, so I will be with you; I will never leave you or forsake you. Be strong and courageous." (Joshua 1:5-6) This was the same message given to all God's leaders.

Threader: We have heard numerous testimonies with regard to this same message. "Do not fear, for I am with you; Do not anxiously look about you, for I am your God ... " (Isaiah 41:10) Actually, the background of this verse was given when the Israelites were taken into captivity in Babylon. In the same context, Apostle Paul also said something similar to his inmates when he was imprisoned. "Rejoice in the Lord always; again I will say, rejoice!" (Philippians 4:4)

How was it possible for him to say that when he was in such a bad shape? It was because he was in Christ. He was totally convinced of God's promise of "You are Mine." God's Word of "I will never leave you or forsake you" recovers and brings us back to the original state of being. Initially, we have been chosen by God before the foundation of the world (Ephesians 1:4) but through corruption of mankind, we have all been living under the spell of Satan and by receiving Jesus, we have been shifted back to our original position.

The Response of the People

The people of Israel all responded positively to the new leadership. As Joshua assumed the command, he said to the Reubenites, Gadites and to the half-tribe of Manasseh who had settled in the eastern part of the Jordan River whether they would be together with the conquest and they all agreed by saying, "All that you command us we will do and wherever you send us we will go." Now this was a significant reaction since it had been such a long time during the 40 years of journey that the entire people agreed in something all together.

God is in the midst among us when the members and the leaders of the church are aligned together with one another. (Joshua 17:8-16) What's the use when you say "we want the Holy Spirit in our church" when you are not united with one another. We must realize that the Holy

Knowledge Search 11

How Different is Islam's Jihad and the Conquest of War of Canaan?

The word 'Jihad' is frequently used by the Islamic people. It means 'Holy War' in Arabic and appears numerously in today's newspaper. In order to maintain peace, the Muslim had no choice but to fight against the anti-Islamic people but when the word 'Jihad' is found around us today, we automatically connect it with terrorism of Islam.

In reality, the Holy War originated from the battle to conquer Canaan. What does the 'Holy War' mean when God said to Joshua to conquer Canaan? The land of Canaan was God's promise to Abraham but it was not yet the time for judgment since the sins of the Amorites were not ripe yet. It was finally after 400 years that the land was ready and so basically, the conquest of Canaan was God's judgment towards the Canaanites. This war, 'unlike the Muslim who decide to conduct suicidal terrorism towards many other countries just because they have different faith and conviction' is at a totally different level.

Spirit works when we, the whole congregation, are all one in heart with our pastors in Christ. The Israelites along with their new leader Joshua set out to spy the city of Jericho.

Spies to Jericho and Rahab, the Prostitute

_Joshua 2-6

In order to conquer any territory, one must spy the land first. Joshua sends two men to do the job. Probably, by his own experience of spying the land of Canaan from Kadesh Barnea during the days of

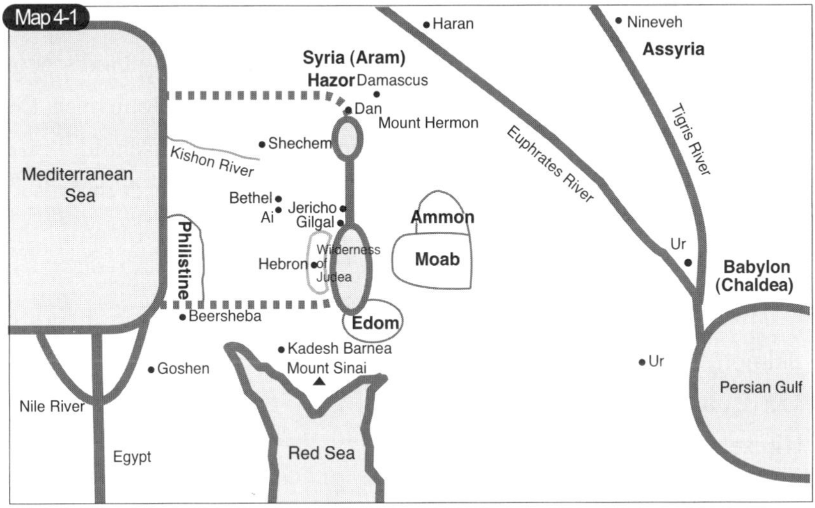

Period of Conquest The city of Jericho lies just west of the Jordan River alongside the Dead Sea. Jerusalem is on the left of the Dead Sea. This time period is before the temple of Jerusalem was built. The valley of Ayalon where Israel attacked the southern alliance is located on the way from Tel Aviv to Jerusalem. The capital of Israel today is Tel Aviv where it used to be the harbor of Joppa.

Moses, he might have judged that two men who had faith (believing in the invisible God's promise than the visual aspects) would be sufficient to carry out the task.

By the time when the two spies were inside of Jericho, the people in that city were noticeably scared in guarding the city. They had heard about the fall of the kingdoms of the Amorites, Bashanites, and Moabites by the Israelites. The two spies hid inside the house of the prostitute, Rahab. Her action in harboring the spies stemmed not from fear, but from belief that Israel's God is the true God which commends her faith.

Obviously she had never met any Israelites before but she had heard of God's work through His people. Faith comes from hearing. The house of a prostitute was no doubt a good place to pick up information. Faith comes from hearing/listening and since she heard about God, therefore, she believed in Him. "I believe that God will certainly give this land to you. The hearts of people of Jericho have been melted down and they are in a daze."

As Rahab saved the lives of the spies, so she and her family come under God's protection - finding permanent home among God's people and becoming part of the great salvation story. "Believe in the Lord Jesus, and you shall be saved, you and your household." (Acts 16:31) But why did the spies tell her to tie a 'cord of scarlet thread' as a symbol of promise? (See Joshua 2:18-19) It symbolizes the blood of the Lamb, blood of Christ.

Threader: The biblical scholars interpret that Rahab married Salmon who was one of the two spies sent to Jericho and through her son Boaz became an ancestress not only of David but of Jesus Himself (Matthew 1:5).

Advance across the Jordan_Joshua 3

After completing the spying in the city of Jericho, the people of Israel are finally poised on the border of the Promised Land ready to advance across the Jordan River.

The impact of the Jordan River was great during the days of Joshua. The origin of the Jordan River comes from Mt. Hermon's melted snow and it is said that almost 65 tons of water flow into the Jordan River per day. The width of the lower part of the Jordan River was approximately 800 meters (approx. 1 kilometer) which reflects that it was quite a big river. Especially, it was known to overflow over all of its banks when the heavy late rain poured right before the days of harvest season, drowning the fields of crops. Many people who visit the Holy Land imagining the adventurous cross of the Jordan River by the Israelites are disappointed when they actually see what the river has become. It is more of a streamlet (brook) now and literally a 'jump' away. The water streaming from Lake Galilee into the Jordan River flows underground through a conduit pipe and is used for developing the irrigation channel in the Negev Desert so the water has dried up over the years.

During Joshua's days, how did the people cross over such a great river as the Jordan? As you recall, God had separated the Red Sea by stirring easterly winds throughout the night and the Israelites witnessed it in front of their eyes. But unfortunately, the praises and the memory of miraculous event were soon forgotten. So God did not separate the Jordan River this time.

God's Strategic Order

Before the Israelites crossed over the Jordan River, God prepared the people of Israel through Joshua. Basically before the conquest of Canaan, they had to believe that the seven tribes were going to be destroyed since God was with them.

God prepared their faith by:

First, by commanding the priests to step into the water while carrying the Ark of the Covenant and stand 'still' when they approached to the edge of the water which symbolized that it is God who leads and guides. As believers today, we can go forward to Father through the blood of Christ but the people in the Old Testament period had to follow the Ark by looking at it from a distance.

Second, by consecrating the people. Meaning 'to prepare ourselves before God' by purification and self-examination in the light of what God requires. In the last days when we stand in front of the Lord, we must also "Be holy and blameless." (Ephesians 1:4) God's Kingdom may be experienced by being born again through baptism and the Holy Spirit.

Third, by believing the presence of the living God. Joshua's action in leading the people across the Jordan on dry land parallels Moses' crossing of the Red Sea: Joshua's position was established and the nation honored him. It was a sign to show the Israelites the presence of the living God.

Stepping into Jordan with God's Word

After consecrating their bodies and believing that God was with them, the high priests stepped into the Jordan River carrying the Ark of the Covenant. This was different from the crossing of the Red Sea. The people of Israel were being chased at the time so God cleared the way in haste by separating the waters by blowing the easterly wind all night so that they could cross over quickly into safety. But this time God worked together with the high priest and the people of Israel.

The minute the high priest dipped their feet into the water, it says in the Bible that 'the waters that were flowing down from above stood and rose up.' This is very true scientifically as well. The Jordan River did not split into two like the Red Sea but the water that was coming down went upstream which left the river bed dry. God had blocked the flow of the downstream water! When the high priests carrying the Ark of the Covenant (the Word) stepped in the water the pathway opened. What does this symbolize? The Promised Land opens by the energy of God's Word. It was the high priests with the Ark of the Covenant that led the Israelites across the Jordan just as God separated the waters and land by His Word on the third day of creation.

Worship in Gilgal_Joshua 4-5

A memorial stone altar consisting of 12 stones from the Jordan river symbolizing the 12 tribes was set up to mark the place where the priests stood and 12 to recognize the Israelites' first base camp in the new land at Gilgal. Taking over the city of Jericho was more of an offering to God than a mere achievement, a 'first fruit' of the conquest.

Also, before breaking into the enemy line, the Israelites performed circumcisions. The rite of circumcision had not been practiced for a long time because the covenant itself had been neglected for 40 years as a result of people's disbelief and disobedience to God. Now the sign of circumcision marks the new generation of Israel as God's own people. But can you imagine from the point of view of military strategy, this is a crazy act! After being circumcised, all men were lying down on their back and what if the enemies attacked them with swords. They would have been destroyed without even having a chance to fight at all.

It was a symbolic gesture of faith worship to God through their physical bodies. It was the Lord who is the Conqueror and not them. They believed that the victory comes through faith in God and obedience to His word, rather than through numerical or military superiority.

Shortly thereafter, they celebrated Passover with the first taste of the products in their own land. The meaning of 'Passover' is literally to pass over commemorating the exodus and the grace of redemption that the Israelites experienced. Through their 40 years of semi-nomadic life in the wilderness, they were not able to celebrate it so there had never been a Passover like this one.

All of these actions were worship, praising and glorifying the Lord of the highest.

Encounter with the Captain of the Lord_Joshua 5:13-15

The conquest of Canaan was a holy war and no one knew this better than Joshua, after his encounter with the 'captain of the army of the Lord.' Who was this captain? It was the angel sent by God which meant that God was at the head of the army. It is the same message as "Be anxious for nothing, but in everything by prayer and supplication with thanksgiving let your requests be made known to God." (Philippians 4:6)

This applies to us because we are confronted with all kinds of problems in our lives. And the only thing we must do is to kneel down and give worship to God. There is no need to cry or be anxious about anything. God sends His angel who arrives 'now' when we pray and worship Him and our problems start to resolve.

Who should have been standing in the frontline if it wasn't for Joshua and the captain of the Lord? Most likely, it should have been the tribes of Reuben, Gad and half of the Manasseh tribe who had crossed over the Jordan in battle array before the Israelites. The way in which the entire line up was: 5,000 men from the tribes that settled already in the east side of the Jordan, then, the seven priests carrying the seven trumpets of rams' horns, next, followed by the priests carrying the Ark of the Covenant and finally the security guards and the rest of the people of Israel thereafter.

Threader: The captain of the Lord (angel) stood in front because it was during the Old Testament period. But today, just like the hymn (hymn #398) verse, it is Jesus who stands in front of us now.

Joshua then commanded the people saying, "You shall not shout nor let your voice be heard, nor let a word proceed out of your mouth, until the day I tell you." (Joshua 6:10) Why such a command? We must recall how the people of Israel behaved during the journey in the wilderness. They were constantly grumbling and blaming Moses for bringing them to suffer in the desert. But they all obeyed by the word 'silence.' It was a war of nerves for the men of Jericho: day after day the encircling troops, the trumpet blasts, the silent army, building up to the great climax of the seventh day. The walls of Jericho collapsed. It has been a mutual understanding by scholars and scientists that the wall collapsed due to the resonance of an earthquake. But God's order to the people was to obey in silence by 'encircling the wall' which was actually a very simple method.

The Power of Worship

The wall had collapsed but the army of Jericho did not come after the Israelites with swords or anything. It was because the captain of the Lord had fought ahead of them. This is the power of worship. Who fights? Humans. We, humans, are not only made of dust but of

The Power of Resonance, Collapsed by Earthquake?

How do you think the walls of Jericho collapsed? According to the common grounds of the experts of methodology of construction and scientists, the resulting collapse was due to the 'power of resonance and an earthquake.'

First, the wall of Jericho collapsed due to the effect of resonance. In truth, the power of resonance is way beyond our imagination. The classic example is the Tacoma Narrows Bridge in Washington, D.C. that was built in November 7, 1940. The bridge was constructed with superstructure that was designed with the newest technology to sustain typhoons of any sort but it collapsed at the slightest wind. It was also recognized for its design worldwide and was a pride of U.S. technology of engineering. It was constructed to sustain a windshield factor of 190km speed but collapsed at only 70km speed after three months of completion.

In order to find the cause of the bridge's collapse, F. B. Farquharson, a Professor of the University of Washington and other top notch University engineers in the U.S. were hired. After their investigation, the cause was revealed that the collapse was due to the power of the resonance vibrations and not the strong gust of wind. All steel or concrete consist of its own oscillation and when a tremor comes from the exterior coinciding with its own vibration, the amplitude increases tremendously and this is what is referred to as resonance. It is said that if the resonance continues repeatedly, no matter how strong a material may be, the destruction of the object is inevitable. Since the Tacoma Bridge was a suspension bridge, whenever a wind blew, a slight vibration occurred and the tremor matched with its own oscillation frequency. In other words, the strength of the wind was not the issue but that the slightest wind and the tremor of the bridge's oscillation were in resonance, which caused the bridge to collapse.

Apparently, this was not the only bridge that collapsed due to resonance. It is recorded as an accident of resonance when the British Calvary troops marched over the suspension bridge near Manchester in 1831. The march in cadence and the bridge's oscillation amplitude coincided that it collapsed. This is the same principle as that a voice of a soprano can break a crystal glass.

Second, the collapse of the wall of Jericho was due to an 'earthquake.'

It has already been revealed by the geologist that the valley of Jordan was set up as one big single story. Jericho is located in between the two plates that are moving to the opposite direction which causes especially frequent earthquakes. The mud bricks that are ruined by severe erosion have left trace of earlier periods of life in Jericho.

At the time of Exodus in 1446 B.C., the number of Israelite men was 603,550 (Numbers 1:46) and if women and children were included, the number would be estimated around 2 million people altogether. With this in mind, probably the approximate number of people during the conquest of Jericho would have been around 1 million. The repeated impact of these people circling the city once a day for six days must have triggered the resonance weakening the ground. Finally on the 7th day, when the priests blew the trumpets, Joshua said to the people, "Shout! For the Lord has given you the city." (Joshua 6:16) The fall of the wall of Jericho may possibly be explained in a scientific approach either resonance or earthquake but the most important message that we must focus on is that the people of Israel obeyed God's command by keeping silent while encircling Jericho.

spirit in us. The words of Rahab, "I know that the Lord has given you the land, and that the terror of you has fallen on us, and that all the inhabitants of the land have melted away before you." (Joshua 2:9) The word 'melted away' means that they had lost consciousness. God had grasped the spirits of the people of Jericho.

The walls of Jericho did not collapse by mere encircling of the people. Victory is in the hands of God and it was the captain of the Lord who caused the wall of Jericho to collapse. God had received the worship given by the people of Israel in Gilgal and sent His captain. The emphasis must be given to the power and importance of worship at all times.

Spiritual Search 13

The Sense of Belonging

The essence of all spirits attributes to love. Therefore, human spirit is bound to love another person. For the same reason, God created Eve as 'Ezer' (Helper) for Adam for it is not good for a man to be alone.

What this all means is that we, as humans, love ourselves. It is essential to love yourself. If not, you would become self-destructive. But, on the other hand, if you were to love only yourself and not others, then your spirit becomes the spirit of Satan -- spirit of the world. Based on loving yourself, you must have a loving nature for others as well.

The spirit of the world (Satan) makes you love the world. Ultimately, you end up becoming self-centered in the end. If so, you would constantly seek out for your own interest only and not care for others as long as you are satisfied. The down turn of it is that you become lonely since there is no one but yourself. That is why the spirit of the world is a spirit of solitude. Being alone is not good because it allows. Satan to grab you into a captivity of solitude. Hell is a place of eternal solitude. There is no one but you and this status is what we call 'hell.'

What is God's spirit? It is a spirit of love. When the Spirit of God comes inside us, His love fills our heart. It is not us holding on to God but God who fills our hearts with love. That is why our heart is content and nothing is lacking when the spirit of God is in us.

We come across the so-called self-righteous people in our lives. They normally do not listen to others. Among them, there are also people with God given special gifts. Initially, they do great works of God but as time goes by, the spirit of Satan penetrates and they forget that their role is to be a God's angel' (servant) and become self-righteous in the end. Those who have become self-righteous after receiving the gifted works of the Holy Spirit start to have dull ears and also ignore the pastors in church. They claim that they listen to God's voice directly so no one, whether it is from a church member or even from the pastors, can tell them anything.

The same thing applies to those who are seeking power of authority. "Whoever is below me, obey!" is their attitude. Success has made them lose their sense of belonging, with others. Why? One cannot become enemies with someone who is physically far away. It happens when the sense of belonging breaks with someone close to you either by disappointment or betrayal and when the despair starts to creep inside. Ultimately, it makes you feel as if there is no one in the world except you. Feelings of hatred is stirred by Satan's spirit. We have witnessed many couples who became enemies with the other, which all stemmed from losing the sense of belonging. Next in line would be the friends and then the business partners.

We must understand that there are limitations in feeling the sense of belonging but at the same time, we cannot live alone. One of the Ten Commandments is: To love God first and then love others. True sense of belonging comes from when we feel the love of Jesus. God's love is eternal and never changes. Because it is spirit, it does not sway according to the five senses of the body unlike humans who have limitations. When we are filled with the Holy Spirit (Helper), we are able to let go of all the bitterness and anger and instead be kind; to forgive one another, just as God in Christ has forgiven us. (Ephesians 4:31-32)

By doing so, only then do we really experience true peace, joy and harmony in our heart. That is why we want all the people of the world to believe in Jesus. Those who do not believe in Jesus cannot experience the real joy and instead live in the midst of all the ups and downs once the sense of 'belonging' is shattered. Ultimately leading to eternal hell. There is no salvation without the Spirit of Jesus.

The reason why Jesus emphasized "to love your God with all your heart, mind and soul" is because without the Spirit of Jesus one cannot have the heart of honoring parents or loving neighbors.

PEOPLE CONFRONTED AT THE CROSSROAD OF BLESSING AND CURSE

Joshua 7-24

The people of Israel had successfully taken over the biggest city of Canaan, Jericho and yet were defeated in a much smaller city of Ai. The 'new' generation had stepped into the land of Canaan after the death of all the unbelieving 1st generation but an event occurred. Through this incident, the faith of Israel became stronger and eventually distribution of land took place after Ai was conquered.

An Incident in Ai_ Joshua 7-8

Defeat in the City of Ai_Joshua 7-8

Achan Defies God's Ban

Jericho is known to be the oldest and the biggest city of Canaan. According to the archeologist, the Israel's attack took place around 5000 years ago either 1250 B.C. or 1350 B.C. which is about the 13th or 14th century B.C. That is about 3000 years or more ago from now. Some parts of the city walls still exist even to this day. In any event, the point is that the people of Israel had conquered a big city.

The Israelites now felt confident that Ai, a small city which was only a short distance away from Bethel, could easily be conquered so to that end, Joshua did not pray to God as he did in the past. "We don't need to pray to God for such a small matter as this. Just send 3,000 men." How easily human minds fall into self-absorbing attitudes! This was a trap and an act of the good and evil.

We are bound to have negative aspects after the positive. Israel was struck down by the men of Ai and was defeated. If the news traveled to other tribes in Canaan, the fate of Israel would be at stake. One must knock on the doors of heaven when the shadows of hell surface. At that point, Joshua fell on his face before the Ark and prayed fervently to God, "O Lord, you have promised to give us Canaan and all the inhabitants of the land as well as promised to wipe out the seven tribes of the Canaanites. What will You do for Your great name?" (Joshua 7:9) Joshua prayed in tears for the sake of God's name. Then, God answered, "Israel has sinned, and they have also transgressed My covenant which I commanded them. And they have even taken some of the things under the ban and have both stolen and deceived. Moreover, they have also put them among their own things." (Joshua 7:11)

Joshua then realized what had happened and picked out the one who had sinned against God's law as mentioned in the book of Deuteronomy. His name was Achan who defied God's ban.

God had commanded 'three killings' upon entering the land of Canaan. The 'three killings' does not mean to kill three times but to kill three things. First, to kill all those that was breathing. Anything that was alive whether it was human beings or animals. Why did God pass on such a severe judgment? Judgment time had come for the Amorites since their sins were overflowing so everyone and everything had to be wiped out. The idolatry of Baal would come in if the Amorites were kept alive. Second, towns were to be burnt down because temples of Baal existed in all villages. Third, they were to destroy and burn all confiscated items except for gold and silver since they were to be used for the tableware for the Holy Place.

Achan defiled God's ban. The looted items, a leather mantle (in today's term, it would be a 'mink' coat) made in Babylon, 200 shekels of silver and a gold bar of 50 shekels in weight altogether were hidden underneath his tent. Probably, these items were not much, but to Achan, it meant a tremendous opportunity to become rich. The whole nation was shamed before their Canaanite enemies and according to God's command, the Israelites put to death not only Achan but his entire family clans and burned them with fire after they had stoned. They raised a tower of stones over him, symbolizing the curse of Achan's disobedience and named it as 'the valley of Achor' to this day. The disobedience of one individual touches the whole community; where wrong has been done, there is corporate, as well as individual, accountability.

Victory is in the Hands of God - Even the Smallest is at God's Will

I recall from my early childhood days a hymn (Hymn #355) when I mispronounced the word 'Achor' and thought nothing of it but as I became an adult, I discovered that it was the place where Achan was stoned to death by following the materialistic things of the world rather than the Word of God. The prime message of this hymn was "to keep the Word of God even where worldly temptations exist."

Why were the Israelites defeated in Ai? It's because they assumed that they could easily take over a small city as Ai by sending only 3,000 men. But battles were won only when they followed God's strategy. This was all in God's plan. The lesson here is that God's word is the tree of life and that we must prevent from eating from the tree of the good and evil. The eternal truth of the Word applies to our daily lives and the core message to us from the defeat of Ai(Israel to Ai) is that even though it may be the smallest or an insignificant matter, we must not rely on our own thoughts.

In the earlier days soon after their exodus and right before entering the Mt. Sinai, Joshua was in the battle with the Amalekites. While they were in the battleground, Moses prayed with his hands raised. When his arms were raised, the Israelites won and defeated in the battle when his hands were down. So Aaron and Hur supported his hands and ultimately won the battle. Realizing the importance of prayer and worship to God, Joshua's flight and ambush strategy makes capital out of Israel's previous defeat.

In God's name he took possession of the land and the covenant was sworn as Moses had commanded in Deuteronomy 27. Joshua was given a light spear whereas Moses was given a staff as a symbol of leadership and throughout his battles the spear did not leave his hand. "Joshua did not withdraw his hand with which he stretched out the javelin until he had utterly destroyed all the inhabitants of Ai."(Joshua 8:26) If you wish to succeed then you must pray.

Conquering Entire Territory of Canaan

The Cunning Act of the Gibeonites_Joshua 9

Gibeon was an important city that was located about 5 miles north of Jerusalem. The Israelites had been forewarned against any alliance with local people. The Gibeonites employed such a cunning, disguising (even to the pretense as if the news of the recent victories at Jericho and Ai has not reached them) that they not only concluded the treaty for themselves but included three other cities in it. Setting out as envoys in worn out appearances, the Gibeonites approached the men of Israel and said, "We have come from a far country and have no desire to fight with you. We want to have a treaty with you. Our wish is to become your slaves, so please accept us."

The decision was not consulted with God and Israel could not draw back from a treaty sealed in friendship (meal eaten together). The worst they could do was to reduce the Gibeonites to slave status. Ultimately, other tribes of the Canaanites heard about their betrayal and it led Israel promptly to get involved into war.

● ● Attack by the Kings of the South _Joshua 10

The kings of the south attack Gibeon but at the command of the Lord, all five Amorite kings are killed and their city states (all except Jerusalem) are destroyed following the root at Beth-horon. "The battle is not yours but God's." (2 Chronicles 20:15) Per God's command, every breathing human were to be slaughtered as they fled towards the valley of Aijalon.

Let's visualize how time consuming it must have been chasing after them. It's not like today where you could throw bombs at them but the fact that they had to be killed one by one with swords or spears. Basically a day was not enough to do the job! Out of desperation, Joshua pleas to God, "O sun, stand still at Gibeon, And O moon in the valley of Aijalon." (Joshua 10:12) So the sun stood still, and the moon stopped.

Obviously it is not the sun nor the moon that moves but the earth itself. In truth, it is God who "Upholds all things by the word of His power" as written in Hebrews 1:3. But what would be the outcome if the earth stopped for 24 hours? It would explode. In order to find whether this was actually happened or not, a research from an astronomical observatory was done and it revealed that the earth which should have circled within 24 hours did, in fact, actually took 48 hours to revolve at one point. "There was no day like that before it or after it, when the Lord listened to the voice of a man; for the Lord fought for Israel." (Joshua 10:14) Hence, how strong the power of Joshua's prayer!

The powerful king of Hazor, commanding his vassals, assembles an even more formidable alliance than that of the south. Although the strategic cities were in Israel's hands within a short time of their entry into Canaan, mopping up operations took a great deal of time.

With the commander of the Lord on their side, Israelites defeated the kings of the north as well. Now kings of south, central and northern Canaan were all defeated under Joshua. The people of Israel have now conquered the entire land of Canaan completely.

Division of Land

Promise Being Fulfilled_Joshua 13~21

After the conquest of the land of Canaan, the latter part of the book of Joshua talks about the dividing the land among the tribes. The promise of Abraham, Isaac and Jacob is about to be fulfilled now. God appeared to Abraham when he arrived in Shechem and said, "To your descendants I will give this land." (Genesis 12:7); God also appeared to Jacob in Bethel when he laid down on one of the stones, "I will give this land to you and to your descendants." (Genesis 28:13) A promise of almost 500 years old is about to be fulfilled.

The time has come for the Israelites to finally receive the inheritance originating from the promise of Abraham, Isaac and Jacob. Distributing the land among the clans for settlement symbolizes how it takes on a sacred identity. Its possession is seen as the covenant gift of God. As we know, the land east of Jordan had already been allotted to the tribes Reuben and (half) Manasseh during Moses' time.

But before dividing the land to the 12 tribes, God had set up three governing principles:

First was the blessing of Jacob (Genesis 49). Before Jacob's death, he had specifically expressed to his 12 sons the blessing and curse through the division of the land.

Second was the size and number of tribe. Each tribe had different

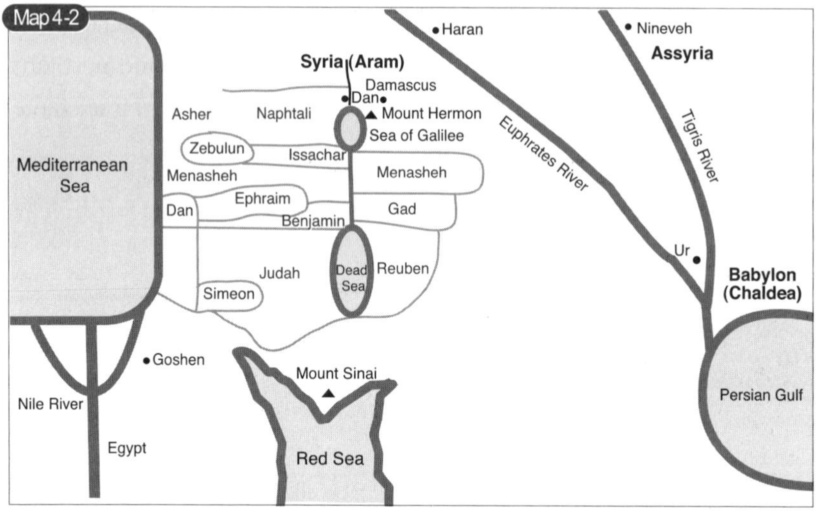

Period of Conquest-Division of the Land: After the battle, the distribution of the land (God's inheritance) is given to the 12 tribes of Israel. It is) distributed according to the blessings of Jacob. Joseph's two sons, Manasseh and Ephraim receives the portion of the tribe of Levis.

counts.

Third was the relationship between each tribe. Distribution of land was determined on the relationship they had with one another. Rueben, the firstborn, had defiled his father's bed (Genesis 49:4) and was given the land east of Jordan. He later gets absorbed by the tribes of Moab.

Simeon, the 2nd son, received the furthest south and eventually scatters away. Simeon and Levi had used their swords in slaughtering the men of Shechem out of anger due to their sister's rape. "I will disperse them in Jacob, And scatter them in Israel." (Genesis 49:7)

Levi, the 3rd son having collaborated with his brother Simeon failed to receive any land. Levi's portion went to the two sons of Joseph, Manasseh and Ephraim. The Levites were set apart for priestly service; their portion was to be God Himself. However, they were provided 48 cities with pasture, by the other tribes.

Judah, the 4th son, received the most blessing. They received the largest land near the Red Sea. Not only were they big in numbers but also received abundant blessings from Jacob. The tribes of Judah became the ancestor of David and Jesus Christ. "Judah, your brothers shall praise you ..." (Genesis 49:8)

Dan, the 5th son, received a land upwards of Judah. During the period of the Judges, the assigned land which brought them up against the Philistines and other tough enemies in the south, the tribes of Dan failed to conquer it and eventually settled in the far north.

Naphtali, the 6th son, received the land next to the Lake Galilee. The town of Nazareth where Jesus grew up was around this region.

Gad, the 7th son, had already received land on the eastern part of Jordan.

Asher, the 8th son, also received a good coastal land of the Mediterranean.

Zebulun, the 9th son and Issachar, the 10th son received the inner land in the north.

Joseph, the 11th son received the blessing of the firstborn and inherited the land for two tribes. The tribes of Manasseh received the land facing one another with the Jordan River in between. The tribes of Ephraim received the upper land of Jericho.

Jacob's most beloved wife, Rachel and her two sons, Joseph and Benjamin were combined and given land together. But the tribes of Benjamin later got absorbed by Judah. (The Northern Kingdom is formed with the tribes of Judah and Benjamin.)

The division of the land to the 12 tribes was completed as God had promised. They all hold on to their tribal inheritance firmly acknowledging that it was forbidden to sell or give away since it was God's gift to them.

Threader: That is why Naboth refused to sell his inheritance (vineyard) to Ahab and said, "The Lord forbid me that I should give you the inheritance of my fathers." (1 Kings 21:3)

Loyal Pledge at Shechem_Joshua 24

Some years have elapsed since the division of the land and Joshua has reached the end of a long life and leaves no single successor. It is therefore vital to ensure that the leaders keep the law and remain faithful to God. God who keeps His promises; God who gave them the land; God who has driven out great and powerful nations. Joshua assembles the elders at Shechem to renew the covenant as follows: "If it is disagreeable in your sight to serve the Lord, choose for yourselves today whom you will serve: whether the gods which your fathers served which were beyond the river, or the gods of the Amorites in whose land you are living; but as for me and my house, we will serve the Lord." (Joshua 24:15) The stipulations are made, with the warnings about the consequences of disobedience. God is love so He never forces anyone to respond to His love. God pours His love and patiently waits until the person voluntarily responds. Based on this same concept, Joshua asks the people of Israel to 'choose' at their own freewill. His own readiness to commit himself wholly to God remains unwaveringly and the people are eager to follow him in renewing the covenant, showing the sufficient tribute to his leadership. His 'we shall serve the Lord' is echoed by the voice of the people, "We too shall serve the Lord; He is our God" (Joshua 24:18) and it is an indication the strength of Joshua's influence for good fulfilling his duty of call until his last days. But unfortunately, even after the loyal pledge at Shechem, the elders and the people of Israel forsake the Lord which marks the new beginning of a sad period of the Judges on this same land. "The sons of Israel did what was evil in the sight of the Lord, and forgot the Lord their God, and served the Baals and the Asheroth." (Judges 3:7)

Offering Basket is for the Devil?

"For the love of money is a root of all sorts of evil, and some by longing for it have wandered away from the faith, and pierced themselves with many grieves." (1 Timothy 6:10) People who love money do not want anyone whether it's family, children or even God. Money is all they need because it takes care of pretty much everything in the world such as physical lust, visual satisfaction and comfort. There is no space for God for them.

For this reason, we give offerings at church because that's when the devil (self-interest) departs from us. One pastor even made a symbolic comment that an offering basket is for the devil.

The moment you give an offering, selfishness departs from you. By the same token, it is not right to be forced to give when you are incapable of giving it in the first place. In the book of Acts, a fate of Ananias and Sapphira is written. This couple voluntarily makes a pledge that they will give all the money from their property sold but leaves something behind for themselves resulting in death in the end. This is not the proper way to commit. An offering must be given at one's ability and discretion. It is the willing heart of gratitude that must follow with an offering, not the amount.

Spirits travel between humans unlike animals so when there's a group of people gathered at one place, the work of spirit is bound to occur whether it is God's Spirit or Satan's. If you hold on to money then the spirit of Satan starts to work. Often times we think that money will solve all the problems in life. Money brings wealth but once your health goes down, nothing matters anymore. The wealthy give enormous inheritances to their children and the outcome of their lifestyle doesn't necessarily guarantee happiness. Instead, there's always something negative going on in their lives. This is what happens if you become slaves of money.

Material blessings follow when we live according to God's Word. Look at the universe and marvel at the power of God's creation. No matter how we try to own the estate or leave footmarks on the earth-it's beyond our control. No matter how much we eat there'll always be something to eat. It's an endless creation. We're living in a day that traveling to space and mars is possible but there are still countless stars around us that have yet to be explored.

According to the Hebrews 1:3, it is God who upholds all things by the Word of His power. So basically, it is God who controls everything on this earth. The Spirit of God, the Creator, who is in our hearts, reveals Himself through the Word when we admit and confess to Him through prayers. The only thing we can do is to connect the incidents and the environment that surround us with God through prayers, realizing that it is God who is in control, not us.

A rich man needs not to carry anything but a credit card. In the same manner, as believers of God we only need to continuously reaffirm God who is already in our heart. "I thank you Lord for taking care of all the necessities of my daily life. You provide all things I need appropriately at the right time. Praise you, O Lord! And, thank you." Once you are convinced in your heart, you have nothing to fear because God is your provider.

The Blessing and Curse - Two Different Paths

Since the Old Testament is a shadow of the New Testament, numerous ceremonies are mentioned. It is teaching us the way to worship God and how our lives must be led.

Upon entering the land of Canaan, Joshua had taken over the two cities, Jericho and Ai. There were still many more cities to be conquered ahead of them. Through the defeat in the city of Ai, Joshua had learned that without God's interference, nothing can be achieved. So Joshua called to the nation and repeated Moses' words to Israel, reciting the covenant of blessings and curses to them in Mount Ebal. (Joshua 8:30) "I have set before you life and death, blessings and curses."(Deuteronomy 11:26-28)

Knowing it was not enough, God wanted the people to remember it in their heart through ceremonial assembly. So Joshua gathered the people at Shechem which was above Bethel; on the left of Shechem was Mt. Gerizim and Mt. Ebal on the right. "Ebal" sounds very close to the word 'evil' in English. Apparently, blessings were proclaimed in Mt. Gerizim and curses in Mt. Ebal. (Joshua 8:33) The 12 tribes were divided into two groups, the ark was left behind in Shechem and the six tribes each walked separately towards Mt. Gerizim and Mt. Ebal.

Two different paths are the roads of blessing and curse. The blessings would follow 'if you obey the word of God' and 'if you leave God's word and worship foreign gods, there will be judgment and curse.' The blessing of obedience and the consequences of disobedience is loud and clear. This is the exposition of the law referred in the book of Deuteronomy, the heart of the old covenant. In essence, it is the core message of the entire Bible for all Christians. Remember to obey and keep faith. This is the key to God's blessings. Forgetting God in the new life is the same as courting disaster. "It shall come about, when the Lord your God brings you into the land where you are entering to possess it, that you shall place the blessing on Mount Gerizim and the curse on Mount Ebal."(Deuteronomy 11:29) Upon entering the Promised Land, this ceremony was to be observed and carried out. This message was to be sealed in their hearts through the ceremony since knowledge was not sufficient enough to keep and act in it.

The 17 books of prophecy also talk about the two paths. The underlying background of these books lies when the nation was in the midst of destruction after the end of the period of the divided kingdom. The Israelites had thrown away God and were deeply into worshipping idols at the time. These books stir the Israelites through the message that it is not too late for them to return to God. Throughout the Old Testament, this message challenges us to make a choice which path we want to follow regardless of your return whether it is God's way or idolatry.

The two different paths are also mentioned in the New Testament. "Enter by the narrow gate; for the gate is wide, and the way is broad that leads to destruction, and many are those who enter by it. For the gate is small, and the way is narrow that leads to life, and few are those who find it." (Matthew 7:13-14) There is definitely a gate that leads to life and destruction. More fearful words follow. Jesus said, "Not everyone who says to Me, 'Lord, Lord,' will enter the kingdom of heaven; but he who does the will of My Father who is in heaven will enter." (Matthew 7:21) There is a clear distinction between the two paths: one for those who obey God's Word (those in Spirit) and the other for those who don't (those in flesh) - the narrow and wide gates.

All the parables of Jesus clearly talks about the two paths. For instance, the parable of the ten virgins: five virgins were ready with oil in their lamps and the other five without oil where all are related to the believers of God. The part saying "They will not enter the wedding feast of the Little Lamb" refers to the five virgins without oil in their lamps. (Matthew 25:1-13) Similar parable of the marriage feast where a man was found not dressed in wedding clothes is the same message regarding the two paths. "Friend, how did you come in here without wedding clothes? And he was speechless. Then the king said to the servants, 'Bind him hand and foot, and cast him into the outer darkness; in that place there shall be weeping and gnashing of teeth.'"(Matthew 22:12-13)

It clearly states that on judgment day, a distinctive separation of the sheep from the goats will take place as well as those who have and have not fed, clothed and took care of the sick as mentioned in the passages. (Matthew 25:31-46)

Majority of the books and letters in the New Testament all relate to those who act according to the Holy Spirit and to those who follow their flesh. Paths for these two different types of people are clearly explained. Even among the believers, there are some who act according to the Holy Spirit and those who follow their flesh. The conclusion of the entire Bible (both the Old and New Testament) is whether you act according to the Holy Spirit or follow their fleshly needs these are the two paths. Following the 'flesh' means doing whatever you please and desire. In other words, following wherever the Satan drags you. (1 Corinthians 12:2) The Bible tells us to become Christians who follow the Holy Spirit wherever it leads us. Obviously, this is something that cannot be achieved easily and the only way to succeed in it is to pray in Spirit at all times. (Ephesians 6:18) We become a true Christian when we pray in Spirit and frankly there is no other alternative. To a true Christian, the fruit of the Holy Spirit starts to appear in our daily life. (Galatians 5:22-23).

SINFUL PERIOD CONTINUES

Judges

The people of Israel were led to the land of milk and honey. They conquered the promised land and divided the land between the 12 tribes. It was now up to them to make this land into God's Kingdom or not but Israel began to sin from the beginning. Israel's sin during the period of Judges was this: God was no longer their King.

The Worst Sinful Period

Doing Whatever Was Right in His Own Eyes_Judges 21:25

The Promised Land was delivered to Israel, but it did not mean that the Promised Land became God's Kingdom automatically. Only when God becomes the leader of the nation that it can be referred as 'God's Kingdom.' This was the homework left for the Israelites at the moment. It was a difficult and unsettled time, when the scattered tribes were without central leadership, held together only by their common faith. Loyalty to God meant a strong united nation.

There are three elements to become a nation: territory (land), nation (people) and ruler. That is why God multiplied Israel into a great nation first and then delivered the land to them. The only thing that was left for them in order to become a nation was a ruler, God's reign. Through the loyal pledge at Shechem, God

[Chart 3] The Pattern of Sinful Days during the Period of the Judges

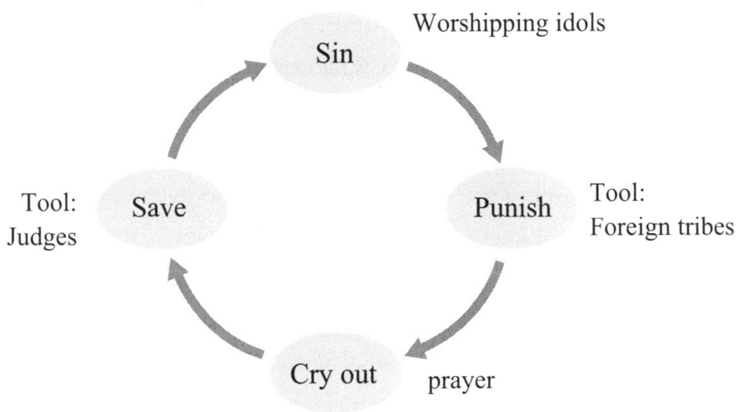

gave 100% freewill to the people of Israel. It was God's intention that the Israelites would voluntarily at their own freewill select Him as their leader. In other words, a world that is governed by God is a true God's Kingdom.

Threader: It was God's mercy and intervention in response to the cries of the people of Israel.

Through the battles of Joshua, it was God's salvation of justification that they were able to conquer the land. If conquering the Canaan was the salvation of justification then the process of making the land into God's Kingdom could be referred as the salvation of sanctification.

The period of the Judges from the beginning to the end was recorded as: "In those days there was no king in Israel; everyone did what was right in his own eyes." (Judges 21:25) The regularity and persistent sinfulness of the human scene in Judges was a depressing one. The nation's fortunes followed a monotonous, repetitive cycle. Israel deserted God for the local gods - forgetting all the trainings received during their 40 years of journey in the wilderness. The deteriorating lifestyle led them to destruction in the end. Actually, this is the same outcome for Christians today because after believing in Jesus, they fail in the process of sanctification. The 400 years of Judges is known as the worst sinful period.

God wanted theocracy which means that He governs people directly rather than through another ruler. The mid-ruler would be a king. The people of Israel did not want God to rule. Why? The spirit of Satan interfered so as a result they didn't like it. Satan's spirit has given us 'Demo' (general public) which is referred to as 'Democracy' today rather than "Theo" (God) which is referred to as "Deocracy." The general public becomes the master. In reverse, it meant people became their own master rather than God. God's Kingdom (salvation of sanctification) could not be formed since everyone did what was right in their own eyes. But God wanted Israel to acknowledge Him as the supreme commander because God's Kingdom cannot be accomplished when the general public takes over. Minority belongs to God, not majority. We have clearly witnessed that it is the minority not majority through the incident of the spies sent to Canaan. If the so-called 'Democracy' took over, then God should have listened to the 10 unfaithful spies and have the Israelites returned back to Egypt but as we know the outcome -the two faithful servants' (Joshua and Caleb) hands were lifted instead.

Tools of Salvation and Tools of Sin

There was a reason behind God's command that all the seven tribes of Canaan had to be driven out. It was to prevent Israel from the idolatry of Baal and worshipping of the Baal. The Israelites still had much work to do to secure the land and to drive out the inhabitants there but they failed to do so. The remaining Canaanites lived on the coast and were great traders. So much that the word 'Canaanite' came to mean 'merchant' in Hebrew. The Israelites were disadvantaged against the superior iron weapons and iron-clad chariots of their enemies at the time so instead of persisting to drive the Canaanites out, they lost their courage completely and were content to settle alongside of these people. As a result, they were increasingly under the great political influence of the people around them and lured by unacceptable religious practices. Baal and other gods were adopted into Israelite worship along with God, thus compromising the ideals God had set forth in the law. Forgetting the words of Joshua "Choose for yourselves today whom you will serve ... " (Joshua 24:15) Israel chose Baal instead of God as their king. Forsaking God and turning to the local gods around them brought weakness and division into Israel but most importantly as prophesied in Deuteronomy 28 regarding the two paths. Curse was inevitable.

God continued His program of revelation by showing Israelites that He was faithful to the covenant of curses and penalties as He was to the covenant of benefits and blessings. His grace did not negate His justice. Whenever Israel sinned, God used the neighboring nations as a tool of punishment. We must realize that when God punishes, we experience all kinds of turbulences in our personal lives such as health problems, bankruptcy, loss of jobs, and sudden changes making us run away. God's message must be heard loud and clear through the book of Judges. If we fail to fulfill God's Kingdom, our physical body will be hit. We tend to cry out "Oh please, save me!" only at the last minute when our body hurts.

At the last stage of the Judges, Israel does not even cry out because they have completely abandoned God. Once your faith hits rock bottom, you don't even bother to call out to God even when you're desperate. But know this, God is patient, just, and merciful; God is always ready to save you when you call upon Him.

Judges were people who had the Spirit of the Lord in them. It was not up to an individual to become a judge on their own by saying, "I'll become a judge and a warrior to fight against the foreign tribes since I'm strong." The judges of Israel were not simply legal advisers but also had other duties. They acted as a substitute of the king and delivered the tribes or nation from the enemy's oppression, winning their laurels in active service and also acted as a high priest. A judge was not a king but a substitute, playing king's role for 'one-time' whereas kings were hereditary.

The Israelites suffered at the hands of the Canaanites and cried out to God for help and each time, God periodically raised deliverers (judges) as His tool to save His people. Through the judges, God demonstrated His power and mercy by delivering the Israelites. All went well for a while; but once the judge died then the old pattern of infidelity reasserted itself. This shows the limitation of mankind. Once God takes care of a problem, bringing peace into our lives, the sinful nature of humans is ready to sprout once again. So having said that, it would be better to be thankful if a problem is unresolved because it is God's way of preventing us from further sinning.

Threader: Faithfulness and failures are basically the summary of the Old Testament. The wonder is God's constant love and concern. Despite unfaithfulness, God knows what will happen again. He answers and chooses to work with the most unpromising people. After exodus, from the period of the Judges, United Kingdom and up to the period of the Divided Kingdom, the Israelites went into exile and eventually destroyed by a foreign nation (Babylon).

The worst sinful days continue throughout each period; the book of Judges contains the sinful period of 400 years. Basically, the Israelites were experiencing a political, social and religious time of crisis. Having only recently gained their foothold in the Promised Land, they struggled to control the Israelites, maintain tribal unity and religious purity. In these turbulent times, there were inevitably battles for the land, tribal conflicts and lapses into paganism and idolatrous cult sites.

Knowledge Search 13

Reasons Why the Israelites Were Not Able to Throw Away the Idolatry of Baal

It was a great turmoil for the Israelites relating to the idolatry of Baal and other gods which existed during the period of the Judges. The Israelites started to worship Baal as soon as they entered Canaan and the Baal became increasingly influential to the Israelites until the period of the Divided Kingdom. What triggered them to worship Baal when they had witnessed the power and existence of living God?

1. The Israelites Believed God to be the God of War

The Israelites were nomadic tribes just as Abraham who traveled in donkey caravans. Isaac did some farming for a little while but for Jacob, pasturage (cattle farming) brought him great success. They took care of Pharaoh's cattle stocks in the land of Goshen in Egypt as well. They also assumed that God was the provider for food because of their experience with Him in the wilderness. Through their first victory against the Amalekites when entering the Mt. Sinai and through winning at all the major battles from the days of Joshua up to the period of the Judges, Israelites believed God was in control of all the battles.

As a result, the Israelites thought God was not in control of weather which was closely related to farming. Instead, they joined the Canaanites in their worship of Baal, believing this local god to be in control of the weather and the fertility of the land. (See 1 Kings 18 - challenge of 850 v. 1: high priests of the Baal against Elijah in Mt. Carmel)

2. Worshipping Baal was Extremely Stimulating Whereas Worshipping God was Painful

The father of the local god Baal is 'El' which originally means 'God.' Under this spirit "El" there are several sons and Baal is one of them. The Canaanites believed the drought was caused because the Baal, god of storm was downcast by the dominating power of the Baal, god of the ocean. In order to let the Baal, god of storm, escape from death, they believed that they had to do anything possible to wake up the Baal, god of storm, so he would pour rain and the Canaanites thought sexual stimulation would wake up the Baal's spirit. It is said that one would get aroused by looking at the sexual act of others. But in this case, in order to wake up the Baal spirit, they thought the massive groups of people conducting sexual acts would satisfy the needs. For this purpose, they built a temple, placed the statue of the Baal in the middle and performed group sex in front of it. The Canaanites regarded the Baal pouring out the sperm as the 'rain' and the act of group sex was regarded as their pure offering ceremony to Baal. Women working in the temple were referred as the religious caretakers, not prostitutes. Obviously, these kinds of acts could not be easily performed in a 'normal' state of mind so they inhaled or drank various types of substance beforehand (so-called narcotics in today's term). Prophet Hosea expressed these acts as "You are all adulterers like a heated oven stirring up fire." (Hosea.7:4)

On the contrary, what kind of worship did the Israelites perform for God? It was very difficult for the Israelites to give worship to an invisible God inside the temple. Not only were the animals brought to the sanctuary for the offerings but the Israelites had to kill it with their own hands. Their clothes were smeared with blood and sweat from peeling animal's skin all day long; then they also had to separate the intestines and chop the meat into cubes. From this process, one can imagine the odor and the hard work that these people had to endure to give the offering to God. This required an incredible sacrifice from their part.

So obviously, giving worship to Baal was no comparison to

God's worship -it was too easy. How convenient and great it was! All they had to do was relieve their physical lust whenever they were pleased and everything was taken care of. Regardless of the length of the training and the warnings the Israelites received, it was not easy for them to turn away from the Baal. Quite simply, it was easier to choose the physical needs rather than an invisible spirit.

In the ancient myth, a male commander of the earth was called the 'Baal' and a female god 'Baalite.' The myth of Baal spread throughout Asia and eventually created sexual promiscuity in India which is the reason why you can find the drawings of people conducting sexual acts around the male's genitals when you travel to the temples in India. You will also frequently find similar situations in the Buddhist temples of lamaseries. The idolatry of Baal then was transmitted to Europe and can be found in the Greek myths. The symbolic female flame bearer who is clothed transparently in the Olympic Games is actually the goddess of the temple of Baal. We must realize that this flame is not holy, but rather it is a flame of lust. Ashtaroth/Astartes who appears in the Greek myth as well as Venus in Roman myth are all the female gods of Baal. The immoral sexual acts of the world are all based on the Baals.

The ongoing problem throughout the Old Testament is: Who sends the 'rain' on this earth? It is why the Bible repeatedly tells us that it is God who sends the rain. (Deuteronomy 11: 8-17) Whatever we need to sustain ourselves boils down to this: "Is it God or the Baal?," "Is it me or God's doing?" Let us remember that the spirit of Satan vigorously encourages us to think that it is our ability and effort that we live because he wants us to reject the fact that it is by God's grace that we live. Ultimately, the Northern and Southern Kingdom of Israel were completely destroyed by following the Baal idolatry in the end. Let us remember this fact.

The 12 Judges

There were 12 judges raised during this period. The number is slightly different whether it is 12 or 13 depending on whether to include the military leader, Barak who fought in the battle with prophetess Deborah or not. The easiest way to remember the number of judges is to think of the 12 tribes of Israel. But the number is only for the purpose of easy reference and does not necessarily mean that the judges came out from each tribe.

Threader: Six of the 12 judges mentioned (namely: Othniel, Ehud, Deborah/Barak, Gideon, Jephthah and Samson) are described in some detail while the remaining names and their activities are restricted to a few lines. The judges that are mentioned in detail are referred to as the 'great judges.' I recall one church member who said that he would like to be recorded at length rather than in a 'restricted' few lines in the book of life by doing many works of God. This is an admirable attitude but on a serious note, if you read the book of Judges in depth, you will realize that the judges mentioned in detail did not necessarily have a good ending. Often times people who claim to do the great works of God made many mistakes along the way. The stories of local heroes which are told and retold down the years leave us with one message. The only 'true' judge is Jesus just as the conquests during Joshua's time imply that Christ is in control of their endeavors.

Othniel, Ehud and Shamgar were the first judges that appeared during the period of the Judges. The first judge, Othniel, was the brother of Caleb and was a valiant man. Ehud had formidable reputation for being a left-handed slinger and Shamgar was a farmer who wiped out 600 Philistines with his metal tipped pole (the ox-goad) and saved Israel. This shows us an example of how God periodically raised the most unpromising people by anointing each individual with the Holy Spirit at the most appropriate time to save Israel.

Prophetess Deborah and the Military Force of the Canaanites_Judges 4-5

Attack of the Canaanites_Judges 4:1-3

God's plan was to simultaneously wipe out the Canaanites as well as to punish the Israelites for abandoning Him in favor of the idolatry of the local gods. The Canaanites who continuously lived in God's promised land of milk and honey even after Joshua's distribution of land were used as a tool for God. The Israelites thought they wiped out all the Canaanites but instead, the Canaanites had 900 iron chariots and oppressed them severely for 20 years. The Canaanites assembled in an area called Megiddo, crossed the Kishon River and advanced towards Mt. Tabor where the Israelites were concentrated. So the Israelites cried out to the Lord and repented. (Judges 4:1-3) "God! Save us. Please forgive us for our sins."

The Faith of Military Leader, Barak

Deborah the prophetess was raised as a judge in the judicial sense,

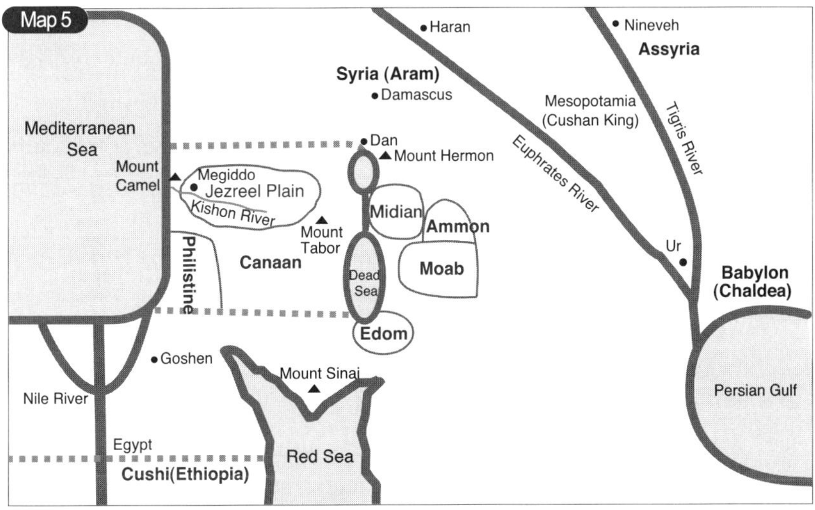

Period of the Judges Kishon River flows down from Mt. Carmel. Along the surrounding streamline is a valley where beaneath it is a rich plain field of Jezreel. This area is where the Canaanites lived.

a person of authority but being a female, she needed a man to fight with her. She sent for Barak, a military leader associated with the tribes of Zebulon in the upper part of Lake Galilee and gave him God's instruction: "Behold, the Lord, the God of Israel, has commanded, 'Go and march to Mount Tabor, and take with you ten thousand men from the sons of Naphtali and from the sons of Zebulun. And I will draw out to you Sisera, the commander of Jabin's army, with his chariots and his many troops to the river Kishon; and I will give him into your hand.'" (Judges 4:6-7) Rather than accepting the order, Barak said, "If you will go with me, then I will go; but if you will not go with me, I will not go." (Judges 4:8) Deborah responded, "I will surely go with you; nevertheless, the honor shall not be yours on the journey that you are about to take, for the Lord will sell Sisera into the hands of a woman." (Judges 4:9)

At a glimpse, it appears that Barak lacked in faith but we must focus in his humility more closely. He believed that God was with Deborah and knew that the victory was in God's hand. Realistically, this battle was not in shape at all because the Israelites had no proper weapons to defend themselves whereas the Canaanites were equipped with 900 iron chariots ready for full force attack. But what use is it if the wheels of iron chariots don't turn?! God sent the 'late rain' and a cloud burst turned the Kishon River into a raging torrent, sweeping away many of the chariots and the rest were completely bogged down in the mud. Then Barak charged the army to go down the steep slopes of Mt. Tabor to attack the armies of Sisera and killed them. (Judges 4:12-16) Both Deborah and Barak defeated the armies of Sisera and the Canaanites.

Sisera, the commander of the Canaanites fled away on foot and hid in a tent near the Jordan River. A resourceful woman by the name of Jael went out to meet him and brought him inside her tent to rest. While the mighty Sisera was sound asleep, Jael took a handy tent-peg and with a mallet, she smashed it down into his temple killing him instantly. Just imagine the blood that must have scattered all over the place!

Through the events that happened to Israelites after winning this battle, we can find the deceitfulness of humans once again. Now that Israel has tasted victory and taken over more land, life becomes comfortable for them. "And the land was undisturbed for forty years." (Judges 5:31) When abundant food is available people start to sin immediately. This applied to the Israelites without losing a beat.

Gideon and Midian_Judges 6-9

The Lord is with Us

"The sons of Israel did what was evil in the sight of the Lord; and the Lord gave them into the hands of Midian seven years." (Judges 6:1) The nomadic Midianites were used as a tool to punish the Israelites. They swept through southern Israel as far as to the Philistine city of Gaza and the terror spread by these fierce camel riders who are like locusts destroying the produce of the earth and animals and wiping them out clean leaving behind total devastation. "So Israel was brought very low because of Midian, and the sons of Israel cried to the Lord." (Judges 6:6)

Gideon was raised as the deliverer of Israel when the Midianites were regarded as the most fearful people at that time. The Midianites confiscated all the harvested grains each year and killed all people mercilessly right on the spot when they found that some crops were left behind. Bearing this circumstance in mind, Gideon had no other option but to thresh his meager grain harvest secretly in the wine press when God called upon him. The angel of the Lord appeared to Gideon and said, "The Lord is with you, O valiant warrior." (Judges 6:12) He was naturally surprised but not impressed. Instead, he was upset. He said, "O my lord, if the Lord is with us, why then has all this happened to us? And where are all His miracles which our fathers told us about, saying, 'Did not the Lord bring us up from

Egypt?' But now the Lord has abandoned us and given us into the hand of Midian." (Judges 6:13) In other words, he was venting out to God, saying this: "If there is God why is this all happening to us? All year long -we work hard in farming and when the harvest time comes thousands of vultures (nomadic tribes) come and wipe us out each year. Are you really there for us? If so, show me a 'sign.'" Gideon said, "If now I have found favor in Your sight, then show me a sign that it is You who speak with me. Please do not depart from here, until I come back to You and bring out my offering and lay it before You." And God said, "I will remain until you return." (Judges 6:17-18)

Then Gideon went inside and prepared a young goat and a piece of unleavened bread. Putting the meat in the basket and the broth in a pot, Gideon brought them out to God. Then, the fire from heaven sprang up from the rock and consumed the meat and the unleavened bread. After witnessing what happened in front of his eyes, Gideon believed that God was with him. Callings are given to those who meet God in spirit. From this point on, Gideon obeyed God.

That night God said to him, "Take your father's bull and a second bull seven years old, and pull down the altar of Baal which belongs to your father, and cut down the Asherah that is beside it; and build an altar to the Lord your God on the top of this stronghold in an orderly manner, and take a second bull and offer a burnt offering with the wood of the Asherah which you shall cut down." (Judges 6:25-26)

In today's term, Gideon's father was the high priest of the biggest temple of Baal and since he was afraid of the Baal worshipers, he took 10 men of his servants and destroyed the altar of Baal during the night. Obviously it was chaos the next morning. Early the next morning, the men of the city arose and found the altar of Baal torn down, Asherah was cut down and the second bull was offered as a sacrifice on the altar. They yelled and said, "Who did this thing? Bring your son so that he may die for what he has done." (Judges 6:30) But the amazing thing is that God had turned Gideon's father into a man of faith overnight. Instead he spoke to the crowd, "Will you contend for

Baal, or will you deliver him? Whoever will plead for him shall be put to death by morning. If he is a god, let him contend for himself, because someone has torn down his altar." (Judges 6:31) In other words, if Baal is alive, let him judge; if he will judge, why then bother to make noise? This statement quieted everyone and the crowd left.

After this incident, God hit the Midianites through Gideon. But then again, the opponent was too big in numbers so Gideon asked for a sign again. "If You will deliver Israel through me, as You have spoken, behold, I will put a fleece of wool on the threshing floor. If there is dew on the fleece only, and it is dry on all the ground, then I will know that You will deliver Israel through me." (Judges 6:36-37) And God did so. Then Gideon asked God to reverse it by showing him a sign once again and God did so. (Judges 6:39-40)

Gideon and 300 Chosen Men_Judges 7

Gideon gained confidence after seeing the signs from God and gathered people which totaled 32,000. People assembled but God instructed Gideon that there were too many of them. Gideon obeyed and kept behind 10,000 people, sending 22,000 men back. But then, again, it was too many in the eyes of God for the reason of that the Israelites might become boastful and claimed that it was their own power winning the battle. "The people are still too many; bring them down to the water and I will test them for you there." (Judges 7:4)

Thirst was always experienced since water was scarce in the region so majority of them knelt down to drink it when they were brought down to the water. Those who knelt were dismissed by God because it symbolized that once flesh is faced with hardships, they would easily give in without any hesitation. On the other hand, those who scooped up the water and lapped it from their hands were the ones who are more alert to danger than those who knelt. So, as a result, 300 men had passed the test of God by their method of drinking water.

The faith of Gideon for all his initial caution is seen in his readiness to face the Midianite hordes with a force of only 300 men. God instructed them to hold trumpets on one hand and the empty jars on the other hand with the torches inside. Fully aware that the people (including Gideon) would have a hard time believing that they were going into the battle with no weapons except a torch and a trumpet in their hands, God let Gideon hear a dream about a loaf of barley bread tumbling into the Midianites' camp and struck it flat. Upon hearing this dream, Gideon gained confidence that victory was theirs. He used his wits in attack to surprise them by surrounding the campsite of the Midianites in the middle of the night, blowing the trumpets and smashing the pitchers that were in their hands. With this, the Midianite armies started killing one another out of confusion and fled as far as they could go. The victory was theirs but the ensuing rout was God's.

Bearing the torches inside of the jars, the Holy Spirit comes into our heart in the same manner. "You are the light of the world" (Matthew 5:14) since the Holy Spirit has come inside of us. The reason why the light is not shining through is because 'you' (we) have not been broken yet. Without breaking ourselves, the Holy Spirit cannot work. We must also realize that without prayers our flesh will neverbreak. Though you believe in Jesus, go to Bible studies and attend all kinds of revival retreats, it does not mean that your flesh goes away. The only short cut to break ourselves away from the flesh would be to pray not with our senses but led by the Holy Spirit.

Money, Power and Woman_Judges 8-9

Upon his victorious return, people shouted "Gideon, you're our hero and our king. Rule over us for both you and your son have delivered us. We want to serve you as our king now because in the past, having no king made us vulnerable from the neighboring countries." To this suggestion, Gideon responded, "I will not rule over you, nor shall my son rule over you; the Lord shall rule over you." (Judges 8:23) But, since people were persistent, he said to them, "I request that each of you give me an earring from his spoil (For they had gold earrings, because they were Ishmaelites)." (Judges 8:24) Maybe, in his mind, he thought he would accept the prosperity and refuse to take the power completely ignoring the fact that gold and silver were to be offered to the Holy Place.

Upon his request, substantial shekels of gold were brought to him; he made a gold ephod out of it (a short tunic worn by the high priest when praying to God on behalf of the people of Israel). Eventually the people of Israel played the harlot (fortune telling) with the ephod, so it became a snare to Gideon and his household. This was the way Gideon became corrupted which resembles the fall of those who are so-called 'specially gifted' people of God today.

In addition, Gideon had 70 sons from his "many wives" (Judges 8:30) which inevitably created a situation where a problematic descendent is to be found. In Gideon's case, it was Abimelech, a brutal and ambitious son from one of his concubines. The name "Abimelech" appears in the Bible in many passages but this Abimelech is a different person of the same name. Although his father Gideon could have some claim to the kingship but yet firmly rejected it, he, on the other hand, showed no such scruples. He thought, "Hey ... if I can get rid of my 70 brothers, I could be a king!" With conspiracy and all, he killed his 70 brothers and proclaimed himself to be a king. There is something we must learn from this incident. The massacre of Gideon's sons seems obvious in saying that if a servant of God who had received the Holy Spirit falls, it was God's way of punishment towards sin.

Regardless of whether he claimed himself to be the king or not, Abimelech was not a God's choice as his father was. But he ruled over Israel for three years. And along the way with his army, he arrived at Shechem where they dealt with people treacherously. After fighting against the city, he captured it and killed the people in it. Then he also razed the city and sowed it with salt symbolically consigning the city to a permanent desolation. Then Abimelech fought against a tower of the city and approached the tower to burn it with fire when a woman threw an upper millstone (grain was ground between the two heavy circular stone slabs) on his head. This millstone crushed his skull. Still conscious and concerned that it would be a mocking death so he commanded his armor bearer to pierce him with his sword and he died.

Threader: Through this incident, it became a rule for the armies of Israel that whenever they fight against a tower, they made certain not to stand beneath it. Later in David's time, Joab wrote a letter to King David saying, "Why did you go so near to the city to fight? Did you not know that they would shoot from the wall? Who struck down Abimelech the son of Jerubbesheth? Did not a woman throw an upper millstone on him from the wall so that he died at Thebez? Why did you go so near the wall?" (2 Samuel 11:20-21)

The last years of a great judge Gideon ended in this way. His major mistake was taking God's work as if it were his own doing. One thing we need to understand is that we must refrain ourselves from treating God's servant (i.e., pastor/reverend) as if he/she is a super-hero or some sort. We must definitely respect our pastors as God's anointed person to head the church but need not to focus on the person. God is teaching us from this chapter that a person who has experienced the Holy Spirit can also easily fall as well. If we accept people in ministries are just like us human beings who make mistakes as well, then there would be no expectations, whatsoever. No criticisms or disappointment. As a result, there would be no need to leave a church, searching for another one. Rather, our duty is to pray for God's servants for their dedication and devotion.

The Ammonites and Jephthah_Judges 10-12

A Valiant Warrior Becomes a Judge

Israel is now caught in a vice between the Philistines on the west and the Ammonites on the east. Once again, God uses the Ammonites as His tool. The elders of Gilead cried out to the Lord for help but God refused to hear them. "Did I not deliver you from the Egyptians, the Amorites, the sons of Ammon, and the Philistines? Also when the Sidonians, the Amalekites and the Maonites oppressed you, you cried out to Me, and I delivered you from their hands. Yet you have forsaken Me and served other gods; therefore I will deliver you no more. Go and cry out to the gods which you have chosen; let them deliver you in the time of your distress." (Judges 10:11-14)

The elders continuously cried out to the Lord, "We have sinned, do to us whatever seems good to You; only please deliver us this day. So they put away the foreign gods from among them, and served the Lord; and He could bear the misery of Israel no longer" (Judges 10:15-16) In order to prove their repentance, they went out and destroyed the foreign gods around the town and started to worship God.

Then God instructed them to call for Jephthah. The Bible introduces him as a valiant warrior (Judges 11:1) but in today's term he was more like a 'gangster.' He was the son of a harlot and was treated as an illegitimate outcast when he was growing up. He then mingled with people so-called worthless guys in town and eventually became a reputable leader of a gang in the eastern part of Jordan. As per God's instruction, the elders of Gilead went to get Jephthah and said, "Come and be our chief that we may fight against the sons of Ammon." (Judges 11:6) Then Jephthah replied, "Did you not hate me and drive me from my father's house? So why have you come to me now when you are in trouble?" (Judges 11:7) But realizing that the command came from God, Jephthah accepted it and received the power of the Holy Spirit. He sent messengers to the king of Ammon, saying "What is between you and me, that you have come to me to fight against my land?" Then king of Ammon said, "Because Israel took away my land when they came up from Egypt, from the Arnon as far as the Jabbok and the Jordan; therefore, return them peaceably now." (Judges 11:12-13) The question that was raised by Jephthah despite his background that was considered unworthy makes us realize that he certainly was knowledgeable of Israel's history. But most importantly, we get the glimpse of how he trusted in God. Against Ammon, the new champion was the brigand-chief, Jephthah, who God raises as the next judge. The Moabites were driven out but the Ammonites were left intact since they were to be used as God's tool of punishment down the line.

The Mistaken Vow

Jephthah on his way to fight against the Ammonites made a vow to God. Often times, people of his nature, gangster type, makes a vow as a 'man of integrity.' Today, in the world of gangsters such acts are done by chopping off their pinkie to show their loyalties (Asian style). Actually, this certain type of vow that Jephthah made originated from the religion of the foreign gods. "If You will indeed give the sons of Ammon into my hand, then it shall be that whatever comes out of the doors of my house to meet me when I return in peace from the sons of Ammon, it shall be the Lord's, and I will offer it up as a burnt offering." (Judges 11:30-31) It was the culture of the foreign gods at the time to give a human as a sacrifice. Even though Jephthah relied on God he followed the customs of foreign gods. Yet, though ignorant and mistaken, the vow was made in good faith.

This applies to us as well. We must be able to continuously wash away the bad habits we were exposed to prior to believing in Jesus through the Holy Spirit and prayer. If not, it will remain with us. Threader: During the Old Testament period, the Holy Spirit could not come into us because it was before the cross of Jesus. Hence, the history of the Old Testament ended in failure. Even though the works of the Holy Spirit were greatly revealed outwardly to the Israelites, the process of becoming sanctified was not well proportioned. In other words, it was not possible for them to be changed inwardly.

Upon victory when Jephthah came to his house his one and only daughter ran out to meet him with tambourines and dancing. "When he saw her, he tore his clothes and said, 'Alas, my daughter! You have brought me very low, and you are among those who trouble me; for I have given my word to the Lord, and I cannot take it back.'" (Judges 11:34-35) The vow that he had made to God was that whatever comes out of the door he would offer it to God as a burnt offering. It was his one and only daughter!

If he had truly believed in God properly, upon seeing his own daughter coming out of the door, he should have knelt down and repented: "God! Please forgive me. I was a fool to make such a promise." In spite of his heartbreak, Jephthah did not break faith his word to God. This can be interpreted that his 'self pride' was not broken. He probably thought, "Look at me. I'm the leader of this great army and have defeated the great force of the Ammonites. How can I break my promise with God?" Again, this idea applies to us as well. The problem is the 'I' which is magnified from within. It becomes an obstacle to surrender in front of God. We must admit and confess that 'I am nothing I am a sinner' to God. Then, there will be no problem at all. The great challenge to us is that 'I' do not die easily. Ultimately Jephthah offered his daughter to God.

There is a slight conflict between theologians on this issue about the fact that the battle was not won because of Jephthah's vow to God. It must be understood that his vow was wrong.

Surprisingly, the daughter's response is astonishing; instead of getting upset at her father, she was saddened that she had to die as a virgin and asked her father if she can be left alone with her friends for two months in the mountain to weep. Jephthah gave permission. "At the end of two months she returned to her father, who did to her according to the vow which he had made; and she had no relations with a man." (Judges 11:37-39) There is no record of what happened at the end of two months and this part is where the conflict is raised between theologians. It appears that Jephthah's daughter came back from the mountain and spent her life as an errand girl in the Holy Temple because it is clearly written in the book of Leviticus that human sacrifices were forbidden. The reason why Isaac was to be sacrificed as a burnt offering was that it was strictly a God's test for Abraham to make him the ancestor of faith. As we all know, Isaac was not sacrificed. In those days, if a virgin vowed to work in a temple she had to remain as a virgin for all her life. This is the way I would propose to interpret 'die' rather than reading it literally.

Tragic Result

Jephthah had to deal with the jealousy of the powerful Ephraim. "Why did you cross over to fight against the sons of Ammon without calling us to go with you? We will burn your house down on you." (Judges 12:1)

Jephthah gathered the men of Gilead, took up the sword and destroyed almost all the tribes of Ephraim. In fact, the Ephraimites were the ones who interfered when Gideon was fighting with the Midianites. These people were from the mountainous district of Ephraim and were proud since Joshua was one of the Ephraim. On the other hand, Gideon, who was from the tribe of Manasseh overcame the difficult situation by humbling himself towards Ephraim. "The men of Ephraim said to Gideon: 'What is this thing you have done to us, not calling us when you went to fight against Midian?' And they contended with him vigorously. Gideon responded: 'What have I done now in comparison with you? Is not the gleaning of the grapes of Ephraim better than the vintage of Abiezer? God has given the leaders of Midian, Oreb and Zeeb into your hands; and what was I able to do in comparison with you?' Then their anger toward him subsided." (Judges 8:1-3)

So therefore, Ephraim assumed that Jephthah was the same person as Gideon and raised the identical remark as before. "Why didn't you call us to go with you?" And without giving Jephthah a chance to explain, they threatened to kill him. However, by his own tough past background, Jephthah literally wiped them off by gathering his men to guard the fords of Jordan. Anyone who tried to escape the territory by crossing the river was stopped by his men and was asked, "Are you an Ephraimite?" If the answer was 'No,' they had to say 'Shibboleth.' When pronounced incorrectly as 'Sibboleth,' Jephthah's men seized them and killed them on the spot. As a result, almost one entire tribe out of 12 tribes of Israel was destroyed. This became a tragic beginning of a break up of the Israel's united nation of the 12 tribes.

At the calling of God, Jephthah judged Israel and experienced many victories under his belt but he also made a mistake in saying his vow and almost killed off one entire tribe of Israel. A leader is extremely important in every way. In this connection, one must never boast about his or her experience of the Holy Spirit in the past. As we know, all judges experienced the Holy Spirit and acted with great power against the enemies. The work of the Holy Spirit was shown outwardly through the victorious battles at the time but judges failed to have their individual hearts changed by God's love from within. It becomes crystal clear why Christ had to come as a man, shed blood and die on the cross so that He could send the Holy Spirit into our hearts. Throughout the Old and New Testament, the Bible teaches us continuously about the works of the Holy Spirit. The Holy Spirit is neither a theory, theology or philosophy. The Bible tells us that whoever has experienced the Holy Spirit received the power from above to do great works of God. Simultaneously it teaches us that the experience of the Holy Spirit must not end as a one-time effect.

Samson and the Philistines_Judges 13-16

Loss of One's Calling

Samson was the last judge during the period of the Judges. Many of the Canaanites had moved north by this time. But the Philistines were pushing inland and became a major threat to Israel.

Threader: To this day, Philistines remain as a problematic country - issues relating to the peace of Middle East, Freedom Movement of

Philistines, etc. The nation's repeated pattern (for 400 years) of disobedience to God for the local gods prompted God to use the strongest tool ever, Philistines, as His tool of punishment on the Israelites.

Samson was raised to deliver the Promised Land against the Philistines. He was called at a time when Israel had completely forgotten about God. The power of the Philistines were getting stronger than ever so God was desperate and promised a son to a childless couple (husband's name was Manoah) and instructed them to raise the boy as a Nazarite. There were three conditions for Samson to keep as a Nazarite: first, not to use razor on his head; second, not to drink wine or any other fermented drinks and third, not to eat or touch anything unclean.

Samson lived in a small valley called Zorah next to where the city of Jerusalem was to be built later. His parents got upset when their son confessed that he had fallen in love with a woman in Timnah. About this, the Bible records "However, his father and mother did not know that it was of the Lord, for He was seeking an occasion against the Philistines." (Judges 14:4) The people of Israel lived in the midst of the Philistines at the time and they were not aware that in reality, the Philistines were actually rising to rule over them. God's plan was to stir up the resentment in the heart of Samson against the Philistines by marrying a Philistine woman and to be betrayed by her. Eventually Samson's marriage was formally arranged by his parents, but instead of the bride returning to the Samson's house, as she would normally do after the wedding, she stayed with her family. Because of the deceit over the riddle he started, there was no consummation of the marriage. He is then hastily bounded by the people of Judah to be handed over to the Philistines but the Spirit of God came upon him with mighty strength that he released the ropes that were on his arms and killed 1,000 men with a jawbone of a donkey.

Samson became a judge over Israel but used all of his God-given strength in leading a life of sexual promiscuity instead and because of it, he fell and was corrupted in the end.

Result of a Sin Lasts Long_Judges 16

A judge is a king, a high priest and a prophet. Samson went to a prostitute in Gaza (town in Philistines) in order to avoid any rumors in the land of Judah. In the valley of Sorek, he fell in love with a woman named Delilah. During my freshman years in college late, a pop singer Tom Jones had a hit song called, 'Delilah' and a Korean singer also sang it in Korean as well. My memory tells me that I myself also sang it quite frequently not realizing who Delilah was not to mention how little I knew about the Bible at the time.

Samson madly got involved with a Philistine woman when by right he should have led a sanctifying life as a high priest as well as being a prophet. His role of protecting the Israelites against the Philistines was forgotten at this point. It appears that Delilah also loved Samson but at the persistent request from her own people to seek where his great strength was coming from, she ended up standing on the Philistine's side since Samson was the obstacle in taking over Israel. Delilah gladly agreed with a reward for her if she successfully finds out about it. Day in and day out, she seduced Samson to extract the secret of the source of his great strength.

In the end, Samson opened his mouth and told Delilah that the secret was his hair. In truth, however, the secret of his strength was the Spirit of the Lord. By exposing his secret, locks of his hair were shaved off while he was sleeping on Delilah's knees. After shaving his hair and witnessing that Samson was weak, the Philistines seized him and gouged out his eyes, and then set him to the task of a beast, turning the mill in his prison at Gaza in bronze chains. In this midst of misery, Samson repented to God. While the Philistines were giving offerings to their god, Samson was called in to amuse them by standing between the pillars. Samson asked a boy who was holding his hand and said, 'Let me feel the pillars on which the house rests that I may lean against them.' And he prayed to God to give him strength for the last time. With the Holy Spirit upon him, he grasped the two pillars and bent with all his might until the house collapsed, killing 3,000 people including himself. Samson ended his life in a tragic way and decorated the end of the period of the Judges.

Threader: From this point on, the history of Israel goes side by side with the Philistines. Israel continuously fights against the strong Philistines, having battles ceaselessly from the opening of the period of the kingdom of Israel. The Philistines killed King Saul but were narrowly controlled during the time under King David on the other hand. This is the historical background of the Middle East war today which is mainly caused by the conflict between the PLO and Israel. We must reflect on this reality in the Middle East which is originated from one person, Samson's mistake of forgetting his duty.

True Reality of the Sins During the Period of the Judges_Judges 17-21

There are two major types of sins during the period of the Judges: spiritual and sexual sin. In reality, if one commits spiritual sin, the sexual sin comes automatically. The latter part of the book of Judges explains these two types of sins in this time period in detail.

Spiritual Sin: Micah's Idolatry_Judges 17-18

There was a man named Micah who lived in the hill country of Ephraim. Apparently, he stole 1,100 pieces of silver from his mother and she cursed at whoever took it. Out of guilt, Micah returned it claiming that he had 'found' it. His mother was so proud of her son and said, "Blessed be my son by the Lord. 'I wholly dedicate the silver to the Lord for my son.'" (See Judges 17:2-3) Then his mother took 200 pieces of silver to the silversmith to make a graven image and a molten image to put in their household shrine.

The molten image set up by Micah and use of an ephod and the teraphim household gods for divination were strictly prohibited. This is the spiritual sin. God had clearly indicated through the 10 Commandments that no other gods must be served, therefore, idolatry was forbidden. The state of religion and morality in the lawless days of the latter period of the Judges reached to the point that everyone did as they pleased. They had no recollection of God anymore and made idols claiming them to be god. People put up household shrines with the ephods (the same kind with the one that was made in Gideon's days) as well as with the teraphim (that was regarded as an important family jewel, the idol that Rachel's father worshipped) in it.

Threader: Unfortunately, this spiritual sin is repeated during the reign of King Saul as well as many kings of the Divided Kingdom era. The first king of the Northern Israel, Jeroboam, started off his reign by making a gold calf in the shrine. Even today, the responses of non-believers when we approach them to say to believe in Jesus are, "Well, I suppose it may be necessary to have one religion at least during our lifetime." In other words, the perception of many people are such that they acknowledge their weakness at times so consider having one god around would not be a bad idea when one needs it which means that who that god is doesn't make any difference whether it is Jesus or a Buddhist statue in that regard. This is what we refer as the wrongful mixed faith. Recall what Joshua said to his people: "Choose who you want to serve as God." (Joshua 24:15) Even though the Israelites had agreed to serve the Lord already, they instead chose to become their own masters. Alternatively, they were willing to serve any god whoever bailed them out when necessary. The key word that repeats over and over again here is that it was a time of 'do as you please.' This was corruption itself and also a religion of King Saul.

Sexual Sin: The Concubine of a Levite the High Priest_Judges 19-21

As soon as one commits spiritual sin, sexual sin is followed promptly thereafter. We must realize that spiritual adultery (mixed religion) leads us to physical adultery. Similar case as Samson's, chapter 19 in the book of Judges relates to the story of a Levite lived in the remote part of Ephraim and his concubine who apparently took off with another man. In search of his concubine, the husband set off to her home town and was greeted with a warm hospitality of the concubine's father who feared that his daughter might be killed otherwise. The long drinking sessions went on for six days.

At last, the Levite and his concubine left for home and stayed overnight at a town called Gibeah where the tribes of Benjamin lived. They were visited by local men in town who demanded the 'Levite man' and said, "Bring out the man who came into your house that we may have relations with him." (Judges 19:22) Afraid for his life, the Levite's concubine was handed over to them instead and they gang-raped her all night. The woman was found dead at the doorway the next morning.

In doing a second terrible atrocity, her husband cut her body up into 12 pieces and sent it to the 12 tribes to summon them to avenge her on her death by sending messages through it: "Elders look at this. Israel has fallen to this disgraceful level of sexual corruption." His personal sins, such as having a concubine as a high priest and the fact that he spent days in drinking were set aside, instead, he was pointing fingers at the deeds of the Benjamites. The Israelites who were busy worshipping the Baal in the first place got together for a civil war against the Benjamites. "We will take 10 men out of 100 throughout the tribes of Israel, and 100 out of 1,000, and 1,000 out of 10,000 to supply food for the people, that when they come to Gibeah of Benjamin, they may punish them for all the disgraceful acts that they have committed in Israel." (Judges 20:10) Jephthah had destroyed the tribe of Ephraim in the past and now, all of Israel gathered to wipe out the tribe of Benjamin. All these actions compounded to a great national grief, causing the division of Israel down the road.

The pitiful result by sinners, a sinner pointing fingers at each other, is shown to us in this situation as an example. Our eyes were opened when we ate from the tree of good and evil and that's when we started to judge others. Rather than pinpointing faults of others, we must realize that we are all sinners in front of God. This is what God is trying to teach us.

The human sins in Judges are very depressing. The nation's fortune follows a repetitive cycle. After God's blessing, people sin and they suffer at God's punishment of their sins, then they cry out to God for help. Despite of unfaithfulness of people, God answers and delivers them. The conclusion of Judges is: "In those days there was no king in Israel; everyone did what was right in his own eyes." (Judges 21:25) Simply put, they lived as they were pleased. It shows how Israel tried to make use of God for their own ends, and it was so even when they acknowledged God's choice in the matter that His word proved faithful. Trying to get God to work for you is a folly and it is well exposed throughout the book of Judges.

We must understand that it is important for us to receive the Word daily and through prayers. The only way to prevent and overcome the same consequences of evil doings like in the days of Judges is acting with the wisdom and strength that come from above through the Word of God. By doing so, we will be able to enjoy the promised eternal life.

Reason Why the Period of the Judges Failed

Obviously, Israel failed to choose God as their leader (King) and as a result, an idolatrous cult site is set up within Israel, which includes the forbidden images and mercenary priest within was set up in Israel. What happened to them?

God's tent was situated in Shiloh, north of Bethel and on the east side of the path that goes up from Bethel to Shechem. We notice there are no records of the 12 tribes of Israel gathering to worship from the days of kingship until Solomon built the temple. Failing to give worship, they could not digest the invisible God (the Word) and instead, their eyes were focused on the things that were visible (prosperity, productivity and sexual pleasure). "Faith is the assurance of things hoped for, the conviction of things not seen." (Hebrews 11:1)

This also applies to us today. If we (Christians) are lazy in giving worship, it is extremely difficult for us to go beyond the assurance of things that we cannot see. Instead, we turn our interest into the visible things and start to complain or grumble in our given situation. David knew the importance of the unforeseen elements and therefore spent his days yearning to meet God in the temple. "One thing I have asked from the Lord, that I shall seek: That I may dwell in the house of the Lord all the days of my life." (Psalms 27:4) In return, God poured abundant blessings and love upon him.

It is important for us to remind ourselves of how we were created in the first place and put our utmost efforts in giving worship to God. We have come into this world from the 'unforeseen' (Son of God = Word) and strive to become like Jesus through the process of sanctification to return to the unforeseen (inside the Lord). Believe and trust that if we seek God's righteousness and His kingdom, all things (what to eat, drink or clothing) will be added to you. (Matthew 6:33)

. . .

You are the light of the world. A city set on a hill cannot be hidden; nor does anyone light a lamp and put it under a basket, but on the lampstand, and it gives light to all who are in the house. "Let your light shine before men in such a way that they may see your good works, and glorify your Father who is in heaven.

Matthew 5:14-16

BEGINNING OF MONARCHY AND KING SAUL

1 Samuel 1-15

The period of the United Monarchy covers a broad range of scale -starting from 1 & 2 Samuel through 1 & 2 Kings. As one opens the book of Samuel, the last two judges of Israel, Eli and Samuel, come into the scene. As Samson being the last, the twelve judges appears in the book of Judges but Eli and Samuel play the role of being the last judges who link the period of the Judges to the period of kingship in the history of Israel.

Beginning of Kingship

Two Last Judges_1 Samuel 1-8

Eli, the Weak Judge

Eli, the judge (high priest) is portrayed as a very weak person in the Bible but we must realize that it is strictly from God's standpoint and not from the worldly point of view. In other words, he was not in tuned with God but loved his sons more than God. He also experienced the humiliation of losing the Ark during the battle with the Philistines. The Ark was Israel's most precious possession and Eli assumed that keeping the Ark in the camp site of the battlefield utilizing it as a talisman would be an ultimate protection for it against the enemy. The result was a total disaster; the army defeated and the Ark was in the hands of the Philistine.

During Joshua's day, the reason why the Jordan River split

opened when the high priests stepped into the waters while carrying the Ark on their shoulders was because they had obeyed God's word. It was not the Ark itself that caused the miracle but Eli was not aware of this fact. Fulfillment of God's judgment on Eli's family fell upon them: Eli sitting on a chair inside the temple died instantly with his neck broken when hearing the shocking news that the Ark had been seized by the Philistines, and to make things worse, his two sons also died in the battlefield the same day. (1 Samuel 4:17-18)

In our generation today, there are believers who necklaces with a cross pendant or hang crosses as an accessory in their cars thinking that it might bring them good luck. But we must realize that the cross itself does not have the power. "If anyone wishes to come after Me, let him deny himself, and take up his cross, and follow Me." (Matthew 16:24) Simply, in order to experience God's grace and blessing, we must be able to sacrifice for others as a reflection of God abiding among people.

The Great Works of Samuel

Samuel was born as a God's answer to years of prayer of his mother, Hannah. Pouring her heart out to God in prayers in the temple Eli was quick to jump to the wrong conclusion that she was drunk since only her lips moved. (1 Samuel 1:12-14) But the devoted Hannah did not dispute with him and gave proper respect to Eli as a high priest whether he was worthy or not. She received God's blessing in the end. (1 Samuel 1:15-16)

Prophet Samuel had a special role to play in the great plan of God. From this time on, Samuel was God's messenger who protects the Promised Land and guides the Israel to return to God in repentance of their sins for 400 years during the period of the Judges. (1 Samuel 7:3-17)

There were three great major works of Samuel in the history of Israel:

First, as the Israel's last greatest judge and prophet, he played a role in linking the two time periods together, the period of the Judges and the period of Kingship.

Second, he led Israel to an act of spiritual repentance and cleansing. That is the reason that whenever we have a revival gathering today, we call it as the "Movement of Spiritual Repentance." Foreclosing the sinful period, Samuel explained why Israel was attacked by the foreign tribes for 400 years; it was because they had turned away from God for the images of Baal and Ashtoreth, the Canaanite fertility gods. Then he gathered all the people of Israel to Mizpah for national revival which is named as the '1st assembly at Mizpah.' (1 Samuel 7:3) Immediately the test came. The Philistines were advancing and God used the occasion to show Israel what He will do for His people who keep faith in Him. (1 Samuel 7:10-13)

Third, he became Israel's 'kingmaker' under God's direction which highlights his credentials for all his work. History repeated itself and Samuel's sons turned out a little better than Eli's. Their bribery and corruption provided the people with a ready-made excuse to lobby the aging man for a king, like the nations around. "You have grown old, and your sons do not walk in your ways. Now appoint a king for us to judge us like all the nations." (1 Samuel 8:5)

Samuel felt rejected and resisted to listen to the Israelites' request but God advises him to hear them out. In truth, it was not the prophet who was being rejected but the whole concept of theocracy. The Lord said to Samuel, "Listen to the voice of the people in regard to all that they say to you, for they have not rejected you, but they have rejected Me from being king over them." (1 Samuel 8:7) Unfortunately, the people of Israel assumed that they lost battles because they didn't have a king and a standing army. They failed to understand that their leader was God and the reason why they were pursued by foreign tribes was because God used the foreign tribes to punish them for their idolatry of Baal. Samuel spared nothing and assured them that they only have to look at their neighboring states and find that having a king meant conscription, forced labor, taxation and loss of personal liberty. But even this did not deter them. Finally, God said 'Appoint them a king.'

Why do you think God listened to their request? It was for them to experience what it would be like to be under the ruling of a king so that in the end, they would realize the heart of God why He did not appoint a king for them. The whole purpose was for them to return to God.

Threader: It was God's plan to raise the world as a shadow of His Kingdom ever since Exodus. (Deuteronomy 17). This can be verified by the fact that "Kingdom of Heaven" indicates 'heaven' (God's Kingdom).

What was the result of having kings in the Northern and Southern Israel throughout all those hundreds of years? When they were taken into captivities after the destruction of the period of kingship, understanding of the coming Messiah started to surface in their hearts. They began to wait for the 'true' king to come through the descendents of David. In the end, they finally realized that under a kingship, there was nothing but suffering that followed.

King Saul_1 Samuel 9-31

Saul: Israel's First King

The worldly standard in choosing a king was primarily the candidates' appearance and humble attitude.

First, appearance. During the ancient times of the Middle Eastern countries, the appearance, such as height, quantity of hair locks, intelligent looking eyes and modesty was regarded as a crucial criteria to be a king. Especially the hair had to be long. For instance, David's son Absalom was known to be handsome who only cut his hair once a year and his hair that was cut was 200 shekel.

Second, modesty/humility. Worldly modesty can be a problem because once it becomes unduly excessive, it turns into an inferiority complex which is exactly what happened to King Saul.

God had already indicated the rules and regulations that a king must abide by in Deuteronomy 17:11-18.

First, a king of Israel had to be anointed by God.

Second, a copy of God's word must be kept by the king at all times so that he would be reminded of it daily and live according to it.

Third, multiple wives were prohibited.

Fourth, not many chariots or military units were necessary since God, being their 'true' king would protect them.

But like King Solomon, there were many kings who failed to follow these rules.

According to Israel's request, 'we want a king!' God gave Saul as their first king. Saul's search for his father's lost donkeys led him to the prophet Samuel and to his destiny as the Israel's first king. (1 Samuel 9:3) Samuel anointed Saul with oil, setting him apart for his high office. (1 Samuel 10:1) At the time, an anointed king was not regarded as a king right away. Samuel gathered the people of Israel to choose a king at the '2nd assembly meeting at Mizpah.' Each tribe chose 1,000 representatives to cast lots for themselves. It quite clearly shows that God is the one who chose the king of Israel; it was not left to the people.

The result was obvious but Saul fought with his shyness (modesty) and hid himself behind baggage. "They inquired further of the Lord, 'Has the man come here yet?' So the Lord said, 'Behold, he is hiding himself by the baggage.'" (1 Samuel 10:22) The baggage must have been enormous. Since 12,000 representatives were gathered at one place, there must have been lots of baggages, making a huge pile where Saul hid himself. He was dragged from hiding and didn't need to be afraid of the crowd. A king who was a head taller than the rest met with the people's instant approval. Even though Saul was the official king, there was no crown of any sort but instead a clap of applause as well as a loud shout of "Long live the king!" and he was sent back home.

Saul's actual role as a king was displayed when the Ammonites invaded Jabesh-gilead. The people were reminded that they had a king who could fight on their behalf. God moved Saul for him to make his appeal to the people. Empowered with the Spirit of the Lord, Saul killed an oxen with his bare hands and cut it into 12 pieces to send them out to each tribe of Israel with a message "let's all unite and drive the Ammonites out." (1 Samuel 11:7-8) Perhaps for the first time since the days of Joshua, the nation was united, 330,000 people were gathered in one place: a good beginning to the new king's reign. After Saul's first victory, they made him a king before the Lord in Gilgal.

King Saul's Wrongful Religion

First Standing Army is Established

After battling with the Ammonites, Saul established the first standing army. He left 2,000 men in the temporary capital of Gilgal and left 1,000 men with his son, Jonathan whose role was the commanding officer, in his hometown of Gibeah. (1 Samuel 13:2) What a pitiful sight to watch these armies! In the meantime, triggered by the failures of Samson and Eli, the Philistines had grown into a stronger force. They had destroyed all the blacksmith's shop to prevent the Israelites in making weapons of any sort so, therefore, the Israelites had to go to Philistine for approval and then was able to make swords or tools there.

In this kind of circumstance, Israel had no proper swords or spears and the only sword that Israel had was that of King Saul's representing his entire army. Besides the sword was held by a sword-bearer since a king was not to carry it himself. The same applied to the army in Gibeah: the only weapon they had was the spear of Jonathan held by the spear-bearer in the same manner as King Saul. In spite of this major difference between the two opponents, this was King Saul's first troop of armies.

Threader: This aspect is actually quite the opposite compared to today's situation because Israel had completely dominated the PLO, the descendents of the Philistines. No matter how the Philistines stand against Israel, they cannot do more than self-inflicted suicidal missions because its outcome is that they will be revenged by tanks and plane bombings by Israel.

Under such situation, the Philistines assembled vast armies and camped in Michmash and Gibeah, hometown of Saul, which meant they had control of the whole valley. They came with 30,000 chariots, 6,000 horsemen as well as enormous amount of people backing them up whereas Israel was with only 3,000 soldiers and one sword and one spear as their weapon. They practically had no chance at all and the bottom line, the Philistines' intention was to just wipe Israel away at once and take over their land instantly.

Various thoughts must have crossed Saul's mind: "God! What are you trying to do with me here? Are you trying to humiliate me now after you have chosen me as their king?" But he knew that without God, there would no victory in his hand.

The Difference between Obedience and Offering

At the time, Samuel was traveling back and forth between Gilgal, Mizpah and Lama to carry out his duty as a judge. He told Saul that he would return to Gilgal after seven days but the problem was that he didn't return on the day he had promised. In the meantime, Saul mustered his troops and waited seven days, during which the army steadily dwindled and failed to see the seventh day out. "When the men of Israel saw that they were in a strait (for the people were hard-pressed), then the people hid themselves in caves, in thickets, in cliffs, in cellars, and in pits. Also some of the Hebrews crossed the Jordan into the land of Gad and Gilead. But as for Saul, he was still in Gilgal, and all the people followed him trembling." (1 Samuel 13:6-7)

Saul knew well that he had to wait for Samuel to perform the offering service since only then God would be with them in the battle. In other words, he believed that God would be on their side when worship was given but apparently, Samuel, the prophet did not return on the day he had promised. Ridden by fear and desperation, his disobedience and arrogance in taking over the function of the prophet cost him his dynasty.

The next day Samuel arrived and scolded Saul for he had not kept the commandment of the Lord. "You have acted foolishly; you have not kept the commandment of the Lord your God, which He commanded you, for now the Lord would have established your kingdom over Israel forever. But now your kingdom shall not endure. The Lord has sought out for Himself a man after His own heart, and the Lord has appointed him as ruler over His people, because you have not kept what the Lord commanded you." (1 Samuel 13:13-14)

Why did Saul fail? The first reason was that he had taken over the duty of the high priest. It was made clear by God through the book of Deuteronomy that unlike the period of the Judges, upon setting up kingship, the duties of a king, high priest and prophet were distinctively separated. The role of a king was to fight for the people and judge during normal days. Having the power didn't enable a king to carry out the function of performing the offering service which was strictly set aside for high priest only. It was made law that a king must obey the word of the prophet.

Threader: God continuously sent prophets during the period of kingship and when a king made a mistake, the prophet played his role, pinpointing the wrongdoings through the Word of God. It was God's way to protect His world through His messengers. While there were kings who persecuted or even imprisoned prophets, there was someone like David who knelt down before God to repent even as a king. In this regard, Saul had disobeyed God's command.

Why? It was because he had a wrong concept of religion. He

believed in God and knew of the power of worship but the problem of his faith was that it was based on Shamanism. Through 1 and 2 Samuel and the book of Chronicles, the Bible tells us the wrongful religion of King Saul. Out of fear and desperation, he failed to wait for Samuel the high priest and conducted the offering service which was prohibited. The misconception of his belief was that by giving offering (worship) he thought God would help them whenever necessary. The correct attitude of a believer is to 'wait until the high priest comes' or obey the Word of God even at the most crucial moment. As Christians, rather than being caught up with own thoughts in urgent situations, we must trust in God first.

Ignoring the Prophet's Command

There was another God's command to be completed through Samuel which was to attack the Amalekites. To Israel, the Amalekites were old enemies whose punishment had long been forecasted and there was one specific cautionary instruction when attacking them. "Samuel said to Saul, 'The Lord sent me to anoint you as king over His people, over Israel; now therefore, listen to the words of the Lord. Thus says the Lord of hosts, 'I will punish Amalek for what he did to Israel, how he set himself against him on the way while he was coming up from Egypt. Now go and strike Amalek and utterly destroy all that he has, and do not spare him; but put to death both man and woman, child and infant, ox and sheep, camel and donkey'" (1 Samuel 15:1-3)

According to the command, Saul defeated the Amalekites but there was one problem. He kept Agag the king of the Amalekites alive and spared the best of the sheep, oxen, the fatlings, the lambs and all those that were good. Then Saul said to Samuel who came to him, "I have carried out the command of the Lord." (1 Samuel 15:13) But Samuel responded, "What then are these noises of sheep and oxen in my ears?" (1 Samuel 15:14) To this,(, added) Saul said, "The people spared the best of the sheep and oxen, to sacrifice to the Lord your God; but the

Religion of Shamanism versus Religion of Christianity

People who go to shrines of tutelary deity (local gods) or worship mountain gods are following the religion of Shamanism ('religion of request'). They acknowledge that there is a god but have no interest at all whether the god they rely on is of a good character or not. Their main interest is to be satisfied with the things they want.

One may easily think that dethroning Saul just because he performed the offering service instead of Samuel is too severe. What's the big mistake in taking over the function of a prophet in an urgent situation? But the issue is that Saul had a mentality of Shamanism. Having no interest in God's Word but only focused on own needs is the religion of Shamanism. Unfortunately, many Christians fall under this category today. For instance, many people gathered in the early dawn services during the period of college examination period but as soon as it's finished, the drastic reduction of attendance proves it all.

There is a major fundamental difference between these two types of religion. The center of the universe is God in the religion of Christianity whereas the religion of Shamanism regards 'self' (Me) as the center of the universe. As a Christian, you and I have a loving relationship with the living God (which, in fact, distinguishes differently from the aspect of 'mercy' in Buddhism). We believe that God will provide us with all the necessities in life since we have been created as his beloved children. We worship God who is of character. We are thankful for His love bestowed upon us which is why we obey His command.

This is the reason why we must live according to His Word. "He who has My commandments and keeps them, he it is who loves Me." (John 14:21) And Jesus also said, "Those who say 'Lord, Lord' are not the ones who will enter my Father's kingdom but those who do the will of Father." (Matthew 7:21) So God took away the kingship from King Saul and shifted to the one who sought out His heart. Obviously we cannot possibly carry out all the Word of God but doing our utmost to abide by it is the process of sanctification to fulfill salvation.

rest we have utterly destroyed." (1 Samuel 15:15)

The following words of Samuel are well known to many: "Has the Lord as much delight in burnt offerings and sacrifices As in obeying the voice of the Lord? Behold, to obey is better than sacrifice, And to heed than the fat of rams." (1 Samuel 15:22) What this means is that obeying God's word is more important than giving offerings for your own needs.

In truth, Saul was keen in impressing the people rather than keeping the animals alive for the sake of the burnt offerings. He regarded the people more important than God. Having this type of religion of Shamanism is very dangerous. Rather than obeying the Word of God out of love, putting efforts to win a favor from the people to reign as a king for a longer period of time was more important to him. Even today, many people fall under this category.

Ultimately, King Saul did not love God. He was more interested in seeking popularity than obeying (loving) God's word. This time, Saul's disobedience was a deliberate decision and he was rejected by God as the king of Israel. Plus, Samuel paid him no more official visits.

Reason Why Obedience is Better Than Offering

To believe in God is not through the knowledge but through the love of God. To put it more precisely, to respond to God's love. After entrusting the human species with the gift of free choice, God invited its representatives to act as partners, even to argue and wrestle with the One who created them.

Love is expressed through mind, heart and action: Think of your loved ones who make you happy and imagine of yourself acting according to that person's wish. The problem with King Saul was that his faith was limited. Limited in thinking of God and being happy and content. He believed his victories in the battles were in the hands of God. But on the other hand, God's interest was in Saul whether he would move in full obedience of determination according to God's command.

This applies to many believers of God today. It is more important to start your day by giving thanks and love to God rather than giving worship (for personal request). God loves those who surrender their own thoughts and strive to live in obedience to His Word.

All other religions (such as Buddhism, Hinduism and others) also pursue to overcome 'self.' Therefore, they claim that it is no different to Christianity but in fact there is a significant fundamental difference. In order to overcome 'self', meditation or monasticism are conducted which involves your mind (in other words, traveling in the midst of dust) based on your own efforts. But the more you try, the more you get in deeper into yourself 'being.' (To the state of formless, void and darkness as written in Genesis 1:2)

Love is the only way to overcome self but a human's love has its limit. There is no other way to overcome self but through the love of

Christ who came into our hearts through the cross and resurrection. That is why Jesus said, "I am the way, and the truth, and the life." (John 14:6) To this extent, a determined decision making is required in order for us to become one with God. This is only possible through the Word and prayer along with the power of the Holy Spirit so that obedience would come ahead of our own thoughts.

. . .

We love, because He first loved us. If someone says, "I love God," and hates his brother, he is a liar; for the one who does not love his brother whom he has seen, cannot love God whom he has not seen. And this commandment we have from Him, that the one who loves God should love his brother also.

1 John 4:19-21

TEMPLE WORSHIP, KING DAVID

1 Samuel 16-31, 2 Samuel, 1 Chronicles 11-29

The first king of Israel dies a miserable death. God has already chosen David as the 2nd king of Israel. The prophecy has been heard by David that he will become king of Israel. For the following 13 years, he spends his days in suffering. But through this process, he finally becomes a king 'who seeks the heart of God.'

Training School of Suffering

_Until Becoming the King

How was David the Shepherd Boy Raised as a King?

_ 1 Samuel 16

God sends Samuel to anoint David. On the basis of the first choice of king, Samuel might well have been looking for someone tall and handsome. But this time, God makes it plain that he looks deeper. Samuel visits the home of Jesse who brings out seven sons only thinking his youngest son, David, the shepherd, is the least of his family. If you visit Rome, you will come across a statue of handsome David sculptured by the famous Michelangelo unlike his real appearance. In this regard, I believe Jesse had thought David was not that great looking to his worldly standard but what God saw was not his outward appearance but the heart.

David was a shepherd in Bethlehem, a small village located southwest of Jerusalem, in the wilderness land of Judah. From young, he was dedicated to the Word and always confessed his faith to God and wrote many psalms. As a young shepherd, how in the world did he become a king? He was anointed at the age of

17 but was not made the king right away. Instead, 13 years of journey of suffering awaited him.

At first, he was hired as a harpist in the palace. When the Spirit of God left Saul, evil forces took charge and he was at the mercy of his own ungovernable temperament. His disordered mind plunged him into black depression and violence. But music can push back the shadows and so Saul's need became David's opportunity. In a modern sense, he worked as a part-time harpist in the king's court.

Goliath's Challenge_1 Samuel 17

The Philistine champion challenges Israel by saying, "I defy the ranks of Israel this day; give me a man that we may fight together." (1 Samuel 17:10) And Saul, who has fought valiantly against the Philistines, is as terrified as his men to answer the giant's challenge. David's time in the hills alone with the sheep has added faith to courage so he stands in front of this 'uncircumcised Philistine' with a stick and mocks him. The giant curses and says to David, "Am I a dog, that you come to me with sticks? ... Come to me, and I will give your flesh to the birds of the sky and the beasts of the field." (1 Samuel 17:43-44)

Without fear, David responds, "You come to me with a sword, a spear, and a javelin, but I come to you in the name of the Lord of hosts, the God of the armies of Israel, whom you have taunted." (1 Samuel 17:45) David kills Goliath with a sling and a stone but in truth, Goliath has died by the struck of David's faith. David becomes an instant hero through this incident but then again, a hero brings forth an enemy. The minute he became a hero, his journey of suffering just begun.

Upon his heroic victory, the women come out of all the cities of Israel and sing, "Saul has slain his thousands, And David his ten thousands." (1 Samuel 18:7) As David's prestige grows, Saul's jealous suspicion that David is the 'next king' prophesied by Samuel increases and he plots David's death. Samuel said, "The Lord has torn the kingdom of Israel from you today, and has given it to your neighbor who is better than you." (1 Samuel 15:28) The downfall of Saul was that his thoughts superseded God's will and challenged God. If he were told that his kingship had ended, he should have immediately repented to God for his mistake. This act proved that he did not accept God as a being of character. Instead, regardless of what God thought of him, his interest was to maintain his kingship as long as possible.

Death Threat to David

Since Saul had turned against David, his life was turbulent from this point on. The first thing Saul did was to put David near his side. Before, when David played the harp, Saul's mood swings were comforted but now he only pretended to listen and then suddenly hurled a spear towards David with the intention to kill him. David narrowly escaped from it twice. How was this possible when in fact he had knelt down in front of the king playing the harp? It was God who had blocked the spear so Saul kept missing David.

This made Saul more afraid of David for he knew that the Lord was with David but had departed from him. He then thought of another scheme, asking David to bring hundred foreskins of the Philistines, Israel's chief enemy and promises his daughter, Michal, to David as his bride. The foreskin is the skin of male's private part taken from the circumcision. It meant that David had to kill 100 Philistines men. Saul wanted David to be killed by them. "Saul then said, 'Thus you shall say to David, The king does not desire any dowry except a hundred foreskins of the Philistines, to take vengeance on the king's enemies. Now Saul planned to make David fall by the hand of the Philistines.'" (1 Samuel 18:25)

Instead, David doubles Saul's demand and returns unharmed to claim his royal bride. Again, Saul has no choice but to comply with his suggestion and David becomes his son-in-law. But Saul's black moods follow and another attempt to kill David fails when Michal's deception saves David's life. Finally David realizes Saul's evilness, the extreme measure of his attempt to kill his own daughter's husband.

There was no place for him to hide in Israel except the temple so for a time he joined Samuel and his school of prophets at Ramah. Eventually he went to Nod and went to Ahimelech, the priest, who fed David with sacred bread (each Sabbath, 12 fresh loaves of bread were placed on the altar and the 12 stale ones were removed. Only the priests were entitled to eat them.) (1 Samuel 21:1-6) He then asked for a spear or sword since he was without a weapon. So the priest handed him the sword of Goliath which David had used, indicating that it was the only one in the temple. In those days, all spoils of war were kept in the temple. David took the sword and started to escape once again.

In the meantime, Saul and his army came after David and when he found that Ahimelech had aided David's escape, he slaughtered 85 priests and their families in Nod. An for the sake of keeping his position as king, the bloodshed he committed!

Fortunately enough, one son of Ahimelech escaped and fled to inform David. Just imagine, what fear David must have felt? For a king to kill a young man was certainly not a difficult thing to do at the time. In modern days, there are people who wake up in the morning and say, "Wow! What a great weather for golf!" But as for David, when he awoke in the morning, he must have said something like this, "Wow... my neck is still intact today." Each morning he was thankful to God that he was still alive. Because of this terrifying situation, David was able to entrust in God completely which meant that he had overcome himself (self-denial). That big 'me' had been crushed during the process of his suffering.

There was no place to hide from the sword of Saul in Israel. In the end, he escaped to the enemy's land of the Philistines where he woke up each morning with fear and the circumstances forced him to focus on God. He wrote, "Even though I walk through the valley of the shadow of death, I fear no evill; for You are with me; Your rod and Your staff, they comfort me." (Psalms 23:4) Of the 150 psalms, it is said that David had written 73 of them. The common theme of his writing is "The Lord is my rock and my fortress and my deliverer, My God, my rock, in whom I take refuge." (Read Psalms 18) His confession was that there was nowhere to hide, rely or defend his life except God.

Through this process, David had become a man of steadfast faith who sought out the heart of God. "After He had removed him, He raised up David to be their king, concerning whom He also testified and said, I have found David the son of Jesse, a man after my heart, who will do all My will." (Acts 13:22)

First Refuge to the Philistines

After fleeing from the temple, David escaped to Gath, a five-city nation which was regarded as the capital city of the Philistines at the time. But there's a problem: King Achish greeted David but his cabinets were disapproving of the king's decision. The servants of Achish said, "Is this not David the king of the land? Did they not sing of this one as they danced, saying, 'Saul has slain his thousands, And David his ten thousands?' " (1 Samuel 21:11) Recognizing the danger, David feigned that he was mad playing so effectively that Achish was completely convinced. "So he disguised his sanity before them, and acted insanely in their hands, and scribbled on the doors of the gate, and let his saliva run down into his beard." (1 Samuel 21:13)

Escape to Engedi Cave_1 Samuel 24

After departing from Gath, David escaped to the cave of Adullam where the tribes of Judah were gathered in exile since the Benjaminites, the smallest tribe of Israel and Saul's family had begun persecuting them. 400 men gathered and they made David the captain over themselves making a great opportunity for David to revenge against Saul. (1 Samuel 22:1-3)

Due to Saul's relentless pursuit, David kept moving continuously from cave to cave and ended up in the cave of Engedi. The word 'Engedi' means "stream of a baby goat" in Korean. In the middle of the wilderness of Judah, there was a small waterfall in the cave of Engedi. Saul had come into the cave to have a bowel movement so most likely he must have had a one guard with him to watch while he was doing his business. In the cave, Saul was completely at David's mercy because that was where David and his men were hiding. Obviously the men thought this was their moment to kill Saul. "Shall we kill him?" But David persuaded them not to touch him. Instead he secretly cut off the edge of Saul's robe. "The men of David said to him, 'Behold, this is the day of which the Lord said to you, 'Behold; I am about to give your enemy into your hand, and you shall do to him as it seems good to you.' Then David arose and cut off the edge of Saul's robe secretly." (1 Samuel 24:4)

David Again Spares Saul's Life_1 Samuel 26

The pro-Saul Ziphites again laid information against David and for the second time, Saul found himself at David's mercy and was shamed into repentance. David found where Saul had camped and at night, he and Abishai went down to find Saul sleeping inside the camp with a spear stuck in the ground at his head. David could have easily struck him down but spared his life again. Instead, he took the spear and the jug of water with him as a proof. Then Saul realized and said, "I have sinned. Return, my son David, for I will not harm you again because my life was precious in your sight this day. Behold, I have played the fool and have committed a serious error." (1 Samuel 26:21)

Probably because David found exactly where Saul had camped in the wilderness of Ziph, the postal code in America is referred as a 'Zip Code.'

Second Refuge to the Philistines_1 Samuel 27

Hypothetically, let's imagine a potential candidate for our country's new leader has taken refuge in North Korea. Is it possible for this person to return later to South Korea and become a leader?

Knowledge Search 15

Reasons Why David Spared the Life of King Saul

1. It was because of his faith in God. "Far be it from me because of the Lord that I should do this thing to my lord, the Lord's anointed, to stretch out my hand against him, since he is the Lord's anointed." (1 Samuel 24:6) God's punishments are inevitable when church members dismiss God's anointed servants (pastors/ministers). We must learn the ways in which David handled such situations. Life threatening pursuit of Saul must have urged David to harm him but he believed that Saul was anointed by God. This meant that it was not up to him but God to judge. Therefore, he spared Saul's life even to the very end. "May the Lord judge between you and me, and may the Lord avenge me on you; but my hand shall not be against you." (1 Samuel 24:12)
2. If he had killed Saul, he would not have been able to embrace the remaining 11 tribes.
3. He did not want to leave a mark in the history of Israel that a king had been assassinated.

Absolutely not! But this was exactly what David did. A person who would be Israel's future king fled to his enemy's country. This was an enormous mistake on David's part. The reason behind this was obvious. It was an act of desperateness to take refuge a second time amongst the Philistines. At the same token, let's not forget how David prayed to God each moment throughout his fugitive life but he forgot and made his own decision in thinking that he would be safe in the enemy's country. This was an act of eating from the tree of the good and evil which brought him to the peak of his suffering that he had not experienced before. "But from the tree of the knowledge of good and evil you shall not eat, for in the day that you eat from it you shall surely die." (Genesis 2:17)

There were two major sufferings that David experienced during his refuge in the Philistines. Pretending to raid Israel and her allies, David fooled King Achish completely once again. Achish trusted David to the extent that he and his families were permitted to live in Ziklag, the land beneath Gath, along with providing 600 men under David's control. In fact, David wiped out enemy's cities leaving no one alive to tell the tale. "Now David and his men went up and raided the Geshurites and the Girzites and the Amalekites; for they were the inhabitants of the land from ancient times, as you come to Shur even as far as the land of Egypt. And David attacked the land and did not leave a man or a woman alive, and he took away the sheep, the cattle, the donkeys, the camels, and the clothing. Then he returned and came to Achish. Now Achish said, 'Where have you made a raid today?' And David said, 'Against the Negev of Judah and against the Negev of the Jerahmeelites and against the Negev of the Kenites.'" (1 Samuel 27:8-10)

The Philistines gathered their army for war against Israel and Achish asked David to fight with him. David assured him that he would. But the other Philistine overlords were less gullible than Achish so David was spared from this awkward predicament of facing his fellow countrymen to battle. God had moved the other commanders' heart to be suspicious. "But the commanders of the Philistines were angry with him, and the commanders of the Philistines said to him, 'Make the man go back, that he may return to his place where you have assigned him, and do not let him go down to battle with us, lest in the battle he become an adversary to us. For with what could this man make himself acceptable to his lord? Would it not be with the heads of these men? Is this not David, of whom they sing in the dances, saying, Saul has slain his thousands, And David his ten thousands'?" (1 Samuel 29:4-5)

Achish then told David, "As the Lord lives, you have been upright, and your going out and your coming in with me in the army are pleasing in my sight; for I have not found evil in you from the day of your coming to me to this day. Nevertheless, you are not pleasing in the sight of the lords. Now therefore return, and go in peace, that you may not displease the lords of the Philistines." (1 Samuel 29:6-7) One thing we must learn from this event is that prayers to God are made into a hedge by angels in which case, David's prayers in the past have saved him from another close call. Basically, David had no time to pray in this desperate moment and we can relate to that because it's quite natural that prayers are the last thing you think of when you are in a crisis. The importance of prayers must be emphasized here since all prayers that we do are made into somewhat like a shield over us protecting us when we are in trouble.

"I love you, O Lord, my strength. The Lord is my rock and my fortress and my deliverer." (Psalms 18:1-2)

The Revenge of the Amalekites_1 Samuel 30

David's return was perfect timing since another major suffering was waiting for him after a narrow escape from the battle. At this point, he was married with two wives and there were also family members of the 600 men which meant that David had approximately 2,000 people under him. After hearing that David was going to participate in the battle, the Amalekites raid the village in Ziklag where they burnt down the houses and looted the entire place as well as kidnapped the women and children to make them slaves. The exact people who had made David their leader were now about to stone him to death since their families were in danger. They blamed the disaster to David. This shows the real character of a human being. There's no problem when things go well but once something drastic happens, the blaming starts. David was greatly distressed with the people's reaction but strengthened himself in the Lord God. (1 Samuel 30:6)

David's confession is expressed in Psalms 18: "I call upon the Lord, who is worthy to be praised, And I am saved from my enemies. The cords of death encompassed me, And the torrents of ungodliness terrified me. The cords of Sheol surrounded me; The snares of death confronted me. In my distress I called upon the Lord, And cried to my God for help; He heard my voice out of His temple, And my cry for help before Him came into His ears." (Psalms 18:3-6)

David wrote Psalms 18, 20, 23, 30, 31, 40 in the midst of his troubles which portrays his prayers of outburst cries and gratitude towards God. When David finally came to the throne, it was clear that God, not his own political ambition, had brought him there. A great king was to be born after going through tremendous hardship.

Death of Saul_1 Samuel 31~ 2 Samuel 1

The last battle with the Philistines caused Saul's death. If David had participated in this battle, probably the people of Israel may have said that he had killed Saul. But then again, God prevented this altogether. Saul was a man who only thought of himself. The most important aspect of his life was his throne and striving with all his might to protect 'himself.'

There was a pastor who compared our religious life to an umbrella that was left back at home. On an ordinary day, the umbrella is completely forgotten but when it suddenly rains you start searching for it. In other words, you only need an umbrella when it rains. God is not like an umbrella where you need only when necessary. He is our rock and refuge but many times we put God aside and completely forget about Him just like a forgotten umbrella. People falling under this category tend to go pretty much everywhere. Claiming to be Christians and yet they visit fortunetellers. Rather than accepting God as a character of love, they become self-focused and egocentric. In other words, as long as you are satisfied, nothing matters anymore. But we must realize that in the end, their result would be the same as Saul's life.

"Then they asked for a king, and God gave them Saul the son of Kish, a man of the tribe of Benjamin, for forty years." (Acts 13:21) What kind of life did Saul lead for 40 years? He strived throughout the years to keep his kingship and never was content. During his lifetime, he experienced hell and ended in hell after death.

We must look at David's remarkable outreach towards his valued friendship with Jonathan, son of Saul after his father's death. He wrote a song of comfort for Jonathan which is referred to as the 'song of the bow.' The lament for Saul and Jonathan is one of the most moving and beautiful piece of all David's poems. Sword, bow, eagles and lions are used to express Saul and Jonathan in the song. "From the blood of the slain, from the fat of the mighty, The bow of Jonathan did not turn back, And the sword of Saul did not return empty. 'Saul and Jonathan, beloved and pleasant in their life, And in their death they were not parted; They were swifter than eagles, They were stronger than lions. O daughters of Israel, weep over Saul, Who clothed you luxuriously in scarlet, Who put ornaments of gold on your apparel.'"(2 Samuel 1:22-24)

His regret for the king seems wholly sincere; his distress at the loss of Jonathan was deep and genuine. Let us not forget that Saul's 13 years of pursuit to kill David and imagine David commemorating a song of lamentation for Saul! This is certainly not possible for an ordinary person and quite frankly, he must not have liked Saul in the first place. But David is revealing the meaning of loving one's enemy that is referred in the New Testament here. It was not because he was a great man but because of his strong conviction that the king's life was sacred since he was God's anointed one. He is asking everyone to mourn for the death of Saul who was after his own life. In our modern days, when a supervisor from a company passes a nasty remark towards us we automatically get upset and a thought of "when will that person drop dead!" crosses our mind. Through David's lament and the way he handled himself earned him great respect from the people of Israel.

David Was Made the King of Judah_2 Samuel 2

David inquired God where he should go and received an answer.

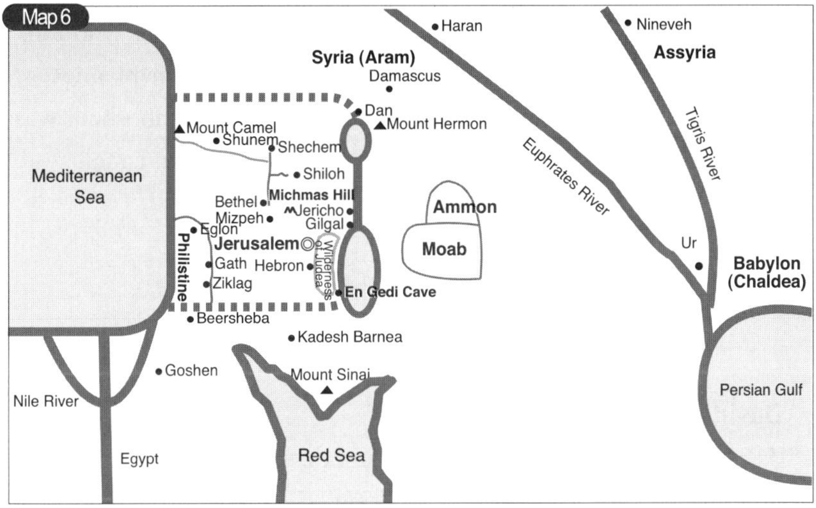

Period of United Kingdom_David David flees from King Saul and escapes to Gath in Philistines. David asks God where he should go and receives an answer.

"'Shall I go up to one of the cities of Judah?' And the Lord said to him, 'Go up.'" (2 Samuel 2:1) The place God directed him to go was Hebron, a land in the wilderness of Judah and was also the founding place of Abraham, Isaac and Jacob. Hebron was David's capital before he took over Jerusalem and this was where the reign of King David began.

When David became a king, he was 30 years old. It was 13 years later since his young days as a shepherd when he was anointed at the age of 17; he killed Goliath and soon thereafter, his fugitive journey began at King Saul's life threatening pursuit. God did not make David the king over Israel right away after King Saul's death. At this point, he was made as a king in the small southern tribe of Judah. In other words, there were still other kings other than David in the 11 tribes of Israel. Even though King Saul was dead, the other eleven tribes followed the lead of Abner, Saul's army commander and gave allegiance to Ishbosheth, Saul's son.

For two years the nation was divided and Israel experienced another full scale civil war approximately for 7 years. Ishbosheth was not the man like his father was but Abner was the real power who took Saul's concubine as his wife. Abner eventually died in revenge of Joab, David's nephew and his army commander and Ishbosheth was assassinated which results in the downfall of the northern Israel.

David Becomes King Over All Israel

_2 Samuel 5-6, 1 Chronicles 11-16

David Rules from Jerusalem

All the eleven tribes of northern Israel came to David at Hebron and requested him to become their king. He finally became a king over Israel at the age of 37. He reigned over Israel and Judah for 33 years until the age of 70.

In a shrewd political move to give him independent power, David takes the Jebusite city of Jerusalem and makes it his capital. It was an impregnable fortress with a height of 770m above sea level with natural water and was also the place where Abraham had offered Isaac, Mt. Moriah. This territory had not been conquered for hundreds of years since Joshua's days through the period of the Judges. And now finally David's men took the Jerusalem citadel by means of a tunnel which brought water into the city from an outside spring. Jerusalem was a first-rate choice of capital since it was centrally situated, tribally neutral, had a distinguished pre-history from Abraham's time and could, therefore, provide the 12 tribes with a unifying center. Threader: During King Hezekiah's time, the water supply is channeled from the Spring of Gihon to the surface level of the Pool of Siloam.

It was approximately A.D. 1,000, exactly 1,000 years since Abraham, when David made Jerusalem as his capital. It is written that Abraham, Isaac and Jacob lived in tents rather than in a city. "By faith Abraham, when he was called, obeyed by going out to a place which he was to receive for an inheritance; and he went out, not knowing where he was going. By faith he lived as an alien in the land of promise, as in a foreign land, dwelling in tents with Isaac and Jacob, fellow heirs of the same promise; for he was looking for the city which has foundations, whose architect and builder is God."(Hebrews 11:8-10)

While David was in the midst of proceeding with God's foundation, the Philistines came in but they were totally oppressed by David's army. (2 Samuel 5:17-25) From this point on, there is no record of the Philistines attacking Israel anymore. We see the glimpse of the great heroic works of David. Even today, the Philistines are completely dominated by Israel which is basically due to David.

What becomes of the city is more important than the historical fact of David making Jerusalem as his capital. After the Philistines returned the Ark, it remained at Kiriath-jearim but now David brought it to his new capital after lo. The occasion is marked with all the exuberance of Jewish worship. The Ark was kept in the Most Holy place and the high priests would go inside once a year and sprinkle the blood of sacrifice against the altar to signify that by the blood that is shed, people can come into the presence of God. Sin inevitably means death, being cut off from God. But when the death penalty has been satisfied, the people can be brought to God and established permanently in His presence.

The word "Shalom" means peace and comes from "Jerusalem" which can be referred to as the 'house of peace.' "Pray for the peace of Jerusalem: 'May they prosper who love you. May peace be within your walls, And prosperity within your palaces.'" (Psalms 122:6-7) Another word for Jerusalem is Zion which means the 'city of God.' The holy city, the 'new' heaven and earth is mentioned in the book of Revelation and through David the Ark finally comes to Jerusalem. In a sense, the city of Jerusalem is being proclaimed that it belongs to God. God's promise to Abraham, Jerusalem becomes the capital of God's Kingdom, is now being fulfilled through David by bringing the Ark to Jerusalem.

Many animals are sacrificed in the temple in Jerusalem as well as our Savior Jesus who shed His blood on the cross for the sins of mankind. The city of Jerusalem becomes the city of salvation. It also carries a significant spiritual meaning that the second coming of Christ will come in the holy 'new' city of Jerusalem. "And I saw a new heaven and a new earth; for the first heaven and the first earth passed away, and there is no longer any sea. And I saw the holy city, new Jerusalem, coming down out of heaven from God, made ready as a bride adorned for her husband." (Revelation 21:1-2) God and His throne is the city of Jerusalem. "To which the tribes go up, even the tribes of the Lord - An ordinance for Israel - To give thanks to the name of the Lord. For there thrones were set for judgment, The thrones of the house of David." (Psalms 122:4-5)

God's Covenant with David_2 Samuel 7:8-16, 1 Chronicles 17:4-14

After moving the Ark into the city of Jerusalem, David confessed to Nathan the prophet, "See now, I dwell in a house of cedar, but the ark of God dwells within tent curtains." (2 Samuel 7:2) He was living in a palace built with cedar transported from Lebanon by Hiram, king of Tyre. The sea-port of Tyre was the capital of the Phoenician kingdom and was known for commercial prosperity with arts and crafts. It was the Phoenician craftsmen who helped build David's palace. David felt guilty for living comfortably when the Ark of God was inside the tent and thought how cold God must be. Obviously, God who is the Spirit does not need any dwelling space but it shows how passionately David loved God.

But, in any event, God did not allow David to make his dream of building the Temple come true, to build the temple for his son, a man of peace, not a warrior. But the disappointment is followed by a promise that goes way beyond anything David could have asked. No wonder his response is a great outpouring of love and praise. "I have been with you wherever you have gone and have cut off all your enemies from before you; and I will make you a great name, like the names of the great men who are on the earth." (2 Samuel 7:9) David may not be allowed to build the house of God, but God will build him a house - a dynasty - which will last forever. (2 Samuel 7:16)

Basically God wanted David to remain as a respectful king. David's son, Solomon, did build the Temple but David contributed a great deal to it; he drew up the plans, provided materials, and organized and assigned Temple duties including music and worship. The blessing overflowed to his son as well who committed sin down the road. But his kingship would be intact and judgment would not be carried out; instead fatherly warnings would be given to him. This was a tremendous blessing from God for David.

On this promise, rests a hope which runs right through the remainder of the Old Testament, the hope of a Messiah. And when Christ came, the promise was fulfilled. He was born in Bethlehem, David's birthplace, and as "Of the house and lineage of David." (2 Samuel 7:16) David was able to receive such a great blessing from God because of his dedication, obedience and love to God. "He who has My commandments and keeps them, he it is who loves Me; and he who loves Me shall be loved by My Father, and I will love him, and will disclose Myself to him." (John 14:21)

Obedience to the Word of God should be reflected in our daily lives. God's main interests are love and blessings so if we obey His Word and obey Him, we will receive blessings. "He who does not love Me does not keep My words." (John 14:24) We really must be sensitive and be alert to the Word of God and put our efforts to obey it.

David's Mistake

Adultery with Bathsheba_2 Samuel 11

"Then it happened in the spring, at the time when kings go out to battle." (2 Samuel 11:1) David's army was fighting the Ammonites, but this spring, the king was not with them and instead was resting in his palace at the urging of his generals. "You shall not go out again with us to battle, that you may not extinguish the lamp of Israel." (2 Samuel 21:17) This was the problem. In the past, through many hardships and turbulent life through his ordeal, David only held on to God. And now, the Ark was returned to Jerusalem and life became comfortable for him. He was taking an afternoon siesta, strolling in the cool part of the palace roof.

There is no chance of sinning during the difficult times since we focus on God. We do not realize that the problematic situations are actually the blessing to us. Without difficult periods in our life, we would not hold on to God. From his vantage point, David could see down into the open courtyard of a nearby house, where the lovely Bathsheba was taking a bath. "David sent messengers and took her, and when she came to him, he lay with her; and when she had purified herself from her uncleanness, she returned to her house." (2 Samuel 11:4) She was brought to him by force and David committed adultery.

After finding out that she was pregnant, David sent for her husband, Uriah, who was at the battlefield fighting against the Ammonites, to return to his wife. In other words, he wanted Uriah to spend the night with his wife but being a loyal soldier, he stayed in the palace claiming that it would be unwise to go home while his men were fighting in the battlefield. David had no choice but to plot for Uriah's death by sending a letter to the commander in chief requesting to place Uriah in the front line of the fiercest battle and withdraw from him so that he may be struck down and be killed. David committed murder.

We normally think of David as a great king but he had committed the worst sins of all according to the Bible. Not only one but two, adultery and murder. There is no other greater sinner than he! The Bible is trying to reveal to us that "There is none righteous, not even one." (Romans 3:10) No matter how righteously David led his life in God, wrote many poems and received great blessings, the possibility of committing a great sin was always there even after experiencing God' special blessing.

But what redeemed David here is the fact that in the face of prophet Nathan's rebuke, he repented immediately and admitted his double sin. The most important thing is the attitude when you repent. In other words, the moment you sin, you must kneel down and confess to God, "I have sinned." The attitudes of the kings of the Northern and Southern Kingdom were such that when mistakes were addressed by the prophets, instead of repenting, some imprisoned and persecuted them. One of them even sawed the prophet to death. There were no excuses uttered from David showing his greatness once again and not commit such sin again even until his death.

True repentance means not only are you confessing your sins but never committing the same sin again. After shedding tears of remorse and saying that it would be the last time, few days later if you find yourself saying, 'I had no choice but to sin,' that is not what we call repentance.

We must realize God forgives our sins but the sins that we've committed in the world will remain as our own scores. For instance, if a person who have committed adultery or murder repents to God then his sins are forgiven and salvation is received which means that the person will not go to hell. But at the same time the sins that have already been committed will be dealt according to the laws of the world.

The consequences of David's sin are prophesied through Nathan, the prophet. "Behold, I will raise up evil against you from your own household; I will even take your wives before your eyes, and give them to your companion, and he shall lie with your wives in broad daylight. 'Indeed you did it secretly, but I will do this thing before all Israel, and under the sun.'" (2 Samuel 12:11-12)

"The sword shall never depart from your house, because you have despised Me and have taken the wife of Uriah the Hittite to be your wife." (2 Samuel 12:10) The prophecy of Nathan was fulfilled. Three of David's sons are murdered, two by their own brothers and the rebellion of Absalom.

The Rebellion of Absalom_2 Samuel 13

David was well respected as a strong king in Israel but as predicted by the prophet Nathan, David's son, Absalom, started to scheme a rebellious act against his father. The family feud amounted to a civil war, and David's life was under threat. Absalom's hatred towards his father was so tremendous that it was to the degree of killing his father with a sword.

The appalling rape of his sister Tamar by her half-brother Amnon stirred hatred and revenge of Absalom who was eventually sent into exile. But by the mercy of David, Absalom returned back to Jerusalem and his conspiracy took place against his father. David wept, this time for himself, as he fled Jerusalem from his castle to Mount Olive so hastily that he walked away barefooted along with his servants and guards. When David reached Bahurim, Shimei, Saul's relative, came out, passing vindictive curses at him and started to throw stones at David and all of his servants.

Then one of the aid said to David, "let me cut off his head!" But the king said, "What have I to do with you, O sons of Zeruiah? If he curses, and if the Lord has told him, 'Curse David,' then who shall say, 'Why have you done so?'" (2 Samuel 16:10) David was a great king since he thoroughly reflected upon his sins. Not to mention that running away from Saul for 13 years was not enough, he was now in a situation where he had to run away from his own son - all because of his sin of adultery. David had secretly committed adultery with Uriah's wife but his own son, Absalom, raped David's 10 wives in the broad daylight out in the open place.

Death of Absalom _ 2 Samuel 18

Absalom must have been a tall handsome man with long hair almost touching his feet. David's order to his commander Joab was to spare Absalom's life but he was shrewd enough to see that only the death of the pretender or the king can settle the issue.

The irony was that Absalom was riding his donkey in the forest during the battle and his beautiful long hair got tangled in the oak tree and the donkey moved on without him leaving him dangling as a helpless prey. One of the soldier spotted this and alerted Joab who went and struck him dead with his sword. David was torn with anguish upon Absalom's death but he came back to his senses once again and eventually returned to his city, Jerusalem.

Records of David's Reign

Destruction of the Philistines_2 Samuel 21:15-22

One of the achievements of David was the extermination of the Philistines. The descendants of the giant Goliath and potential warriors were all struck down. Even though it might appear as a bloody massacre, the Israel were not attacked by the Philistines anymore.

Promise Kept with the Gibeonites_2 Samuel 21:1-14

We must recall the cunning alliance of the Gibeonites during Joshua's period which Israel could not draw back from a treaty. But 200 years later, King Saul had broken the treaty, trying to destroy the Gibeonites and God punished the nation for breaking their word. King David allowed the Gibeonites to kill seven of Saul's sons to settle down the matter.

The Census_2 Samuel 24, 1 Chronicles 21

"Then Satan stood up against Israel and moved David to number Israel." (1 Chronicles 21:1)

"The anger of the Lord burned against Israel, and it incited David against them to say, 'Go, number Israel and Judah.'" (2 Samuel 24:1)

The census in ancient times was very cruel. It indicated reliance on numbers instead of God. By taking the census, the glory went to the king and secondly, through the census one would determine how much taxes could be collected as well as determining the numbers of men who would be drafted in case of war. This resulted in tremendous burden and hardships on the people.

Threader: During the New Testament period, the reason why Joseph and a very pregnant Mary traveled from Nazareth to Bethlehem was for family registry because the census of Rome was being performed at the time. We get the glimpse of how impractical and hardships that people had to go through at the time.

A plague was sent from God because of David's census. A pestilence upon Israel for three days where 70,000 people died. The angel stretched out his hand toward Jerusalem striking down the people and David knelt down in repentance. "Behold, it is I who have sinned, and it is I who have done wrong; but these sheep, what have they done? Please let Your hand be against me and against my father's house."(2 Samuel 24:17) This is a true attitude of a shepherd who loves his sheep. Just as David had shown his obedience towards the anointed King Saul, churchgoers must also obey God's anointed messengers (pastors/ministers) at church under no circumstances. The sensitive issues arising from churches must be dealt with Godly attitudes rather than persuading who's right or wrong in a worldly way.

Preparation to Build the Temple_2 Samuel 24

After repenting, at the suggestion of Gad as God had commanded, David went and bought the threshing floor from Araunah for 50 shekels of silver to build an altar to God. This was David's last achievement before his death and on this threshing floor that is close to the place where Abraham prepared to offer up Isaac, the temple was built. Even though the actual temple was built by David's son Solomon, every detailed preparation (starting from design, construction and materials including area) was provided by him. Clearly we feel the passion of David and his desire in building a temple of God. 'One thing I have asked from the Lord, that I shall seek: that I may dwell in the house of the Lord all the days of my life, to behold the beauty of the Lord and to meditate in His temple. (Psalms 27:4)

Path of David vs. Path of Jeroboam

"Be careful that you do not offer your burnt offerings in every cultic place you see, but in the place which the Lord chooses in one of your tribes, there you shall offer your burnt offerings, and there you shall do all that I command you." (Deuteronomy 12:13-14) God clearly instructed His chosen people the distinctive place to worship and told them not to give any offerings at any place other than the designated place - which is the Temple in Jerusalem. It was a temple that was designed by God and David facilitated it in the city of Jerusalem.

God was most pleased with David because of his dedication in giving worship and prayer in the Temple. David sought out only for one thing, which was to dwell and meditate in the house of God. (Psalms 27:4) God was happy with David's religion of temple worship.

On the other hand, in order to sustain his throne, Jeroboam built the temples as he wished (an act of eating from the tree of good and evil), which were built in Bethel and Dan, forcing the people to give their burnt offerings there. Outwardly, the formality of giving offerings (service) to God was performed but in truth, it was done according to Jeroboam's way which God detested. A curse will be given to anyone who follows the paths of Jeroboam that they will be "swept away like dung."(1 Kings 14:10)

In today's world, a church that was bought and raised by the blood of Christ is the place for us to worship. So a church is "Is His body, the fulness of Him who fills all in all." (Ephesians 1:23) In a simpler term, it means that a church is a place where Jesus fills you up in all different ways. Obviously you can sing praise, pray and even study the Bible at home as well but it is God's promise that He will fill our hearts in whatever method He deems appropriate through the church service. People who don't believe in the importance of church are the same as those following the path of Jeroboam.

By giving daily worship in God's temple (especially the early morning service) and experiencing God's presence through the church, we must become the body of Christ. We then receive the power from above that fills our heart so that we may share the blessings with others in the world. Ultimately we must become the channel of blessings to others.

The History of Israel is the History of War

The history of Israel in the Old Testament is completely filled with wars.

Exodus and Period of the Wilderness

Spiritual war whether they are being guided properly to enter the Promised Land or not.

Promised Land, their lives should have improved in the Promised Land, but having no water, food and in the wilderness suffering brought war of complaints and frustrations instead.

Period of Conquest

War with the Canaanites (evil foreign idols: Baal) in order to establish God's Kingdom in the Promised Land. Spiritual war against inner self (casting away self-absorbing lifestyles and lustful thoughts, etc.) by holding on to the Holy Spirit within us.

Period of the Judges

War against attacks from neighboring tribes as God's tool of punishment. Spiritual war compelling to trust in God as your only judge.

Period of Kingship

War of protecting God's Kingdom.

Spiritual war whether you seeking the invisible God through temple worship or following the visual things in life (Division of believers: those who are in spirit or in flesh).

Through the historical wars of Israel in the Old Testament, regardless of the boundaries of time or place, we learn that the only way to overcome the spiritual war is fulfilling God's Kingdom in us first and then expanding God's Kingdom on this earth through our daily worship (Bible, praise and prayer). We can win over the spiritual war only through worship.

EVEN IN KING'S POSITION IS VANITY OF VANITIES, KING SOLOMON

1 Kings 1-11, 2 Chronicles 1-9
Solomon is the king who enjoyed his reign in the peak of Israel's United Kingdom. King Solomon had received blessings of prosperity due to his faithful parents but in the end, he failed to sustain his loyalty. The cause of his downfall was his turning from God to worship idols. By writing the books of Ecclesiastes, Proverbs and Lamentations, he led many people to the road of salvation but sadly failed to save himself.

Solomon's Peak of His Power

1,000 Burnt Offerings_1 Kings 3, 2 Chronicles 1

Solomon was not an immediate successor of David since he had other elder brothers. Besides, his mother was Bathsheba which made him even more of an obstacle for kingship.

But Solomon had inherited his father's faith and gave 1,000 burnt offerings to God. Since it was before the temple was built, he went to Gibeon, a town northwest of Jerusalem to make his sacrifice. We must understand that it was 1,000 individual burnt offerings offered not 1,000 sacrificial services. The time spent on these offerings must have been extremely long. That night God appeared to him in a dream, offering a gift which was for him to choose. "Ask what you wish me to give you." (1 Kings 3:5)

He asked for wisdom to rule his people justly. It was the choice of a man whose heart was right before God and so he was given more than he asked for. Solomon was renowned for his wise judgment that uncovers the true facts of the cases even when they are particularly hard to solve. The case of the two women who were against each other over the baby is famous for his revealing and using the special insight in human nature to solve the issue. His fame spread far and wide even to the foreign countries upon the visit of the Queen of Sheba as his kingdom enjoyed unprecedented economical prosperity.

Ceremony of the Temple_1 Kings 8, 2 Chronicles 6

Upon his strong faith inherited from his parents, Solomon builds the temple after completing his offerings to God. As we know it was David's great ambition to build God a temple, finally God's promise to David is being fulfilled through Solomon.

Works are completed and the Ark is brought from the citadel and installed in the inner sanctuary. The whole temple building shines with the light of God's presence, the same bright cloud that once rested on God's Tent in the desert. The prayer of dedication for the temple takes place. The famous confession, Solomon's prayer for the royal house and for the nation echoes the language of Moses. (1 Kings 8:22-55; 1 Chronicles 6:12-42).

He asks God to hear the prayers and forgive the sins of his people and whoever focuses on the temple and to answer their prayers. "Listen to the supplication of Your servant and of Your people Israel, when they pray toward this place; hear you in heaven Your dwelling place; hear and forgive." (1 Kings 8:30)

His remarkable faith is displayed in this prayer. Let us take a moment and imagine a young man kneeling down with his two hands raised up high and praying out loud. Whenever I picture this in my mind, my heart is filled with compassion and my eyes well up with tears of emotion each time. After his prayers, the temple is filled with God's glory and His blessing followed after it; blessing by sacrifice, sacrifice by feasting and rejoicing throughout the land.

What a beautiful sight of service and the loving character of

Solomon! That night, after the consecration festival, God speaks to Solomon again. The 'if...if not'- God repeats the promise made to David with a warning. (1 Kings 9:4-5)

Unfortunately, Solomon ignored this and followed the foreign gods and suffered the consequences, though God did not break His promise of keeping David's family line. (2 Chronicles 7:12-22)

Again, receiving God's blessing is totally up to us whether we obey His words or live according to the worldly ways. The freedom of choice is ours.

King Solomon's Wisdom_1 Kings 10

There was no greater splendor that any king has experienced than King Solomon. He was the first of Israel's kings to create a merchant navy. The fabulous wealth and revenue through trade and taxes were just enormous that all the neighboring countries came to give a tribute to Israel. As promised by God, Israel prospered and Solomon tasted all fortunes that a person could experience on this earth. Even queen of Sheba visited Solomon to find out for herself the truth after hearing intriguing reports of his wisdom and splendor.

"King Solomon gave to the queen of Sheba all her desire which she requested, besides what he gave her according to his royal bounty. Then she turned and went to her own land together with her servants." (1 Kings 10:13) The queen requested for a seed of wisdom and Solomon gave it to her. This meant that they had spent the night together and she conceived.

Solomon came to realization that the more wisdom and knowledge one has the more grief and pain it brings. (Ecclesiastes 1:12-18) He had sought out all the desires of the world. Remember now. He had 1,000 wives! "He had seven hundred wives, princesses, and three hundred concubines, and his wives turned his heart away." (1 Kings 11:3) Solomon had lived his life to the fullest especially through sex. But just like one can never be satisfied with materialistic things, the greed can never fill up one's heart.

The life learning conclusion of Solomon was "Vanity of vanities! All is vanity." (Ecclesiastes 1:2) It was repeated five times. He also expressed that life without God is same as having nothing even if you have everything and warned us with "Remember also your Creator in the days of your youth, before the evil days come and the years draw near when you will say, 'I have no delight in them.'" (Ecclesiastes 12:1) This is the conclusion of the book of Ecclesiastes as well as the beginning.

"For you have been born again not of seed which is perishable but imperishable, that is, through the living and abiding word of God. For, all flesh is like grass, and all its glory like the flower of grass. The grass withers, and the flower falls off, but the Word of the Lord abides forever." (1 Peter 1:23-25) This confession of Apostle Peter was also spoken by Solomon when he was reigning as a king 1,000 years ago. The message is loud and clear; the glory of the world is nothing. "The conclusion, when all has been heard, is: fear God and keep His commandments, because this applies to every person. For God will bring every act to judgment, everything which is hidden, whether it is good or evil." (Ecclesiastes 12:13-14) Only the Word of God is eternal.

King Solomon's Downfall_1 King 11

Marriage of Convenience

When Solomon was young, he honored God and wrote the books of Proverbs, Ecclesiastes and Song of Solomon. But in his old age, he quickly turned from God to worship idols. Why did he fall? It was due to many women in his life "... his wives turned his heart away." (1 Kings 11:3) For this particular reason, the kings of Israel were warned to refrain themselves from having many wives according to Deuteronomy 17.

During his reign, the land of Israel expanded all the way from Egypt to the upper part of Euphrates. In spite of earlier warnings,

Solomon did all evil things in the eyes of God. Having a mind to protect his country by himself rather than relying on God. He started to fortify his cities with chariots and created a merchant navy. One can still see the remains of the site of Solomon's chariot city if you visit Megiddo today.

His political marriage alliances no doubt contributed to the country's peace and security but then again, young foreign wives brought with them foreign gods. Although he wrote 'vanities, vanities brings nothing' as a young man, he completely forgot everything as an old man. He became totally captivated by his young wives. Each of them requested their own temple to serve their foreign god and probably at first, he might have scolded them but in the end gave in. Eventually the whole city of Jerusalem was filled with temples for foreign gods. Even today, if you go up to Mt. Olives in front of Jerusalem, you can still see some of the remaining temples that Solomon had built. Loathsome acts of worshipping these foreign gods, such as Milcom, the god of the Ammonites, involved child sacrifice (by boiling a child in hot water), fertility rites, prostitution and sexual practices which were forbidden in Israel were all permitted by Solomon because of his love for his young wives. (1 Kings 11:3)

How quickly God was forgotten! Solomon's devotion to God diminished rapidly because of his worldly desires. The focus on visual blessings blinded him from the invisible God and His Words. Once he was bitten by the physical attraction of the world, it was natural for him to distance himself from God. This applies to us as well that if we fail to keep the Word of God, neglect to pray and give worship, we will also end up like Solomon.

Man's Promise and God's Promise

Solomon completely fell in his last years. God warned him twice. "Because you have done this, and you have not kept My covenant and My statutes, which I have commanded you, I will surely tear the kingdom from you, and will give it to your servant." (1 Kings 11:11)

Remember how King David repented promptly when the prophet Nathan warned him but Solomon's attention were all stolen by his women. God's warning was completely ignored. God's blessings of wealth (i.e., glory of the world) overshadowed the presence of God and the wisdom God gave. The mindset of self-reliance started to sink into him leading to think that he could run the country without God.

"My loving kindness shall not depart from him, as I took it away from Saul, whom I removed from before you." (2 Samuel 7:15) God would have said, 'I will judge Israel and destroy it' if it was other kings. But in order to keep His covenant with David, God tore the kingdom into two. Internal strife weakened both kingdoms and the nations were preyed to stronger neighbors. Eventually, they were devoured by the great powers. The final split of the kingdom occurred not during the Solomon's days because of God's promise but during Solomon's son, Rehoboam.

Threader: The main core of David's promise was the permanence of David's dynasty. The Jews believe in the continuity of David's dynasty even today so Jerusalem remains as their crucial point of place since its recovery has yet to be accomplished. It is noted that peace in the Middle East becomes difficult for this specific reason. When Jesus said that He will return, one of the disciples asked, "Is it at the time when Israel will be restored?" The belief of God's promise to David for the people of Israel is tremendous. Jesus fulfills David's lineage by His birth as you open the book of Matthew, as it reads: "The book of the genealogy of Jesus Christ, the son of David, the son of Abraham." (Matthew 1:1) But unfortunately, the Jews do not accept this so they are still waiting for David's kingdom to be restored in Israel.

Solomon had good faith when he was young by following the footsteps of his parents but failed to keep his own. This tells us that no matter how strong faith our parents may have, we must have our own faith. Not only do we need to study the Word but daily prayers are essential to experience His presence so that we awaken ourselves.

“As for you, the anointing which you received from Him abides in you, and you have no need for anyone to teach you; but as His anointing teaches you about all things, and is true and is not a lie, and just as it has taught you, you abide in Him.” (1 John 2:27)

Apostle Paul reminded himself not to make the same mistake as Solomon who glorified himself in the end. A man who saved many others and yet failed to save himself “I protest, brethren, by the boasting in you, which I have in Christ Jesus our Lord, I die daily.” (1 Corinthians 15:31)

David was much smarter than Solomon in every way because he did not seek the blessings of the earth but sought God instead. “One thing I have asked from the Lord, that I shall seek: That I may dwell in the house of the Lord all the days of my life, To behold the beauty of the Lord, And to meditate in His temple.” (Psalms 27:4)

I would like to throw a challenging question to my readers: Which lifestyle would you choose for yourself - David who yearned to enter into God’s heart by praying and worshiping daily or Solomon who became blinded with all the glorious blessings of the world but thrown out by God in the end? The choice is yours as always.

Lessons from the Three Kings - Saul, David and Solomon

By anointing three kings in Israel, God wanted to recover the Garden of Eden (God's Kingdom). Only those with God's direct anointment were made as the king of Israel. They had to obey the law and God's command as a dutiful 'servant' of God.

But unfortunately during the period of the United Kingdom, all three kings sinned right after receiving great blessings from God. Basically all of them committed sin because of 'Me.'

Saul was a young man from the countryside and became Israel's first king. His disobedience occurred because of his thought to maintain his pride as a king. He performed offerings when it was prohibited. As for David, right after receiving great blessings from God that his household, country and kingship would continue forever, he committed adultery to satisfy his lust and then to cover his sin, the conspiracy of murder took place. And Solomon having received wisdom from God experienced great prosperity and good fortune in an unprecedented and splendid way, but his glory was magnified to the point that he established the prohibited chariot armies as mentioned in the book of Deuteronomy. He committed the greatest sin of all by distancing himself from God entirely due to worldly marriage with the foreign princesses to form political alliances and even worshipping idols.

Ironically, the sins of these three kings appear more like a repeated version of the original sin of mankind during the period of creation (Genesis 1-11). The kingship that was given to Saul was like that in the Garden of Eden where he could eat and rule everything except the forbidden tree of the good and evil - but the command of God was disobeyed by Saul much like those in the Garden. David's murder due to the result of his adultery was same as Cain's killing of his brother Abel and Cain being thrown out of the Garden of Eden resembled David's hasty escape in tears from the city of Jerusalem. Solomon's sin resembled the challenge to God by building the Tower of Babel as the ancestors who fell into worshipping idolatries and ultimately turned away from God. That is why the Garden of Eden (God's Kingdom) must be "cultivated and kept" - to work it and take care of it (Genesis 2:15).

God's response to sin is consistently a blend of judgment and mercy. He clothed Adam and Eve with leather after they sinned and threw them out to the east side of the Garden of Eden. An opportunity to repent to God was given to them through their sufferings.

In the same manner, even though the kingship of Saul was switched over to David in the end, he continued to reign for 40 years giving him ample time to repent. Just as Cain was given an opportunity to repent by the seal of protection of his life after his murder, God also spared David's life and gave him sufferings through his own son Absalom's conspiracy which enabled him to repent completely. Again, in a similar way as the confusion of tongues at Babel scattered the nations, God split the kingdom into two and giving ample time to Solomon to repent and return. God tempered his justice with generosity. Beyond the immediate punishment, there is always God's ultimate intention for humanity's well-being and blessing.

In a world of disorder and corruption, we long to receive 'blessings' from God but then again, we must realize that there is a greater chance for us to sin than not. Thus, we must put our efforts in giving worship to God and praying to God so that even though we may fall at times, we should not be discouraged but repent immediately just as David had done. Our true repentance means to 'change' ourselves and not fall into the pattern of repetitious cycle. I pray for all my readers that each of you may please the heart of God and trust in Him with all your mind, soul and heart.

. . .

In Gibeon the LORD appeared to Solomon in a dream at night; and God said, "Ask what you wish me to give you." Then Solomon said, "You have shown great lovingkindness to Your servant David my father, according as he walked before You in truth and righteousness and uprightness of heart toward You; and You have reserved for him this great lovingkindness, that You have given him a son to sit on his throne, as it is this day.

1 Kings 3:5-6

HISTORY OF THE NORTHERN ISRAEL, JEROBOAM'S WAY

1 Kings 12-22, 2 Kings

The above chapters are one of the most difficult parts to read among all the books in the Bible. It becomes quite confusing since it goes back and forth between the two kingdoms: Northern Israel and Judah. In this book, I will separate the history of the Northern Israel and Southern Judah completely in order to fully help you to understand the works of God during this period.

The History of Northern Kingdom of Israel, Jeroboam's Way

Reason for the Division of the Kingdom _1 Kings 12

There may be various reasons why Israel was divided but in a broad sense, there are two:

First, it was due to Solomon's sin. In spite of the warnings, he turned away from God and worshipped various foreign gods brought by his foreign wives. To keep God's promise with David, He did not destroy Solomon but instead split Israel into two.

Second, it was due to the arrogance of Solomon' s son, Rehoboam. It took 7 years to build the Solomon's temple and another 13years to build his own royal palace afterwards. The vast labor force was needed for new building and defense works required heavy taxes from the people. The people were exhausted

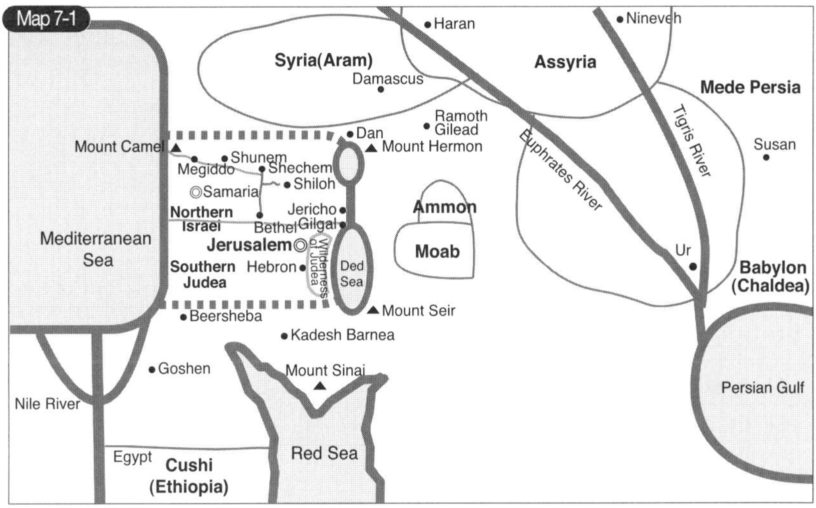

Period of Divided Monarchy Worshipping idols were the ways of Jeroboam of Northern Israel and God worshipping were the ways of David of Southern Judah. The figure of Divided Monarchy is a foreshadow of our identitles.

after working in labor for 20 years. So they brought their complaints to the newly appointed King Rehoboam to request for relief from their hard labor and taxation. Rather than listening to the elders of Israel, Rehoboam consulted with the young men who he grew up with and responded to the people, "My little finger is thicker than my father's loins! Whereas my father loaded you with a heavy yoke, I will add to your yoke; my father disciplined you with whips, but I will discipline you with scorpions." (1 Kings 12:10-11, 14) Realizing their request was denied, the people of Israel left their land except the tribes of Judah. "When all Israel saw that the king did not listen to them, the people answered the king, saying, 'What portion do we have in David? We have no inheritance in the son of Jesse; To your tents, O Israel! Now look after your own house, David!'" (1 Kings 12:16)

The division of the kingdom was permanent-the Northern Israel and Southern Judah. When we read the book of Kings, we must pay attention to the word 'Israel' because the Bible does not specify whether it's Northern or Southern Israel but make a note that when you read the book of Kings whenever 'Israel' is mentioned it refers to

Northern Israel. Otherwise you will be confused if you think of it as the 'united' Israel.

● ● Northern Israel - Jeroboam's Way_1 Kings 12:25-33

The Temple of Jerusalem and Temple of Golden Calves in Bethel

For approximately 200 years (B.C. 920-722), there were 19 kings in Northern Israel. Jeroboam, the first king of Northern Israel, set Israel on the wrong downward path of sin against God so that many kings followed his way. The Bible refers any evil doings of a king as 'Jeroboam's path'. Kings who did evil things of worshipping idols in the eyes of God.

Jeroboam was originally one of the Solomon's men. He was in charge of the laborers(tribes of Benjamin) in the copper mines near the Red Sea. The northern tribes found a leader and spokesman in Jeroboam but negotiations they initiated for a separate kingdom broke down at the face of Rehoboam's strong arm tactics. The rebelling tribes declared their independence and set Jeroboam up as the king of Israel. Due to Solomon's sin, Israel was split into two and the half was given to Jeroboam just as God had promised.(1 Kings 11:29-35)

Even though Jeroboam was made a king, there was a problem of lacking in lineal descent. The king of Israel had to be anointed by God. Jerusalem had been the religious center of the united kingdom but now that it was divided, King Jeroboam turned Tirzah as the capital of Northern Israel. Jeroboam, being fearful that his people visiting Jerusalem for the pilgrim feasts will lead to defect, created new sanctuaries for the northern kingdom. (1 Kings 12:26-27) He also created an unlawful priesthood(non-Levites) and made bull calves, the symbol of fertility, for the people to worship. One was set up in Bethel and the other in Dan. His actions encouraged idolatry and as time passed,

Israelite worship became more and more degenerated. The temple of golden calves that is mentioned several times in the Bible is actually the 'Jeroboam's way.'

Sadly the Northern Israel started off in the path of doom right from the beginning. When Jeroboam's son Abijah became sick, he sent off his wife to the blind prophet to find out whether his son was going to live or not. But she got no chance to ask him her question. Ahijah, the blind prophet predicted Jeroboam's rise and since he had not been loyal to God, as David was, he said Jeroboam's whole dynasty will be swept away like dung. God spoke through Ahijah, "Behold, I am bringing calamity on the house of Jeroboam, and will cut off from Jeroboam every male person, both bond and free in Israel, and I will make a clean sweep of the house of Jeroboam, as one sweeps away dung until it is all gone." (1 Kings 14:10)

The religion of Christianity is responding to God's love. Responding to love means doing things the other person wants you to do and refraining yourself from doing things that upsets them. For instance, as a married couple, the relationship sours when a spouse continues to do the things the other partner dislikes. Having no interest in what God wants from us but continuing to carry on with our own religious lifestyle is what we refer to as a religion of 'Shamanism.' This is exactly the same as worshipping the golden calves.

The fate of the Northern Israel was already fixed by the sanctuaries of the golden calves. Ever since the first king of the northern kingdom was cast out by God, the successors of kingship were short-lived and constant rebellion outbroke inside the kingdom. The history of blood bath continues for 200 years and ultimately gets destroyed by Assyria. All the kings of Israel were automatically bad though some were worse than others, therefore, the history of the kings of the Northern Israel do not serve its purpose to go into detail for this particular reason. Loyalty to God and true religion is the only measure of a king's success.

Omri Dynasty, King Ahab and Queen Jezebel

There were two major dynasties in the Northern Israel - Omri (Ahab) and Jehu.

The 7th king of Israel, Omri is one of the Israel's most powerful kings, politically. He introduced a new dynasty and ruled for 12 years fortifying Samaria as his new capital. For 150 years from this point, Assyria referred Israel as 'the land of Omri.' King Omri married off his son Ahab to Jezebel, princess of Sidon (now known as Lebanon). This queen Jezebel is known to be a wicked woman in the Bible who turns Israel completely into Satan's kingdom. The Ahab's marriage to Jezebel effects an alliance between Israel and its northern neighbor Phoenicia, and brings political strength and trade benefits. But she is strongly attached to her own religion and persuades Ahab to sin against the Lord by imposing worship of the Baal on his people. As we know, Baal idolatry includes worshipping of Ashtoreth, the lesbian goddess of Sidonians.

This is the same Baal idolatry that the people of Israel worshipped discreetly in the period of the Judges but now the people could worship it publicly. Baal was worshipped as a weather god who could give or withhold the produce of the land. In the namesake of a ritual for rain, people spent their days in the temple having group sex while smoking marijuana. King Ahab brought down Israel completely.

Now suddenly, rather than listing the activities of the kings in the following chapters, as if from nowhere and at a critical time, God's prophet makes sudden and dramatic entrance. Elijah will be known as the greatest of all the prophets. The writer of the book of Kings has no interest in the kings anymore since the religious life in Israel has reached an all time low in Ahab's reign. Instead, the scene is set for the appearance of Elijah and a classic conflict of 'church versus state' unfolds. From this point on, it tells us of the redemptive work of God through the prophets. It is a spiritual war between the family of Ahab and God as God reveals His presence to the people of Israel.

Prophets Who Fought against Ahab's Household

The latter part of the Old Testament is the 17 books of prophecies. The authors of Isaiah, Jeremiah, Lamentations of Jeremiah, Ezekiel, Daniel and Hosea are referred as the prophets. The prophets Elijah and Elisha who appear in 1 & 2 Kings did not leave any prophecies behind but instead played a special role in preparing the groundwork for the prophets to come. The writer of 1 & 2 Kings is introducing them to us now.

The people of Israel were far gone into worshipping Baal and totally engrossed with their sexual pleasures that both Elijah and Elisha knew that whatever they say would be a loss. What use would it be to tell the people to repent and return to God when they had totally lost their interest in God! So, God now proves His presence to the king and the people of Israel through Elijah and Elisha whose main activities were performing miracles as they traveled place to place. In a modern sense, they performed powerful signs and wonders (healing). Threader: Actually, these two prophets in the Old Testament are already showing us the foreshadow of the coming Messiah, Jesus Christ. Majority of the miracles performed by Jesus during his ministry are the same as these two prophets had shown while confronting the King Ahab (Omri dynasty).

ELIJAH

Elijah and Widow of Zarephath_1 Kings 17

Elijah forecasts the drought in front of Ahab. "As the Lord, the God of Israel lives, before whom I stand, surely there shall be neither dew nor rain these years, except by my word."(1 Kings 17:1) Baal was being worshipped as a weather god who could give or withhold the produce of the land while despicable immoral acts were being practiced simultaneously by the people. Just as God had shown His power over the gods of Egypt through the plagues, God prepared Elijah as His tool to risk depicting the mighty empires since He alone has power over the sun and rain without which nothing will grow.

God then told Elijah to go and hide by the Cherith Brook (1 Kings 17:3-4) which was in the east of the Jordan and ravens were sent to feed him until the brook dried up. Let's take a moment here and imagine what Elijah went through. Waiting around in the wilderness for food by ravens is certainly not something one can easily do. Besides, how much can a bird actually deliver food in the first place? We must be able to focus on God's love. God who provides for Elijah's needs first from nature and then through a most unlikely person in the unlikeliest of places.

When the brook had dried up, God told Elijah to "Arise, go to Zarephath, which belongs to Sidon, and stay there; behold, I have commanded a widow there to provide for you." (1 Kings 17:9) He must have traveled for about 10 days to finally meet this widow who was a foreigner with no one to support her. Zarephath was in the heart of Baal's own country! The first thing he spoke upon meeting her was, 'please give me food' and her reply was "I have no bread, only a handful of flour in the bowl and a little oil in the jar; and behold, I am gathering a few sticks that I may go in and prepare for me and my son, that we may eat it and die." (1 Kings 17:12)

A great famine was over all the land at the time and the nerve to ask her 'last' food was unthinkable. Yet Elijah commanded her to do so. "'Do not fear; go, do as you have said, but make me a little bread cake from it first, and bring it out to me, and afterward you may make one for yourself and for your son.' For thus says the Lord God of Israel, 'The bowl of flour shall not be exhausted, nor shall the jar of oil be empty, until the day that the Lord sends rain on the face of the earth.'" (1 Kings 17:13-14) So the widow obeyed according to the word of Elijah and surely for 3 1/2 years the bowl of flour and jar of oil was not exhausted just as according to the word of the Lord which He spoke through Elijah.

Threader: Later in the New Testament, Jesus refers this incident as an example and praises the widow's faith. This miracle could be interpreted as the shadow of Jesus feeding the five thousand people. By providing Elijah in this way, God also shows His care for the poorest of the poor. "Elijah was sent to none of them, but only to Zarephath, in the land of Sidon, to a woman who was a widow." (Luke 4:26) Cherith Brook appears as you follow the valley from Jerusalem and Jericho; Zarephath is in the heart of Sidon which is the northwest land of Lebanon.

Elijah's Challenge on Mount Carmel_1 Kings 18

King Ahab was desperate since famine was severe in Samaria so the king himself along with his prophets sought out to survey all springs and valleys in the land in search for water. Now in the midst of this, Elijah returned, one against 450, giving a challenge to Ahab,

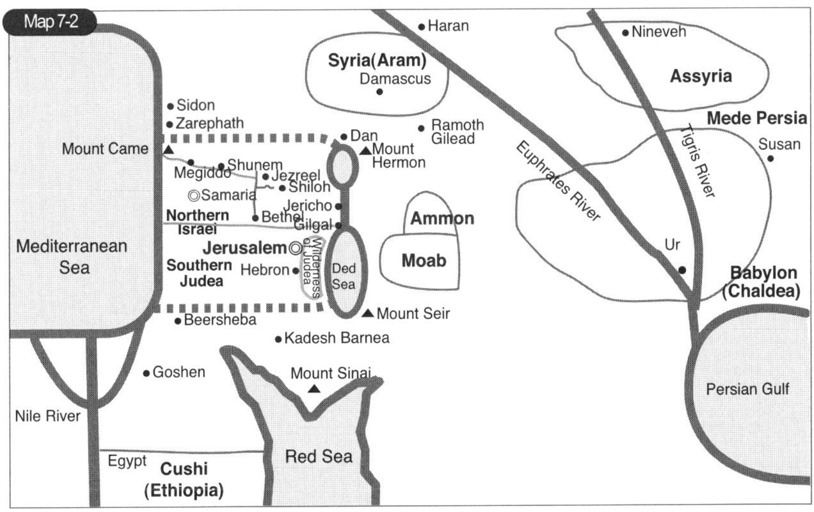

Period of Divided Kingdom - Place of Activities of Elijah and Elisha The upper part of the Mediterranean that sticks out is Mt. Carmel. This is the place where Elijah prayed. Cherith Brook can be found as you follow the valley that runs through from the city of Jericho and Jerusalem. Zarephath which is in the vicinity of Sidon is the western land of Lebanon today. A territory of Shunem can be found as you follow the Kishon River from Mt. Carmel. Aram is referred to as Assyria in the Bible which is Syria today.

putting the test who is the real God. "Now then send and gather to me all Israel at Mount Carmel, together with 450 prophets of Baal and 400 prophets of the Asherah, who eat at Jezebel's table." (1 Kings 18:19) King Ahab accepted the challenge. Regardless of any kind of god, Ahab was eager to do anything as long as it was to bring rain to the land. Elijah's contest challenged the 450 prophets of Baal plus 400 prophets of Asherah which amounted to 850 against one person!

The prophets leaped around in front of the altar with a loud voice but nothing happened until midday. So, according to their custom, they cut themselves with spears and swords until blood gushed out from them but nothing happened until the evening. (1 Kings 18:28-29) Let's visualize what's going on here for a moment. Elijah was challenging 850 prophets all by himself. What a lonely war. If he failed, it meant that not only God fails to receive His glory but his life would be at stake! But, so far, Baal was it as he was no more able to produce the fire than to send the needed rain.

It was Elijah's turn now. In order to avoid the accusation that the fire might have broken out due to the dry woods on the altar, Elijah made a trench around the altar and then arranged the wood and placed the pieces of meat on the wood. The water flowed over the altar and filled the trench. Then as Elijah prayed, the fire of the Lord fell and burned the saturated offering. When all the people saw it, they fell on their faces and shouted, "'He is God, who is the living Lord.' The prophets of Baal and Asherah were taken to Kishon brook where they were all slaughtered. (1 Kings 18:37-40)" Threader: The history of the Old Testament continuously addresses the two paths to choose from-God's or the idolatry of the Baal.

After all was done, Elijah went up to the top of Carmel and crouched down, putting his face between his knees and prayed. (1 Kings 18:42) He asked his servant to check the sea whether there was any sign of cloud or not. No signs of cloud. Nothing at all but after 7th try, the servant came back and reported that a cloud as small as a man's hand was coming up from the sea. Elijah then knew that God was going to send heavy rain.

We must realize that the ability to understand the signs of fulfillment to the answers of our prayers is given to us when we pray. On a personal note, I was getting a bit concerned about my eldest daughter's belated marriage. She was already 31 years old at the time and yet there were no signs of proposal. Then one day, during my early dawn prayer session, I heard the voice of the Holy Spirit. "My loving son, I'm sorry for the delay in giving blessings to your three children. But surely I will bless them." Without knowing what it meant at first, I just shed tears of thankfulness at the time. Then a couple of months down the road, my eldest daughter met a young man of faith which led to marriage. During one of my early dawn service, the Holy Spirit recalled the incident of Elijah on Mount Carmel to me, I knew then enormous blessings were forthcoming to my other two children. Tears rolled down my cheeks out of gratitude.

Not only did God prove that He was alive but through Elijah, he brought heavy rain and ended the 3 1/2 years of drought. King Ahab told Jezebel what Elijah had done and how the prophets were slaughtered. She couldn't believe her ears and demanded how he could allow 850 prophets to be killed just because this man of God brought fire down. She sent soldiers to kill Elijah. "Then Jezebel sent a messenger to Elijah, saying, 'So may the gods do to me and even more, if I do not make your life as the life of one of them by tomorrow about this time.'" (1 Kings 19:2)

Elijah Flees to Mt. Horeb, Receives a New Calling_1 Kings 19

Even a great prophet as Elijah, ran for his life out of fear when Jezebel held the whip hand. Spiritual and physical strain leaves him in the grip of depression, fear and disappointment. He journeys into the wilderness of Kadesh Barnea and sit down under a juniper tree "It is enough; now, O Lord, take my life, for I am not better than my fathers." (1 Kings 19:4) An angel brings him bread cake baked on hot stones and a jar of water and God comforts him, "Arise, eat, because the journey is too great for you." (1 Kings 19:7) After drawing fresh strength, he travels 40 days and 40 nights, escaping south to the desert and Sinai (Mt. Horeb) in the place where God made Himself known to Moses. He finds a cave and lodges there.

God speaks to Elijah, not in any spectacular way but out of the stillness. "What are you doing here, Elijah?" (1 Kings 19:9) And Elijah responds, "I have been very zealous for the Lord, the God of hosts; for the sons of Israel have forsaken Your covenant, torn down Your altars and killed Your prophets with the sword. And I alone am left; and they seek my life, to take it away." (1 Kings 19:10) In other words, he is saying his life was at stake in delivering God's message against the people of Israel and the king because of his zeal. This is rather an arrogant confession because what he is saying is that since all prophets have been killed he is the only one left. Then God said, "Go, return on your way to the wilderness of Damascus, and when you have arrived, you shall anoint Hazael king over Aram; and Jehu the son of Nimshi you shall anoint king over Israel; and Elisha the son of Shaphat of Abel-meholah you shall anoint as prophet in your place. And it shall come about, the one who escapes from the sword of Hazael, Jehu shall put to death, and the one who escapes from the sword of Jehu, Elisha shall put to death. Yet I will leave 7,000 in Israel, all the knees that have not bowed to Baal and every mouth that has not kissed him."(1 Kings 19:15-18)

Normally when a person receives persecution while doing God's work, he/she becomes afraid thinking that they are all alone. But that is not true. Even Apostle Paul, during his mission trip to Corinth, was chased out from the synagogue but God's spirit appeared in vision to Paul and comforted him, "I am with you, and no man will attack you in order to harm you, for I have many people in this city" (Acts 18:10) You have experienced 'paradise' if you understand this. You are comforted because you know that you are not alone. On the other hand, if you say "I am alone" then you are experiencing hell and, therefore, you become solitary. God's people are never alone because there are

7,000 people who have not knelt down in front of Baal yet. Self-pity is dealt with a sense of proportion restored. Elijah feels intolerably lonely and thinks his work is finished but God sees different path ahead - hope of salvation through him is mapped out. Besides he is given a companion and successor, Elisha. God's work goes on.

God specifically gave three types of work to Elijah.

First, he is to anoint Hazael as a king over Aram. God plans to punish the fallen Northern Israel through the king of Aram but the king at the time, Benhadad, is too soft that he fails to reprimand Israel properly. So God commands Elijah to anoint Hazael who was the chief commander of Aram as king. Each leader of a country is raised by God because all political matters and power are in the hands of God.

Second, in order to remove the dynasty of Ahab, God instructs Elijah to anoint Jehu who was also the chief commander of Ahab's army and changes Israel's political figure as well. Through a riot, a new Jehu dynasty appears into the scene. We are now witnessing that not only God interferes with Israel but also changes the king of Aram.

Third, Elijah's successor is named and is to be anointed. The first thing that Elijah did after coming out of Mt. Horeb is to call upon Elisha who was plowing the fields at the time of his visit.(1 Kings 19:19-21)

Naboth's Vineyard and the Death of King Ahab_1 Kings 21-22

One day, King Ahab approached Naboth in Jezreel who had a vineyard beside the palace asking him to liquidate his vineyard because he wanted to build a summer castle for his wife, Jezebel. Naboth refused to sell his land since it was inherited to his family from the days of Joshua and a man's heritage had to be handed on to the next generation. But Ahab couldn't do much to take the land from Naboth because seizure or compulsory purchase of the land was illegal in Israel. This outcome was known to Jezebel who had no concern of other people's right. While her husband sulked, she quietly arranged for Naboth's death. She had only to contrive a blasphemy charge-backed, of course, by the statutory number of witnesses and the land was forfeited as a result. Not only was the land robbed but also Naboth was stoned to death. (1 Kings 21:10)

Elijah was in Samaria at the time and was the only one who speaks the truth. He delivered the curse message from God to both King Ahab and Jezebel. "Thus says the Lord, 'Have you murdered, and also taken possession?'", and towards Jezebel, "Thus says the Lord, 'In the place where the dogs licked up the blood of Naboth the dogs shall lick up your blood, even yours.'" (1 Kings 21:19, 23-24)

Israel and Judah were temporarily allied against Syria. The warning on the king's death was ignored. Ahab could not cheat death by disguising himself as if he were not the king and died in the battle at Ramoth-Gilead, east of Jordan, as God had said. A random arrow struck him through his armor and since the battle raged throughout the day, there was no way he could get out and receive proper treatment. Eventually the king was propped up in his chariot and bled to death. (1 Kings 22:34-35) The dead king was brought to Samaria and was buried. As they washed the chariot by the pool of Samaria the dogs licked up his blood. It happened just as God had spoken and the pool was where the harlots of Baal bathed.

Death of King Ahaziah_2 Kings 1

After King Ahab's death, his son Ahaziah took over the throne. He consulted the Philistine god, Ekron (a.k.a. Baalzebub), after a fall from the flat roof of his palace. This particular god was the one so-called 'Lord of the flies' a derogatory pun on the god's real name, Baalzebul. Again, Elijah pronounced God's judgment on his idolatry. Elijah challenged the entire household of Ahab, delivering God's presence and then was taken up to heaven.

Elijah's Ascension_2 Kings 2

The final scene of Elijah. Without facing death he is taken up to heaven by God. Elisha's vision of a fiery chariot and horses is played out east of the Jordan, close to the place where Moses died. It is a remarkable end to a remarkable life. This symbolizes the scene of believers of God at the 2nd coming of Christ. Elisha asks not only for double amount of Elijah's spiritual power but for the share which would mark him out as the prophet's successor. Elijah replies, "You have asked a hard thing. Nevertheless, if you see me when I am taken from you, it shall be so for you but if not, it shall not be so." (2 Kings 2:10) And as they are walking and talking, a chariot of fire and horses of fire separates the two of them and Elijah is taken up by a whirlwind to heaven.

The last portion of 1 Kings and the first part of 2 Kings wrap up the bitter ending of King Ahab who spent his entire life focusing on fleshly needs while simultaneously prepares the ascension of Elijah who risked his life in proclaiming God's presence on Mount Carmel.

The pastors who have conducted many funeral services have shared their stories of the last breath of unbelievers. Majority of them end up saying, "This dark angel of death has come to take me away. I'm not going. I don't want to go!" But the reactions of Christians are different in their last moments. They reflect upon their lives and confess with their lips voluntarily what kind of life they had led as Christians. They realize how important it is to lead a sanctified life and start to confess before they die. Confessing about not giving tithes, about not living according to God's word, and about their hatred towards someone, etc.

This is what the Bible is referring to about our last days in front of our Lord. A full accounting of our deeds in front of God. "Obey your leaders, and submit to them; for they keep watch over your souls, as those who will give an account. Let them do this with joy and not with grief, for this would be unprofitable for you." (Hebrews 13:17) This accounting will be done through our lips first. Naturally on the last judgment day, all accountings will be done but we confess this beforehand before we die. This concept is expressed very accurately in insurance where 'deductibles' are mentioned. Before entering heaven, before we die, the amount of confession with our lips is deducted from the crown that we're supposed to receive in heaven. But let's face it, after all the deductions, do you expect anything to be left? Probably nothing except our own hair! On the other hand, those who have lived and shared the love of God with others will be recommended by them; receive the glory of obtaining not only one crown but many more from the Lord according to those recommendations.

● ● ELISHA

Elisha's Spring of Water_2 Kings 2:19-22

Upon receiving spiritual powers from Elijah(2 Kings 2:9), Elisha performed the most wonders among all the characters in the Bible except Jesus. He healed the sick and saved the dead as well. But surprisingly, there is no mention of crowds following him. This is the shadow of Jesus' work of salvation in the New Testament.

"Where is the Lord, the God of Elijah?" (2 Kings 2:14), Elisha struck the waters of Jordan just as Elijah had done with the mantle of Elijah that fell from him when Elijah was taken up to heaven. Then the waters were divided and he crossed it. This was the beginning of Elisha's wondrous work. In the city of Jericho where Elisha was staying, men came and informed him that the water was so bad that the land was unfruitful. Elisha then went out to the spring and purified it by throwing salt into it. Even today if you go to Jericho, you will find "Elisha's Spring Water" and people drink from it.

Threader: Just as the bitter waters were changed to sweet water by Moses after crossing the Red Sea, the first miracle that Elisha performed was to purify the water as it was the source of life. The first miracle of Jesus was also changing the water into wine at the wedding festivities in Cana. The common ground of these two miracles was that it was the 'transformation of water.' God's interest is in the source of life the water we can drink from and changing it to His blood (wine). "Therefore if any man is in Christ, he is a new creature; the old things passed away; behold, new things have come." (2 Corinthians 5:17)

When Elisha was on his way to Bethel some boys were yelling severely at the prophet and His God, telling him to 'go up' like Elijah. "Go up, you baldhead." (2 Kings 2:23) So Elisha looked up and cursed at them in the name of the Lord. Then two female bears came out of the woods and tore them up. This is rather a puzzling situation but it could be interpreted as prophets were so precious at the time that God did not permit Baal worshipping people to mock the man of God.

Elisha Ends Drought in the Wilderness of Moab_2 Kings 3

A punitive expedition against Moab by the allied forces -- allied by Jehoshaphat, king of southern Judah, Jehoram, king of northern Israel and king of Edom were faced with hazardous drought. Seven days of journey left them with no water for the army nor for the cattle that followed them. And Jehoram, the king of Israel, complained "Alas! For the Lord has called these three kings to give them into the hand of Moab." (2 Kings 3:10) But then Jehoshaphat said, "Is there not a prophet of the Lord here, that we may inquire of the LORD by him?" (2 Kings 3:11) So Elisha who prophesied for the king of Judah was brought to them. The evil king of Israel received salvation by the fact that he was with the man of God.

Elisha, with his faculties stimulated by music (a common prophetic custom) promised an end to the drought and a victory. "'Thus says the Lord, Make this valley full of trenches.' For thus says the Lord, 'You shall not see wind nor shall you see rain; yet that valley shall be filled with water, so that you shall drink, both you and your cattle and your beasts. And this is but a slight thing in the sight of the Lord; He shall also give the Moabites into your hand.'" (2 Kings 3:16-18) As Elisha prophesied, the valley was filled with water and they ended up with slaughtering the Moabites and won the battle.

Just as the prophet was moved by the Holy Spirit after listening to the sounds of praise, we must also open our hearts and give praise to the Lord before listening to the Word so that we could ultimately hear the voice of God as well.

Elisha and the Widow's Oil_2 Kings 4:1-7

Now Elisha was on his way to Bethel when he heard the news of his disciple's death. The widow was so poor that their children were to become slaves to discharge her debts. Elisha felt pity for them so he offered his help to the widow who said that the jar of oil was all she had. He said, "Go, borrow vessels at large for yourself from all your neighbors, even empty vessels; do not get a few." (2 Kings 4:3) So upon gathering the vessels as instructed, the widow and her two sons shut the door and started pouring oil into all the vessels. The jars were soon filled with olive oil which was treated like money in those days so she was able to pay off her debt by selling the oil and lived on the rest.

Like the miracle of Jesus feeding the 5,000 people, Elisha's miracles show God's care for the ordinary people and their needs as well. Having the fatherly love towards others allows us to experience similar 'filling' of oil (materials) into our empty vessels. This similar miracle is not limited to the days of Elisha or Jesus. It is happening even today wherever the love of God exists.

The Childless Woman of Shunem_2 Kings 4:8-37

Elisha was passing over to Shunem one day when a prominent woman extended generous hospitality to him. Even a small chamber was set aside for him so whenever he passed by, he stopped over at this woman's house. Remind that it was during the days when majority of the northern Israel was worshiping Baal so anyone who served God was persecuted and put to death. After receiving such a kind hospitality, Elisha asked his servant to find out whether she needed anything even though she was wealthy. No matter how wealthy one may appear there's bound to be something lacking or difficulty for everyone. His servant, Gehazi said, "Truly she has no son and her husband is old." (2 Kings 4:14)

Through Elisha's prayers, she conceived and bore a son. The child grew but died of a sun stroke. The woman saddled a donkey and went to Elisha in Mount Carmel and blurted out to him, "Did I ask for a son from my lord? Did I not say, 'Do not deceive me'?" (2 Kings 4:28) Then Elisha brought her dead son alive. Threader: This is a preview of the miracle of Jesus-raising up the dead to life. Jesus was in Galilee at the time but visited Jerusalem each year for Passover and stayed at the house of Mary and Martha in Bethany. Jesus brought Lazarus, brother of Mary and Martha, back to life when he was dead.

Removing Poison from the Stew_2 Kings 4:38-44

Elisha returned to Gilgal and there was a famine in the land. His prophets were preparing stew when one man gathered wild gourds and sliced them into the pot of stew without knowing what it was. It was actually colocynths, a powerful laxative, bitter and poisonous in large quantities. Again, a miracle similar to the one of Jesus' feeding 5000 was performed. It is said that 100 were fed with 20 loaves of barley bread. One may question "Why not? If you cut it into 1/5th then it's possible to feed 100. It's not a miracle." But it is a miracle indeed because they had leftovers after eating it to full capacity! Through these incidents, Elisha was testifying God's presence that He is alive and was revealing the previews of the works of Jesus.

Healing of a Syrian General, Naaman_2 Kings 5

Syria (Aram) was often at war with Israel and Naaman was the commander of the enemy's army who had caught leprosy. A young

Israelite slave girl, captured in a border raid, told Naaman's wife about Elisha's power. "I wish that my master were with the prophet who is in Samaria! Then he would cure him of his leprosy." (2 Kings 5:3) The news traveled into the ears of the master. This shows that even though Naaman was a high ranking officer, he actually listened to his slave girl which reveals his character, a kind hearted man even towards servant level people.

A visit was arranged through the diplomatic channels. The king of Syria wrote a letter to the king of Israel saying, "I have sent Naaman my servant to you, that you may cure him of his leprosy." (2 Kings 5:6) Upon reading this, the king of Israel tore his clothes and said, "Am I God? How can I cure a man of his leprosy?" (2 Kings 5:7) Obviously he had no faith. It happened that Elisha heard the news and sent the word to the king to send Naaman to him.

General Naaman went to Elisha's house but to his dismay, the prophet didn't even bother to come out of his house. Naaman had assumed the prophet would come out to greet him and put his hand over him and pray to cure him. Instead, the prophet's instructions were not what he had expected. A messenger was sent to him from Elisha saying "Go and wash in the Jordan seven times, and your flesh shall be restored to you and you shall be clean." (2 Kings 5:10) Naaman became angry. "Naaman was furious and went away and said, 'Behold, I thought, He will surely come out to me, and stand and call on the name of the Lord his God, and wave his hand over the place, and cure the leper. Are not Abanah and Pharpar, the rivers of Damascus, better than all the waters of Israel? Could I not wash in them and be clean?' So he turned and went away in a rage." (2 Kings 5:11-12) He was so arrogant.

Then his servants persuaded him to try and said, "My father, had the prophet told you to do some great thing, would you not have done it? How much more then, when he says to you, 'Wash, and be clean'?" (2 Kings 5:13) He finally put down his rank as general on the ground and dipped himself in Jordan as instructed and was healed.

Threader: Another preview of Jesus' miracle is shown here through Elisha by healing leprosy.

Whenever Jesus healed the sick, He said, "Do you believe that I am able to do this?" (Matthew 9:28) We must learn from here that whoever wants to be healed or cured of any sickness or disease, we must first let go of our thoughts, position and believe in the Word of God with an obedient attitude. I was instructed to go under chemotherapy for one year after my surgery of stomach cancer. In the mist of receiving treatment for 6 months, I had caught jaundice. My white blood cell level was not being reproduced properly so my entire skin was turning literally black like a dead corpse. At that crucial moment in my life, I met a healer sent by God. I was challenged to stop all the treatments and believe that God would cure me. My decision was to believe God wholeheartedly and I obeyed. To this day, it remains as one of my testimonies that with God's grace I was completely healed. A child-like heart that simply believes God without figuring out what's right or wrong will enable you to experience the blessing of God's miracle.

The Floating Axe - Head_2 Kings 6:1-7

The thick woods of the Jordan Valley provided a ready source of timber which was needed by the prophets for the new community building. As they were cutting down the trees, someone fell from a beam and his axe head dived into the water. Elisha then cut off a stick and threw it where the axe head had fallen and the iron started to float above the water. This miracle may appear as a simple act but it has a message for us. God's compassionate heart for people who try to return what was borrowed is shown here through the Elisha's miracle.

Miracle in Dothan_2 Kings 6:8-23

The Aramean army had surrounded the city to capture Elisha who was staying in Dothan. The attendant of Elisha had risen early and went out to find army with horses and chariots circling them and rushed inside shouting, "Master, what shall we do?!" Elisha's confidence was in God's protection. A very real thing for those who have spiritual eyes to see. He prayed "O Lord, I pray, open his eyes that he may see." (2 Kings 6:17) Then the servant's eyes were opened and he saw that the mountain was full of horses and chariots of fire, the army of God all around Elisha to protect him. It was God who protects His servant and Israel. I have also experienced on numerous occasions the power of angels' hedge (Job 1:10) to those who pray by opening my spiritual eyes when confronted with major obstacles.

As the armies approached, Elisha then prayed once again "Strike this people with blindness." (2 Kings 6:18) Far from being doomed, Elisha had them in the palm of his hand as he led them back to Samaria. Then the king of Israel said to Elisha, "My father, shall I kill them?" (2 Kings 6:21) The answer was "You shall not kill them. Would you kill those you have taken captive with your sword and with your bow? Set bread and water before them, that they may eat and drink and go to their master." (2 Kings 6:22) The king, too, showed mercy and so the Aramean ongoing raids came to an end. Elisha's action is a classic preview of the words of Jesus: Love your enemy.

Prophecy of the Fleeing Syrian Army_2 Kings 6:24 - 7:20

The peace secured by Elisha did not last forever. Benhadad of Syria returned to lay siege to Samaria and the people suffered from starvation and cannibalism. One day, as the king was passing by on the wall, a woman cried out to him for help. Apparently the two women had an agreement earlier on and now they were arguing heavily. The king inquired further. The woman replied, "This woman said to me, 'Give your son that we may eat him today, and we will eat my son tomorrow.' So we boiled my son and ate him; and I said to her on the next day, 'Give your son, that we may eat him'; but she has hidden her son." (2 Kings 6:28-29) Upon hearing this, the king tore his clothes and blamed Elisha for telling him to hold out and promising deliverance. The king said, "May God do so to me and more also, if the head of

Elisha the son of Shaphat remains on him today." (2 Kings 6:31)

King Joram recalled not only of Elisha's healing of General Naaman's leprosy but also the fact that he had let the Aramean armies go home unharmed. He assumed that being too generous towards them resulted in the siege. In spite of the desperate hunger around them, Elisha promised food the next day that 'a measure of fine flour will be sold for a shekel.' At the time 'a measure of fine flour' was about a pound and if it was to be sold for a shekel, it meant that it was extremely cheap. This indicated that a great miracle was about to happen.

The four leprous men at the entrance of the gate were exchanging words with one another. "Now there were four leprous men at the entrance of the gate; and they said to one another, 'Why do we sit here until we die? If we say, 'We will enter the city,' then the famine is in the city and we shall die there; and if we sit here, we die also. Now therefore come, and let us go over to the camp of the Arameans. If they spare us, we shall live; and if they kill us, we shall but die.'" (2 Kings 7:3-4) The lepers were prohibited from living inside the city so they hung around outside of Samaria at the time. They depended on gifts of food and were worse off than most. But their desperate hunger made them the first to discover the truth of Elisha's prediction. Amazingly enough, the Aramean army had fled, leaving food behind so they spread the good news to everyone.

As Elisha predicted, God had worked along with His angels overnight, making stentorian sounds of chariots and horses that the Aramean army was overwhelmed with fear that they fled in haste, leaving everything behind. "For the Lord had caused the army of the Arameans to hear a sound of chariots and a sound of horses, even the sound of a great army, so that they said to one another, 'Behold, the king of Israel has hired against us the kings of the Hittites and the kings of the Egyptians, to come upon us.' Therefore they arose and fled in the twilight, and left their tents and their horses and their donkeys, even the camp just as it was, and fled for their life." (2 Kings 7:6-7)

The promise was fulfilled. In the midst of our troubles or tribulations, do not be discouraged but be encouraged by the man of God near you who delivers the good news and responds in "Amen" rather than ignoring it so that all of us may experience the miracle and lead a victorious life.

Anointment of Hazael

Elisha fulfills God's commission given to Elijah when Elijah was in the cave of Mt. Horeb. He goes to Damascus and anoints Hazael, the chief commander of Benhadad, king of Syria. After doing so, Elisha fixes his gaze on Hazael until he is ashamed and weeps. "Why does my lord weep?" says Hazael. Elisha predicts the evil from Hazael and answers, "I know the evil that you will do to the sons of Israel: their strongholds you will set on fire, and their young men you will kill with the sword, and their little ones you will dash in pieces, and their women with child you will rip up." (2 Kings 8:12) God had chosen an evil king as His tool to punish Israel.

Anointment of Jehu_2 Kings 9

There were constant battles between Syria and Israel to take over the land of Ramoth-gilead - the region of granary. Elisha carried out Elijah's last commission while the armies of Israel and Judah were defending Ramoth-gilead against Syria. He sent one of the sons of the prophets to Ramoth-gilead to anoint Jehu, the captain of Joram's army, as the next Israel's king, who was found in the frontline of the battlefield at the time.

While King Joram, the youngest son of King Ahab, was conveniently recovering from his wounds at Jezreel, Jehu did not lose any time to kill the king and became king. He opened his reign with a blood bath. Not only was Joram killed but also Ahaziah, King of Judah who was visiting his uncle at the time. When Ahaziah saw what happened to his uncle, he fled but was pursued by Jehu and was killed. Ultimately, all of Ahab's family including royal house of

Judah, and the prophets, priests and worshippers of Baal were wiped out fulfilling the prophecy of Elijah. It was God's judgment against Ahab's household. (2 Kings 10:10-11)

After killing Joram, Jehu set out towards the castle of Queen Jezebel. Inside the castle, Jezebel was putting makeup and fixing her hair to meet Jehu. "When Jehu came to Jezreel, Jezebel heard of it, and she painted her eyes and adorned her head, and looked out the window. And as Jehu entered the gate, she said, 'Is it well, Zimri, your master's murderer?'" (2 Kings 9:30-31) She had put on her last makeup before being thrown out the window and died. "Then he lifted up his face to the window and said, 'Who is on my side? Who?' And two or three officials looked down at him. And he said, 'Throw her down.' So they threw her down, and some of her blood was sprinkled on the wall and on the horses, and he trampled her under foot."(2 Kings 9:32-33) In 1997, I was conducting a bible study of 'Threading the Bible' in Beijing and apparently, out of all the names, a new Korean cosmetic brand came out with a label of 'Isabelle' at the time.

Death of Elisha

Finally the prophet died. Throughout his extensive travel around Israel he performed many miracles in the Old Testament, showing us the preview of the works of Jesus during his ministry. Jesus, the invisible spirit and Father God who is love had been revealed to all mankind. The living Father God and His love towards Israel were proclaimed through the works of Elijah and Elisha. Through them, the house of Ahab, four generations, who were responsible for worshiping Baal had been completely destroyed and a new dynasty was installed.

Prophets Amos and Hosea

The reign of Jehu continued until the fall of the Northern Israel. One of the primary works of Jehu was destroying the house of Ahab, his descendants and the objects connected with Baal worship. But the shrines of the golden calves at Bethel and Dan which were built by Jeroboam, Israel's first king, remained and the house of Jehu also neglected God's law in the end. Ongoing battles continued as a result and during his reign, Israel's territory in the east of Jordan was lost to Syria. In the midst, there was a king who only reigned for a month- and then Hoshea, the 19th king became the last king of Israel. Samaria fell unto Syria after a terrible three year long siege and the whole remaining population was deported. In B.C. 722, approximately 200 years after the division of the kingdom, Northern Israel collapsed.

Before the fall of the Northern Israel, God sent the prophets Amos and Hosea. Prophet Hosea proclaimed a powerful and touching words of advice. "Come, let us return to the Lord. For He has torn us, but He will heal us; He has wounded us, but He will bandage us. He will revive us after two days; He will raise us up on the third day That we may live before Him. So let us know, let us press on to know the Lord." (Hosea 6:1-3)

Israel's fate was seen as the direct consequence of longstanding idolatry, of pursuing heathen practices and disobeying God's law so in connection to this, prophet Amos proclaims, "But let justice roll down like waters And righteousness like an ever flowing stream."(Amos 5:24)

The righteousness of God had to be revived.

God showed His presence through the works of Elijah and Elisha before the fall of Israel and through the words of Hosea and Amos, God revealed his unchangeable love, recovery and hope towards Israel. Israel's ignorance and failure to return to God resulted their fall in the hands of Syria.

As Israel was fallen by Syria, Judah also fell to Babylon and down the line, Babylon took over Syria and became the kingdom of Babylon-which is Iraq today. Conclusively, Israel was destroyed by Iraq. Interestingly enough, God had called Abraham from Ur of the Chaldeans which was another name for Babylon. Considering from this aspect, the history of Israel originated from Iraq and ended there. Threader: President Bush spoke in one of his speeches related to the Iraq war that if Jerusalem fails to stop Babylon from charging in the last days, then the Amageddon war cannot be won in the end time-emphasizing the war in a historical aspect in the end time and interpreted America as the 'new' Jerusalem. In other words, the 'old' Israel has been destroyed and if America, a new Christian country raised by the Puritans, fails to block Iraq and its terrorism, then the so-called Amageddon war cannot be prevented in the end. President Bush is looking at the present war with Iraq through this historical angle. Whatever it may be, we must understand that Iraq is the originating country who played a significant role in Israel's destruction.

The Activity of the Brain and Believer's Spiritual Lifestyle

The book *Revolution of the Brain* (Author : Haruyama Shigeo) explains that only humans have the ability to choose between the two paths.

Vegetables have no brain as well as insects. Insects only have a mouth and intestines. They are only interested in food. They eat or get eaten. The concept is that those who are only interested in eating will be eaten eventually by others.

God gave brains to animals, too. They are capable of feeling their emotions. A wagging tail indicates that the dog is happy and if not, it makes a sound of discontent. But animals are only interested in eating, drinking and excretion. Sometimes, even a human who are only interested in these three types of activities is referred as living a 'life of a dog.' In the end, animals are taken up by the stronger existence than them.

Only humans have cerebral cortex. We have left and right brains. Even though the blood of an animal and a human may appear to be the same, blood transfusions are impossible between a human and an animal. Apart from the biological factor, there is a distinctive difference between the blood of a human and an animal. God created human from dust and breathed His breath of life. Therefore, human blood started to move according to one's senses. If you are feeling good, the blood is healthy but if you are depressed, the blood receives stress and once it starts to accumulated it develops into cancer. If you are embarrassed, your face turns red. Similarly, anger also makes your face red but partially since the blood is racing up and down.

Only humans are aware of 'self.' With our left brain, we capture things that move and are visible. Our experience or knowledge is controlled by our left brain due to this fact. When we learn or practice something, it is all done through our left brain. The more we use our left brain, the more 'self' we are pursuing. The emphasis on 'self' is due to the competitive world we live in. It is said that the more we use our left brain, the more a Beta wave is produced resulting in hormone called 'adrenaline.' This adrenaline enables the blood to flow rapidly and stimulates excitement to human. Playing sports for a long period of time is not recommended since the body produces adrenaline which enables you to perform well but ultimately it shortens your life span.

The activity and interest of the right brain is on the things that are invisible. The pursuit of invisible, beauty, truth and kindness is done through the right brain. This is unique and something only humans are capable of. This is not something we can practice or learn. It's more like an instinct that are stirred through feelings. This part of our brain has no interest in self. The right brain produces Alpha wave when it relates to instinct and feelings. The hormone that comes out as a result of Alpha wave is called 'endorphin.' A great amount of endorphins are produced when we shed tears while praying through the inspiration of the Holy Spirit.

When I finished my lecture at a church in New Zealand, one doctor approached me and explained that endorphin is produced not only when we're happy or cheerful but also when we are sick. He said if our body is not well, then a small amount of endorphin comes out along with the white blood cells in order to fight against the bad germs. So when a sick person prays and recovers from their sickness, it is due to the great amount of endorphin that was produced by the energy of God's love through the deep movement of the Holy Spirit.

I had an opportunity to receive supplemental explanation on this by a doctor in New York. According to a recent medical publication, endorphin does not cure illness but when the endorphin is produced, a secretion (morphine) that is released and travels through the brain. It searches for cancerous cells and attacks the harmful cells to dissolve them. This internal morphine in the brain is produced in the body of people who sleep between 10 pm and midnight, and approximately works for 2 to 3 hours in search for cancerous cells killing them. This proves the benefit of sleeping early (10 pm) to attend the morning service at dawn and simultaneously become healthy!

I am totally convinced and believe this explanation through my own personal experience. Whenever I pray more than usual, my heart is moved by the Holy Spirit and it feels like a stream of life overflowing within me. I know this for a fact because my body itself is my proof.

According to the recent medical survey, majority of the people have stopped using their right brain and only 1/10th of their left brain is utilized. Therefore, the flow of the blood stream is not smooth which causes the brain cells to die and many suffer from stroke or brain hemorrhage. Heart attacks are also caused because people don't use the right brain enough. Most of the paralysis effect comes on the left side of the body due to the lack of use of the right brain. We use the left brain on a daily basis and it includes our Bible reading as well.

But the important fact is that the right brain overpowers the left brain. In order to send blood towards the right brain, it is necessary for us to shift our interest to intuitional and inspirational things that are invisible so that we may be responsive to the inner world. We are able to do this through prayers. The Bible refers to the two paths and tells us to go towards the narrow gate which actually means us to 'open our right brain.' In other words, it means that we must pray daily. Just compare quickly in your head with a person who goes to church on Sunday and pray once a week with a person who prays daily. The differences of the right brains of these two people are tremendous. It would only take a moment to distinguish which person is healthier: a person who opens their 'right brain produces endorphin and the morphine in his/her brain or a person who continues to live with a dull pulling sensation in his/her back brain. Surely we must realize that we reap whatever we sow.

Between the left and right brain, there is an inter-brain which is also referred as the 'back brain.' People who drink excessively or smoke heavily feel a pulling sensation in their 'back' head because their back brain is reacting. It is medically evidenced that the impact of smoking and drinking travels to the back brain and in some worst cases, it results in death. Majority of people (especially in Asia) eat a certain type of soup after a hangover assuming that it would soothe the pulling sensation in their back head. But this is strictly limited to a sense of calmness and effect only psychologically. It is known that blood flows into the back brain when erotic feelings of sensation occur during adulterous or immoral acts. But then again, ultimately the blood is being accumulated in the back brain which results in life-threatening effects.

In this connection, it is advisable to refrain yourself from excessive drinking, smoking or adulterous act even when you are young since whatever harms the back brain suffers it cannot be repaired. There is also a nerve that connects the left and the right brain. It is said the interpretation of tongue is possible when this particular nerve becomes activated. When you pray through the guidance of the Holy Spirit, the right brain gets hooked up with the left brain and the spiritual activity of the right brain is transpired to the left brain. The content of the spiritual prayer (tongue) is traveled to the outer person's conscious physically and ultimately enables the person to interpret the prayer of tongue.

THE BEGINNING AND END OF THE KINGS OF SOUTHERN JUDAH

2 Kings 12-25, 2 Chronicles 10-36

The following are the stories of the kings of Southern Judah. There are 20 kings who reigned for approximately 350 years during the period of B.C. 920-586.

The Beginning was a Good Start

The kings of Israel who walked in the ways of Jeroboam are not recorded in detail in the Bible. But on the other hand, the stories of the kings of Judah are told specifically in detail. Why? It is because the lineage of David must be preserved for God's promise (David's covenant).

There are some good kings who served God and some bad kings but majority of them started off well and in the end abandoned God completely. The common characteristics of the kings of Southern Judah is that 'they believed well in the beginning.' Both the books of Kings and Chronicles record the stories of the same kings but in a contradicting way. The same Southern Judah kings are recorded as faithful towards God in the book of Chronicles but in the book of Kings, they are portrayed as idol worshippers. Why is that? The kings who were evil in the eyes of God are briefly mentioned in the book of Kings whereas activities of them in the book of Chronicles begin with their faith in God.

The story of the kings who start off well but turn evil in the end is a universal message to us and explains the reason why the Messiah, Jesus Christ, had to come. No man can boast the work of salvation without the help of the Holy Spirit. The history of the kings proves it. For this purpose, the Son of God had to come into the world to carry the cross, and resurrected so that the Holy Spirit can be sent to help and guide us. This is accurately evidenced and explained through the book of Kings and the book of Chronicles so that we may reflect and learn from it.

There are believers who say 'I have lost my first love.' If so, then it is a big problem. The reason why God sent the Holy Spirit to us is to feel His presence and love now. Not to dwell on the past 'lost love.' Our religion is both present and future. Our God is present, living and eternal God! If you feel your heart has lost its passion for God's love then your faith has become ill. That is why I emphasize on the willpower and commitment. You must repent through prayers and hold on to the Word so that the Lord may come inside of you again. Then God will truly heal you.

Rehoboam-1st King of Judah
_1 Kings 12, 2 Chronicles 12

Rehoboam who grew up seeing his father King Solomon abandoning God for idolatries became a king of Judah. Israel was a divided kingdom at the time. He also built temples for foreign gods and did wicked things in the eyes of God. At the time, the priests fled to Judah from Israel to avoid Jeroboam's persecution to break the religious ties with Jerusalem. (2 Chronicles 11:13) Ironically, this situation resembles Korea's division, the North and South. It is said that one of the reasons why there are many Presbyterians in the South (Korea) is due to a large Presbyterian assembly associated with the Pyungyang (capital of North Korea) Union who decided to flee to the South.

Due to the influence of the priests who fled from Israel, Rehoboam walked in the ways of God for three years. But he eventually fell into the pleasures of the world and failed to recover God's Kingdom. He lived as a worldly king and died as the first king of Judah. Faith cannot sustain itself through the help of others. As we have seen a similar situation with King Solomon, the religion inherited from his father David did not last. This teaches us that our faith relies upon our own determination, meditation of the word and prayer. It will last through the process of sanctifying lifestyle. In order to bear fruit, we must be able to control our freedom of choice and align with God in our daily lives.

Abijah-2nd King of Judah_1 Kings 15, 2 Chronicles 13

In the book of 2 Chronicles, King Abijah is referred as the son of Rehoboam (but he is referred as Abijam in the book of 1 Kings). There were frequent battles between the two divided kingdoms and obviously, Judah had fought with Israel during King Abijah's reign. Here's how the book of Chronicles portrays Abijah: When King Abijah was at war with Israel, he began the war with great faith and exhorted, "So now you intend to resist the kingdom of the Lord through the sons of David, being a great multitude and having with you the golden calves which Jeroboam made for gods for you." (2 Chronicles 13:8) The armies of Israel fled upon hearing this powerful warning and eventually, Abijah and his army defeated them.

But in 1 Kings, it is written conclusively that Abijah was an evil king. "He walked in all the sins of his father which he had committed before him; and his heart was not wholly devoted to the Lord his God, like the heart of his father David." (1 Kings 15:3) Abijah, like the other kings of Judah, believed and walked in God's ways in the beginning but as time passed, he lost his faith and went further away from God.

Similarly, King Asa's faith was also good in the beginning. A prayer to God resulted in victory for Asa when an army of a million and 300 chariots of Cush came against him. "Lord, there is no one besides You to help in the battle between the powerful and those who have no strength; so help us, O Lord our God, for we trust in You, and in Your name have come against this multitude. O Lord, You are our God; let not man prevail against You." (2 Chronicles 14:11) With this one prayer, the battle was won.

This king was a man of prayers but soon forgot the grace of God and his faith weakened under the test in his later years. Under the threat from Israel, he called in foreign aid from Syria, costing him all the silver and gold from his palace and the Temple. "Then Asa brought out silver and gold from the treasuries of the house of the Lord and the king's house, and sent them to Ben-hadad king of Aram, who lived in Damascus, saying, 'Let there be a treaty between you and me, as between my father and your father. Behold, I have sent you silver and gold; go, break your treaty with Baasha king of Israel so that he will withdraw from me.'" (2 Chronicles 16:2-3)

Then Hanani, the seer came to Asa and scolded him. "Because you have relied on the king of Aram and have not relied on the Lord your God, therefore the army of the king of Aram has escaped out of your hand." (2 Chronicles 16:7) After hearing this, Asa imprisoned the prophet and develops a disease on his feet. In his sickness, he turned, not to God, but to the physicians instead and eventually died. (2 Chronicles 16:12)

King Asa was among the 8 'good' kings of Judah but unfortunately, this has no significant impact because in the end, he ended up sinning and became totally deviated from God.

There is no perfect king as Jesus Christ. Through the life of King Asa, we must learn that we should not stop praying once an urgent matter has been resolved but continue to pray at all times, making it as our routine of life. Rather than a prayer of request but a prayer of confession of the love for God must be embedded in us.

Jehoshaphat - 4th King of Judah

_1 Kings 22:41-50, 2 Chronicles 17-20

There are only three kings in Judah who were faithful towards God and Jehoshaphat is one of them. He walked in the ways of David and was successful in building up a strong army and in defending his country since God was with him.

During his reign, the alliances of Moab and Ammon-in a modern sense, the vast armies of Jordan invaded the land of Judah. At this time, Jehoshaphat's prayer resembles Solomon's prayer of dedication for the temple. His prayer was "When your people go out to battle against their enemy, by whatever way You shall send them, and they pray to the Lord toward the city which You have chosen and the house which I have built for Your name, then hear in heaven their prayer and their supplication, and maintain their cause." (1 Kings 8:44-45) God spoke through Jahaziel, a Levite, who answered his prayer, "Do not fear or be dismayed because of this great multitude, for the battle is not yours but God's ... You need not fight in this battle; station yourselves, stand and see the salvation of the Lord ..." (2 Chronicles 20:15-17)

Upon hearing this answer, Jehoshaphat formed a line of people to sing praises in front of the assembly of the army which had never done in the past and as they did so, God ambushed the enemies and the victory was in their hands. The Bible states that Jehoshaphat walked in the ways of David and records him as a 'good' king but there was one great mistake that he committed. From a humanly standpoint, he loved his people from the North which is truly commendable but the problem was that his underlying compassion was to recover the glory of unifying Israel as one and united kingdom again.

We must recall that during this particular period of Jehoshaphat, God's messengers, Elijah and Elisha, were sent to Northern Israel who risked their lives to proclaim the word of God in order to remove the wicked king Ahab. But Jehoshaphat continued to fight the battles together with the sons of King Ahab as allied forces. If he had loved the kings of the North with the same heart of God, he should have stirred them to return to God by proclaiming His word but instead for political purpose, an alliance through marriage between his son and Athaliah, Ahab's daughter took place which was far from reuniting the kingdom. For this, Prophet Jehu rebuked Jehoshaphat by saying, "Should you help the wicked and love those who hate the Lord and so bring wrath on yourself from the Lord?" (2 Chronicles 19:2)

Even though this marriage didn't appear to be that significant, this link with king Ahab actually brought tremendous disaster to Judah for four generations. Bringing an unbeliever (in this case, Athaliah as a daughter-in-law) into a family brought fatal outcome in the history of Judah.

From a preventive standpoint, spending time with people who deny God or do evil things (i.e., only interested in socializing and in worldly activities) according to God's standard is something we must avoid or distance ourselves from no matter how much we like them on a human level. Majority of them claim that it is for evangelism's sake that they end up mingling with this type of people. But in many cases, they lose their faith instead. The temptation and the power of what the world can offer are so strong that without firm faith, we would be challenged to overcome it. Bearing this in mind, we must be cautious with whom we associate with at all times.

Jehoram - 5th King of Judah
_2 Kings 8, 2 Chronicles 21

While Northern Israel was being wiped out due to the idolatry of Baal by King Ahab, the evil influence of Jehoram's wife, Athaliah (daughter of King Ahab and Jezebel) deterred Jehoram, son of Jehoshaphat, to worship Baal. He led the nation into idolatry and nobody was sorry when he died. A simple line is recorded in the Bible for him: "He did evil in the sight of the Lord." (2 Kings 8:18)

Ahaziah - 6th King of Judah_2 Kings 8, 2 Chronicles 22

Ahaziah is the son of Jehoram and Athaliah, King Ahab's daughter. Ahaziah learned nothing from his father's horrible end. Friendship with Israel led him directly to his death when Jehu purged the house of Ahab. Ahaziah died at Megiddo before his nephews' death.

Athaliah - 7th King of Judah
_2 Kings 11, 2 Chronicles 22-23

Queen Athaliah becomes the 7th king of Judah. As mentioned earlier, Athaliah proves to be far more ambitious and wicked than her mother Jezebel. The death of Ahaziah had no impact on her. Rather than mourning, she wiped out the offsprings of the royal line of David to take the throne and secure it for herself. These were some of the darkest days in the nation's history just like the dark periods of King Ahab in Northern Israel. This woman drove the nation completely into the Baal idolatry dirtying the temple of God and making it into a tunnel of lewdness. It is known that she raised Baal statues inside God's temple and used offering plates/goblets for drinking and smoking pot while conducting detestable immoral acts.

After witnessing the despicable conducts, the priest Jehoiada (husband of princess Jehosheba, who rescued Joash) led the well planned and virtually bloodless coup which put Joash on the throne after 6 years of Queen Athaliah's reign. The constitutional monarchy was restored and loyalty to God was reaffirmed in the swearing of a new covenant. Jehoiada then anointed Joash as the new 8th king of Judah, who was seven years old at the time. (2 Kings 11:20-21)

Joash - 8th King of Judah_2 Kings 12, 2 Chronicles 24

Joash became a king when he was only seven years old. The Bible records Joash as "He did what was right in the sight of the Lord all the days of Jehoiada the priest." (2 Chronicles 24:2; 2 Kings 12:2) Joash is regarded as one of the Judah's good kings and under Jehoiada's guidance, he ruled well. People recalled the covenant of loyalty and the temple that was damaged during his grandmother's disastrous leadership was repaired. For some years money intended for temple repairs gets no further than the priests. For some years, collecting money for temple repair didn't make much progress so a new method of collection was devised and the work was put in hand. Funds came from tax and freewill offering.

But unfortunately, after Jehoiada's death, Joash's later years faced a decline in political, moral and religious spheres. He was exposed to unhealthy influences of the officials of Judah and abandoned God for Asherim and the Baal idolatry. People gathered and committed immoral acts. Upon witnessing such sinful acts, the son of Jehoiada, Zechariah spoke in front of the king and the people, "King, why are you abandoning God and committing such evil acts?" Joash sank to the level of murdering Zechariah for his outspoken criticism. "Then the Spirit of God came on Zechariah the son of Jehoiada the priest; and he stood above the people and said to them, 'Thus God has said,

'Why do you transgress the commandments of the Lord and do not prosper? Because you have forsaken the Lord, He has also forsaken you.'" So they conspired against him and at the command of the king they stoned him to death in the court of the house of the Lord." (2 Chronicles 24:20-21) Threader: The blood of the righteous prophets is later raised by Jesus in the New Testament. "So that upon you may fall the guilt of all the righteous blood shed on earth, from the blood of righteous Abel to the blood of Zechariah, the son of Berechiah, whom you murdered between the temple and the altar."(Matthew 23:35)

King Joash was a man who had received the grace of Jehoiada, the high priest which parallels with the grace of God and yet he committed murder. It indicates that King Joash kept his faith through the influence of the high priest during his threatening days and in critical time. But once the high priest died, he was unable to sustain his loyalty to God and gradually gained self-confidence which led him to fall into the temptations of immoral lewd sexual activities as people in his grandmother Queen Athaliah's days did. In the end, he died at the hands of his servants. (2 Kings 12:20)

Amaziah - 9th King of Judah

_2 Kings 14, 2 Chronicles 25

Amaziah, the son of Joash succeeded him as king. Lacking in men, he hired 100,000 valiant warriors of Israel for 100 talents of silver in order to defeat the Edomites. But a man of God came to him and told him not to rely on the army of Israel but in God. So Amaziah dismissed the troops and defeats Edom. (2 Chronicles 25:11-13) He slaughtered the Edomites, throwing 10,000 men to their death from the top of the citadel cliff crushing them into pieces. King Amaziah experienced prosperity when he was aligned with God but in the end his faith withered and walked in the ways of Jeroboam.

Amaziah's total victory over Edom led to downfall. He brought home the foreign gods. “Now it came about after Amaziah came from slaughtering the Edomites that he brought the gods of the sons of Seir, set them up as his gods, bowed down before them, and burned incense to them.” (2 Chronicles 25:14) Most likely, this foreign god was also an idol of obscenity. And in his bumptious pride, he threw down the gauntlet to powerful Israel. The disastrous challenge to Jehoash brought the forces of Israel right into Jerusalem, looting the temple and other treasures. Defeat turned the people against him and a conspiracy ended Amaziah’s life which can be seen as a punishment for worshipping the gods of Edom. “He did right in the sight of the Lord, yet not with a whole heart.” (2 Chronicles 25:2) Basically, we must learn that those who do the work of God half-heartedly rather than as a loyal servant will fall just like Amaziah.

Uzziah - 10th King of Judah_2 Kings 15

The next king is Uzziah (whose name appears as Azariah in the book of Kings). He also received a blessing of becoming the longest reigning king in Israel for 52 years including a time as a co-regent. He was a strong king, aided by his religious adviser Zechariah. He started off well, seeking God and extending his sovereignty as far as to the Red Sea and experienced prosperity. He defeated the Philistines and Arabs and reduced Ammon to a vassal state; his army was well equipped and armed with the latest in guided missiles.

But as with many good people before and after him, power and success were his undoing that his pride took over. When only a priest was allowed to enter the Temple of God, he took on the role of a priest. (2 Chronicles 26:16) Then Azariah the priest and 80 priests entered after him opposing and reminding Uzziah that the burning of incense was strictly the role of the priests. He then not only ignored their warnings but also became furious. At that moment, and leprosy broke out on his forehead right in front of the priests in the temple, beside the altar of incense. (2 Chronicles 26:19) God stroke him with leprosy, a visible proof of unseen defilement of sin which made him unfit for God's presence. Normally, a person with leprosy would be sent away to a distanced and secluded place out of reach with ordinary people. But being a king, he was assigned to a separate house cut off from everyone while his son Jotham ruled over Judah. Pride had brought him down to an unpleasant end, a life in solitude for approximately 10 years making him rule as a regent for Jotham.

It is so easy to be disobedient towards God's commands. Not only is it limited to the kings of Judah who thought living in disobedience is alright but it is also very tempting to us. The result of disobedience is serious. If you disobey, you can actually experience life in hell on this earth prematurely. Alternatively, abundant blessings are given to those who are obedient to the Word of God. We must hope for the blessing of God's peace and His presence which roots from obeying.

Jotham - 11th King of Judah

_2 Kings 15, 2 Chronicles 27

After witnessing his father's leprosy, Jotham proved to be a good king, faithful to God. He maintained and increased the power his father has established, adding Ammon to his tributary states. "So Jotham became mighty because he ordered his ways before the Lord his God." (2 Chronicles 27:6) Rather than becoming prosperous quickly and being arrogant, it is better to have a fearful heart towards God and gradually become strong which is the key in receiving blessing.

Ahaz - 12th King of Judah_2 Kings 16, 2 Chronicles 28

The fallen days of King Ahab of Israel were long gone and buried but King Ahaz brought back the pagan gods again. He built altars for Baal and Asherah and turned Judah into a hotbed of obscenity. God used the idolatrous northern kingdom to punish His people and to show them the clemency to the prisoners of war that is almost unheard of before. Judah was under attack from all quarters: Syria and Isracl in thc north; Edom and Philistia in the south. During this invasion, 120,000 people of Judah died in one day. Not only was this a curse but indeed was a God's judgment. They also lost 200,000 of them as captives.

Some of Isaiah's prophecies dated from this time. There was still some good left in Israel. Crisis brings some people to the deeper level of faith but not Ahaz. God is now focusing on Judah and sends his messengers. God spoke through the two prophets: Amos and Hosea after sending Elijah and Elisha to the Northern Israel who walked in the ways of Jeroboam. But unlike the Northern Israel, God spoke to Judah through many prophets including Isaiah and Jeremiah because Jesus Christ was to come as the descendant of David.

Prophet Isaiah started to work vigorously during King Ahaz's time. Just like Elijah and Elisha who challenged King Ahab of Israel, now Isaiah was in a similar position in front of King Ahaz. These two kings were that they had spread the idolatry of Baals in the land of Israel.

In turning to Assyria for help, Ahaz ignored Isaiah's advice. He even stripped the temple of its silver and gold to pay the heavy tribute demanded by Assyria in return for their help. Ahaz became more unfaithful to God and compromised his faith to worship the gods of Damascus. He even sacrificed his own son as a burnt offering to prove his loyalty to the king of Assyria. Desperation made him more distant to God failing to realize that it was God Himself who had raised Israel all along. Undoubtedly, he was a wicked king. Ahaz rejected Isaiah's advice telling him to wait for God's sign, "Take care, and be calm, have no fear and do not be fainthearted because of these two stubs of smoldering firebrands, on account of the fierce anger of Rezin and Aram, and the son of Remaliah." (Isaiah 7:4) Smoke comes out when you hold a charcoal or a briquette with a stub (poker) since the flame is still intact inside the charcoal. But sooner than you think it cools down rapidly. This means a smoke is not a real threat even though it may appear alarming.

Isaiah prophesied to King Ahaz, "Therefore the Lord Himself will give you a sign: Behold, a virgin will be with child and bear a son, and she will call His name Immanuel." (Isaiah 7:14) This was great news -- the birth of Jesus! "For a child will be born to us, a son will be given to us; And the government will rest on His shoulders; And His name will be called Wonderful Counselor, Mighty God, Eternal Father, Prince of Peace." (Isaiah 9:6) These were challenging words of God spoken through Isaiah to King Ahaz. The proclamation is being made here - the history of Israel has ended and a child born through the descendant of a woman (Genesis 3:15) will now create a new kingdom. "Then a shoot will spring from the stem of Jesse, And a branch from his roots will bear fruit." (Isaiah 11:1) After King Ahaz, the history of Judah was already diminishing away like a dimming light of a lamp stand but a promise of the Messiah, the son of God, was being proclaimed.

Ahaz was one of Judah's worst kings. He is among the three wicked kings of Israel. The terrible apostasy of Ahaz brings Judah close to destruction.

Hezekiah - 13th King of Judah

_2 Kings 18-20, 2 Chronicles 29-32

Hezekiah is the son of the evil King Ahaz. He is one of Judah's finest kings and is among the three 'good' kings of Israel. God was with him since he walked in the ways of David. His first concern was to restore the temple to its proper use that his father Ahaz had robbed and closed it. "For he clung to the Lord; he did not depart from following Him, but kept His commandments, which the Lord had commanded Moses. And the Lord was with him; wherever he went he prospered. And he rebelled against the king of Assyria and did not serve him." (2 Kings 18:6-7) "He did right in the sight of the Lord, according to all that his father David had done." (2 Chronicles 29:2)

Having dealt with Israel, the Assyrians (Iraq) turned their attention to invade Judah in Hezekiah's 12th reign. The Northern (kingdom) Israel had been wiped out by Assyrians during Hezekiah's 4th year and Samaria the capital caved in. But surprisingly, the Assyrians did not take the ten tribes of the northern Israel into captivity at the time. Instead, God spread them to all different parts of the land as slaves and filled up the northern kingdom with Arabs. This was in 722 B.C. period which tells us that for approximately for 700 years, Arabs were living in the land of the Northern Israel up until the coming of Jesus, the Messiah. Threader: There's a scene in the New Testament where Philip, a disciple of Jesus, said to Nathanael, "We have found Him of whom Moses in the Law and also the Prophets wrote, Jesus of Nazareth, the son of Joseph." (John 1:45) And Nathanael responded, "Can any good thing come out of Nazareth?" (John 1:46) The reason for this comment was because the ten tribes of the Northern Israel had disappeared from the Promised Land for 700 years. Since the ten tribes of Israel had walked in the ways of Jeroboam, God had spread them apart. That is why we refer the people of Israel as Jews today instead of the people of Israel because only the people of Judah had returned to Israel after 70 years of captivity in Babylon.

The three Assyrians (the king's supreme, the king's chief officer and the field commander) were the masters of psychological warfare. They refused private talks with Hezekiah's cabinet and insisted on a public speech and played on the people's fear by speaking in Hebrew, not the diplomatic language of Aramaic so that everyone could understand. King

Sennacherib failed to take Jerusalem since King Hezekiah put his trust wholly in God during the crisis. (2 Kings 14-19) The angel of the Lord struck 185,000 men in the camp of the Assyrians overnight making Sennacherib to retreat entirely the next day. (2 Kings 19:35-36) Hezekiah's faith in God was strong because the prophet Isaiah, a man of God, was on his side. God answered his prayer and responded to his trust so Isaiah's prophecy was fulfilled. In the same manner, our faith gets strengthened when we spend time with God's people.

The next significant prayer of Hezekiah was given when he became mortally ill of skin cancer. (2 Kings 20:1) Prospect of death from Isaiah reduced Hezekiah to tears of prayer. "Remember now, O Lord, I beseech You, how I have walked before You in truth and with a whole heart, and have done what is good in Your sight. And Hezekiah wept bitterly." (2 Kings 20:3) He claimed that he had walked in the ways of David and kept his faith. God responded to the king's distress, "I have heard your prayer, I have seen your tears; behold, I will heal you. On the third day you shall go up to the house of the Lord. And I will add fifteen years to your life..." (2 Kings 20:5-6) This is a clear evidence that God listens and saves people who pray to Him.

But according to the book of Chronicles after receiving an extension of 15 years to his life, Hezekiah's heart became proud. (2 Chronicles 32:25) He must have felt that God had saved his life because he was such a great guy. In any event, Babylon, a small state located in the south of Assyria at that time was looking for allies and visited Hezekiah after learning that he had been sick. Hezekiah exhibited his treasures to the envoys of the rulers of Babylon with foolish pride and with a mindset of "Look at all this and see for yourself what a powerful guy I am. God has specially cured me from a deadly disease."

After learning what happened, Isaiah warned the king of his hasty and foolish act and delivered God's word: "Behold, the days are coming when all that is in your house, and all that your fathers have laid up in store to this day shall be carried to Babylon; nothing shall be left, says the Lord." (Isaiah 39:6) Hezekiah's attitude was "as long as it does not happen during my days it is fine with me." This is a normal reaction for anyone who has become proud. As a result, all the treasures that were boasted to the envoys from Babylon at the time were all confiscated without leaving a trace when Babylon invaded Jerusalem.

Normally we ask God to heal us when we're sick but it is more important to keep our faith. We must continue to humbly worship and love God even after we have become healthy. If one holds on to God while being sick then it is better off being sick rather than committing sin while one is healthy. What's I'm trying to say is that living in God's presence is so much more important than living in sin.

Manasseh - 14th King of Judah

_2 Kings 21, 2 Chronicles 33

To Judah, Manasseh is what King Ahab was to Israel. For almost all of his long reign period, Manasseh was one of Judah's least God-fearing kings. He desecrated the Temple, raised Baal idolatries and practiced human sacrifice. But most of all, he persecuted and killed prophets in a most cruel way. According to Israel's tradition, it is said that prophet Isaiah was sawed to death while he was still alive. The Bible records him as, "He did much evil in the sight of the Lord, provoking Him to anger." (2 Chronicles 33:6) Even though God answered the king's desperate prayer in between, He brought Judah to the point of no return. All due to Manasseh's sin who had provoked God to anger.

A good king as Hezekiah having such an evil son as Manasseh is alarming which again confirms that a father's faith does not necessarily get passed down on to his son. It shows us that salvation can never be achieved through bloodline.

Amon - 15th King of Judah

_2 Kings 21:19-26, 2 Chronicles 33:21-25

Amon is another bad king. He followed his father Manasseh's evil example and was murdered by his servants after being on the throne for two years. There's not much said about him except that he had served and worshipped all the carved images of Baal just like his father.

Josiah - 16th King of Judah

_2 Kings 22-23, 2 Chronicles 34-35

Josiah is among the best of Judah's kings. He was loyal to God and His laws and carried out thorough religious reform. He desecrated and demolished the places and objects of pagan worship and repaired the Temple. "He did right in the sight of the Lord and walked in all the way of his father David, nor did he turn aside to the right or to the left." (2 Kings 22:2)

As any reforming king in Judah who worshipped God properly did, his first task was to repair the temple - the restoration of worship to God. Through worship a new 'value' (worth/merit) is being created. In the course of repairing the Temple, a book of the law (an original copy of Deuteronomy) is discovered, the law that was written by Moses some 800 years ago. When the King Josiah heard of it, he trembled and tore his clothes. Why? Because the core message of the book of Deuteronomy; 'Choosing God or the Baal' was the choice of the two distinctive roads of Israel's blessing or curse mentioned in the book.

Then the king sent the book to Huldah, the prophetess, who delivered God's message: "Thus says the Lord, Behold, I bring evil on this place and on its inhabitants, even all the words of the book which the king of Judah has read. Because they have forsaken Me and have burned incense to other gods that they might provoke Me to anger with all the work of their hands, therefore My wrath burns against this place, and it shall not be quenched." (2 Kings 22:16-17) Josiah tore his clothes and God answered to his prayer. "'Because your heart was tender and you humbled yourself before the Lord when you heard what I spoke against this place and against its inhabitants that they should become a desolation and a curse, and you have torn your clothes and wept before Me, I truly have heard you,' declares the Lord."(2 Kings 22:19) God's judgment was delayed for four generations but not reversed. Josiah lost no time in acting on God's message through the prophetess Huldah. Public reading of God's law was followed by renewal of the covenant pact with God. Despite the king's lead, the people's response was too lukewarm and too late to avert the judgment.

As a matter of fact, Josiah was Judah's last king. In spite of his loyalty to God, he lacked in political leadership as a king. Ever since the armies of Pharaoh of Egypt had been swept away while crossing the Red Sea following the Israelites in their exodus in Moses' days, Egypt was not able to rise for 500-600 years. But now Necho, the Pharaoh of Egypt had regained strength and was marching north to join Assyria passing through the land of Israel to fight off Babylon.

The good faithful King Josiah attempted to block them. Why? The futile conflict was that Assyria had destroyed the northern Israel and on top of that during Hezekiah's period, Assyria had also attacked Judah as well. The rising power of Babylon was beginning to appear and pressure from it was gradually upon Assyria. Nineveh, the Assyrian capital had already fallen to the Babylonians and the king of Assyria had escaped to Haran, indicating the fall of Assyria was approaching. If Pharaoh Necho of Egypt had joined forces with Assyria and fought against Babylon then the fall of Judah might have been delayed because eventually Judah falls in the hands of Babylon.

King Josiah was not capable of making the right decisions regarding the international affairs so he died in the battle. (2 Chronicles 35:20-24) His death was not merely a death of a king but the fate of Judah.

From this point on, Judah was like a flickering candlelight harboring in front of the strong winds of neighboring countries. This incident carried a symbolic warning that the kingdom of Judah was about to perish. The neighboring countries influenced and dethroned the kings of Judah who followed from hereafter until the end of the kingdom of Judah. There were four more kings after the king Josiah, but they were just a figurehead.

We live by God's Word, doing His work in the world but the leaders of countries at least must be aware of the world affairs and make the correct judgment accordingly.

Jehoahaz, Jehoiakim and Jehoiachin 17th-19th King of Judah

Josiah's son Jehoahaz, the 17th king of Judah, was on the throne for only three months and was deported to Egypt by Pharaoh Necho. Instead, Jehoiakim was put on the throne by Necho as the 18th king of Judah who was more of a puppet. He is regarded as one of the three 'bad' kings. It is because of his evil ways prophet Habakkuk wrote in his book, "If you are a living God, why are you not punishing this wicked king and let him live?" "How long, O Lord, will I call for help, And you will not hear? I cry out to you, 'Violence!' Yet you do not save. Why do you make me see iniquity, And cause me to look on wickedness? Yes, destruction and violence are before me; Strife exists and contention arises. Therefore, the law is ignored And justice is never upheld. For the wicked surround the righteous; Therefore, justice comes out perverted." (Habakkuk 1:2-4) To his outcry, God responded, "Look among the nations! Observe! Be astonished! Wonder! Because I am doing something in your days you would not believe if you were told. For behold, I am raising up the Chaldeans, That fierce and impetuous people Who march throughout the earth To seize dwelling places which are not theirs." (Habakkuk 1:5-6)

Jehoiakim was a wicked king whose heart was far away from God. He oppressed his people and was easily subjected to Egypt and then became Babylon's target after Egypt is defeated. Surprisingly, he ruled for 11 years. Eventually Babylon discovered the king's wavering position and invaded the country and killed him in captivity. Jehoiakim's son, Jehoiachin became Judah's 19th king. He was 18 when he became a king but was removed from the throne after three months by Nebuchadnezzar and was taken captive to Babylon with the treasures of Jerusalem and all the leading men of Judah. The Bible records that he was released from prison and kindly treated after 37 years. (2 Kings 25:27-30)

Zedekiah - 20th and the last King of Judah

Zedekiah is the brother of Jehoiachin who ruled for 11 years. In the eyes of God, he was also a wicked king. This new puppet king also rebelled. Jerusalem suffered a terrible siege and Zedekiah attempted to escape to south but was caught and taken captive to Babylon with his eyes taken out and bounded in shackles. (2 Kings 25:7) The city fell to the Babylonian army, was looted and utterly destroyed. This was the last days of King Zedekiah of Judah in 586 B.C. Prophet Jeremiah who was active from Jehoiakim's days witnessed his own prophecy of Israel being taken captive to Babylon, the last days of Israel with his own eyes. That is why he is known as the 'prophet of tears.'

In the midst of Israel and Judah's history coming to an end, what is the Bible telling us? All the prophets including Isaiah are proclaiming, "Then a shoot will spring from the stem of Jesse, And a branch from his roots will bear fruit." (Isaiah 11:1) "Therefore the Lord Himself will give you a sign: Behold, a virgin will be with child and bear a son, and she will call His name Immanuel." (Isaiah 7:14) The coming of the Messiah, the prophecy of God who will be with us forever; and who will come through the lineage of David is being proclaimed.

Many prophets were sent and they performed signs and wonders as well as delivering God's word just as Jesus had done during the latter period of the divided kingdom. But there is a significant difference between the prophets and Jesus. In the Islamic religion, Jesus is regarded as one of the many prophets like Mohammed. But the role of prophets were to prophesize or deliver God's plan and love verbally or through their actions. Basically they urged people to choose between blessing or curse. As for Jesus, he died on the cross for our sins and showed God's love through his body. Our Lord has fulfilled the message of the prophets the blessing and curse-through His body.

The Conclusion of the Stories of the Kings

If we summarize the stories of the kings of the Northern Israel and Judah, 19 kings of Northern Israel all walked in the ways of Jeroboam (temples of golden calves) and the ways of Ahab (worship of Baal) confirming there was no hope under their reign whereas the Bible portrays a positive evaluation of the kings of Judah. Among the 20 kings of Judah (southern Israel) Hezekiah (13th king) and Josiah (16th king) were the only ones who walked in the ways of David (religion of temple worshiping). King Asa (3rd), Jehoshaphat (14th) and 8, 9, 10, 11th kings: Joash, Amaziah, Uzziah and Jotham, all six kings were graded as 'partially' good kings. Obviously there are differences in degrees but the bottom line is that both kingdoms eventually were destroyed because of their disobedience to God.

After the division of the united kingdom, God was patient towards the faithless Israel for approximately 200 years (933~722 B.C.); the reason why additional 130 years (933~586 B.C.) were given to Judah was not because of the kings like Hezekiah and Josiah, whose hearts were reasonably aligned with God. More importantly, it was because of God's promise to David that his house and kingdom would endure forever. (2 Samuel 7:8-16)

This background is well explained by the writer of the book of 1 Kings where the sins of Abijam, the 2nd king of Judah, are exposed. "He (Abijam) walked in all the sins of his father which he had committed before him; and his heart was not wholly devoted to the Lord his God, like the heart of his father David. But for David's sake the Lord his God gave him a lamp in Jerusalem, to raise up his son after him and to establish Jerusalem." (1 Kings 15:3-4) The message that a lamp, a descendant of David will be raised in Jerusalem to light up the darkness that is overcastting both kingdoms of Israel was being proclaimed. The reason why Jesus had to enter the city of Jerusalem, died on the cross Mt. Moriah and resurrect is clearly being revealed through the stories of the kings. At the triumphal entry of Jesus on a donkey into the city of Jerusalem, praises were given to him. "Those who went before, and those who followed after, were crying out, 'Hosanna! Blessed is He who comes in the name of the Lord; Blessed is the coming kingdom of our father David; Hosanna in the highest!'" (Mark 11:9-10)

All the kings of Israel were anointed and raised by God but the truly anointed one was to come to rule over the nation in a righteous way. Through the stories of the kings (1 & 2 Kings and 1 & 2 Chronicles), the people of Israel were given the hope of waiting for the truly anointed one, the Messiah.

. . .

"Therefore the Lord Himself will give you a sign: Behold, a virgin will be with child and bear a son, and she will call His name Immanuel." He will eat curds and honey at the time He knows enough to refuse evil and choose good.

Isaiah 14-15

DO NOT TAKE GOD'S WARNING LIGHTLY

2 Chronicles, Jeremiah, Daniel, Ezekiel

The reason why the Bible separates the period of exile with others is because even though the country was destroyed and people were taken into captivity, they were to return to their land based on God's recovery plan. The ten tribes of the northern Israel were scattered throughout the world and was not able to return to their land but for Judah-it was different. Judah was recovered after 70 years of captivity in Babylon all because of God's faithful promise to David.

Prophet Jeremiah Who Prophesized the Exile

You Will Be Ruined

There is a consistency in the prophecies of the Bible. The word of God states, "When you become the father of children and children's children and have remained long in the land, and act corruptly, and make an idol in the form of anything, and do that which is evil in the sight of the Lord your God so as to provoke Him to anger, I call heaven and earth to witness against you today, that you shall surely perish quickly from the land where you are going over the Jordan to possess it. You shall not live long on it, but shall be utterly destroyed. And the Lord will scatter you among the peoples, and you shall be left few in number among the nations, where the Lord shall drive you." (Deuteronomy 4:25-27) As we know, Israel was founded on God's promise to Abraham and the Israelites were expected to be faithful to the Lord God only and to fashion their lives according to the Law. A warning for the consequences of worshipping foreign gods was already expressed that they would experience exile resulting from their unfaithfulness. This message is repeatedly mentioned throughout the book of prophets.

By serving foreign gods (idolatry) instead of God, the book of Isaiah records, "Behold, the Lord lays the earth waste, devastates it, distorts its surface, and scatters its inhabitants." (Isaiah 24:1) The period that Isaiah worked actively was around 700 B.C. The Word of God that was given to Moses in 1,400 B.C. had traveled through the period of the Judges and the Kingdom period. And now God sends a series of messengers to remind them of His prophecy. Simply put, God's message was disobedience to God would not only bring destruction of the country but also an exile to a foreign land.

Right from the beginning, people proved to be rather poor at keeping their side of the covenant and were incapable of hearing what God had to say. They chose to worship idols instead. Why? It is because of self-gratification. Idolatry only focuses on self satisfaction. In order to achieve self-serving desires, you distance yourself from God and follow foreign gods which is what 'idolatry' is all about. It is a religion of Shamanism, worshipping an idol for something in return. This type of religion is even more dangerous than an atheist.

The most important theme messages from all the prophets were on God's judgment: people being taken into captivity, living in exile. And it was Jeremiah who warned of the impending exile in detail and appealed in vain to the nation to turn back to God. He was also in the midst of the religious and political affairs that was worsening for Judah after the death of godly King Josiah under Jehoiakim's reign. At various intervals he prophesied of the Babylonians who will conquer Israel and the fall of Jerusalem was inevitable to him. To make it worse, he witnessed King Zedekiah being taken into captivity bounded in chains with his eyes pulled out.

God showed a vision and explained to Jeremiah what he must tell the people. "The word of the Lord came to me saying, 'What do you see, Jeremiah?' And I said, 'I see a rod of an almond tree.'" (Jeremiah 1:11) In Hebrew, the two words 'almond/watching' sound similar as 'shaqed/shoqed.' In the book of prophets and psalms, we frequently come across the wit of Hebrews regarding the way how they interpret the words through 'sounds.' This is the case in this situation. Upon seeing the vision, Jeremiah instantly understood what 'shaqed'meant. It was to 'carry out' and he was extremely shaken. He knew that God was going to fulfill His prophecy given to the people during the Moses time -- the warnings on the destruction and the exile if they abandon God for idolatries.

Jeremiah suffered great pain and sadness. But then again, God showed him another vision. "The word of the Lord came to me a second time saying, 'What do you see?' And I said, 'I see a boiling pot, facing away from the north.'" (Jeremiah 1:13) This vision was of a cooking pot that was about to tip over. Destruction was 'boiling over' onto God's people from Babylon, the great power of the north, devastating the city of Jerusalem and burning the temple where the Ark was kept.

One may wonder how it is possible for the destruction to 'boil over' from the north when Babylon is actually situated in the east. Looking from the historical background will enable you to understand this quite easily. The power of Assyria was already crushed away by Babylon during the days of Jeremiah. Therefore, King Nebuchadnezzar of Babylon emerged as a supreme power to become the instrument of God's judgment on His own people at the time which coincides with the vision of the boiling pot ready to tip over on Judah who was caught in the crossfire between the two contending world powers: Babylon in the north and a resurgent Egypt in the south.

Reason Why Jeremiah Shed Tears

The message of the prophets was like Joshua's: Choose the way whether to serve God or to worship foreign gods. Prophets enter into the scene during the latter part of the kingdom of Judah which was going downhill towards destruction. After King Uzziah, the 10th king of Judah, God intervened decisively in the life of the Nation by sending His own special representatives. Prophet Hosea of the Northern Israel spoke as if a woman had left her husband for another man referring Israel that she had forsaken God for Baal and instead worshiped golden calves. God pointed out numerously that His people had served the lewd idol of Baal.

In spite of Israel's unfaithfulness, God encouraged them through the prophets that it is still not too late to return to Him. God gave every available opportunity and chance. Even though the life may appear as if it has ended, God's message is 'I still love you' and He waits for us to return to Him. The prophesy is that there will be salvation if we return to God but if not, destruction, judgment and wrath await us.

All the prophets prophesized about 'choices' but among the 17 prophets in the Old Testament, only Jeremiah prophesied about 'shaqed' - 'the word of God being fulfilled.' In other words, the time limit for Israel to choose had expired. With this knowledge, Jeremiah could not help but to declare the terrible fate of his nation that he saw and grieved over their stubborn refusal to take notice. The primary role of a prophet is to deliver God's message by encouraging and giving hope to people that it is still not too late to return to God. Message with no hope would be useless but in Jeremiah's situation, he was left with no choice but to deliver in tears the anguished warnings of God's judgment to come within the years leading people up to exile-God's word was to be fulfilled. "You are now finished. History of Israel has ended-kingdom of Judah and Jerusalem will be barren and void. God is going to use Babylon to take you into captivity."
(See: Jeremiah 25:9-11)

The prophecy of Jeremiah was basically the following: "Babylon's attack is God's judgment and they are being used as a 'tool' of God so obey and do not resist." For example, just imagine what the reactions of the people would be like if North Korea comes down with tanks to attack the South and a prophet like Jeremiah comes into the scene with a microphone shouting, "People! We must not fight back but surrender." People would start cursing at him and think he has lost his mind. This is why Jeremiah became known as a weeping prophet because of his dismay at the message of judgment that he is obliged to bring to his people, who are now poised precariously on the brink of destruction. He longed to end his mission but the power of God would not leave him. "But if I say, 'I will not remember Him Or speak anymore in His name,' Then in my heart it becomes like a burning fire Shut up in my bones; And I am weary of holding it in, And I cannot endure it." (Jeremiah 20:9)

Yet he had to make God's word known so his role as prophet put him under tremendous pressure. It was too much for him to bear that he even cursed that he was born. But God said to Jeremiah, "Before you were born I consecrated you; I have appointed you a prophet to the nations." (Jeremiah 1:5) "Behold, I do not know how to speak, Because I am a youth" (Jeremiah 1:6) was the reply from Jeremiah's mouth unable to fathom God's work through him. What Jeremiah must tell the people was what they would not want to hear. They will be against him from the outset.

The book that follows after Jeremiah is Lamentations and the author is unknown. One of the reasons many people assume that it is the lament of Jeremiah is probably because he is known for his tearful mixture of literary forms; prose and poetry, taunt and lament.

The Word of God Will be Written in Your Hearts_Turning Point of the Work of Salvation

Jeremiah advises that the Israelites will return from exile in Babylon after 70 years. "For thus says the Lord, 'When seventy years have been completed for Babylon, I will visit you and fulfill My good word to you, to bring you back to this place.'" (Jeremiah 29:10) God promised their return not because of the efforts of the people of Judah but because of Him for who He is.

When it looks like total extinction caused by sin, God promises a future that He will save them again. Failing to return to God in spite of warnings will bring forth judgment but afterwards our merciful God restores His people with comfort and hope once again. According to the Jeremiah's prophecy, when the people of Judah were chained and taken into captivity from Jerusalem to Babylon which was approximately 1000 miles away, God comforts them, "Comfort, O comfort My people" (Isaiah 40:1) "Behold, days are coming,' declares the Lord, 'when I will make a new covenant with the house of Israel and with the house of Judah ... I will put My law in their minds and write it on their hearts." (Jeremiah 31:31, 33)

A new covenant was promised to replace the old one made at Mt. Sinai, which they had broken. Throughout the history of Israel, we have learned God's law written on the stone tablet that was kept inside the Ark had no significant effect to the people of Israel. God was shifting His work of salvation here. This time, God was going to remake them from within, giving them the power to do His will. We must realize that the meaning of the 'new covenant' (New Testament) is Jesus Christ, the full realization of Jeremiah's prophecy. The 'new covenant' is the work of Holy Spirit through Christ, to write God's laws on the hearts of all believers.

Even today, for us, the words written in the Bible are just like the God's law on the stone tablet as it was for the people of the Old Testament period. The words of God, being moved through the Holy

Spirit, must be carved into our heart so that God's message comes alive in us. This is what we call 'lament.' There are many words in the Bible but without the Holy Spirit, you cannot hear God's voice. From this point on, God promises that He will intervene directly into the lives of people through the Holy Spirit so that one may hear His voice and be transformed. This was the new hope God gave to Israel after the northern and southern kingdoms had fallen. Hallelujah!

The meaning of 'lineage community' the descendants of Abraham who carried the Ark and gave offerings in the Tabernacle, has now ended and instead replaced with a church, a 'community of the Holy Spirit.' The recovery of God's Kingdom was going to be accomplished via churches where one hears the voice of God through the movement of the Holy Spirit and by receiving Jesus, growing together into a dwelling of God in Spirit. (Ephesians 2:22) Perhaps the greatest contribution of Jeremiah can be found in his proclamation of the new covenant-God is shifting the direction of His work to give salvation to us. (Jeremiah 31:31-33) As history unfolds, this prophecy becomes the basis of the covenant initiated by Christ with his church.

TRUE FACTS OF THE PERIOD OF EXILE

What was the condition of the people of Judah during the period of exile? The history does not record how they lived during their captivity but through Daniel and Ezekiel we are able to learn the actual aspects of the exile period since the prophets were also among the people in the exile.

The book of Daniel falls into two parts. The first six chapters relate to Daniel's loyal faith to God who overrules no matter how powerful the opposing forces are. Through the life threatening events, he trusts in the Lord God and at the same time, he has ample opportunities to declare God's sovereignty as He demonstrates His power over the kings and gods of Babylon. The remaining chapters 7 to 12 are the prophecies written in the genre known as 'apocalypse' - setting out a world view of history with the great purposes of God.

Nation's Exile

The 1st Judean exile to Babylon took place during the 3rd reign of King Jehoiakim in 605 B.C. This is referred as the "1st captivity" and Daniel was a boy at the time of the first batch of the exile. We must realize that not everyone was taken into captivity. Exceptionally able and intelligent people were taken as hostages and farmers or field-keepers (laborers) of the kind were left behind.

Request for Vegetarian Diet_Daniel 1

King Nebuchadnezzar selected men with good looks and natural ability to educate them as the king's personal assistant in the court of Babylon. Daniel and his friends were among those selected for this special training. They were brought to the palace to be trained with a Babylian world view and culture which included eating Babylonian food as well. But instead of eating their food, Daniel, with his friends requested for vegetarian diet. It was not because he disliked meat but because of the fact that Babylonians did not observe Jewish rules on clean and unclean food nor did they drain away the blood when they slaughter animals but essentially because the king's food were the offerings to the idols. Daniel was determined not to compromise his faith with their religion. Imagine, this young man was a captive not a regular visitor of the king, what courage! Obviously one cannot be this bold without faith. Daniel asked the overseer, "Please test your servants for ten days, and let us be given some vegetables to eat and water to drink." (Daniel 1:12) Reluctantly the overseer agreed because if Daniel and his friends who were with him turned frail, it would be his responsibility. Ten days later, he noticed their faces were shining. What is more, they graduate from the king's school with honors. Through this incident, they stood as the witnesses of God's sovereignty over even to the greatest empire the world had known.

Interpretation of an Image in the Dream_Daniel 2

Daniel interprets King Nebuchadnezzar's dream. There was another person other than Daniel who succeeded in life because of dream interpretation -- it was Joseph. They were in similar situations: both were relatively young and in a foreign country. In Joseph's case, he interpreted Pharaoh's dream in Egypt after hearing about it but as for Daniel, he had to interpret the King Nebuchadnezzar's dream without even hearing it. In a way, it was a test which the king himself devised. 'I just had a horrible dream-can anyone interpret it for me?' Besides there was a threat that followed after if things went wrong. "If you do not make known to me the dream and its interpretation, you will be torn limb from limb, and your houses will be made a rubbish heap." (Daniel 2:5) Magicians and the rest could not possibly interpret the dream. How could they when they didn't even hear the dream in the first place?

But then God showed Daniel a vision and revealed the dream as well as its meaning. The image represented four different empires, beginning from the situation in those days and stretching into the future. The interpretation was that Nebuchadnezzar and Babylon will be ruined by Persia (now Iran).

Threader: This particular dream becomes the background of the New Testament and the fact that Christ (the kingdom of God) comes in the Roman period. After the fall of Israel until the birth of Christ, the change of the world is clearly revealed through Daniel's vision. The book of Malachi is the last prophecy and the Word of God literally stops for 400 years until the coming of Christ. This period is referred as the 'silence period.' Through this dream, it revealed how God worked for 400 years in order to send the Messiah, Jesus Christ into the world. Chapters 7-12 contains the apocalyptic message. This portion (the changes after Babylon until the Roman Empire) will be explained in more detail in the New Testament.

How can anyone say "your country will perish"even if a person had authority and power? But in faith Daniel boldly expressed it and King Nebuchadnezzar praises to the people that Israel's God is the 'living God' and commands that God be honored.

Daniel and Three Friends in the Furnace _Daniel 3

As years passed by, the king Nebuchadnezzar forgot that he once acknowledged Daniel's God and set up his gold-covered image demanding his people to worship it. Whoever refused it were to be put into the fiery furnace as a punishment. Daniel and his three friends, Shadrach, Meshach and Abednego refused and so they were put into the furnace. Nebuchadnezzar was furious and ordered "Heat the furnace seven times more than it was usually heated." (Daniel 3:19) Daniel and his companions believed God can deliver them from a terrible death and did not compromise. (Daniel 3:16-18)

Originally a fiery furnace was used for melting down steels or probably for baking bricks and with the flames that was set seven times higher than the normal temperature would have easily burnt them to ashes. But they saw a god-like figure walking through the flames along with them. The angel of God had protected them during the ordeal. As they came out unharmed, the king honored them and praised the God of Israel. (Daniel 3:28) Even though the king Nebuchadnezzar was compelled to worship God, he failed to do so. Many people want to witness miracles and are amazed when they experience it but in reality, it has no effect when it comes to believing in God. Salvation is not easily obtained.

Death of King Belshazzar_Daniel 5

King Nebuchadnezzar became mad and finally died after roaming around eating grass like a cow for seven years. His son, Belshazzar, took over the reign and his dream was to conquer the world which he successfully carried out by unifying the territory in the Middle East. Then he became restless. Boredom captures the heart of a person once things become comfortable and we must realize that these types of feelings are sparked by the spirit of Satan. Then automatically a person starts to think "Is there anything (sin) I could do?" and the irony is that never once does it dawn on a person's mind to read the Bible nor pray even after admitting that one is bored.

Out of boredom, King Belshazzar held feasts day after day. Since drinking alone was no fun, he hosted a great feast for over 3000 of his nobles at the palace-drinking from the gold cups and bowls plundered from the Temple when they burnt down and destroyed Jerusalem. The feast was at full swing when a mysterious hand began to write on the wall "Mene, Mene, Tekel, Upharsin" (Daniel 5:25).

People started to gather around it wondering what it was. No one was able to interpret it so Daniel was summoned in. He went to the root of the three words: Mene-numbered; Tekel-weighed on the scales; Upharsin: divide (lack of quantity) which meant that the king's days were indeed numbered. That very night, the king was killed and King Darius of Mede took over the kingdom of Babylon.

Daniel in the Lions' Den_Daniel 6

Babylon was already attacked and fallen before Mede and Persia joined the forces. As the period of kingdom of Babylon ended, King Darius of Mede entered into the scene. He is also recorded as Cyrus the Persian in the Bible. A new government had taken over and yet Daniel continues to serve as the king's commissioner. Being able to maintain his position in spite of the changes in ruling power is quite remarkable!

Especially King Darius admired and respected Daniel that he

appointed him as one of the top commissioners over the entire kingdom. Other commissioners got jealous and wanted to get rid of him. His enemies still could not fault him and can only attack Daniel through his religion. Failing to find any grounds of accusation, they finally decided to go up to King Darius and tell him about the laws of Daniel's God since they knew that he prayed three times daily facing towards the city of Jerusalem. They spoke, "All the commissioners of the kingdom, the prefects and the satraps, the high officials and the governors have consulted together that the king should establish a statute and enforce an injunction that anyone who makes a petition to any god or man besides you, O king, for thirty days, shall be cast into the lions' den." (Daniel 6:7) The next day, Daniel knew that the document was signed but he continued to pray to God in the same manner as he had been doing previously.

So his enemies had him and the king's hands were tied by his own decree. After Daniel was thrown inside the lions' den, the king spent the night fasting and could not sleep. He knew how important Daniel was to him; without Daniel as his advisor, it would be tough for him to conquer the world and govern the kingdom. The king arose at dawn and went hastily to the lions den and called out, "Daniel, servant of the living God, has your God, whom you constantly serve, been able to deliver you from the lions?" (Daniel 6:20) He actually prayed in his heart to God asking Him to keep Daniel alive when he went to the lions' den. Even though Daniel was a captive in a foreign land, he was able to deliver the living God through his life to the foreign kings.

Eventually Mede was absorbed by Persia and fell down at the rise of the Greek Empire of Alexander the Great. The Medians spread throughout the world and became a nation without a country-which is the worldly problematic tribe of the Kurds today. Even now more than 200,000 people are spread throughout various countries and especially in Iraq and Spain, they are persecuted tremendously.

The Book of Ezekiel-The Book of the Holy Spirit

Ezekiel is known to be the smartest man in his time. Probably being such an extraordinary and visionary man, unlike those of other prophets, Ezekiel's prophecies are meticulously ordered and the message is consistent throughout the book.

Generally it is said that the book of Joel is the book of the Holy Spirit in the Old Testament but in truth, it is the book of Ezekiel where the prophecies are filled with the Holy Spirit. The history of Israel has ended and we desperately need to catch Ezekiel's vision of Almighty God. We need to see sin as God sees it. He is delivering a message of the coming Messiah who is to come in Spirit after dying on the cross and upon resurrection. "Moreover, I will give you a new heart and put a new spirit within you; and I will remove the heart of stone from your flesh and give you a heart of flesh. And I will put My Spirit within you and cause you to walk in My statutes, and you will be careful to observe My ordinances." (Ezekiel 36:26-27)

Ezekiel is telling us that the Spirit of God will come into our heart but in the Old Testament period, it was before the crucifixion of Jesus Christ so the Holy Spirit could not enter into the hearts of the people yet. It is why the Holy Spirit in the Old Testament is expressed as the 'presence of God's Spirit' (outwardly upon a person's head). Just like when the Spirit of God came upon Saul, he took a yoke of oxen and cut them into pieces; also enemies were overthrown during the period of the Judges. The total transformation of a person was not accomplished since the Holy Spirit did not enter the heart of man.

Ezekiel's body was lifted up by the Holy Spirit who took him to the third heaven where God was. "Then the Spirit lifted me up, and I heard a great rumbling sound behind me, 'Blessed be the glory of the Lord in His place.'" (Ezekiel 3:12) Just like apostle Paul, Ezekiel also heard the angel's praises of glory in the third heaven. "He stretched out the form of a hand and caught me by a lock of my head; and the Spirit lifted me up between earth and heaven and brought me in the visions of God to Jerusalem, to the entrance of the north gate of the inner court, where the seat of the idol of jealousy, which provokes to jealousy, was located." (Ezekiel 8:3) Here Ezekiel expressed the power of the Holy Spirit as a 'hand' pulling him upwards to heaven.

The same promise given during Jeremiah's days, "I will make a new covenant with the house of Israel and with the house of Judah"(Jeremiah 31:31) and "I will put a new spirit within you." (Ezekiel 36:26) It is a promise that through the Holy Spirit, the hardened heart will be replaced with the soft one. In other words, the Holy Spirit will wash away all the filth within our hearts and replace it with the 'new' spirit. "I will put My Spirit within you and cause you to walk in My statutes." (Ezekiel 36:27) This means that we will be able to keep God's word only when the Holy Spirit enters our heart.

God's work of salvation through the Holy Spirit was being proclaimed through Ezekiel. The God's method of giving salvation through temple worship that was conducted by the Israelites was now going to be carried out through the Holy Spirit.

Threader: The salvation work in the New Testament is fulfilling God's Kingdom on this earth through loving God (upwards) and loving neighbors (sideways). It is up to each individual to experience the Holy Spirit and the Word from our community of churches, where we ultimately can become Christ-like. When we are touched by the inspirational power of the Holy Spirit, all the evil energy within us will be wiped away. Only then will we be able to keep God's word and live according to His standard. This message was proclaimed to the people of Israel through Ezekiel at the time of exile. (Ezekiel 36:26-27)

The Spirit of God Gives Life to the Dry Bones_Ezekiel 37

This chapter is filled with stories of skeletons which are coming alive. God gives Ezekiel a vision in the valley of dry bones.

A quick recap of the history of the Israelites: they were slaves in

Egypt for 400 years, lived during the period of the Judges after entering Canaan for 400 years and another 400 years in the period of the kingdom. God punished Israel and gave them physical suffering by using foreign countries in the neighbor as His tool when they abandoned Him for idolatry. And now, after living in exile, physical suffering was not a matter since they were financially stable but were mentally tormented. With Jerusalem destroyed, the people have given up hope because there were no temples to give worship. They finally came to realize how cruel it was to live apart from God and how miserable they were.

Their torment is well described in Psalms 137:2-4 "Upon the willows in the midst of it We hung our harps. For there our captors demanded of us songs, And our tormentors mirth, saying, 'Sing us one of the songs of Zion.' How can we sing the Lord's song In a foreign land?" The Hebrews normally played harps while singing praise to God at the time and the Babylonians urged them to sing for them since it was good in their ears but the Hebrews refused to entertain them with their song. Instead they hung their harps on the willow tree and wept daily facing towards the temple of Jerusalem. Unable to worship is great pain.

When I worked in Gabon, Africa, there were no churches around since it was a Muslim country. They only had temples and Catholic churches. I then realized for the first time how painful it was not to have a church around. Luckily, I met an American missionary and went to his house daily and gave worship along with other foreign missionaries. But, unfortunately, two months later the missionary returned to the U.S. for his sabbatical year and I was left with no place to go to worship again. I felt totally at a loss. We must truly realize how blessed it is to be able to give worship at a church. The relationship with God gets cut off when you stop giving worshiping. Even though you are alive physically but spiritually, you are like the dry bones.

Years of living in exile were like the dry bones in the valley for the people of Israel. The nation was dead. But it is the Spirit of God who gives life and makes them into a living army. God was promising Israel that they will be remade and live again. The promise of restoration after the exiles merged into the full blessing of the golden age in the future through the vision. When you are spiritually down or weary, just like dry lifeless bones, pray to God so that He may breathe into you His Spirit so that you may come alive again. Then you will experience the Lord's breath of life of resurrection.

Life-Giving Water from the Temple_Ezekiel 47

Another vision was given to Ezekiel by God. Out of God's Temple came a great life giving river flowing towards all four directions of the house. The water kept overflowing into all directions reaching the ankles, knees, waist and finally it became a river big enough to swim in. (Ezekiel 47:1-5)

One starts to evangelize when the life-giving water of the Holy Spirit reaches the ankle. But from the ankle to the head, one goes about the way he/she wants and is not considered to be full of the Holy Spirit. A person prays daily, kneeling down when life giving water reaches the knees and the water will reach the waist if one continues to pray. The person is totally absorbed by the Holy Spirit and at this point, you are no longer living freely but your life is aligned with God. When it becomes like a river enough to swim then your thoughts are totally surrendered and you give your life 100% to the Holy Spirit and led by it.

This vision is also the prophecy of the coming of the Messiah, Jesus Christ. His water of the Holy Spirit will wet Jerusalem, Judah, Samaria and spread to the ends of the world. God is giving a preview of what is to happen approximately 500 years later after the crucifixion of Christ. The promise of restoration and a hope of salvation to the people of Israel is being proclaimed by God through His messenger.

Benefits from the Period of Exile

Synagogue was formed

Israel had benefited a few things while they lived in exile. Worshipping in Synagogues and prayer places near the river side started since there were no temples to give worship during their exile. This was the origination of Israel's synagogue culture. Nowadays a synagogue can be found in any Jewish neighborhood. Whenever more than 10 Jewish people gathered, they started to form a synagogue while they were living in exile. Normally the Ark of God was supposed to be inside the temple but in a synagogue they recited the law and whoever was capable delivered the Word of God.

After the fall of Judah, the Israelites lived in exile in Babylon. After their return from this exile, they were all scattered throughout the world once again by the conquest of the Romans. And they took the culture of synagogue along with them at this time. Due to this effect, Apostle Paul was able to bear fruit from his mission trip since he delivered the Word of God to the Jews in the synagogue. Through the laws of the Old Testament and the prophecies, God had hope for Israel to accept His promise that He was going to send Christ as the Messiah at an appropriate time. But the result was the opposite. The Jews did not believe and instead, persecuted Apostle Paul. Rather it was the Gentiles who believed in Jesus first. Not only did God promise the 'new' covenant and the 'new' spirit but also prepared the method, via synagogues, in which His message would be spread throughout the world.

Prayer Place of the Riverside was formed

It was difficult to build a synagogue when there were less than 10 Jews. So the other alternative was setting up a prayer place near the riverside where they gathered and prayed. Apostle Paul crossed the straits of Samothrace and was on to Philippi during his 2nd missionary journey and found no synagogues there. So he automatically assumed that the people were at the prayer place near the riverside. It was at this place where Apostle Paul met a Jewish business woman, Lydia, who received the Word of God and helped the church of Philippi to be born.

Synagogues and prayer places played a significant role in spreading the news of the gospel.

Transcription of the Bible was made

During the years of exile, the people of Israel started to think of their identities. For instance, if a one year old child was taken as captive he would have turned 70 years old in Babylon. Such reflecting thoughts would have crossed their minds: "Who am I? Where did we come from? What does a 'Jew' mean? Why are we living in a foreign land?" In any event, the people of Israel started to record the Bible for the purpose of finding their identities and background during their lives in exile. There were no printing materials or printers at the time so everything was written by hand. The Bible was referred as the Scripture and the person who recorded it was a scribe. Finally, scribes were born from this point on.

Naturally the scribes became masters in writing the Scriptures and because of their knowledge, they started to teach it as well. Threader: In Matthew 23, Jesus scolded the scribes and the Pharisees for they only had literal knowledge of the Word of God rather than observing it.

The Chronicles are the records of the exile period. The author's purpose of writing this book was to make Israel understand the roots of their origin, namely, 'the root of David's kingdom is Abraham, who was the descendant of Adam and Eve; and that Adam was the first man that God created' in addition to God's promise of giving them hope and courage that they will return from captivity.

On the other hand, Jeremiah is assumed to be the author of the book of Kings which emphasizes that Israel had fallen because they had sinned against God. The book of Isaiah and other prophecies follow throughout the period of exile.

. . .

Comfort, O comfort My people, "says your God." Speak kindly to Jerusalem; And call out to her, that her warfare has ended, That her iniquity has been removed, That she has received of the LORD'S hand Double for all her sins. "A voice is calling," Clear the way for the LORD in the wilderness; Make smooth in the desert a highway for our God.

Isaiah 40:1-3

LOOK FORWARD TO THE RESTORATION

Ezra and Nehemiah

God's promise through Jeremiah was fulfilled when the people of Israel were allowed to return to their homeland and to their holy city of Jerusalem after 70 years of exile by the decree of King Cyrus of Persia (today's Iran). The leadership of Middle East was now shifted over to Iran from Iraq.

The Decree of King Cyrus_Ezra 1:1-4

God's promise through Isaiah was made approximately 170 years before King Cyrus was born. "Cyrus His anointed, Whom I have taken by the right hand" (Isaiah 45:1) "I have given you a title of honor Though you have not known Me." (Isaiah 45:4). Even a foreign king obeyed the bidding of God and as a result the Jews were allowed to return to their homeland. All leadership and power are in the hands of God. God took the hands of King Cyrus of Persia (Iran) and opened the gates for them to easily win the battles with Babylon (Iraq). Interestingly enough, the war between Iran and Iraq continues to this day.

"Therefore thus says the Lord God, 'Now I shall restore the fortunes of Jacob, and have mercy on the whole house of Israel; and I shall be jealous for My holy name.'" (Ezekiel 39:25) "Thus says Cyrus king of Persia, 'The Lord, the God of heaven, has given me all the kingdoms of the earth, and He has appointed me to build Him a house in Jerusalem, which is in Judah. Whoever there is among you of all His people, may the Lord his God be with him, and let him go up!'" (2 Chronicles 36:23) God saw to it that the exiles, like the Israelites at the exodus, did not leave empty handed. It was the king's order that the Israelites in exile would leave with silver, gold and goods enough to build the temple of Jerusalem but their return was delayed.

Reason for the Delay of the Return from the Exile

One of the major reasons for the delay was because of the economic stability. Even though they lived in exile in Babylon, they were reluctant to leave since life was comfortable and stable. Knowing that the grounds of the temple in Jerusalem were in rubbles, they were not anxious to go and start their life all over again in a desolate land. The other obstacle was the journey ahead of them. As they needed to walk the long journey (approximately 1,000 miles), it was known there were bandits and thieves who would rob their valuables or even rape women in some instances, so they could not even conceive the idea of leaving Babylon. In the past when they were taken captives, at least they were protected by the soldiers of Babylon but now since they would travel by themselves through their journey, they were terrified even though freedom was in their hands.

God raised three leaders. Zerubbabel, Ezra and Nehemiah and through their leadership, the Israelites finally returned to Jerusalem. A herd of sheep needs a shepherd to guide them.

Zerubbabel and 1st Stage of Return from Exile: Rebuilding the Temple_Ezra 1-3

Return in 70 Years_Ezra 1-3

The return took place in three stages. The main party, approximately 52,000 people returned with Zerubbabel in B.C. 538-7 to rebuild the Temple. The first captivity that Daniel was in took place in B.C. 605 and according to Jeremiah's prophecy, Israel returned approximately 70 years later. God's clock never fails and His promise is always fulfilled.

The 1st returnees upon their arrival in Jerusalem went straight to the grounds of the Temple and gave burnt offerings. They were mortified at the site of ashes where it once used to be the Holy Temple of God and wept for the glories that had been destroyed.

The purpose of rebuilding and laying the foundation of the Temple was not because they lacked the space to worship or felt melancholy for their homeland but because, just as Solomon's prayer when he built the Temple, a Temple symbolized a 'House of Prayer to God'a place where God existed. God kept His promise by restoring His people back to their homeland and was with them as He had proclaimed.

Opposition Brings Foundation Work to a Standstill_Ezra 4

The Jews started to build the temple after a year had passed since they gave burnt offerings. And the settlers from Samaria, capital of Northern Israel, offered to help, saying, "Let us build the Temple with you since we have been sacrificing to God like yourselves."

But the Jews did not want to have none of it. These people in Samaria, their adversaries were actually not one of the ten tribes but the mixed people of Assyria who had settled in the land at the fall of the northern kingdom in B.C. 722. From that period on, the Arabs started to live in that land later known as the Samaritans. They worshipped God but alongside of other deities.

The rejection stirred them to interrupt the construction of the Temple. In the meantime, King Cyrus died and his son took over the reign. This new king issued a decree terminating the construction of the Temple. The year that was spent on the foundation work had gone astray.

The 52,000 Jewish exiles had returned to Jerusalem to restore their temple and left behind the comfortable life they had led in Babylon. But because of the influence of the king's power and other obstacles to continue with their plan, they gave up and stopped the restoration work completely forgetting their original purpose of their return. Instead, they shifted their interest in their own dwelling homes. In order to deter their attention on building their homes and to remind them of building the Temple, God sent severe drought and calamity (Haggai 1:5-6) but the people were more discouraged and rather came to a conclusion that it was not yet the right time to rebuild the Temple.

Another 14 years passed by. God was impatient and sent a warning through prophet Haggai, "Is it time for you yourselves to dwell in your paneled houses while this house lies desolate?" (1 Haggai 1:4) Basically, the message was that no matter how much efforts they put in, there would be no fruitful results because the temple work had been suspended. God showed eight prophetic visions to Zechariah at the time when the Temple was rebuilt: the vision of four horse-drawn chariots, a lampstand and olive trees among others which symbolized judgment and salvation for Judah and the nations. Rebuilding of the Temple was a sign of God's presence among His people. All together, they supply what God's people need to shine with God's light in the world, which ultimately points to the coming Messiah.

At the urging of prophets Haggai and Zechariah, the people started building the Temple again-14 years since the official authorization by King Darius. In four years since they restarted the construction, the Temple was finished, in 20 years since the 1st group of Jews had returned from exile. This was a significant accomplishment for the Israelites as a nation since they were delivered by God from their bondage to Babylon through the 2nd exodus. The Temple that was restored through Zerubbabel might have been an empty shell since the Ark was missing but the essence of it was to prepare the coming of Christ as the head of the church. Without blood shed, there would be no redemption (Hebrews 9:22) so the Temple had to be restored for God to enter into His Holy place.

The 1st Temple in Jerusalem is Solomon's Temple, the 2nd is the Zerubbabel Temple and the 3rd is the Herod's Temple built during the period of Christ.

Spiritually speaking, the Temple is Christ Himself and since He is in our heart our body is the temple. That is why our body must be kept holy and blameless until the coming of Christ. (Ephesians 1:4, 2:22) If we leave the temple(our body) barren and busily go around focusing on our business or home, then we will hear the same warning message from God as "You have sown much, but harvest little; you eat, but there is not enough to be satisfied; you drink, but there is not enough to become drunk; you put on clothing, but no one is warm enough; and he who earns, earns wages to put into a purse with holes." (Haggai 1:6) This is the reason why it is important for us to hold on to the Word and kneel down at church to wash away the barren temple within us with living waters and edifying ourselves on a daily basis.

Ezra and the 2nd Stage of Return from Exile: Recovery of the Law_Ezra 7-8

A building alone does not make it a temple. The Law (the Word of God) must be recovered in it. In the past, the high priests delivered the Word of God to the people at the Temple in Jerusalem but since there was no temple, the Jews had no way of learning it.

About 80 years later after the temple was rebuilt, the 2nd group of exiles of approximately 5,000 people returned with Ezra in B.C. 458. (Ezra 7:1-28) Ezra was a scholar of God's law and was given an official sanction to teach the law, and to appoint magistrates in his homeland, who can offer sacrifices and to beautify the Temple. In today's term, a seminary is where he taught the new community of God's people and it is where scribes and high priests were born.

The Jews began to give worship in the Temple and started to observe the Sabbath since they did not keep the Sabbath or the Seventh year properly throughout the 450 years of the kingdom period because of their pagan ways. They also thought the reason for their exile in a foreign land was that God wanted to give the land of

Judah 'rest' for 70 years. According to Judaism, this was one of the reasons the emphasis is on the Sabbath in order to reflect that they do not repeat past mistakes. For instance, on the Sabbath, one is limited only to walk for a certain distance and is not allowed to work or conduct any kind of business. Instead, one has to sit all day and read the Scripture and is only restricted to talk about God and pray.

Threader: The development of Judaism teachings originating from B.C. 450 that produced high priests and scribes ended up persecuting Jesus. These people were the masters of the Scripture and therefore, persecuted Jesus for not observing the Sabbath. They took the Law literally. It is truly commendable of Ezra that he revived the Word of God back among the Jews but the irony was that they ended up persecuting Jesus. But then again, it was based on God's plan of salvation that Jesus was to shed His redemptive blood for mankind.

Since their return, priests, rulers and people alike have intermarried with the heathens around them which was forbidden by God. Ezra's bitter distress at the disclosure is not surprising and deep grief of his prayer pricks the nation's conscience. They are addressed to 'leave the foreign women' behind and the blame for all the unhappiness of broken marriages rests not on Ezra but on the list of offenders (recorded in Ezra 10:18-44) men who contracted those marriages in defiance of God's law. Through this incident, a message is loud and clear that we must keep ourselves pure both physically and spiritually just like a bride awaiting for the bridegroom.

Nehemiah and the 3rd Stage of Return from Exile: Jerusalem's Wall Rebuilt

_Nehemiah 1-13

Upon the exiles' return, the Temple was rebuilt in Jerusalem and the Word of God was restored. But there were no walls around the Temple to protect the grounds making it vulnerable against the foreigners and the enemies who could easily dirty the holy Temple. Nehemiah's brother Hanani brought the sad news of the colony in Jerusalem at the time to him who was a cup-bearer of King Artaxerxes of Persia at the time. Although far from his homeland, he was so concerned for his people that he continued to grieve and pray over the situation. God answered his prayer and Artaxerxes granted his request to leave to return to Jerusalem. Unlike Ezra, the 3rd stage of return from exile took place (B.C. 445) under a military escort.

When the walls of Jerusalem were being rebuilt under Nehemiah's inspirational leadership, there were oppositions from various enemies-especially Sanballat the Samaritan, Tobiah, the Ammonite and Geshem from Arabia. Threader: The Samaritans opposed when the temple, as well as the walls was being rebuilt and because of their actions, the Jews referred them as the 'dogs' at the time of Jesus. The Jews despised the Samaritans based on their foul experience with them. Apparently, this kind of conduct was not a wise move so Jesus spoke a parable regarding a good Samaritan: The high priests and the scribes including the Jews, on their way to Jericho from Jerusalem, came across a man who was almost dying stripped and beaten by thieves. But they passed by without offering any help despite their knowledge of the Law. But a Samaritan who the Jews labeled as the 'dogs' had the compassion to stop and took care of him. Jesus spoke this parable to people to relay the message that one must not be boastful of their knowledge of the Word of God or be proud of being a lineage of Abraham.

The people had the will to work. With a sword on one hand to fight off the enemies and with a shovel on the other hand to build the wall. With so much opposition they worked 24 hours with night shifts and with Nehemiah's dynamic leadership, they spent only 52 days to complete the walls despite all the obstacles.

Why do you think God restored Jerusalem? As Ezekiel had prophesied, it was because the living waters of the Holy Spirit had to flow and spread from the Temple of Jerusalem throughout Judah, Samaria and to the end of the world. Also Jesus had to shed his blood on the Mt. Moriah in Jerusalem where Abraham had offered his son Isaac. "Then a shoot will spring from the stem of Jesse, And a branch from his roots will bear fruit." (Isaiah 11:1)

The Jews thought making Jerusalem a fortified city by rebuilding the Temple and walls and recovering the Law would restore David's kingdom once more. But that was not the case. The restoration of Jerusalem had nothing to do with political recovery of David's kingdom. Instead, it was a preview of the second coming of Christ with His Word and the Holy Spirit to the 'new' heaven and the 'new'earth-the new holy city of Jerusalem. (Revelation 21:1-2)

Sin

Deviation from the Word of God is Sin

The people of Israel failed because of sin. This applies to us as well. After the period of the Judges, the Israelites distanced themselves from God for foreign gods and worshipped only for their own prosperity as they experienced through various kingdoms.

It is a sin when you deviate yourself from God which is the same thing as being ignorant. Since God is spirit and invisible, you go about living the way you want according to your own desires and have no interest in returning God's love to Him. As the result of sin, you have cut yourself off from God and since you are deviated from the Word of God, your neighborly relationship also suffers. A person who has not received God's love cannot love others. Thoughts creep into your mind such as 'what efforts have I gone through to make this money? How can I share it with others?' Not possible. But on the other hand, those who have received God's love can easily share with others.

Being deviated from the Word of God makes you become a believer of 'Shamanism'- a belief that as long as you become prosperous you don't care who or what it is. God does not want this sort of devotion-a devotion to achieve your own needs. A true faith has been shown by King David's acknowledgement towards God's love.

'God, thank you for loving me such an unworthy person that I am.'

Confess Your Weakness to Sin

It is the first step towards repentance to confess your weaknesses to sin. Memorizing verses in the Bible does not mean repentance. The Satan will not budge when you say, "Why do I still feel like a sinner even after knowing Jesus have washed away my sins? You evil spirit, move away from me!"

Repentance comes from our lips when we are moved by the Holy Spirit. "Come now, and let us reason together, Says the Lord, Though your sins are as scarlet, They will be as white as snow; Though they are red like crimson, They will be like wool." (Isaiah 1:18) True repentance must come from deep within our heart when the Holy Spirit moves us rather than through the confession coming from our thoughts. You will then experience God's love and comfort like the living waters that fills you up.

A person who seeks self-interest cannot be thankful for no reason. They are only thankful when things turn the way they had hoped for. Prophet Habakkuk said, "Though the fig tree should not blossom, And there be no fruit on the vines, Though the yield of the olive should fail, And the fields produce no food, Though the flock should be cut off from the fold, And there be no cattle in the stalls, Yet I will exult in the Lord, I will rejoice in the God of my salvation." (Habakkuk 3:17-18) This is what faith is all about to be able to give praise and thankfulness to God regardless of your situation.

Even David confessed his weakness to sin. "Behold, I was brought forth in iniquity, And in sin my mother conceived me." (Psalms 51:5) As the descendants of Adam, we are all born in sin. And this is exactly what wears us down. People who have not dealt with this kind of despair or felt it will never repent. Unbelievers of God become quite upset when they were told that we are all sinners. "Why am I a sinner? The so-called Christians are more corrupted and unrighteous in many ways." There are many unbelievers who are kind, have good characters and live morally in a worldly sense but they are not aware of the despair of sin. In order to make them understand the concept of sin is what we call 'evangelism.'

God sends signals to people when they have a deaf ear to His Word through accidents or environment and make them realize there is nothing they can do on their own when confronted with unexpected situations. At this point, people kneel in front of God.

When we kneel before God, it is first because of despair from the idea that we are weak to sin and second, it is because of the fact that we cannot save ourselves from sin. 'I kneel in front of the cross of our Lord because I know I am helpless' is the way in which we must confess daily. Let's face it. We sin knowingly and unknowingly. It is one of the reasons why I emphasize on rising up at early dawn to kneel in front of God; confessing our sins and being rejuvenated by the Word of God to lead another victorious day ahead. Without God's assurance, how can we overcome a day, living without sin?

. . .

Now in the first year of Cyrus king of Persia - in order to fulfill the word of the LORD by the mouth of Jeremiah - the LORD stirred up the spirit of Cyrus king of Persia, so that he sent a proclamation throughout his kingdom, and also put it in writing, saying, "Thus says Cyrus king of Persia, 'The LORD, the God of heaven, has given me all the kingdoms of the earth, and He has appointed me to build Him a house in Jerusalem, which is in Judah. Whoever there is among you of all His people, may the LORD his God be with him, and let him go up!'"

2 Chronicles 36:22-23

MEET GOD WHO LOVES YOU TO THE END

Amos and Hosea

So far, we have divided the 17 books of history in the Old Testament into 10 periods and gone over the journey of Israelites which began with God's creation, the calling of His people and the exile due to their unfaithfulness and their return. Then a line of 17 books of prophecy follow thereafter. Not only do prophecies supplement the history but it is also the conclusion of the Old Testament as well. Fundamentally, the books of prophecy must be read with the divided kingdom in the background. Let's first look into the prophecies of the Northern Israel.

What is the Difference Between the Fortune Telling and the Prophecy?

Prophecies relate to the future. Prophecies in the Old Testament relate to the future of Israel which can also be interpreted as our own future.

But what is the difference between the fortune telling and the prophecy in the Bible? Worldly people go to fortune tellers because they believe in fatalism. They believe that a destiny/fate of a person's life is already fixed. For instance, 'one is bound to fail in one's business because one's fate is not in business.'

However, we must realize that fortune telling is a trickery of a false spirit. Conclusively, fortune telling is a 'fallacy about one's destiny.' Satan holds on to our past since all mankind's past is filled with sin. It is the reason why Satan is able to pinpoint all that has happened in the past. People fall into the trap when they visit fortune tellers who reveal their past and are marveled by the accuracy. They think, "Wow! This person knows my life like a mirror! So then he/she will know my future as well." Then before they realize, they already have stepped into the trap.

On the other hand, the prophecy in the Bible tells us that the final days of our life lies in our freewill. When we choose not to live according to God's way but our own (as a result of eating from the tree of the good and evil) and encounter failure and suffering, we think, "My life is finished. I have no hope now," but God tells us, "It is not late yet. Repent and return to Me where recovery, comfort and salvation awaits you."

All the prophecies in the Bible are the messages of comfort and hope. Our life does not end in misery but worthwhile to live to the very end. Our journey of life will change completely depending on our decision whether we choose God or the world. Let's think about the thief on the right side of the cross of Jesus for a moment. If a fortune teller had predicted his life, then obviously the response would have been that he was destined to receive a death penalty. But at his last breath of life, he received God and became a citizen of heaven. This is the message that is being told to us through the prophecies in the Old Testament.

The background of the prophecies in the Old Testament is the bitter ending of Israel, a fallen nation and the exile of Israelites resulted from their unfaithfulness to God by walking the ways of Jeroboam and Baal. But through the Prophets, the good news is delivered to them as well, giving them hope for renewal and prosperity if they return to God. For today's church and today's Christian, the challenge of prophecy- the message of hope- remains the same. Hallelujah!

The Message in the Prophecy: Two Split Roads and the Birth of the Messiah_Advent of the Holy Spirit

First, the prophecy is about the two split roads which is different from the two roads mentioned in Deuteronomy "whether it is God or the idol." The historical background of the period of the prophecy takes place right before the fall of Northern Israel and Judah. God sends prophets to the land of Israel and Judah with a message. 'It is not late yet. Repent and return to God for there is salvation.' Therefore, the two roads in the prophecy is basically the choice of 'if or if not.' If one repents and returns to God, there will be salvation; and if not, there will be eternal curse and judgment.

At the time of crisis, when you think 'there's no hope for me anymore, it's finished. My business is ruined and my road of success is kaput. The only thing left is to die.' However, it is actually the time for your salvation. "Seek the Lord while He may be found; Call upon Him while He is near." (Isaiah 55:6) When do you think is the right time to meet God? It is when we are at the rock bottom of our life. God is near you and reaching out to you when you're down and out. You should call out and seek Him.

Even at the last breath of our life, it is all about choices. It's just like a referee at a boxing match when one player is about to be 'knocked out,' and God, the Judge, is counting down by saying "One, Two, Three ... Nine!" And rather saying "Ten" to announce 'defeat,' He is repeating "Nine!" as if He is waiting for some delayed reaction. Our God is telling us that there is still a chance to walk the way towards salvation. We must meet our Lord.

Some might say "Listen, I already believe in Jesus so it has nothing to do with me" but it doesn't necessarily mean that you have met the Lord. The word of prophecy exists to encourage us to make up our mind to humbly accept this fact as the truth and to experience the existence of our Lord within us through the Holy Spirit by praying and holding on to the Word on a daily basis. While continuing our studies of the Old Testament, I have talked about the Holy Spirit and emphasized on prayer along the way. It was primarily because a lot of believers of Christ have not experienced the Lord yet. "At one point in the past I have also experienced the Holy Spirit" does not mean anything. Why? Because the Holy Spirit is alive now. Our Lord does not resurrect on Sundays only and dead for the next 6 days. In order to walk with God, we must call and reach out to Him at all times by continuously praying and longing for the Holy Spirit to work within our heart.

Second, it is a prophecy about the coming of the Messiah, Jesus Christ, the descendant of David, who will rule with heavenly peace and righteousness. Generally, it is said that the prophecy is declaring the coming of the Messiah but truthfully, it clearly talks about not only of the birth of the Messiah but also the advent of the Holy Spirit (Jeremiah 31:31). Therefore, we must remember that the prophecy is not only about 'Jesus is to come' but also the advent of the Holy Spirit.

Structure of the Periodic Prophecy

The books of prophecy are divided according to its voluminous contents(volume) namely 5 major books of prophecy and 12 minor ones. Isaiah, Jeremiah, Jeremiah's Lamentations, Ezekiel and Daniel are regarded as the great books of prophecies. The book of Isaiah consists of 66 chapters and Jeremiah 52 chapters. The author of Lamentations is known to be Jeremiah and it contains only 5 chapters so the book of Jeremiah and Lamentations have been lumped together; Ezekiel has 48 chapters and the book of Daniel contains 12 chapters. The remaining books of prophecy are less in quantity so they are called as the 'minor' books of prophecy. Regardless whether major or minor, each prophecy contains an important message but especially the weight of the major prophets are substantial in every sense of the way.

There are prophets who actively worked before the fall of Israel and the others worked before the fall of Judah. Let's first look at the prophets of the Northern Israel. God sent prophets Elijah, Elisha, Amos and Hosea to the Northern Israel. Prophets like Elijah and Elisha worked through miracles and signs whereas Amos and Hosea who had no real training to become a prophet delivered the message through the Word that God was alive. They all told about the same God and described the same responsibilities given to those who want to maintain a relationship with God. They were God's spokesperson by saying "There is still a chance so return to God."

Prophecy in Northern Israel-

[Chart 4] Historical Setting of Prophecy: Divided into Timeline and Co-Regency.

Country to be sent / Period (Time)	(Northern) Israel	(Southern) Judah	Assyria	Edom
Before (Divided Kingdom)	Amos (760-753 BC) Hosea (740 BC)	Joel (approx. 835BC) Isaiah (740-680 BC) Micah (735-700 BC) Habakkuk (625-587 BC) Zephaniah (625-615 BC) Jeremiah (627-580 BC) Lamentations	Jonah (782-753BC) Nahum (664-611 BC)	Obadiah (845-841BC)
During Exile		Ezekiel (594-571 BC) Daniel (605-532 BC)		
Return from Exile		Haggai (537-515 BC) Zechariah (520 BC) Malachi (400 BC)		

Amos-Seek the Day of the Lord

Amos was a layman, a shepherd and a dresser of the fig trees in the days of the King Uzziah of Judah. God called him as His prophet to the northern kingdom of Israel during the reign of King Jeroboam II. At that time, Israel was at its peak of prosperity and influence to the other countries but beneath its affluence, the nation was rotten. The people had abandoned God for the ways of Jeroboam and Amos was sent to denounce the social and religious corruption, to warn of God's impending judgment, and simultaneously to prophesize the downfall of Ammon and Palestines. As God had wiped out the house of King Ahab through Elijah and Elisha, the people of Israel had fallen to the idolatry of the golden calf set up by King Jeroboam I at the time the nation had first split into two rival kingdoms. Amos warned of their spiritual corruption.

God wants righteousness of His world. "Let justice roll down like waters And righteousness like an ever flowing stream." (Amos 5:24) Once prosperity and affluence arose, people began to turn to luxury and pleasure at the expense of the poor. The gap of the rich and poor became far apart and the order collapsed. There was no justice. Judges were taking bribes and the person giving it was let loose. The prophet was crying out for justice on behalf of the poor and helpless emphasizing God's righteousness, a quality of love with determined act between God and humans, and between one human and another.

From the start, the northern kingdom of Israel walked the ways of Jeroboam and set up a religious center in Bethel and Dan where they worshipped the image of a golden calf. Obscene Baal idolatries were conducted during the days of King Ahab. In the midst of all the evil doing and distortion of human sinfulness, they were still waiting for the ‘days of Yahweh.’ Their assumption was ‘There is no reason why God only exist in the temple of Jerusalem. God will also exist in the golden calf. As long as God helps me and I become prosperous then that's all I care for.’ The mentality of having no relation whatsoever in the Word of God or what God wants from us is a religion of Shamanism.

Unfortunately, even today, there are many church goers who claim they believe in Jesus but have no interest in God or the Word of God. They are only interested in blessings. These types of people attend church claiming, “This is about the right degree of involvement leading a religious life. Besides, I have ‘served’ the church on many occasions.’ It is truly pitiful that there are many people out there thinking that they are Christians and yet assuming Shamanism is a religion. It is, in fact, an alarming reality. The only way we can know God is through the Word. Those who do not learn the Word of God (Bible) will never know who God is, how He wants us to live and what we must do or not do.

The “Day of the Lord” (Amos 5:18 and 20) is the day when God will be coming. If we look at it in the New Testament concept, it is the 2nd coming of Christ. The people who rejected God’s warning are also waiting for the coming of the Messiah but for them, the ‘day of the Lord’ would be the ‘judgment day’ because of their wickedness. The Day of the Lord will not be what they expect.

Hosea-Knowledge of God

Prophet Hosea worked actively from the days of Jeroboam II until the fall of Israel. Through Hosea, God tells us how important it is to know God and His Words. “My people are destroyed for lack of knowledge. Because you have rejected knowledge, I also will reject you from being My priest. Since you have forgotten the law of your God, I also will forget your children.” (Hosea 4:6) The knowledge this verse is talking about is not of the world but of God. Even though the people of Israel were boastful of being the descendants of Abraham, they rejected God so God will also reject them. What this means is that before praying for children's well-being one must hold on to the Word of God first.

Majority of people assume that knowledge of God only comes from reading the Bible but Hosea's interpretation of 'knowing God' is the knowledge not through the head (intellect) but through heartfelt experiences. It is a lasting love and real knowledge of Him that God wants. The religion of Christianity is based on experience, not conception. "So let us know, let us press on to know the Lord."(Hosea 6:3) God wants us to experience Him. Then, how can we experience (meet) God? "His going forth is as certain as the dawn" (Hosea 6:3). It is God's promise that He will meet us when we kneel in front of Him at early dawn just as each morning is promptly greeted with the light of the day. Hosea's moving message to Israel comes straight from the heart that they must return to God even though they are destined to go downhill due to their unfaithfulness. "Come, let us return to the Lord. For He has torn us, but He will heal us; He has wounded us, but He will bandage us." (Hosea 6:1) God wants to heal and care for us through sufferings. God will surely meet us if we confess our sins and repent wholeheartedly to Him. "For I delight in loyalty rather than sacrifice, And in the knowledge (experience) of God rather than burnt offerings." (Hosea 6:6) God wants His people's love, not placatory sacrifices. God is appealing to us, "I love you so please respond to My love." "When you come to appear before Me, Who requires of you this trampling of My courts?" (Isaiah 1:12) God wants to meet us intimately. Therefore, it would be a mistake to understand God conceptually. We must intimately meet Him through the Word and prayer.

Meet God Who Loves You to the End

Not having experienced God and not knowing who God really is makes a person waver in faith due to the lack of assurance in salvation in spite of many years of church attendance. One is challenged with continuous worries and anxieties of the world because the knowledge of the Bible remains intellectually. Apostle Paul said, "May be able to comprehend with all the saints what is the breadth and length and height and depth, and to know the love of Christ which surpasses (overcome) knowledge." (Ephesians 3:18-19) In other words, we must not acknowledge 'God's love' only with our head.

God's love and human love are shown through prophet Hosea. God's first instruction to Hosea was strange: The wife he was to marry was a prostitute. "When the Lord first spoke through Hosea, the Lord said to Hosea, 'Go, take to yourself a wife of harlotry, and have children of harlotry; for the land commits flagrant harlotry, forsaking the Lord.'" (Hosea 1:2)

If you were asked by God to do the same thing, would you do it? Probably not. To marry someone who is immoral would be unthinkable for a normal person. Yet God specifically tells Hosea to marry Gomer, a woman who God knows will prove unfaithful. He obeys and marries the woman who eventually runs away with another man. She ends up being a slave of another man in a brothel house and God calls out to this woman saying "I still love you" who apparently is broken emotionally and physically. God gives a second instruction to Hosea to keep loving his wife even though he may have feelings of hurt, betrayal and anger. God's love is not superficial and sentimental but costly and transforming. Hosea's wife is bought back and put on probation.

Paying the cost is what we refer to as 'redemption.' The cost of our sin is Jesus on the cross. This is the scope of God's love: God had loved the 'virgin' Israel and met them during their days of slavery in Egypt and got engaged with them. Then, after the marriage, they arrived in Canaan to build a 'new' home after the journey in the wilderness but Israel, the bride abandoned God after falling in love with the Baal. Later, Northern Israel was torn apart into pieces by Assyria. Men were sold as slaves and women were sold as prostitutes. The people of Judah also fell in the hands of Babylon and were taken as prisoners in captivity. The prostitution of Israel's religion led them to actual prostitution-pagan religion and its temple brought prostitutes resulting in sexual degradation and the breakdown of law and order in Israel.

Nevertheless, God still loves Israel. The relationship between God and Israel is vividly portrayed in the prophet's own marriage: unfaithfulness, breakdown and healing. The story also is about human's responsibility, about the choices for or against God that Israel had to make, and that we, too, have to make. Wrong choices have consequences for our lives. If your wife had acted like Gomer, would you be able to sell all your treasures to bring back your wife from the brothel house? God's love is freely offered, though grieved by our rejection, yet endlessly forgives, offering a way back into His love through Jesus. No matter how much we break God's heart, God continues to love us to the end and pay the price of redemption to save us.

Knowledge Search 16

Can God's love be weighed or measured?

We praise God by singing "Even though the skies of heaven are wrapped around with His overcoat and the seas as His ink, there is no way to measure the greatest love of God." But is that really true? Apostle Paul told the church members of Ephesus that there is a way to measure the love of God, its width, length, depth and the height. "May be able to comprehend with all the saints what is the breadth and length and height and depth, and to know the love of Christ which surpasses knowledge" (Ephesians 3:18-19)

1. **Width**: The width of the ocean includes all that covers the land and the water. The love of God covers not only our sins but also all elements of our lives. His endless love includes health, materials, happiness in our family, problems of our children and everything relating to our daily lives.

2. **Length**: How long would God's love be towards us? God loved us in Christ even before we were formed, before the creation of the world and He will love us forever.

3. **Depth**: Our Lord died on the cross - "But emptied Himself, taking the form of a bond-servant, and being made in the likeness of men. And being found in appearance as a man, He humbled Himself by becoming obedient to the point of death, even death on a cross." (Philippians 2:7-8) The depth of God's love is with us even though we go down to the lowest level of hell.

4. **Height**: Conquering death our Lord resurrected and when He rose, He raised us up with Him and seated us next to the throne. (Ephesians 2:6) His love raises us up to the right hand of the throne in heaven. Hallelujah!

. . .

so that Christ may dwell in your hearts through faith; and that you, being rooted and grounded in love, may be able to comprehend with all the saints what is the breadth and length and height and depth, and to know the love of Christ which surpasses knowledge, that you may be filled up to all the fullness of God.

Ephesians 3:17-19

WAITING IN SILENCE IS THE GREATEST LOVE

Isaiah, Micah, Joel, Habakkuk, Zephaniah, Haggai, Zechariah, Malachi

God continuously sent prophets so that the torch (people of Judah) of David will not be broken. To keep the promise with David, God sent many prophets to Southern Judah. The 7 books of prophecy were written before the fall of Judah (before exile). Prophets were responsible for speaking out clearly the things that God had given them to say to the people of Israel. However, the listeners also had their own responsibilities to hear the message and heed the things that were said to them: to turn their faith into action; to live out the justice, holiness and love of God. For today's church and Christians, the challenge of the prophecy remains.

Prophecy before the Exile of Southern Judah

Isaiah-Compressed Version of the Bible

Known to be the cousin of Uzziah, the 10th king of Judah, Isaiah knelt in front of God after his power base had collapsed due to King Uzziah's death. Among the prophecies of the Old Testament, the book of Isaiah is the one that the people of Israel focus on the most primarily because it is the message of restoration and hope. The same message applies to the Christians today.

The book provides a template for Messianic expectation as it develops a profile of God's plan, including the exaltation of Jerusalem; the birth of Christ Jesus, who is to come as the Davidic heir to reign with peace and stability; how the ideal Servant of the Lord will carry God's mission through crucifixion and resurrection; the comfort of the Holy Spirit and the second coming of Christ.

Among the 17 books of visions and prophecies, the book of Isaiah invites not only the Israelites but us as well. "Everyone who thirsts, come to the waters; And you who have no money come, buy and eat. Come, buy wine and milk Without money and without cost. Why do you spend money for what is not bread, And your wages for what does not satisfy? Listen carefully to Me, and eat what is good, And delight yourself in abundance. Incline your ear and come to Me. Listen, that you may live; And I will make an everlasting covenant with you, According to the faithful mercies shown to David." (Isaiah 55:1-3) God pledges Himself to His people in tender, unswerving, and enduring love through Isaiah. It is an invitation through the Word and prayer. God repeatedly talks about the Holy Spirit who fills our spiritual thirst.

From the beginning, Isaiah charges Israel like a prosecutor in the court for their sinful acts of rejecting God to worship Baal and that not a single spot is free of disease from head to toe. Yet still God offers forgiveness. Swift and terrible judgment will fall on all who continue to defy Him but God also promises that He will cleanse His people from their sin. "Come now, and let us reason together,' Says the Lord, 'Though your sins are as scarlet, They will be as white as snow; Though they are red like crimson, They will be like wool." (Isaiah 1:18) God will wash away our sins if we confess it with our lips in prayers.

66 Chapters of Isaiah - 66 Books of the Old/New Testament

Many readers find the book of Isaiah difficult to grasp. It contains many well known passages but the overall structure is complicated so it would be helpful in finding some order by noticing the setting of the sections. Amazingly enough, the scope and structure of the book of Isaiah and the 66 books of the Bible are the same. Chapters 1-39 mostly deal with Judah and Jerusalem under the monarchy just like the 39 books of the Old Testament that cover the same period and therefore, the first 39 chapters are referred as the Old Testament of Isaiah. Remaining portion of chapters of 40-66 suits into the period of the Israelites' exile to Babylon and their return to Jerusalem, and this time of the restoration after the exile is referred as the rest 27 chapters of the New Testament of Isaiah. That is why the book of Isaiah is referred as the condensed version of the Bible - (66 chapters of Isaiah = 66 books of the Old/New Testament).

The 'new testament' of Isaiah, chapter 40 starts off with "A voice is calling, 'Clear the way for the Lord in the wilderness; Make smooth in the desert a highway for our God.'" (Isaiah 40:3) and ends with "'For just as the new heavens and the new earth Which I make will endure before Me,' declares the Lord" (Isaiah 66:22). The verses sum up the mission of John the Baptist and end with the message of the 'new heaven and earth' in the Revelation.

Book of Judgment_Isaiah 1-39

The first part (chapters 1-39) or the Old Testament of Isaiah deals with God's judgment as a result of Israel's sin and is referred to as the "Book of Judgment." But a 'holy seed' will bear fruit from a stump that has been kept in the midst of the judgment is the focal point of this part; the message of the Messiah who is to come to bring them salvation. This message, in particular, is as follows:

First, a preview of the 'holy seed' from a stump that was left behind is being proclaimed first in the midst of exposing the sin of Israel and Judah which will bring judgment. (Isaiah 1-6)

"Yet there will be a tenth portion in it, And it will again be subject to burning, Like a terebinth or an oak Whose stump remains when it is felled. The holy seed is its stump." (Isaiah 6:13)

Second, the holy seed is being introduced that a son will be born through a virgin and is a descendant of King David. "Therefore the Lord Himself will give you a sign: Behold, a virgin will be with child and bear a son, and she will call His name Immanuel" (Isaiah 7:14)

King Ahaz defied God and in consequence, his kingdom came under attack from all quarters. When he refused to join the Israel/Syria alliance against Assyria, they attacked Judah. It was at this point when Isaiah offered king Ahaz a sign of God that He will keep His promise to save Judah and its line of kings. Isaiah promised him another sign, a child called 'Immanuel' - in Hebrew it means "God is with us." "For a child will be born to us, a son will be given to us; And the government will rest on His shoulders; And His name will be called Wonderful Counselor, Mighty God, Eternal Father, Prince of Peace." (Isaiah 9:6) A child who has all the authorities, powers and order of the world is Jesus the Messiah who is to come as the descendant of David. "Then a shoot will spring from the stem of Jesse, And a branch from his roots will bear fruit." (Isaiah 11:1)

Third, the prophecy of God's judgment on the specific foreign nations and the kings who gave trouble to Israel is being proclaimed. (Isaiah 13-23)

Fourth, the glory of the coming Messiah in Mount Zion (Jerusalem) is being proclaimed. (Isaiah 24-27) "Then the moon will be abashed and the sun ashamed, For the Lord of hosts will reign on Mount Zion and in Jerusalem, And His glory will be before His elders." (Isaiah 24:23) This is the proclamation of Jesus carrying the cross in Jerusalem and through His resurrection, death is eternally defeated. It also explains the reason why Jesus had to enter into Jerusalem after three years of ministry in the vicinity of Galilee.

"And on this mountain He will swallow up the covering which is over all peoples, Even the veil which is stretched over all nations. He will swallow up death for all time, And the Lord God will wipe tears away from all faces, And He will remove the reproach of His people from all the earth." (Isaiah 25:7-8) A chapter on judgment is followed by rescue and redemption, when God removes 'the cloud of sorrow that has been hanging over all the nations.' A promise to free us from death through Jesus' resurrection is given to those who believe in Jesus. "In that day, the Lord will start His threshing from the flowing stream of the Euphrates to the brook of Egypt; and you will be gathered up one by one, O sons of Israel." (Isaiah 27:12) The day will come when God's purpose for His people will be fulfilled. Apparently, the Jews understood this prophecy as a political recovery of Israel that even today, they firmly believe in it. In reality, through the proclamation of Balboa in 1949, the scattered nation of Israel raised Israel as its country. Therefore, Jerusalem already has been formally restored. But spiritually, the restoration of Israel means the birth of church through the resurrection of Jesus Christ and the advent of the Holy Spirit. The final harvest of all God's people will be brought home through the church that will be risen in Jerusalem. In a way, spreading the gospel to Israel is our role as Christians and God's command.

Fifth, God warns that Judah is protected from Assyria only for a while and gives a prophecy of judgment on them through Babylon because of their disobedience. (Isaiah 39) I have mentioned earlier that the prophecy supplements the history of Israel. The challenge between the prophet and the King Ahaz, the king Hezekiah and Isaiah praying together over the threatening letter when the Assyrian army was hammering at the gates of Jerusalem, the king Hezekiah taking Isaiah's advice and saving the city, etc. are all recorded in the contents of the history. (Isaiah 29-39)

The reason why chapters 1-39 of Isaiah are referred as the Old Testament is because not only Isaiah was a prophet who existed way before the exile took place but he also enumerated the sins of the people of Israel before their fall. His messages are filled with God's voice of warning people of the judgment on sin and comforting them with the knowledge of God's love, His longing to forgive them and all the glories stored for those who repent and return to Him.

Word of Comfort and Hope_Isaiah 40-66

The time of Babylonian exercising its domination over Judah begins with thousands being taken into exile. Isaiah chapter 40 addresses the dispirited exiles and words of comfort and hope are given to the Israelites. This whole section speaks of God's salvation so powerfully that Christians see in it something much bigger than the rescue of Israel at a particular time in the history. Here is God's firm purpose and explanation clearer than in the New Testament that the glory of the coming Messiah who will deliver humankind from the bondage of sin is given through the suffering on the cross. It tells us of our Lord's resurrection, ascension and the 2nd coming of Christ to the new heaven and earth at the end time. In a way, we are given a glance of the entire content of the New Testament. The following is the message of Isaiah's New Testament:

First, it is the 'Promise of Peace.' (Isaiah 40-48) Words of comfort and hope are given to the people of Judah in exile. The people were in distress and had lost hope completely at the time. "Do not fear, for I am with you; Do not anxiously look about you, for I am your God. I will strengthen you, surely I will help you, Surely I will uphold you with My righteous right hand." (Isaiah 41:10) God's tone is infinitely loving and tender to His people and comforts them that they have nothing to fear for He will restore them again. The same message was given through Jeremiah. God works another remarkable road of salvation that we cannot possibly comprehend. "Comfort, O comfort My people." (Isaiah 40:1) "Yet those who wait for the Lord Will gain new strength; They will mount up with wings like eagles, They will run and not get tired, They will walk and not become weary." (Isaiah 40:31)

In other words, we must not complain, saying things like, "God, why aren't you doing something about my situation?" Instead, those who look up to God with hope and focus in Him will pray at the time of despair. A person in total distress who wishes to be strengthened and rise up with wings like an eagle must receive the guidance of the Holy Spirit and pray.

The result of their sin brought fall to the people of Judah (Jerusalem) but they complained that God had forsaken and forgotten them instead. God, with patience and love for faithless Israel, said, "Can a woman forget her nursing child, And have no compassion on the son of her womb? Even these may forget, but I will not forget you." (Isaiah 49:15) God have pre-destined us in Christ before creation. "He chose us in Him before the foundation of the world, that we should be holy and blameless before Him." (Ephesians 1:4) Before we were born, before creation, our spiritual being was in Christ. "I will never forget you" are the Words of God.

God will never forget us since we were in Christ before creation. "But now, thus says the Lord, your Creator, O Jacob, And He who formed you, O Israel, Do not fear, for I have redeemed you; I have called you by name; you are Mine!" (Isaiah 43:1) There is no reason to fear or be alarmed on anything. Our life is in the hands of God. "When you pass through the waters, I will be with you; And through the rivers, they will not overflow you. When you walk through the fire, you will not be scorched, Nor will the flame burn you." (Isaiah 43:2) Not only have we been saved and freed from sin and death by God but have been called by name so no matter what happens, God promises that He will be with us. This message of hope was given to the people of Israel through Isaiah but also remains the same word of hope to us even today.

Second, it is the 'Prince of Peace.' (Isaiah 49-58) The Prince of Peace who is to come to the suffering captives must first become 'God's suffering Servant.' The suffering that the people of Israel went through during their exile was in no comparison to the sufferings the Messiah was to go through for the sake of the sins of mankind. The peace that 'the world cannot give' can be received only through the sufferings of the cross of Jesus.

Isaiah gives warning that the Messiah will receive sufferings when He comes to the world. "But He was pierced through for our transgressions, He was crushed for our iniquities; The chastening for our well-being fell upon Him, And by His scourging we are healed. All of us like sheep have gone astray, Each of us has turned to his own way; But the Lord has caused the iniquity of us all To fall on Him." (Isaiah 53:5-6) Jesus willingly gave His life that we might be forgiven, taking the place of many sinners to reconcile God and His people. As a result of His blood on the cross, we have received His peace.

One of the reasons why we are able to experience peace in our heart during difficult times is because God has already suffered for us. The whipping lashes that Jesus had received from the Roman soldiers are made in leather with nails embedded on them. One lash on the back would strip away lumps of flesh at the same time. When we are healed of illness, it is because of the lashes that Jesus received. 'Like sheep that has gone astray' is the good and evil. As we lead our lives making our own judgments on good and evil, our Lord has made the Messiah to take full responsibility for our sins. "He was despised and forsaken of men ..." (Isaiah 53:3)

God's word relating to the observances of fasting follows. "Is this not the fast which I choose, To loosen the bonds of wickedness, To undo the bands of the yoke, And to let the oppressed go free, And break every yoke? Is it not to divide your bread with the hungry, And bring the homeless poor into the house; When you see the naked, to cover him; And not to hide yourself from your own flesh? Then your light will break out like the dawn, And your recovery will speedily spring forth; And your righteousness will go before you; The glory of the Lord will be your rear guard." (Isaiah 58:6-8) This makes a mockery of religious fasting if we neither love God nor our fellow human beings. God does not want people to sit down with weepy faces claiming that they are fasting. A true fasting results from lack of food since it has been given to others in need.

Threader: This word on fasting falls into the same category as the parable in Matthew 25:31-33:

"When the Son of Man comes in His glory, and all the angels with Him, then He will sit on His glorious throne. And all the nations will be gathered before Him; and He will separate them from one another, as the shepherd separates the sheep from the goats; and He will put the sheep on His right, and the goats on the left." On the last judgment day, God will separate the sheep and the goats among the believers of Him. People who do not live according to God's way are referred as the goats. They are the so-called 'false' believers. "But the sons of the kingdom shall be cast out into the outer darkness; in that place there shall be weeping and gnashing of teeth." (Matthew 8:12) We must not pass over this verse lightly. Those who truly believe in Jesus must be able to share food with those who need to be fed, drink with those who are thirsty and nurse those who need to be cared for and also visit prisoners and console them.

Isaiah also proclaimed the works of the coming Messiah. "The Spirit of the Lord God is upon me, Because the Lord has anointed me To bring good news to the afflicted; He has sent me to bind up the brokenhearted, To proclaim liberty to captives, And freedom to prisoners; To proclaim the favorable year of the Lord, And the day of vengeance of our God; To comfort all who mourn, To grant those who mourn in Zion, Giving them a garland instead of ashes, The oil of gladness instead of mourning, The mantle of praise instead of a spirit of fainting. So they will be called oaks of righteousness, The planting of the Lord, that He may be glorified." (Isaiah 61:1-3) The Spirit of the Lord is upon me means the anointment of the Holy Spirit which is a 'calling' from God. This calling is spreading the good news to the poor, giving console to the broken-hearted and freedom to prisoners. Threader: This word was read by Jesus in the temple in Nazareth right before beginning His ministry.

"To grant those who mourn in Zion, Giving them a garland instead of ashes, The oil of gladness instead of mourning, The mantle of praise instead of a spirit of fainting. So they will be called oaks of righteousness, The planting of the Lord, that He may be glorified." (Isaiah 61:3) It was the customs of the people of Israel to throw ashes over their head at the time of mourning. So it is why God said a garland would be given to them instead of ashes. While in mourning, how can one be poured with happiness? It is only possible through the works of the Holy Spirit. All we can do is to acknowledge the Word of God, confess our sins and pray. Giving praises is the same as praying to God - raising and giving glory to God as we confess our faith to Him. The work of the Holy Spirit is most active when we sing praises. The essence of our faith is contained in all the works of Jesus that He performed during His ministry. There is nothing but the Holy Spirit that washes away our sins and consoles us from sorrow to joy.

Third, it is the 'Program of Peace.' (Isaiah 56-66) The final prophecies highlight two contrasting destinies of light and darkness. God's answer will be two edged: those who are not aligned with God will experience total destruction, and every vestige of evil will be swept away; for His faithful ones, life, joy, peace beyond imagination in heaven and earth will be made new. "For just as the new heavens and the new earth Which I make will endure before Me,' declares the Lord, 'So your offspring and your name will endure." (Isaiah 66:22) Those who walk in their sinful ways will be judged but God has a place reserved in His new world for those with humble faith. The remnants of God's people will participate in praise along with the trumpet sound of the angels at the eternal feast of the Lord who will come in the great glory and power at end time. Whereas those who refused to listen to God will be trembling in fear since it will be their judgment day. God's mercy towards the people of Israel is that they will be saved in a 'new' heaven and earth. Many biblical scholars have agreed that true Christians is interpreted as the 'new' people of Israel rather than interpreting it as the physical descendants of Israel.

Threader: The book of Revelation records the conclusion of the 'new heaven and earth as this: "And I saw a new heaven and a new earth; for the first heaven and the first earth passed away, and there is no longer any sea." (Revelation 21:1) This is the glorifying effect upon the 2nd coming of Christ. It symbolizes the state of glorification of the saints upon the process of salvation and sanctification through the mercy of Jesus' crucifixion. We must strive to be alert and pray in preparation for the 2nd coming of Christ.

Micah - Prophecies of Justice and Merit

Prophet Micah was a contemporary of Isaiah, prophesying in the southern kingdom of Judah, helping King Hezekiah's religious reform. As was the same situation with Amos and Hosea in the northern kingdom of Israel, Judah had become infected with the same sins. So Micah, too, denounced rulers, priests and prophets; deplored the money-grubbing exploitation of the helpless, dishonesty in business and sham religion.

He proclaimed the righteousness of God as follows: "And what does the Lord require of you But to do justice, to love kindness, And to walk humbly with your God?"(Micah 6:8) Don't they know what pleases God? It is to act upon our love towards others. The first 4 commandments in the Decalogue are about loving God with all our mind, soul and heart; and the rest 6 are about loving others just as we love ourselves. So the bottom line is that practicing the 10 commandments is acting upon the justice and merit. Faithfulness, honesty, trust are all gone. Now all human relationships are crumbling but hope remains because Micah knows His God. With God, there is yet light. With God's compassionate love, He will build and deliver the Israel again.

The main highlight of Micah was the prophecy of the ultimate deliverer who will come 700 years later; the birth of the Messiah in the town of Bethlehem. "But as for you, Bethlehem Ephrathah, Too little to be among the clans of Judah, From you One will go forth for Me to be ruler in Israel. His goings forth are from long ago, From the days of eternity." (Micah 5:2)

Joel - The Book of the Holy Spirit of the Old Testament

Considering the place in time range from the 8th to the 4th century B.C., Joel appears to have worked before Isaiah in the land of Judah. The prophet calls the nation to repent at the hay days of King Uzziah. Spiritual low downs occur during when a nation is enjoying its prosperities politically, diplomatically and socially. What prompts the prophet's message is a dire emergency, a plague of all consuming locusts. A plague warns of the Day of the Lord in Judah and Joel calls the nation to repent for God still loves His people and longs to rescue and restore them. "Awake, drunkards, And weep; And wail, all you wine drinkers, On account of the sweet wine That is cut off from your mouth." (Joel 1:5) "'Yet even now.' declares the Lord, 'Return to Me with all your heart, And with fasting, weeping, and mourning; And rend your heart and not your garments.'" (Joel 2:12-13)

Threader: The above verse does not mean literal wine but to be led by the Holy Spirit for true repentance.

The above passage has a similar theme in Ephesians 5:18 "And do not get drunk with wine, for that is dissipation, but be filled with the Spirit." For this reason, the book of Joel is referred to as the 'book of the Holy Spirit.'

"It will come about after this That I will pour out My Spirit on all mankind; And your sons and daughters will prophesy, Your old men will dream dreams, Your young men will see visions." (Joel 2:28) God promises a great outpouring of His Spirit, not just on priests and prophets but on ordinary people, regardless of gender, age or class. Young men grow with great visions once the Holy Spirit is upon them. Just like the young Rockefeller who diligently gave worship in the front seat of the church and began to experience the blessings of wealth through tithing. It is the Holy Spirit that enables young men to have visions.

Threader: As recorded in the book of Acts, the 120 saints who gathered to pray in the attic of Mark were filled with the Holy Spirit. With the advent of the Holy Spirit at Pentecost, tongues of flame started to outburst and all who were watching them said, 'These men are drunk!' Who were these men passing on remarks such as this? They were the Jews who had waited so long for the Messiah! Peter who was transformed by the Holy Spirit addresses the crowd of Jews-representing 'every nation under heaven' gathered in Jerusalem announcing that the prophecy of Joel given 700 years ago is being fulfilled. By Peter's moving speech, 3,000 people were baptized with a new and joyous sense of community. It was under the direction of the Holy Spirit that the first church was born.

Habakkuk - The Psalm of a True Believer

Prophet Habakkuk worked during the reign of Judah's 18th wicked king, Jehoiakim. Habakkuk was battling with the fact that while the good and the innocent suffered, the wicked flourished. Believing that God is just and good, the prophet cried out with questions: "Why, God, why? Why are you deaf to my prayer? Why don't you do something about the breakdown of the law and order and about the wickedness in the land?" (Habakkuk 1:2-4) God's answer seems only to aggravate the problem: 'My punishment will be an invasion of savage Babylonian (Chaldean) soldiers!' Then Habakkuk replies, "Oh no, God! Though the wicked king and people of Judah are not worthy in Your eyes, how can the 'good and just God' use such a vicious instrument of judgment? Will you let Babylon fish the sea of humanity forever?" (Habakkuk 1:12-17)

God has not changed His nature and has not joined sides with the wicked. The response was, "I will also judge Babylon but at my appointed time." (Habakkuk 2:3) The judgment was fulfilled through Cyprus, the King of Persia approximately 100 years later. Then Habakkuk asked, 'what will happen to the righteous ones on the judgment day?' On the Last Day when the final scores are added up, only those who trust God and remain true to Him will live. (Habakkuk 2:4)

Threader: The religious reform of Martin Luther King was based on this verse, "The righteous will live by his faith." (Habakkuk 2:4) Apostle Paul also emphasized this message in Rome. "But the righteous man shall live by faith."(Romans 1:17)

I encourage readers that it is almost mandatory to read the book of Habakkuk who have questions like, "Why does God tolerate injustice in His people? Why doesn't He judge the evil ones in the world?"

It also teaches us about true faith. "Though the fig tree should not blossom, And there be no fruit on the vines, Though the yield of the olive should fail, And the fields produce no food, Though the flock should be cut off from the fold, And there be no cattle in the stalls, Yet I will exult in the Lord, I will rejoice in the God of my salvation."(Habakkuk 3:17-18) This is what true faith is all about. True faith is the opposite of Shamanism. From a Shamanistic point of view, abundant vegetation and flourish of cattle are to be expected after a year long hard labor in the fields. But a true response to God's love is 'even if the blessings of God is wiped out, I will rejoice in God and praise His name.' Prophet Habakkuk shows us the right attitude of a believer who is waiting for the day when God deals with the invader; and he rejoices in God, though life is stripped of all that gives natural joy and satisfaction.

Today, many of us neglect to focus on God and instead try to receive only the blessings - which is why the problems occur in our lives. "The earth was formless and void ... and the Spirit of God was moving over the surface of the waters." (Genesis 1:2) In the midst of formless and void, the Holy Spirit fills our heart when we praise God. If only we realize that once we refrain from dwelling on visible things that is the moment when we experience or encounter God, then surely we will also be able to confess the same kind of faith as prophet Habakkuk.

Zephaniah prophesied about the 'day of the Lord' during the reign of King Josiah (Judah's 16th king). He warned that on that day all evil would be punished, and thus, it will be a black day for many in Israel. He declared that the day is close at hand when all who are guilty of idolatry, violence, fraud, and all who dwell in idle indifference will be set apart for destruction. He proclaimed the day of the Lord that is coming for Judah which would bring judgment to the unbelievers but blessings to the believers who repent and abide by the Word of God.

Simultaneously, as God sends prophets to warn people of the judgment day, God proclaims to save the faithful ones giving them hope and encouragement. As we recall, Lot and his two daughters were saved in the midst of the judgment that fell upon Sodom and Gomorrah. The 'remnants' who Zephaniah is referring to are the people who will return from exile to restore God's temple and the wall of the city of Jerusalem.

For the few who remain faithful even when all their pride and self-sufficiency are gone away and even when the nation is purged, there is still a cause for great rejoicing. God is in the midst of His people, protecting and keeping them safe, pouring out His love on them. (Zephaniah 3:17)

Before the fall of Judah, God sent six prophets: Isaiah, Jeremiah, Micah, Joel, Habakkuk and Zephaniah with the common message: 'It is not late yet so return to Me.' In addition, however, God said the period of the Israel is over and gave His word to send His Son to the world to bear our sins. And through Him a 'Helper' (Holy Spirit) will be sent to our heart.' According to his own prophecy, Jeremiah witnessed the fall of Judah and the captivity taking place. He was not among the Jews who were taken into exile in Babylon but was along with the political leaders of Judah who escaped to Egypt at the time. In Egypt, Jeremiah asked his disciple Baruch to record the events, which is the book of Jeremiah today.

The prophecy that was proclaimed in both Northern and Southern kingdoms of Israel was fulfilled so both kingdoms collapsed and the people of Israel were scattered throughout the region. Ezekiel and Daniel were among the exiles of Israel who lived in captivity. The fact that God was with them reveals God gives messages of hope to His chosen people even at the crucial times of crisis.

PROPHECY TO THE RETURNED EXILES OF JUDAH

Haggai and Zechariah- Psalms of Discipline and Victory

Haggai and Zechariah delivered God's message after 521 B.C., Zechariah in 520-518 B.C. When the first party of exiles returned to their homeland under the leadership of Zerubbabel, the Israelites made an enthusiastic start on rebuilding the Temple but the disturbance by the Samaritans and apathy towards it soon brought the work to a standstill. Sixteen years later after the decree of Cyprus, the Persian Emperor which allowed the people of Israel to return, Haggai and Zechariah began to stir things up again to complete the rebuilding of Jerusalem's Temple with a message. "Is it time for you yourselves to dwell in your paneled houses while this house lies desolate?" (Haggai 1:4) Why was it so important to rebuild the Temple? Because God's honor was at stake and especially, the nations had to know beyond any doubt that God of Israel was still with them. The Temple and the covenant are bound up together so thanks to these prophets that the Temple was finally completed in 20 years.

Particularly, the birth of the church of Christ and its victory were prophesied through Zechariah's eight visions. These visions indicated that after the coming of Christ, many churches will be oppressed in the days of the Roman Empire but in the end it would survive and succeed. The conclusion of the Old/New Testament is the promise of the 'new heaven and earth' but the message that is delivered through the historical setting of the Old Testament, is about the restoration of the people, the coming Messiah (Jesus) and the establishment of the kingdom of God. Without raising the church from heaven and dividing it means only one thing - judgment. But the most important point of Zechariah's message is that even though people are scattered as a result of their sins, God is still telling them, 'It is not late yet. Repent and return to Me.' There would be no hope in our lives without such comforting words of prophecy.

"'Come now, and let us reason together,' Says the Lord, 'Though your sins are as scarlet, They will be as white as snow; Though they are red like crimson, They will be like wool.'" (Isaiah 1:18) Even though we may have done something drastic and deserve judgment, as long as we confess our sin, God will forgive us. This is the essence of God's love towards us and this is exactly the reason why a church will succeed because of God's love. The world consists of money, power, authority and success and the only place that could override all these elements is a church. That is why a church rules over the world. Look around and see all the people who have persecuted churches with their power but a church has remained to revive each time. A church is bound to succeed and this message is being proclaimed to us by Zechariah.

Malachi - Promise of Restoration

Malachi is the last prophet that comes out in the Old Testament and the setting is around 460-430 B.C. which is about 80 years after Haggai and Zechariah spurred the people on to rebuild the Temple.

He delivered God's message to the downcast people who have grown careless. With Malachi, the voice of the prophecy in the Old Testament falls into the long silent period for 400 years until the coming of the Messiah Jesus.

Recovery of Worship

The book of Malachi delivers the message: 'Recover the correct standard of worship.' Approximately 50,000 people returned to restore the Temple in Jerusalem during the first return in 537 B.C. The Temple was completed at a price but it was finally restored in 20 years. It is a difficult waiting period and disillusion has set in. People struggled with economic hardships and the prosperity that was promised by the prophets has not yet materialized for a long time. It was hard for the Israelites to have hope in God as the waiting dragged on. People began to doubt the words of the prophets feeling God had forgotten them and let them down. Their increasingly casual attitudes to worship and the standards God had set forth were deteriorating rapidly. The rule for the offering sacrifices was to offer 'the very best for God' but since nothing happened over time even after the completion of the Temple, people started offering the poor sick animals which the owner was only too glad to get rid of.

Malachi proclaimed, "'You also say, 'My, how tiresome it is!' And you disdainfully sniff at it,' says the Lord of hosts, 'and you bring what was taken by robbery, and what is lame or sick; so you bring the offering! Should I receive that from your hand?' says the Lord." (Malachi 1:13) Threader: The prophecy in Isaiah 59-66 is fulfilled through what is written in Malachi. Amazingly enough, Isaiah had already prophesied what will happen some 300 years later that the returned exiles' worship to God would deteriorate.

The above symptoms relate to the religion of Shamanism. Why did Israel fall? It was because of the Shamanistic ways. Just as Habakkuk had emphasized, we must be able to foresee the amazing blessings that God has in store for us even though at times it is hard to do so when our life in reality unfolds otherwise. Without realizing God's invisible plan, we tend to focus on the things that are visible and our worship becomes tainted as we think blessings are something we can physically experience. It is why Malachi proclaimed desperately the importance of recovering the proper attitude of worship.

Blessings of Tithing

Through Malachi, God promises the blessings of tithing. "Bring the whole tithe into the storehouse, so that there may be food in my house. Test me now in this,' says the Lord Almighty, 'and see if I will not open the windows of heaven and pour out so much blessing that you will not have room enough for it." (Malachi 3:10) Tithing began after Abraham and must not be understood as a 'tax' to God. If one misunderstands the meaning of tithing then automatically you would think "I have earned my wages with my own blood, sweat and tears coping with all kinds of negative attitudes towards me so what do you mean I have to offer 1/10th of my earnings as an offering to God?!"

A true tithe comes from believing and confessing that everything we have comes from God's mercy. As Job had confessed, we have come empty-handed into the world and will leave in the same manner when we depart from the world. We have been created as a receiver of God's love so it is only natural for us to exist in things that God Himself provides. Giving 1/10th of what we have earned to God is the same as confessing, 'You have provided everything for me so the balance of 9/10 is all yours.' As long as we confess that everything comes from God, there is absolutely no loss from our side. But unfortunately, when this is not accepted in the heart of believers, people become very stingy.

One deacon I know confessed that one month, he earned such a great profit that the thought of giving 1/10th of it made him feel uneasy. After tossing and turning, he decided to give only half of the 1/10th. Can you imagine what happened? The next day, his wife who had recently received her driver's license at the time was practicing her driving skills and got into a car accident. This was before she got her car insurance so he ended up paying exactly the same amount of the 'original' amount of tithing that he should have given in the first place.

The spirit of Satan interferes making us to reject God's grace and instead instills our heart with the mindset that 'it is all through my effort so whatever I've earned is all mine.' Not only does this kind of heart make it impossible to give any offering to God but also sharing with others out of the question. Just as the prophets Amos and Micah had mentioned, "But let justice roll down like waters And righteousness like an ever-flowing stream."(Amos 5:24) Blessings received from God must be shared with others. As long as we believe that what we have are by God's mercy and grace, we can easily give to God. When we succeed in doing this, we can then offer and share with others in return. Holding back from giving and focusing on self-interest is to deprive ourselves of all the good things God would otherwise give us.

Prophecy of John the Baptist

The Last Day is surely coming as so many prophets have foretold when God would even things out once and for all. Malachi serves the Old Testament as a prophetic bridge to John the Baptist who would serve with the same heart as Elijah. The last two verses play a role of a postscript, not just in Malachi but in the Old Testament as a whole. "Behold, I am going to send you Elijah the prophet before the coming of the great and terrible day of the Lord. And he will restore the hearts of the fathers to their children, and the hearts of the children to their fathers, lest I come and smite the land with a curse."(Malachi 4:5-6) John the Baptist preached to the children of God to return to Father God whose compassion urges us to respond to Him and find out how His grace offers hope. The Bible is God's revelation of Himself and we read it not to learn about the people but to learn about God so that we might know Him and respond to Him.

Threader: Because of the last words in the book of Malachi, the people of Israel waited anxiously that Elijah must come before the coming of the Messiah as prophesied by many prophets. That is the reason why one of the disciples of Jesus asked, "Are You the Expected One, or shall we look for someone else?" (Matthew 11:3) and Jesus replied, "And if you care to accept it, he himself is Elijah, who was to come." (Matthew 11:14)

PERIOD OF SILENCE

God no longer sends any Word through His messengers. With Malachi being the last prophet, the prophecy falls into the long, silent period for 400 years until the coming of Christ. As prophesied by Isaiah and Malachi, the returned exiles and the remnants had forgotten about God and didn't bother to know about Him. Through this silent period of 400 years, God was preparing to send His only begotten Son Jesus to the world to spread the gospel from Jerusalem, Judah, Samaria and to the ends of the world. We have to recognize God's plan for reconciliation, how He will bring humanity and all of creation back into a right relationship with Him. In order to do that, God placed great blueprint of an 'infra' - a shift in the transition of history-making is referred as the 'silent period.'

Reason Why the Wicked Ones are Left in the World

"Why didn't God get rid of a wicked man as Hitler who had murdered 6 million innocent Jews? Why didn't God do something about it?"

Have you raised any questions like this? I know I have. As I look in the Old Testament, Habakkuk had already raised a similar question to God some 2,500 years ago.

A wicked king Jehoiakim was reigning over Judah at the time and became Babylon's subject. The Northern Israel had already collapsed and its people were in a state of being scattered and murdered. Jehoiakim paid tribute to the king of Egypt with the extorted taxes stripped from his suffering people in exchange for protection against the attack from Assyria.

What kind of a country was Judah in the first place? It was a country raised by God. But Jehoiakim disregarded God who is in control of wars and extorted his own people.

By witnessing what was going on, prophet Habakkuk cried out to God.

"God! If you exist, how can you let this evil king alone?"

God answered,

"I will judge using Babylon so don't worry."

God gave a promise of the rainbow after the judgment of the flood at Noah's time. What this means is that God will delay destroying the sinners until the 2nd coming of Christ - until the last Judgment Day. But in Jehoiakim's case, God said that He will judge him by using Babylon.

Habakkuk rebutted since the people will be killed because of the invasion of the foreigners.

"God, but there are righteous ones among the kingdom of Judah. What would happen to them?"

God answered,

"But the righteous will live by his faith." (Habakkuk 2:4)

What this verse is saying is that even though suffering and persecution are received, the righteous will live by his faith is a remarkable gospel. During the Nazi period, the faithful Jews chanted the word of God while walking towards the gas chambers. Through sufferings, the forgotten psalms were remembered and praises were given to God. "The Lord is my shepherd, I shall not want. He makes me lie down in green pastures; He leads me beside quiet waters. He restores my soul; He guides me in the paths of righteousness For His name's sake." (Psalms 23:1-3) "Even though my flesh may die, my soul will be restored; I thank thee God who guides me in the paths of righteousness for His name's sake." The reason why God has permitted the evil ones to remain on earth and letting His children receive sufferings from them is because there are people who would be called 'righteous' by living by faith in the midst of sufferings.

Germany was a Christian country during the Hitler's time. The Nazis thought that the Jews had to be punished since they had killed Jesus on the cross. In a sense, Hitler came to the conclusion that he would 'judge' the Jews. A Nazi flag symbolizes a cross. During his school days in Vienna, Hitler came across a symbol of the Red Cross of the Middle Ages in his dormitory room and eventually applied it to the symbol of the Nazi flag.

Romans 11 clearly indicates the Jews should not be persecuted. "But if some of the branches were broken off, and you, being a wild olive, were grafted in among them and became partaker with them of the rich root of the olive tree." (Romans 11:17) The 'olive' tree symbolizes the Jews. We are the partakers of the olive tree who have been grafted in among them, therefore, we should never disregard or persecute the olive tree.

Do you think people like Hitler, Kim Jong Il or the Jews are great sinners but not yourself? Questions like "why doesn't God get rid of such a person?" must actually be directed to us. "God, how is it that you do not get rid of such a sinner as myself? How long can you tolerate me?"

Answers to the questions are as follows: "What then? Are we better than they? Not at all; for we have already charged that both Jews and Greeks are all under sin; as it is written, 'There is none righteous, not even one; there is none who understands, there is none who seeks for God.'" (Romans 3:9-11) "Their throat is an open grave, with their tongues they keep deceiving, the poison of asps is under their lips; whose mouth is full of cursing and bitterness; their feet are swift to shed blood." (Romans 3:13-15) Who is this? It is us. It is about our image. Just as God who has tolerated the evil ones for a long time, He is not only tolerating us but through sufferings, He wants us to return to Him. For that reason, I encourage my readers to praise our Lord God!